2 0 0 2
STATE
by
STATE
GUIDE
to
HUMAN
RESOURCES
LAW

MIDYEAR
SUPPLEMENT

This supplement is to be used in conjunction with the 2002 Edition of *State by State Guide to Human Resources Law*. Tables from the 2002 Edition that have been revised in this supplement are reprinted in full.

2002
STATE
by
STATE
GUIDE
to
HUMAN
RESOURCES
LAW

MIDYEAR
SUPPLEMENT

A PANEL PUBLICATION
ASPEN PUBLISHERS, INC.

JOHN F.
BUCKLEY

RONALD M.
GREEN

Copyright © 2002 by Panel Publishers
A Division of Aspen Publishers, Inc.
A Wolters Kluwer Company
www.panelpublishers.com

Printed in the United States of America

ISBN: 0-7355-3187-0

1 2 3 4 5 6 7 8 9 0

About Panel Publishers

Panel Publishers—comprising the former Little, Brown and Company's Professional Division, Wiley Law Publications, the Bureau of Business Practice, Summers Press, Harcourt Professional Publishing, and Loislaw—is a leading publisher of authoritative and timely treatises, practice manuals, information services, and journals written by specialists to assist attorneys, financial and tax advisors, and other business professionals. Our mission is to provide practical, solution-based how-to information keyed to the latest legislative, judicial, and regulatory developments.

We offer publications in the areas of compensation and benefits, pensions, payroll, employment, civil rights, taxation, estate planning, and elder law.

Other Panel products on related topics include:

Books and Manuals

State by State Guide to Managed Care Law
State by State Guide to Workplace Safety Regulation
COBRA Handbook
Employee Benefits Answer Book
Employee Benefits in Mergers and Acquisitions
Employment Law Answer Book
Flexible Benefits Answer Book
401(k) Answer Book
401(k) Answer Book: Forms & Worksheets
Health Insurance Answer Book
Managed Care Answer Book
Mandated Benefits 2001 Compliance Guide
Multistate Guide to Benefits Law
The Pension Answer Book

Periodicals and Electronic Titles

COBRA Advisory
Compensation and Benefits Management
Flexible Benefits
HR Manager's Resource Library on CD-ROM
Medical Benefits
On Managed Care
Panel Employee Benefits Library on CD-ROM
Panel Employee Benefits Library Online
Employment Discrimination Law Library

PANEL PUBLISHERS
A Division of Aspen Publishers, Inc.
Practical Solutions for Legal and Business Professionals
www.panelpublishers.com

SUBSCRIPTION NOTICE

This Panel product is updated on a periodic basis with supplements to reflect important changes in the subject matter. If you purchased this product directly from Panel, we have already recorded your subscription for the update service.

If, however, you purchased this product from a bookstore and wish to receive future updates and revised or related volumes billed separately with a 30-day examination review, please contact our Customer Service Department at 1-800-234-1660, or send your name, company name (if applicable), address, and the title of the product to:

Panel Publishers
A Division of Aspen Publishers, Inc.
7201 McKinney Circle
Frederick, MD 21704

About the Authors

The *2002 State by State Guide to Human Resources Law* was prepared by the attorneys of the National Legal Research Group. Founded in 1969, the National Legal Research Group has provided consulting and research services to attorneys on more than 100,000 cases.

JOHN F. BUCKLEY IV serves as editor and contributing author for the *2002 State by State Guide to Human Resources Law.* Mr. Buckley is a senior attorney on the Public Law team of the National Legal Research Group, where he specializes in civil rights, employment discrimination, and local and state government law; in this capacity, he has advised attorneys throughout the country on legal issues related to equal employment. Mr. Buckley is a member of the Society for Human Resource Management. In addition to his work on the *State by State Guide to Human Resources Law,* Mr. Buckley has served as editor and contributing author for Panel's *Multistate Payroll Guide,* the *Multistate Guide to Benefits Law,* and the *Equal Employment Opportunity Compliance Guide.* He is also the co-author of the second edition of West's *Defense of Equal Employment Claims.*

Mr. Buckley received his Bachelor of Arts degree in History from the University of North Carolina at Chapel Hill in 1983. In 1987 he received his Juris Doctor degree from the University of North Carolina School of Law, where he was a member of the Board of Editors of the Law Review.

RONALD M. GREEN is a partner in Epstein Becker & Green, P.C. A lawyer of national reputation, he is actively engaged in the private practice of employment and labor law on behalf of multinational and do-mestic corporations. Mr. Green has lectured extensively throughout the United States on behalf of public and private institutions, trade associations, and corporations. He is also on the Labor Panel of Arbitrators of the American Arbitration Association and the American Bar Association's Committee on Equal Employment Law and Its Impact on Collective Bargaining.

Mr. Green received a Bachelor of Science degree in Business Management from New York University School of Commerce in 1965. He was graduated from Brooklyn Law School in 1968 with a Juris Doctor degree, having served on the Law Review and participated in the Honors Program. He also earned an LL.M. degree in Labor Law from George Washington University School of Law.

The authors wish to acknowledge and thank the following attorneys and law clerks who served as contributing authors to the *2002 State by State Guide to Human Resources Law:*

Dwight D. Wilkerson, J.D.

Nicole D. Prysby, J.D.

Katherine C. Jenkins, J.D.

The authors also wish to thank Laura Greeney, our editor at Panel Publishers, and the many state labor officials and members of their legal staffs for their assistance in keeping the Guide accurate and current.

Please contact the Editorial Department, Panel Publishers, (212) 597-0200, with comments or suggestions.

Preface

The *2002 State by State Guide to Human Resources Law* is the only comprehensive, authoritative guide to the employment laws of the 50 United States and the District of Columbia. The purpose of the Guide is to serve human resources, compensation, and benefits professionals who work in multijurisdictional environments. Thousands of research hours have been spent to develop this quick-reference chart format, which allows the user to compare and contrast how the various states address any single issue. Assignments that cut across state lines are made easier because the reader at a glance will be able to ascertain whether various states treat an issue in a consistent or incongruous manner.

The 2002 Midyear Supplement incorporates a significant number of substantive changes and valuable additions, as follows:

- Part 2 contains updated tables on the applicability of Equal Employment Opportunity Commission (EEOC) guidelines to state fair employment practice enforcement. In addition, Part 2 discusses the latest judicial decisions that recognize the similarities and differences between federal and state statutes prohibiting discrimination in the workplace.
- New tables in Part 10 cover conduct or events that disqualify employees from receiving workers' compensation benefits. Although disqualifying events vary from state to state, among the disqualifying factors covered are the following: intent to injure or cause death to oneself or others; committing assault; acting with willful negligence or reckless indifference; willfully exposing oneself to risk; engaging in "horseplay"; failing to use safety appliances; committing illegal acts; violating safety rules; engaging in willful misconduct; intoxication or use of controlled substances; refusing to submit to a drug test; refusing to submit to a medical exam; or refusing medical treatment.
- The "Trends and Controversies in Human Resources Law" section contains the following new features:
  - In 2001 the Supreme Court rendered a decision that reaffirmed the judicial recognition of binding arbitration in the employment context. Although the Supreme Court's decision was welcomed as supporting the growing trend toward the recognition of binding arbitration as an alternative to litigation, the arbitration agreement under consideration was ultimately declared unenforceable for other reasons by the Ninth Circuit Court of Appeals. A 2002 decision by the Supreme Court pointed out another limitation on arbitration agreements: they cannot be used to dismiss a lawsuit brought by the EEOC. A new text section discusses these decisions and the various issues related to the enforceability of agreements to subject discrimination claims to binding arbitration.
  - In 2002 the Supreme Court unanimously refused to expand the definition of major life activities to include a limitation in performing manual tasks associated with a particular job. This decision will undoubtedly have an impact on the growing number of claims

being filed under the Americans with Disabilities Act (ADA) based on repetitive motion injuries. New text in the "Trends and Controversies" section discusses how this case affects the growing concern over ergonomics in the workplace.

— An expanded Exhibit I covers the latest developments concerning breastfeeding rights in the workplace, as eight more states weigh in on this important issue.

Business executives and their professional advisors today face an increasingly complex web of law and regulation with regard to the human resources function. Actions of both the federal and the state governments have placed increasing burdens and responsibilities on business relating to the treatment of applicants and employees. And the courts, both federal and state, have also involved themselves in how employers may deal with applicants and employees, importing legal concepts and doctrines of long standing into the domain of the employer-employee relationship.

The information in this book is, for the most part, presented in a tabular format, which is meant to give the reader easy access to information on discrete topics. This Guide is, first and foremost, a reference tool for the professional who needs to put his or her finger on the particulars of personnel law on a state-by-state basis quickly without wading through large amounts of extraneous data. Liberal cross-referencing and an index help the user locate exactly what he or she may need.

What follows is a summary of the information that can be found in each of the parts of this Guide.

Defining the Employment Relationship

This part introduces and describes the major types of employment relationships (i.e., employer and employee, employer and independent contractor, and principal and agent) so that the application of statutory and common-law concepts to the employer-employee relationship can be distinguished.

General information is provided on aspects of the offer and acceptance of employment, including written and oral contracts, the nature of the relationship in the absence of a contract, and the role played by employee manuals. Exhibit 1.2-1, based on the EEOC guidelines, generally sets forth permitted and prohibited topics of preemployment inquiry; Exhibit 1.2-2 provides a closer look at each state's specific statutory provisions.

Also discussed are two important aspects of the dissolution of an employment relationship: breach of contract and alternative dispute resolution.

Fair Employment Practices

Forty-seven states and the District of Columbia have enacted state analogues to Title VII, barring private-sector discrimination on the basis of race, color, national origin, religion, or sex. (The states that have not enacted comprehensive statutes are Alabama, Arkansas, and Mississippi; Georgia's statute applies only to public employment.) A majority of these states have also used their general fair employment statutes to prohibit age and handicap discrimination. States with separate nondiscrimination statutes addressing particular areas—for example, age or handicap—are also identified. In addition, various states have determined that other bases for making employment decisions should be prohibited; for example, political affiliation, sexual orientation, nonsmoker status, or veteran status. The tables in Part 2 make it easy to identify what may be prohibited in a particular jurisdiction.

Other tables indicate who is covered and what actions are prohibited or excepted by the statute; set forth the procedures for bringing and litigating a charge before an administrative agency and a court; identify the time constraints for alleging statutory violations; indicate what statutory defenses may be provided; note the relief available by law, including the penalties and sanctions that may be imposed; and describe in some detail the powers of the state enforcement and regulatory agencies. This part also includes a table that describes any affirmative action obligations the state imposes on employers generally or on those that contract with the state to provide goods or services.

Wages, Hours, and Holidays

The federal government has established certain baseline standards governing employee wages and hours. Minimum wage and maximum hour standards and methods for determining overtime are the most evident and pervasive of the federal rules.

Employers must also know of and comply with myriad state laws governing these same issues. Most states have enacted wage and hour laws that are both consistent with and different from the federal rules, and knowing where the differences are is essential. Tables in this part identify which states have laws setting minimum wage and overtime standards. The tables also note state law recordkeeping requirements for wage and hour matters and the penalties for violating the state statutes.

Most states regulate the ages at which children may work and the types of jobs that children may hold at various ages. A separate series of tables describes state laws pertaining to child labor, recordkeeping rules for both minors and adults, and the penalties for violating the state laws.

Finally, Table 3.10-1 addresses state holidays. The listing in the table does not reflect holidays that private-sector employers must give their employees. Rather, it notes those holidays that a state recognizes for its employees. Many private employers follow their host state's lead, however, in granting holidays to employees, which makes this information of some value to those practicing in the private sector.

Employment at Will

Although the Guide generally is concerned with statutory provisions affecting the employment relationship, issues attendant to employee termination and employment at will, and the various standards and rules applicable in the states, require discussion in this volume. Matters affecting the severing of an employment relationship are among the most troublesome employers face. Challenges to a termination almost always raise issues such as breach of contract or violation of an important public policy concern.

The traditional rule relative to the employer-employee relationship had been (and, in a few states, remains) that either party could terminate the relationship at any time and for any reason. Since the nineteenth century, however, employees have gained a number of important statutory protections, such as those noted in the state fair employment law part. This, in turn, has made it easier for the courts to impose additional obligations on employers seeking to discharge employees. Part 4 identifies the states that have recognized exceptions to the traditional employment-at-will rule. One table notes which states have recognized contractual causes of action as defenses to discharge: for example, statements printed in handbooks or manuals or oral promises of job security.

Another table explains the public policy exception. Specifically, it notes which states have limited an employer's right to discharge employees for serving on juries, exercising a right to seek workers' compensation, informing state officials of health or safety violations, and so forth.

Other tables in this part note several other nonstatutory causes of action an employee may either file to challenge a discharge, such as interference with contractual relations, or include as a separate issue, such as infliction of emotional distress or defamation; defenses that courts have recognized in discharge lawsuits; statutory restrictions on discharging employees; and the remedies available to employees who prevail. This last table is especially important because employees often are able to recover compensatory and punitive damages against an employer deemed to have engaged in an improper termination.

Because the body of law governing wrongful termination is developed almost exclusively by the state courts, the authors have attempted to include citations to the most recent relevant state court decisions; however, inasmuch as this area is one of the fastest changing in employment law, employers will need to consistently monitor judicial determinations concerning contractual and tort theories in the wrongful discharge area.

Employee Benefits

A number of states have enacted statutes requiring that employers offer certain types of benefits to employees. Part 5 identifies those states and describes the benefits.

The part begins, however, with a brief description of the issue of a legal doctrine known as "preemption." By and large, the federal government regulates what employers are required to do for employees in the benefits area. Under a federal law, the Employee Retirement Income Security Act of 1974, as amended (ERISA), Congress states that all state and local laws that relate to employee benefits plans are preempted by the federal law. That is to say, the state and local laws are rendered null and void, and employee benefits plans are governed by a single set of regulations. Unlike unemployment and workers' compensation programs, in which the states are free to set their own standards, employers here are protected from conflicting and inconsistent state requirements. There are limits to the reach of the preemption rule, and, as the introduction to the part notes, an employer subject to state regulation on a benefits plan issue may need to seek assistance in determining whether it must comply with the state provision.

This part describes types of benefits that states may require employers to provide to employees. The principal benefit is group health insurance, covered in 10 separate tables. Most states do not directly require employers to offer certain health insurance benefits, but rather require insurers offering group policies to include certain benefits. Additional tables describe health insurance continuation and conversion rules, regulation of health maintenance organizations, group life insurance and legal expenses insurance provisions, wage payment laws (requiring employers to make certain payments to terminating employees either immediately on termination or within a defined period), and parental leave laws. The issue of parental leave for purposes related to childbirth or adoption or to illness of close family members is one that has just begun to make its way into the social consciousness. A federal law, the Family and Medical Leave Act (FMLA), now requires most employers to allow employees up to 12 weeks of leave for certain specified reasons, and many states have enacted legislation giving employees even greater leave rights.

Unemployment Compensation

An unemployment compensation program is also like insurance. Here, the employer is insuring its employees against the loss of income associated with termination of employment. A state-mandated Social Security program, unemployment compensation provides terminated employees with weekly cash benefits for a period of time, giving employees a cushion during the period they are seeking new positions. States require that employers pay into a state fund (not a private insurance carrier as in workers' compensation) a certain amount per employee. Terminated employees who meet qualification standards are entitled to draw out of the employer's fund for a statutorily defined period. (Also like an insurance program, an employer's unemployment compensation payments are affected by the number of claims made on its account by terminated employees.)

The tables in Part 6 set forth the state requirements. They define who is covered and who is exempted. Most states require that all employers participate in the unemployment compensation program, although a few set different standards for employers in certain industries. Also described are how benefits are calculated, how long an employee must wait before becoming eligible for benefits, the maximum number of weeks one may collect, the weekly benefit amount, the disqualifications for benefits, tax (or premium) rates, and the reporting and recordkeeping requirements.

Workplace Privacy

At common law, the right of privacy has involved four distinct concerns: the right to control and limit the commercial appropriation of one's identity by another; the right to be free from intrusion; the right to control the disclosure of private information about oneself; and the right to avoid being placed in a "false light" in the public eye. Each of these has a relationship to the workplace and the employer-employee relationship. For example, an employer that uses employees in advertising may be violating the first-noted right, that of commercial misappropriation, unless it obtains the employees' consent. The right to be free from the public disclosure of private information may be violated when an employer fails to limit the dissemination of private information about the employee to a "need-to-know" group. An intrusion into an employee's seclusion may result from a search of an employee's desk or locker when the employer failed to reserve the right to conduct such searches or failed to limit the employee's right to the privacy of employer-provided furniture. And the "false light" protection may be violated by an employer that makes statements on behalf of employees without the employees' consent. Because these privacy concepts involve the common law and, as a rule, are not statutory in nature, they are not addressed in this part.

There are, however, a number of discrete issues that are statutory and involve concerns that have a nexus to privacy. Specifically, Part 7 includes tables concerning various types of applicant or employee testing, including tests for use of drugs; exposure to the AIDS virus; and polygraph tests. Additional tables address employer use of consumer credit reporting agencies to conduct background checks, generally of applicants, and an employer's right to use arrest or conviction information about applicants in making employment decisions. Also listed are states with so-called antiblacklisting statutes, which prohibit employers from blacklisting "troublemaking" employees. These statutes may also contain requirements for employers relative to providing references for former employees. Finally, states that make provisions for employee access to personnel records are also listed.

Health and Safety

Part 8 includes a discussion of state occupational safety and health statutes. Some states require employees to provide certain health- and safety-related equipment and, in some instances, medical examinations. The various state requirements in this area are covered in this part. The increasing amount of regulation in the area of workplace smoking is also covered.

Summary of Federal Legislation, Guidelines, and Policies on Human Resources Law

Although the function of this Guide is to provide a quick reference to state laws in a number of important areas, it would nonetheless be incomplete if it failed to address the federal statutes applicable to the employment relationship. Therefore, Part 9 summarizes the major legislation on the federal level affecting personnel law.

Title VII of the Civil Rights Act of 1964, as amended, is the primary federal law prohibiting discrimination on the basis of race, color, national origin, religion, or sex. Although a number of federal statutes preceded it, most notably the National Labor Relations Act (NLRA) and the Equal Pay Act, Title VII marked the beginning of an era in which the U.S. Congress enacted a number of far-reaching laws designed to extend various protections against discrimination to employees in the workplace. The Civil Rights Act of 1991 has not only expanded the remedies available under Title VII but also made jury trials available in such cases. Further, the Americans with Disabilities Act, effective for most employers on July 26, 1992, now provides a vehicle for employees with disabilities to seek redress for discrimination. Both new statutes are discussed in detail. Other statutes include the Age Discrimination in Employment Act (ADEA), the Rehabilitation Act, and the Vietnam Era Veterans Readjustment Assistance Act. The federal government also attacked discrimination through its power of the purse: Executive Order 11246 prohibits government contractors from discriminating on the same bases as Title VII and further requires development of affirmative action plans, which have created a certain amount of controversy related to issues of reverse discrimination.

Other federal statutes with principal purposes other than preventing discrimination also contain components that bar the use of certain criteria to make employment-related decisions. These statutes include the Employee Retirement Income Security Act of 1974 (ERISA) (prohibiting discrimination on the basis of an individual's entitlement to covered benefits), the Immigration Reform and Control Act (IRCA) (citizenship), the Consumer Credit Protection Act (garnishment), and the Jury System Improvement Act (jury service).

Finally, this overview of federal law describes a host of statutes affecting the employment relationship beyond issues of discrimination. For example, the Occupational Safety and Health Act requires that employers establish and maintain safe working environments for employees and sets certain standards for employers to follow in various workplace settings; the Worker Adjustment and Retraining Notification Act (WARN) requires that employers notify employees of large-scale layoffs or business closings; the Fair Credit Reporting Act requires that employers inform employees or applicants of certain efforts to obtain information about them through use of third parties; and the Drug-Free Workplace Act requires that government contractors and recipients of federal grants implement policies barring the use, sale, and manufacture of controlled substances by employees assigned to work on the contract or grant and develop "drug-free awareness" programs to inform such employees of the dangers of drugs in the workplace and where drug-involved employees may obtain assistance.

Finding Aids

A glossary of legal terms that have been used in the tables and text can be found at the back of the main volume of the Guide. This Guide also maintains a traditional index, which should prove helpful in locating information.

We have again labored to make this book as fresh and as timely as possible; however, inasmuch as state laws are constantly changing, we apologize—in advance—for any omission that may occur. We welcome your suggestions for making the Guide even more useful.

John F. Buckley
Ronald M. Green

June 2002

How to Use This Guide

The *2002 State by State Guide to Human Resources Law* is designed to provide quick access to each state's laws on the expanding number of issues and concerns facing business executives and their advisors. The easy-to-use tabular format enables the reader to quickly locate the laws of a specific state, to determine their applicability to specific situations, and to compare how the states approach numerous aspects of personnel law.

Topics that require more extensive discussion appear as two-column text exhibits.

Organization

The annual edition of this Guide is organized into nine major parts. Each part has an overview that introduces the subject area as a whole; within each part, tables are grouped in topical sections, each with its own brief introduction. The Introduction contains a discussion of general principles applicable to human resources law and a section entitled "Trends and Controversies in Human Resources Law," which discusses in detail the major recent developments in human resources law.

Tables and exhibits appear in Parts 1 through 8. Part 9 is a narrative summary of the federal regulation of personnel law.

Introduction
Part 1   Defining the Employment Relationship
Part 2   Fair Employment Practices
Part 3   Wages, Hours, and Holidays
Part 4   Employment at Will
Part 5   Benefits
Part 6   Unemployment Compensation
Part 7   Workplace Privacy
Part 8   Health and Safety
Part 9   Summary of Federal Legislation, Guidelines, and Policies on Human Resources Law

A supplement to the Guide is produced each year, following the publication of the annual edition by approximately six months. In addition to updating changes in state legislation, the supplement features a special comprehensive section on statewide workers' compensation laws.

Table and Exhibit Formats

Each table and exhibit lists in alphabetical order, by state, the provisions of law under discussion. States are listed by standard postal abbreviation. In a handful of instances, where only a few state laws address a particular topic, only those states are listed. Finally, every table is cross-referenced to the text that discusses its content. The cross-reference appears under the table title.

Citation System

Each table and exhibit contains a column titled "Citations to Authority." The information contained within the table is referenced to the state statutes and federal and state court cases that provide the basis for such information. The citations permit immediate access to original sources.

Reference System

Each part has a number, 1 through 9. Within each part, text is identified consecutively by section number; for example, § 1.1, § 1.2, § 1.3, and so forth.

Tables and exhibits are numbered consecutively, but carry the number of the section in which they appear. For example, the tables in § 5.2 are numbered Table 5.2-1, Table 5.2-2, Table 5.2-3, whereas the exhibits in § 1.2 are numbered Exhibit 1.2-1 and Exhibit 1.2-2. For ease of access from the indexes, table, exhibit, and section numbers appear at the top of each page.

Special Reference Features

The *2002 State by State Guide to Human Resources Law* offers a number of special reference features to assist the reader in locating sought-after material of various kinds. These reference guides include the following tables:

- **Frequently Consulted Human Resources Numbers.** This feature presents in a quick-reference chart key information that human resources professionals need to check most often.
- **State Decisions Relying on or Not Following EEOC Guidelines.** These exhibits review state case law applying or rejecting the EEOC guidelines in interpreting state prohibitions against discrimination in employment.

Summary of Contents

Table of Contents

Frequently Consulted Human Resources State Law Provisions

State law provisions relating to human resources are subject to frequent change. The text and tables in this Guide cover a broad range of state laws, including all the key requirements. There are certain key requirements, however, that human resources professionals need to check most often, but which are spread out over different areas of the law and different chapters of this Guide. For the convenience of the reader, the following table gathers together these frequently consulted provisions into a quick-reference chart.

Included in Table i are state requirements for minimum wage, basic overtime requirements, the unemployment wage base, the disability wage base and weekly short-term disability amount (where applicable), and the unemployment compensation benefit formula for each state.

Table i
FREQUENTLY CONSULTED HUMAN RESOURCES NUMBERS

	Minimum Wage	Overtime Compensation Requirements	2002 State Unemployment Wage Base	Disability Wage Base	Weekly Short-Term Disability Amount	Unemployment Compensation Weekly Benefit Amount Formula
AL	—	—	$8,000.	—	—	1/24 of average of 2 high quarters.
AK	$5.65 (50 cents more than federal minimum wage).	8 hours per day or 40 hours per week (subject to DOL approval, an employer and employee may agree to 10-hour days).	$26,000.	—	—	If more than 90% of earnings is in high quarter, base period – (other 3 quarters x 10). If less than 90% of earnings is in high quarter, total wages in base period.
AZ	—	—	$7,000.	—	—	1/25 of high quarter.
AR	$5.15.	40 hours.	$9,000.	—	—	1/26 of high quarter, up to 66⅔% of SAWW.
CA	$6.75.	8 hours per day or 40 hours per week.	$7,000.	$46,327.	$50–$490.	1/33–1/23 of high quarter; if high-quarter wages exceed $2,781.99, the maximum weekly benefit amount will be 45% of those wages divided by 13.
CO	$5.15.	12 hours per day or 40 hours per week.	$10,000.	—	—	60% of 1/26 of 2 high quarters, up to 50% of SAWW, or 50% of 1/52 of base period earnings, up to 60% of SAWW.
CT	$6.70.	40 hours.	$15,000.	—	—	1/26 of high quarter, up to 60% of SAWW, plus $15 for each dependent up to 5 dependents or $75.
DE	$6.15.	—	$8,500.	—	—	1/46 of 2 high quarters if fund is greater than or equal to $90 million, 1/52 if less.
DC	$6.15 (equals federal minimum wage plus $1); $4.25 for employees who have worked less than 90 days.	40 hours.	$9,000.	—	—	1/26 of high quarter, up to 50% of SAWW, plus $5 per dependent up to $20.

State	Minimum Wage	Overtime	Taxable Wage Base			Weekly Benefit
FL	—	10 hours per day for manual laborers, unless contract states otherwise.	$7,000.	—	—	1/26 of high quarter.
GA	$5.15.	—	$8,500.	—	—	1/48 of 2 high quarters or, if alternative qualifying wages are used, 1/25 of highest quarter.
HI	$5.75; $6.25 effective 1/1/03.	40 hours.	$29,300.	Employee's weekly wage, subject to annual maximum set by Division of Labor.	For employees with average weekly wage of less than $26, benefit is wage or $14, whichever is less. For employees with average weekly wage of $26 or more, benefit is 58% of employee's average weekly wage, not to exceed $396.	1/21 of high quarter, up to 75% of SAWW.
ID	$5.15.	—	$27,600.	—	—	1/26 of high quarter, up to 60% of SAWW.
IL	$5.15.	40 hours.	$9,000.	—	—	49.5% of average weekly wage in 2 highest quarters, up to 49.5% of SAWW; up to 58.5% of SAWW if claimant has nonworking spouse; up to 65.5% of SAWW if claimant has dependent child.
IN	$5.15.	40 hours.	$7,000.	—	—	5% of first $2,000 in high quarter plus 4% of remainder.
IA	$5.15 ($4.25 for employees who have worked less than 90 days).	—	$18,600.	—	—	1/23–1/19 of high quarter depending on number of dependents, up to 65% of SAWW.
KS	$2.65.	46 hours.	$8,000.	—	—	4.25% of high quarter, up to 60% of SAWW.
KY	$5.15.	40 hours.	$8,000.	—	—	1.3078% of total base period wages, up to 62% of SAWW.
LA	—	—	$7,000.	—	—	1/25 of 4 quarters of base period, up to 66⅔% of SAWW.
ME	$5.75; $6.25 effective 1/1/03.	40 hours.	$12,000.	—	—	1/22 of 2 highest quarters, up to 52% of SAWW, plus $10 for each dependent up to 50% of weekly benefit amount.

(Table continues.)

Table i (cont'd)
FREQUENTLY CONSULTED HUMAN RESOURCES NUMBERS

	Minimum Wage	Overtime Compensation Requirements	2002 State Unemployment Wage Base	Disability Wage Base	Weekly Short-Term Disability Amount	Unemployment Compensation Weekly Benefit Amount Formula
MD	$5.15.	40 hours.	$8,500.	—	—	1/24 of high quarter plus $8 per dependent up to $40.
MA	$6.75 (minimum wage for agriculture is $1.60 except for children under age 17).	40 hours.	$10,800.	—	—	50% of average weekly wage in base period, up to 57.5% of SAWW.
MI	$5.15.	40 hours.	$9,500.	—	—	67% of average weekly wage.
MN	$4.90 for employers with gross annual sales of less than $500,000; $5.15 for employers with gross annual sales of $500,000 or more.	48 hours.	$21,000.	—	—	The higher of 50% of average weekly wage during base period (up to 66⅔% of SAWW) or 50% of average weekly wage during high quarter (up to 50% of SAWW or $331, whichever is higher).
MS	—	—	$7,000.	—	—	1/26 of high quarter, up to 60% of SAWW.
MO	$5.15.	40 hours.	$7,000.	—	—	4% of high quarter.
MT	$5.15; $4 for employers with annual gross sales of $110,000 or less.	40 hours.	$18,900.	—	—	1% of annual wage or 1.9% of 2 highest quarters, up to 63% of SAWW.
NE	$5.15.	—	$7,000.	—	—	50% of average weekly wage.
NV	$5.15.	8 hours per day or 40 hours per week if working four 10-hour days by mutual agreement.	$20,900.	—	—	1/25 of high quarter, up to 50% of SAWW.
NH	$5.15.	40 hours.	$8,000.	—	—	1.0%–1.1% of annual wages.
NJ	$5.15.	40 hours.	$23,500.	$23,500.	⅔ of employee's average weekly wage, up to 53% of SAWW ($444).	60% of average weekly wage plus dependents' allowance of up to 56⅔% of SAWW.

NM	$4.25.	40 hours.	$15,900.	—	—	—	1/26 of high quarter, up to 52.5% of SAWW.
NY	$5.15.	40 hours.	$8,500.	Employee's weekly wage.	50% of employee's weekly wage, not to exceed $170. Where employee's average weekly wage is less than $20, benefit equals employee's average weekly wage.	—	1/26–1/25 of high quarter.
NC	$5.15.	40 hours.	$15,500.	—	—	—	1/26 of high quarter, up to 66 2/3% of SAWW.
ND	$5.15.	40 hours.	$17,400.	—	—	—	1/65 of the sum of 2 high quarters plus 1/2 of wages in 3rd highest quarter, up to 62% of SAWW.
OH	$5.15; $2.80 for employers with gross annual receipts below $150,000; $3.35 for employers with gross annual receipts between $150,000 and $500,000.	40 hours.	$9,000.	—	—	—	50% of average weekly wage.
OK	$5.15 for employers with 10 or more full-time employees and/or grossing more than $100,000 annually; $2.00 for other employers.	—	$10,500.	—	—	—	1/23 of high quarter.
OR	$6.50.	40 hours.	$25,000.	—	—	—	1.25% of base period wages, up to 64% of SAWW.
PA	$5.15.	40 hours.	$8,000.	—	—	—	1/25–1/23 of high-quarter wage, up to 66 2/3% of SAWW, plus $5 for 1 dependent and $3 for second dependent.
RI	$6.15.	40 hours.	$12,000.	$44,000.	4.62% of employee's highest-quarter wages in base year, not to exceed 85% of SAWW for preceding year. Additionally, employee receives a dependent allowance of $10 or 7% of weekly benefit for each qualifying dependent, up to maximum of 5 dependents. Benefits range from $57 to $527 plus dependent allowance.	—	60% of average weekly wage, up to 67% of SAWW, plus greater of $10 or 5% of benefit rate per dependent, up to 5 dependents.

(Table continues.)

Table i (cont'd)
FREQUENTLY CONSULTED HUMAN RESOURCES NUMBERS

	Minimum Wage	Overtime Compensation Requirements	2002 State Unemployment Wage Base	Disability Wage Base	Weekly Short-Term Disability Amount	Unemployment Compensation Weekly Benefit Amount Formula
SC	—	—	$7,000.	—	—	50% of individual's average weekly wage, up to 66⅔% of SAWW.
SD	$5.15.	—	$7,000.	—	—	1/26 of high quarter, up to 62% of SAWW.
TN	—	—	$7,000.	—	—	1/26 of average of 2 high quarters.
TX	$5.15.	—	$9,000.	—	—	1/25 of high quarter, up to 47.6% of SAWW.
UT	$5.15. *Note:* Recent enactment prohibits localities from enacting provisions requiring employers to pay minimum wage higher than federal minimum wage.	40 hours for public employees and for the employees of companies undertaking government contracts.	$22,000.	—	—	1/26 of high quarter, up to 60% of state-insured average fiscal year weekly wage.
VT	$6.25.	40 hours.	$8,000.	—	—	1/45 of 2 high quarters.
VA	$5.15.	—	$8,000.	—	—	1/50 of 2 high quarters.
WA	$6.90.	40 hours.	$28,500.	—	—	1/25 of average of 2 high quarters, up to 70% of SAWW.
WV	$5.15.	40 hours.	$8,000.	—	—	1% of annual wages, up to 66⅔% of SAWW.
WI	$5.15 ($4.25 for employees under 20 and employed for less than 90 days).	40 hours.	$10,500.	—	—	4% of high-quarter wages, up to 66⅔% of SAWW.
WY	$5.15.	—	$14,700.	—	—	4% of high quarter, up to 55% of SAWW.

Trends and Controversies in Human Resources Law

The laws that define and regulate the relationship between employer and employee are constantly evolving. The rapidity of this evolution has been driven, to a large extent, by the overall pace of social change in this country during the last 30 years. For instance, the media's treatment of issues related to sexual harassment and assault in a variety of settings and evolving social attitudes toward sexual harassment have directly affected legislation defining prohibited workplace conduct. The increasing amount of employment-related litigation has also fueled rapid changes in procedural issues relating to how workplace claims are resolved.

In many instances, judges and legislators may have reached different conclusions regarding the appropriate resolution of such issues, leaving an employer's long-term potential exposure to claims involving these issues somewhat uncertain. This section examines recent and evolving issues in human resources law. Familiarity with current issues will enable employers and human resources professionals to anticipate future changes and to formulate appropriate personnel policies.

[a] Reasonable Accommodation and Seniority Systems

Many lower courts have reconciled the phrases "reasonable accommodation" and "undue hardship" under the Americans With Disabilities Act (ADA) in a practical way, holding that, to defeat a defendant/employer's summary judgment motion, a plaintiff/employee need only show that an "accommodation" seems reasonable on its face (i.e., ordinarily or in the general run of cases). The defendant/employer then must show special (typically case-specific) circumstances demonstrating undue hardship in the particular circumstances. Some courts had recognized an exception to this rule, holding that an accommodation that requires an employer to go against a seniority rule is not reasonable as a matter of law.[1] The Supreme Court has now put its stamp of approval on this exception but has added a caveat that allows an employee still to prevail in certain limited cases, even if the accommodation would require alteration of a seniority rule.

In *US Airways Inc. v. Barnett*,[2] the Supreme Court held that an employer's showing that a requested accommodation conflicts with seniority rules is ordinarily sufficient to show, as a matter of law, that an "accommodation" is not "reasonable." However, the employee remains free to present evidence of special circumstances that makes a seniority rule exception reasonable in the particular case. Not surprisingly, the employee and employer had taken diametrically opposed positions on the issue. US Airways' position was that no accommodation violating a seniority system's rules is reasonable; Barnett's position was that "reasonable accommodation" authorizes a court to consider only the requested accommodation's ability to meet an individual's disability-related needs. The court held that neither position was a proper interpretation of the ADA.

Under the Court's analysis, an employer may meet its burden of demonstrating undue hardship simply by showing that the suggested accommodation would force the employer to alter the rules of a seniority system.

---

1. *See e.g.,* Davis v. Florida Power & Light Co., 205 F.3d 1301 (11th Cir. 2000).
2. No. 00-1250 (April 29, 2002).

Contrary to the decisions of several courts, however, this showing does not necessarily end the inquiry. Rather, the employee remains free to show that special circumstances warrant a finding that, despite the seniority system's presence, the requested accommodation is reasonable based on the particular facts. Special circumstances might alter the important expectations created by a seniority system.

The plaintiff might show, for example, that the employer, having retained the right to change the system unilaterally, exercises that right fairly frequently, reducing employee expectations that the system will be followed—to the point where the requested accommodation will not likely make a difference. The plaintiff might also show that the system already contains exceptions such that, under the circumstances, one further exception is unlikely to matter. The plaintiff has the burden of showing special circumstances and must explain why, in the particular case, an exception to the seniority system can constitute a reasonable accommodation even though in the ordinary case it cannot.

[b] Emerging Issues in Employment Arbitration

As discussed in § 1.6[b] of the annual edition of this Guide, alternative dispute resolution (ADR) has become increasingly common in the employment context. It was not so long ago that some courts held that agreements waiving the right to a judicial forum for claims of discrimination were against public policy. The Supreme Court has made it clear, however, that discrimination claims, like other claims, can be made the subject of binding arbitration agreements. As the Supreme Court has also recently made clear, however, there are some limitations to using arbitration agreements as a means to avoid discrimination claims. Furthermore, as some lower courts have recently held, state law can be applied to nullify an otherwise valid arbitration agreement.

Although the purpose of the Federal Arbitration Act (FAA) was to overcome judicial hostility to arbitration, it is apparent from recent cases that this purpose has not been entirely realized. State courts may no longer be openly hostile to individual agreements to arbitrate employment disputes, but these agreements are certainly not greeted with gusto. In fact, some courts still evince an underlying bias against the validity of arbitration agreements.

The ebb and flow in the enforceability of arbitration agreements in employment is illustrated by a few recent decisions in the area. In *Circuit City Stores, Inc. v.*

Adams,[3] the Supreme Court reaffirmed the judicial recognition of ADR in the employment context, holding that an arbitration clause in an application for employment could be used to compel arbitration under the Federal Arbitration Act. On remand, however, the Ninth Circuit Court of Appeals held that the arbitration clause was unenforceable under state law, which applied to determine the underlying validity of the contract.

[i] Federal Arbitration Act and Employment Disputes

When he was hired by Circuit City, Adams filled out an application that contained a clause requiring all employment disputes to be settled by arbitration. After he was hired, Adams filed a state-law employment discrimination action against Circuit City. Circuit City responded by filing an action in federal court to stop the state court proceedings and to compel Adams to submit his dispute to arbitration pursuant to the FAA. Although the federal district court entered an order compelling arbitration of the claims, the Ninth Circuit Court of Appeals reversed the lower court's decision. According to the Ninth Circuit, a provision in the FAA that excluded from its coverage "contracts of employment of seamen, railroad employees, or any other class of workers engaged in foreign or interstate commerce" applied to all employment contracts, effectively putting any agreement to arbitrate employment disputes outside the coverage of the FAA.

The Ninth Circuit's decision represented a significant departure from decisions by a majority of federal courts, which had held that the FAA applied to individual employment contracts.[4] The decision also seemed to be in conflict with what most courts, including the Supreme Court, had recognized as "a liberal policy favoring arbitration agreements."[5]

In reversing the Ninth Circuit's decision, the Supreme Court held that the exemption from the FAA applied only to transportation workers. Adopting a broader interpretation of the exemption, the Court stated,

---

3. 532 U.S. 105 (2001).

4. *See, e.g.,* Cole v. Burns Int'l Security Services, 105 F.3d 1465 (D.C. Cir. 1997); O'Neil v. Hilton Head Hospital, 115 F.3d 272 (4th Cir. 1997); Rudolph v. Alamo Rent A Car, 952 F. Supp. 311 (E.D. Va. 1997); Asplundh Tree Expert Co. v. Bates, 71 F.3d 592 (6th Cir. 1995); Pryner v. Tractor Supply Co., 109 F.3d 354 (7th Cir.), *cert. denied,* 118 S.Ct. 295 (1997).

5. Gilmer v. Interstate/Johnson Lane Corp., 500 U.S. 20, 35 (1991).

would thwart the FAA's purpose of overcoming judicial hostility to arbitration.

Significantly, the court also rejected the argument that the FAA should not preempt state employment laws restricting the use of arbitration agreements. The Court reaffirmed that "there are real benefits to arbitration in the employment context, including avoidance of litigation costs." For employers with operations in more than one state, the Court noted, these costs are often compounded by the task of sorting out which state's law applies, and which laws apply to different claims. The court therefore reaffirmed the federal role in enforcing agreements to arbitrate employment disputes. To do otherwise, the Court stated, "would call into doubt the efficacy of many employers' alternative dispute resolution procedures, in the process undermining the FAA's proarbitration purposes and breeding litigation from a statute that seeks to avoid it."

In a subsequent decision, however, the Supreme Court recognized that an arbitration agreement cannot serve to completely insulate an employer from a lawsuit based on the violation of federal statutes prohibiting employment discrimination. In a ruling that surprised many observers, the Supreme Court held that a worker's agreement to arbitrate employment-related disputes with an employer does not prevent the Equal Employment Opportunity Commission (EEOC) from obtaining relief for discrimination against the employee.[6] In the 6-3 decision, the Court held that the EEOC could sue for victim-specific relief, including back pay, reinstatement, and damages.

The employee had filed a complaint with the EEOC, alleging that his discharge violated the Americans with Disabilities Act (ADA). He did not submit his claim to binding arbitration. The EEOC then brought its own enforcement action, alleging that Waffle House had engaged in unlawful employment practices on the basis of disability and seeking relief for the employee. Waffle House argued the case should be decided in arbitration, not in the courts. The Fourth Circuit Court of Appeals had partially agreed with Waffle House, holding that while the EEOC could still bring an action for injunctive relief, the arbitration agreement barred any claim for damages on behalf of the individual employee. The Supreme Court reversed the Fourth Circuit's decision, holding that the EEOC could pursue both injunctive relief and victim-specific relief, despite the arbitration agreement.

Although EEOC suits are much less common than suits brought by employees themselves, this decision makes it more difficult for employers to insulate themselves from liability through the use of binding arbitration. In 2001, the Supreme Court indicated a willingness to enforce private arbitration agreements in the employment discrimination context, spurring many employers to incorporate clauses in their employment agreements requiring binding arbitration. Although these agreements are still usually binding on the employee and can be used to preclude a lawsuit brought by the employee, the Court's decision means that arbitration agreements will not be effective in a lawsuit brought by the EEOC.

[ii] Substantive Unconscionability Under State Law

Although the FAA requires even state courts to recognize the enforceability of arbitration agreements, the Supreme Court has stated that these courts should apply ordinary state common-law contract principles in deciding whether the agreement is enforceable. One principle of state contract law that has been applied to invalidate agreements to arbitrate employment disputes is the principle that an unconscionable agreement cannot be enforced.

As previously mentioned, on remand the Ninth Circuit ruled that, although the agreement to arbitrate could otherwise be enforced under the FAA, the arbitration clause before it was unconscionable under California contract law.[7] In reaching this conclusion, the court was guided by Supreme Court precedent directing that arbitration agreements be evaluated pursuant to "ordinary state-law principles that govern the formation of contracts,"[8] and counseling that while arbitration agreements could not be invalidated under state laws applicable only to arbitration, general state law contract defenses such as unconscionability, could serve to invalidate arbitration agreements.[9] The Ninth Circuit's decision in *Circuit City Stores, Inc. v. Adams* underscores the point that, while arbitration can be a useful tool for employers, great care must be taken in the drafting of arbitration clauses in the employment context.

---

6. EEOC v. Waffle House, Inc., 122 S.Ct. 754 (2002).

7. Circuit City Stores, Inc. v. Adams, 279 F.3d 889 (9th Cir. 2002).

8. First Options of Chicago, Inc. v. Kaplan, 514 U.S. 938, 944 (1995).

9. Doctor's Assocs., Inc. v. Cassarotto, 517 U.S. 681, 687 (1996).

In the course of its analysis, the Ninth Circuit observed that:

> [u]nder California law, a contract is unenforceable if it is both procedurally and substantively unconscionable. *Armendariz v. Foundation Health Psychcare Svcs., Inc.*, 6 P.3d 669, 690 (Cal. 2000). When assessing procedural unconscionability, we consider the equilibrium of bargaining power between the parties and the extent to which the contract clearly discloses its terms. *Stirlen v. Supercuts, Inc.*, 60 Cal. Rptr. 138, 145 (Cal. Ct. App. 1997). A determination of substantive unconscionability, on the other hand, involves whether the terms of the contract are unduly harsh or oppressive. *Id.*[10]

The dispute resolution agreement (DRA) Adams signed failed under both prongs of this analysis.

The court found that the DRA was procedurally unconscionable because it was a contract of adhesion (i.e., a standard-form contract) drafted by the party with superior bargaining power, which relegates to the other party the option of either adhering to its terms without modification or rejecting the contract entirely. Circuit City, which the court noted had "considerably more bargaining power than nearly all of its employees or applicants," drafted the DRA and required all of its new employees to use it. Employees were not free to reject or modify the DRA. They could either accept the DRA or decline employment.

The Ninth Circuit easily found that the DRA was substantively unconscionable as well. First, the Circuit City agreement applied only to claims brought by employees and not to employer claims against employees, which Circuit City was free to bring in court or before an arbitrator as it saw fit. Circuit City gave no explanation for this "asymmetry," and the court could glean no business justification for the one-sidedness. Thus, the DRA lacked the "modicum of bilaterality" required by the California Supreme Court in order for contracts to be enforceable.

Second, the DRA limited the scope of employees' claims and excluded damages that would otherwise be available by statute. Specifically, the DRA (1) limited available remedies to injunctive relief, up to one year of back pay and up to two years of front pay, compensatory damages, and punitive damages in an amount up to the greater of the amount of back pay and front pay or $5,000; (2) required the employee to split the arbitrator's fee with Circuit City; and (3) imposed a one-year statute of limitations on arbitration claims, effectively depriving

employees of the continuing violation doctrine. The court noted that the fee-sharing scheme alone would be sufficient to render an arbitration agreement unenforceable.

The Ninth Circuit was careful to point out that its decision was consistent with *Gilmer v. Interstate/Johnson Lane Corp.*,[11] which has been construed to require minimum procedural and remedial protections in order for claimants to pursue their statutory rights. Moreover, the court's opinion did not run afoul of the FAA because the Supreme Court had recognized that unconscionability may be raised as a defense to the enforcement of an arbitration agreement. Finally, the Court opined that its decision was consistent with recent Ninth Circuit precedent.[12] Finding that "the objectionable provisions pervade the entire contract," the court determined that the DRA could not be saved by severing. The court held that the entire DRA was unenforceable and reversed the order compelling arbitration.

California courts have more recently elaborated upon the doctrine of unconscionability and when it applies to invalidate an arbitration agreement. In *Mercuro, et al. v. Superior Court*,[13] the California Court of Appeal, Second Division, reaffirmed the notion that both procedural and substantive unconscionability must be present to invalidate a contract or one of its terms. The court then clarified that the two elements need not be present in the same degree. The greater the degree of substantive oppressiveness, the less evidence of procedural unconscionability that is required to render the term unenforceable, the court held, and vice versa. In *Mercuro*, procedural unconscionability was clearly present, the court wrote, due to the oppressive tactics used by the employer to obtain the employee's signature on the agreement. The plaintiff had allegedly been threatened that the employer would "drive him out" and make it "all but impossible" for him to obtain other employment. The oppressiveness of this conduct was exacerbated by the fact that the employee, aged 52, had only recently relocated to the state, putting him in a position where he could ill-afford to lose his job. Under these circumstances, the court held that a minimal showing of substantive unconscionability was sufficient to invalidate the agreement. The employee made such a

---

10. Circuit City Stores, Inc. v. Adams, 279 F.3d 889 (9th Cir. 2002).

11. 500 U.S. 20 (1991) (holding that employees do not waive substantive rights by agreeing to arbitrate statutory claims but only agree to submit to an arbitral rather than a judicial forum).

12. Circuit City Stores, Inc. v. Adams, 279 F.3d 889 (9th Cir. 2002).

13. 96 Cal. App. 4th 167 (2002).

showing, the court found, in that the agreement was unfairly one-sided because it required arbitration of most claims of interest to employees but exempted most claims of interest to the employer. The agreement also failed to guarantee a neutral arbitrator by designating a small group of potential arbitrators with whom the employer would be a "repeat player." The "repeat player effect," the court found, could put employees at a distinct disadvantage before arbitrators.

Shortly after its decision in *Adams*, the Ninth Circuit addressed a case which raised issues identical to those on remand in *Adams*, except that the arbitration agreement at issue in the subsequent case allowed employees a meaningful choice not to participate in the program. The court found that this difference—the genuine possibility to opt out of the arbitration program—was a crucial distinction and therefore affirmed the decision upholding the arbitration clause.[14]

Ahmed took a job as a sales counselor for Circuit City in March 1995. A month later, the company instituted an "Associates Issue Resolution Program" which called for binding arbitration of legal disputes. Ahmed received a package of documents regarding the new program, including an opt-out form, which had to be submitted in 30 days to avoid automatic inclusion in the arbitration program. Participation in the program was not required as a condition of continued employment. When Ahmed, who had not submitted the opt-out form, sued Circuit City in 1997, the Ninth Circuit refused to enforce the arbitration clause. The Supreme Court, however, directed the court to reconsider the case in light of the holding in *Adams*. This time, the Ninth Circuit enforced the agreement, since it was not a contract of adhesion (an agreement over which a party lacks a realistic opportunity to bargain), and therefore was not procedurally unconscionable, because Ahmed had been free to opt out. The court was unpersuaded by Ahmed's arguments that his lack of sophistication and the 30-day decision period deprived him of a meaningful opportunity to opt out. No case supported these arguments, and Ahmed had ample opportunity to investigate any provisions he did not understand before making his decision. Moreover, as a rule, "one who signs a contract is bound by its provisions and cannot complain of unfamiliarity with the language of the instrument."

Notably, a recent California case has indicated that an arbitration agreement need not be a required condi-

tion of employment to be found unconscionable. In *Packin v. Astra USA, Inc.*,[15] the employer argued that its arbitration agreement was not unconscionable because it was not made a condition of the employee's continued employment, since he could have refused to sign at the cost of forfeiting future allocations to the profit sharing plan. The court disagreed, arguing that "[f]orcing an employee to accept a reduction in compensation in exchange for the right to a judicial forum is as offensive as imposing arbitration as a condition of employment." The agreement at issue was a contract of adhesion and was therefore procedurally unconscionable, since the employee was free only to accept or reject its terms. The court then found the agreement to be substantively unconscionable as well, citing prior case law for the proposition that an arbitration agreement that purports to serve as the vehicle for the enforcement of statutory rights will be enforceable only if it:

> (1) provides for neutral arbitrators, (2) provides for more than minimal discovery, (3) requires a written award, (4) provides for all of the types of relief that would otherwise be available in court, and (5) does not require employees to pay either unreasonable costs or any arbitrators' fees or expenses as a condition of access to the arbitration forum. *Armendariz v. Foundation Health Psychcare Services, Inc.*, 24 Cal. 4th 83, 100–101.

Not all state courts are similarly interested in restricting the use of arbitration agreements. In a recent Florida case, a state appellate court took a strong position in favor of the enforcement of arbitration agreements.[16] Katz, a financial advisor for Prudential, had signed an employment agreement wherein he promised to arbitrate any claim or controversy relating to his employment or termination. In 1999, Katz sent a letter to Prudential expressing concerns about what he perceived to be Prudential's illegal conduct. Shortly thereafter, Prudential responded, denying the allegations and then terminating Katz. Katz brought suit under the Florida Whistle Blower Act, and Prudential sought to enforce the arbitration agreement. The Florida court straightforwardly reasoned that Katz had agreed to arbitrate such claims, that arbitration clauses are applicable to a broad range of actions, and that "arbitration is a favored means of dispute resolution and courts indulge every reasonable presumption to uphold proceedings resulting in an

---

14. Circuit City Stores, Inc. v. Ahmed, 283 F.3d 1198 (9th Cir. 2002).

15. 2002 WL 120563 (Cal. App. 4 Dist. Jan. 29, 2002).

16. Prudential Securities, Inc. v. Katz, 807 So.2d 173 (Fla. Dist. Ct. App. 2002).

award."[17] The court stated that it had a duty to resolve all doubts in favor of arbitration rather than against it. The court noted that "in a steady drumbeat of cases," courts had reversed a number of decisions precluding arbitration for various statutory claims, expanding the permissible scope of arbitration to include antitrust, RICO, securities fraud, and even civil rights cases. If such claims were not inappropriate for arbitration, the Florida court found it "very difficult to imagine a civil claim in which an agreement to arbitrate would not be enforced." Since Katz's claim was expressly covered by the terms of the arbitration agreement, the court could see no reason not to enforce it.

[iii] Consideration Necessary to Support Arbitration Agreements

The concept of consideration is another principle of state contract law that applies to determine the enforceability of agreements to arbitrate employment claims. Because state law may vary on this point, multistate employers and their counsel should carefully consider recent trends in state law before promulgating an arbitration program.

In some cases, courts have had little trouble finding adequate consideration for an arbitration agreement. For example, one court has held that the employer's promise to consider an individual for employment is sufficient consideration.[18] Some courts have held that merely allowing an employee to continue his or her at-will employment is sufficient consideration to support an agreement to arbitrate employment claims.[19]

In *J.M. Davidson Inc. v. Webster*,[20] however, the court held that continued employment of an at-will employee did not constitute sufficient consideration for an arbitration agreement. The court reasoned that such a promise would be illusory because "the company could have fired [the employee] the very minute she signed the acknowledgment form."

It is significant to note that the court in J.M. Davidson indicated that had the arbitration agreement bound both the employee and the employer, it may have found sufficient consideration:

> In its reply brief, Davidson cites In re Jebbia, 26 S.W.3d 753 (Tex.App.—Houston [14th Dist.] 2000, orig. proceeding), and In re Alamo Lumber Co., 23 S.W.3d 577 (Tex.App.—San Antonio 2000, orig. proceeding), in support of its contention that "mutual promises by an employer and employee giving up the right to litigate are sufficient consideration to support an arbitration agreement." However, in both these cases, the language of the arbitration agreement showed that it was binding on both parties. See Jebbia, 26 S.W.3d at 758 ("The language of the arbitration agreement indicates it is binding on both parties."); Alamo Lumber, 23 S.W.3d at 579–80 ("Since the parties surrendered their rights to trial by jury, these mutual promises supply valid consideration."). Because we have held in this case that the "Alternative Dispute Resolution Policy-Employment Application Language" sought to bind only the employee, not the company, we conclude these cases are not controlling.

The importance of the mutuality of obligations imposed under the agreement has been the subject of some disagreement in the courts. At least one court has held that equal rights and remedies are not required to provide sufficient consideration.[21] On the other hand, a court found consideration in the fact that both employer and employee have promised to waive their rights to a judicial forum and submit any dispute arising out of the employment to binding arbitration. Another court has held that mutuality of obligations may be an important factor in considering the adequacy of consideration.[22] For some courts, the mutuality of obligations under the agreement to arbitrate has been the linchpin in the anal-

---

17. *Quoting*, Roe v. Amica Mut. Ins. Co., 533 So.2d 279, 281 (Fla.1988).

18. *See* Morrison v. Circuit City Stores Inc., 70 F. Supp. 2d 815, 824 (S.D. Ohio 1999) (holding that employer's implied promise to consider individual's application for employment and to continue to employ the individual constituted sufficient consideration for arbitration agreement).

19. *See* Quigley v. KPMG Peat Marwick LLP, 749 A.2d 405, 413 (N.J. Super. Ct. App. Div. 2000) (holding that continued at-will employment was sufficient consideration for arbitration agreement); Ex parte McNaughton, 728 So.2d 592 (Ala. 1998) (continued at-will employment sufficient consideration for arbitration agreement even if employer reserves to itself the right to amend the arbitration agreement at any time).

20. 49 S.W.3d 507 (Tex. Civ. App.—Corpus Christi 2001).

21. In re Ball, 236 A.D.2d 158 (N.Y. 3d Dept. 1997) (equal rights and remedies under arbitration agreement are not necessary to provide sufficient consideration for agreement so long as each party provided some consideration).

22. Durkin v. Cigna Property & Casualty Corp., 942 F. Supp. 481 (D. Kan. 1996) (holding that mutuality of rights and remedies under arbitration agreement may be factor in determining whether agreement is supported by adequate consideration).

ysis of whether the agreement is enforceable.[23] A North Carolina court has gone a bit further, stating not only that mutuality must exist in fact, but also that the employee must have been informed of the mutual obligation.[24]

A different twist on the mutuality of obligations question was presented in a case involving an employer who contracted with a third party to provide arbitration of employment disputes. In that case, the Seventh Circuit Court of Appeals held that an agreement to arbitrate employment claims was unenforceable because it imposed no specific obligations on the employer although it contained two pages describing the obligations of the employee. The employer had contracted with another company, Employment Dispute Services (EDS) to provide an arbitral forum for all employment-related disputes between the employer and its employees. When an individual made application for employment, the employer required the applicant to sign an agreement with EDS to submit any claims against the employer to arbitration provided by EDS. The employer was not a party to this agreement. Under the agreement, the description of the EDS's responsibility stated only that the employee agreed to the contract "in consideration of the agreement by EDS to provide an arbitration forum." Under the rules relating to arbitration, which the employee also signed, EDS retained the discretion to determine whether a proposed arbitrator could be struck for cause and also retained complete control over who appears on the lists of proposed arbitrators. The rules also gave the chief executive officer of EDS the power to interpret the rules of arbitration and "any issue which may arise relating to them," and gave the employer the power unilaterally to amend or modify the rules.

Based on these facts, the court held that the arbitration agreement was unenforceable for lack of consideration:

> [T]he arbitration agreement between EDS and Penn contains only an unascertainable, illusory promise on the part of EDS. The agreement is clear enough as to what Penn is promising: he agrees that he will bring any employment-related dispute that he has with Ryan's in the EDS arbitration forum and not in state or federal

court. The agreement restates this proposition several times in various ways, and goes into some detail as to the types of disputes that are covered by the agreement and the duration of Penn's obligation. In marked contrast to the specificity of Penn's obligation is the language describing the consideration EDS is obligated to provide Penn in return: EDS commits itself only "to provide an arbitration forum, Rules and Procedures, and a hearing and decision based on any claim or dispute" that the employee might raise. Nothing in the contract provides any details about the nature of the forum that EDS will provide or sets standards with which EDS must comply; EDS could fulfill its promise by providing Penn and Ryan's with a coin toss. Although Penn was given the EDS Rules along with the contract he signed, and we will assume that the Rules form part of the contract, adding the Rules to the mix does nothing to make EDS's commitment more concrete, because the Rules specifically give EDS the sole, unilateral discretion to modify or amend them. The contract is therefore hopelessly vague and uncertain as to the obligation EDS has undertaken. For all practical purposes, EDS's promise under this contract "makes performance entirely optional with the promisor."[25]

It should be noted that the court held that "the parties could have solved their consideration problem entirely simply by making Ryan's a party to the contract." In other words, had the employer promised to waive its right to a judicial forum for disputes arising out of the employment, such a promise would have constituted adequate consideration for the employee's corresponding promise to submit claims to arbitration.

[iv] Effect of Cost Sharing on Enforceability of Arbitration Agreements

A number of courts have recently addressed the enforceability of arbitration agreements that require employees alleging statutory discrimination claims to share the fees and expenses of arbitration. The Supreme Court has held that fee shifting can render an arbitration agreement unenforceable where the arbitration fees and costs are so prohibitive as to effectively deny the employee access to the arbitral forum.[26] Courts have come to differing conclusions, however, regarding whether fee splitting automatically renders an arbitration agreement unenforceable absent a showing of individual hardship or deterrence.

---

23. Brown v. Rexhall Industries Inc., 1996 WL 662449 (N.D. Ind. Oct. 9, 1996) (holding that sufficient consideration existed to support arbitration agreement signed by at-will employee after she had already been employed where employer waived its right to judicial forum with respect to disputes arising out of employment).

24. Howard v. Oakwood Homes Corp., 516 S.E.2d 879 (N.C. App. 1999) (holding that for consideration to be adequate, employee must be informed of mutual obligation to arbitrate).

25. Penn v. Ryan's Family Steak Houses, Inc., No. 00-2355 (7th Cir. Oct. 17, 2001).

26. Green Tree Financial Corp.—Alabama v. Randolph, 121 S.Ct. 513 (2000).

A number of courts have refused to enforce arbitration agreements with fee-splitting arrangements.[27] Other courts have permitted allocation of fees between employer and employee, based in part on the fact that arbitration is often more affordable than litigation for both plaintiffs and defendants.[28]

The Fourth Circuit has stated that it will evaluate fee-splitting arrangements based on "whether the arbitral forum in a particular case is an adequate and accessible substitute to litigation, i.e., a case-by-case analysis that focuses, among other things, upon the claimant's ability to pay the arbitration fees and costs, the expected cost differential between arbitration and litigation in court, and whether that cost differential is so substantial as to deter the bringing of claims."[29] Applying this analysis, the Fourth Circuit went on to hold that arbitration fees and costs of $4,470.88 were not sufficiently substantial to invalidate the arbitration agreement.

In some other recent decisions, the courts have taken a more restrictive view of the degree to which arbitration agreements can require cost shifting. In *Ball v. SFX Broadcasting*,[30] the court held that the proper analysis of whether an arbitration agreement is enforceable in light of a cost-shifting provision is not whether the plaintiff can afford the costs of arbitration, but whether those costs are significantly more than the costs that would be incurred in a judicial forum. In *Perez v. Globe Airport Sec. Servs., Inc.*,[31] the plaintiff brought suit after the termination of her employment, alleging that she had been subjected to sex discrimination in violation of Title VII. The employer sought to compel arbitration based on an arbitration clause in Perez's employment agreement. Perez argued that the agreement was unenforceable because it improperly shifted the costs of arbitration to the employee. After examining Perez's financial circumstances and the costs of arbitration, the court agreed, holding that the agreement was unenforceable. Furthermore, the court held that the fee-shifting arrangement in

the arbitration clause rendered it unenforceable because it purported to remove "the arbitrator's authority to grant effective relief by mandating equal sharing of fees and costs of arbitration despite the award of fees permitted a prevailing party by Title VII."

In *Mercuro, et al. v. Superior Court*,[32] the California Court of Appeal, Second Division, held that the fee-splitting provision at issue rendered the arbitration agreement invalid, because it required employees to bear a part of the arbitrator's fee, a type of expense that employees would not have been required to bear if they were free to bring the action in court. The California court held that arbitration agreements that apply to an employee's unwaiveable rights under a statute enacted for a public reason are subject to "particular scrutiny," and must, at a minimum, provide for neutral arbitrators, adequate discovery, a written award subject to limited judicial review, and the same types of relief that would be available from a court, and the employees must not be required to bear any type of expense they would not be required to bear if their claims were brought in a court.

These decisions indicate that employers must walk a fine line with respect to cost-shifting provisions in arbitration agreements. Indeed, any benefit an employer may obtain by requiring cost shifting in arbitration may be outweighed by the risk that such a provision will render the arbitration clause or agreement unenforceable. Nevertheless, cost shifting can be a valuable tool in dissuading employees from pursuing frivolous claims. A carefully crafted arbitration clause can include a cost-shifting provision without creating the risk of rendering the clause or agreement unenforceable.

[v] State Court Deference to Arbitral Decisions

Just as court challenges can be an obstacle to the application of an arbitration agreement, further challenges may have to be dealt with after an arbitrator has come to a decision. A recent Texas case is instructive with regard to how state courts may handle such a challenge, and the general tendency of courts not to disturb arbitral decisions. In *Autrey v. Ultramar Diamond Shamrock Corp.*,[33] an arbitrator found in favor of an employer charged with sexual harassment, a decision upheld by the trial court. On appeal, the plaintiff asserted a number of reasons for her contention that the trial court had erred in upholding the award, each of which was rejected by

---

27. Paladino v. Avnet Computer Technologies, Inc., 134 F.3d 1054 (11th Cir. 1998); Cole v. Burns Int'l Sec. Servs., 105 F.3d 1465 (D.C. Cir. 1997).

28. Williams v. Cigna Financial Advisors, Inc., 197 F.3d 752 (5th Cir. 1999); Rosenberg v. Merrill Lynch, Pierce, Fenner & Smith, Inc., 170 F.3d 1 (1st Cir. 1999); Koveleskie v. SBC Capital Markets, Inc., 167 F.3d 361 (7th Cir. 1999), *cert. denied*, 528 U.S. 811 (1999).

29. Bradford v. Rockwell Semiconductor Systems, Inc., 238 F.3d 549 (4th Cir. 2001).

30. No. 00-CV-1090 (N.D.N.Y. Aug. 21, 2001).

31. 253 F.3d 1280 (11th Cir. 2001).

32. 96 Cal. App. 4th 167 (2002).

33. 2002 WL 102198 (Tex. App. Dallas).

the appellate court. The courts, the appellate judges noted, "must review an arbitrator's award with great deference" and review of an arbitration award is "extraordinarily narrow."

Under the FAA, which applies to almost all employment agreements, a court may vacate an arbitration award (1) where the award was procured by corruption, fraud, or undue means, (2) where there was evident partiality or corruption in the arbitrators, (3) where the arbitrators were guilty of misconduct, and (4) where the arbitrators exceeded their powers.[34] Additionally, a court may vacate an arbitration award when the award reflects an arbitrator's "manifest disregard" for the law. The plaintiff took issue with the arbitrator's credibility judgments with respect to herself and her witnesses. The court held that credibility judgments essentially were not reviewable in court. Nor did the arbitrator's alleged inexperience and failure to provide reasons for her decision, as required by American Arbitration Association rules, justify judicial intervention. The arbitrator corrected the omission when it was brought to her attention and therefore did not exhibit "manifest disregard" for the law.

[c] OSHA Withdraws Proposed Rule to Ban Workplace Smoking

In November 2001, a federal appeals court ordered the Occupational Safety and Health Administration (OSHA) to complete the rulemaking timetable for the smoking ban by December 13, 2001.[35] On December 14, 2001, OSHA withdrew the proposed ban, observing that almost 70 percent of American workers already enjoyed smoke-free environments as a result of state and local laws. Interestingly, the withdrawal was encouraged by the American Lung Association, the American Cancer Society, and the American Heart Association. Major anti-smoking groups were concerned that a weaker rule might have been adopted, potentially preempting state and local smoking regulations that have been widely enacted around the country. In making the announcement, Assistant Secretary for Occupational Safety and Health John Henshaw acknowledged the role now being played by state and local legislation. "Of course," Henshaw noted, "this action does not preclude future agency action if the need arises."

State and local legislative bodies have continued to pass smoke-free workplace ordinances. As of 2002, there are hundreds of local ordinances requiring smoke-free workplaces. In addition, several states have imposed bans or partial bans on workplace smoking. For example, Washington has imposed a ban on smoking in office workplaces and Maryland has a ban covering smoking in enclosed workplaces.[36] For more information on state and local smoking laws, see § 8.2 in the *2002 State by State Guide to Human Resource Law.*

[d] Required Interactive Process for the Americans with Disabilities Act

The Americans with Disabilities Act (ADA) requires that employers provide reasonable accommodations for qualified individuals with disabilities. This requirement includes a duty on the part of the employer (and the employee) to engage in an interactive process to determine an appropriate accommodation. In some cases, courts have held that state laws analogous to the ADA create a similar requirement. For example, in *Davis v. Microsoft Corp.,*[37] the court found that the Washington Law Against Discrimination requires employers to engage in an interactive process to determine an appropriate accommodation. In *Davis*, an employee who was responsible for high-level marketing was diagnosed with hepatitis C. His normal workload was between 60 and 80 hours per week, but his doctor advised him to reduce his hours to 40. Microsoft instructed Davis to reduce his hours but did not change his job responsibilities, so he continued to work up to 80 hours per week. Microsoft stated that the only accommodation that would allow Davis to remain in his job would be to hire additional staff to assist him, which it deemed unreasonable. Davis was advised that his only options were to resign or to seek another position at Microsoft. Microsoft took the position that its only duty was to give him a list of possible jobs; in all other respects, however, the company determined that he was to be treated the same as any other applicant. Microsoft would not inform him as to whether any of the jobs on the list could accommodate his 40-hour restriction. Davis attended one interview and discovered that the position required 60 to 90 hours of work per week. Davis applied for no other jobs and was eventually terminated.

---

34. 9 U.S.C.A. § 10(a) (West 1999).

35. Action on Smoking & Health v. OSHA, D.C. Cir., No. 01-1199, order Nov. 13, 2001.

36. Wash. Admin. Code 296-62-12000 *et. seq.*; Code of Md. Regs. § 9.12.23.

37. 37 P.3d 333 (Wash. App. Div. 1, 2002).

Davis sued for disability discrimination under the Washington Law Against Discrimination on two theories, one of which was that Microsoft did not take reasonable steps to identify a vacant position that he could have performed. The jury found in his favor and Microsoft appealed. The appellate court found that Microsoft was required to engage in an interactive process of accommodation, stating that once the disability is known to the employer, the employer must take reasonable steps to determine, and inform the employee of, a vacancy in another position for which the employee is qualified and that could accommodate his disability. The court concluded that Microsoft was not required to guarantee Davis an alternate position, but it was required to take reasonable steps to find an open position for which he was qualified.

A New Jersey court also found that the state law against discrimination requires employers to engage in an interactive process. In *Jones v. Aluminum Shapes, Inc.*,[38] the plaintiff, a crane operator, injured his eye on the job and could not continue as a crane operator due to his lack of binocular vision. The employee experienced difficulty finding another job with the employer. After the employer moved him from position to position, without consideration to his limitations, the employee sued under the New Jersey Law Against Discrimination (NJLAD). The court found that it was well settled in New Jersey that comparable federal ADA cases should be consulted when interpreting the NJLAD. Ultimately, the court found that reasonable accommodation under the NJLAD requires employers to engage in the same interactive process as under the ADA, citing federal cases and the federal regulations on reasonable accommodation.

Conversely, a Massachusetts court found that its state antidiscrimination law did not require employers to engage in the interactive process.[39] In the Massachusetts case, the plaintiff was a security guard who suffered on-the-job injuries that led to his absenteeism. He was eventually terminated for missing work and entered into a dispute with the company concerning workers' compensation and disability. He filed suit on several theories, one of which was a violation of the Massachusetts antidiscrimination law. Specifically, he argued that the employer had failed to engage in an interactive process to determine an appropriate reasonable accommodation. The court stated that no such requirement exists in the

Massachusetts law, and that one would not be adopted as in the federal ADA.

[e] Legislation on Breastfeeding in the Workplace

The American Academy of Pediatrics recommends that mothers breastfeed a child for at least the first full year of its life. Numerous medical studies have found that breastfed babies tend to be healthier, are less likely to become ill, and may be more intelligent than those who are primarily formula-fed. Mothers who breastfeed also have a lower risk of certain cancers as well as osteoporosis. A 1994 *International Journal of Gynecology and Obstetrics* report indicated that two to four billion dollars in U.S. health care costs could be saved annually if women breastfed their infants for as little as 12 weeks.

In response to studies such as these, state legislators have begun in recent years to enact legislation designed to promote breastfeeding and to remove obstacles to both nursing and the expressing of breast milk for later consumption. A majority of states have enacted some form of legislation relating to breastfeeding. A number of states, for example, have passed measures dealing with the permissibility of breastfeeding in public. Other laws exempt breastfeeding mothers from seatbelt laws or jury duty.

Most significant for employers, however, is the growing trend toward states' adopting legislation aimed at protecting the ability of nursing mothers either to breastfeed or to express milk in the workplace. As of this writing, at least seven states had enacted such legislation, including California, Connecticut, Hawaii, Illinois, Maine, Minnesota, and Tennessee. Four of these measures passed in 2001. In addition, Florida, Georgia, Texas, and Washington encourage employers to adopt breastfeeding accommodations.

In addition to state legislation, federal legislation has been introduced to provide tax credits for employers that provide a lactation-friendly workplace for employed mothers who wish to breastfeed or express milk at work. The Breastfeeding Promotion Act, introduced by U.S. Representative Carolyn Maloney (D-N.Y.), would also regulate breast pumps by setting minimum quality standards, and provide protection under civil rights law for women who breastfeed.

Some localities have also begun to promote breastfeeding in the workplace. Philadelphia, for example, has enacted an ordinance barring public accommodations from excluding or segregating breastfeeding

---

38. 772 A.2d 34 (N.J. Super. A.D., 2001).

39. Sullivan v. Raytheon Co., 262 F.3d 41 (1st. Cir. 2001).

mothers from places where they would otherwise be authorized to be.[40] For the past six years, Allegheny County, Pennsylvania's Health Department, has given out its Breastfeeding Friendly Workplace Award to honor employers who accommodate breastfeeding by working mothers.

Nursing mothers have also begun to take their battle to the courts in recent years. Borders Group, Inc. recently settled a lawsuit brought by a California bookstore patron who was directed by store personnel not to breastfeed. The suit was brought under a state law permitting nursing mothers to feed in such public venues. Similarly, two Ohio women are suing Wal-mart for being denied the opportunity to nurse their infants in the retail outlets. In an employment case, the Hooter's restaurant chain has also been sued for pregnancy discrimination recently by an employee who alleged that she had been humiliated by supervisors for expressing breast milk.

Not surprisingly, additional lawsuits, such as one filed recently by a Minnesota employee whose employer denied her a private location to nurse or express milk, are beginning to be brought under state workplace breastfeeding statutes as well.

Nearly 23 percent of employers responding to a 2000 Department of Labor survey indicated that provisions for breastfeeding had been made in the workplace. Over 35 percent of establishments covered by the Family and Medical Leave Act and over 45 percent of establishments having more than 250 employees have put in place some workplace provisions regarding breastfeeding. For these employers, compliance with new state or federal legislation requiring accommodation may be relatively easy. Nevertheless, all employers should be aware of the trend in this area, and the potential compliance issues resulting from this trend. Exhibit I contains a description of state legislation in this area.

---

40. Phil. City Code § 9-1105.

Exhibit I
STATE LEGISLATION ON
BREASTFEEDING IN THE WORKPLACE

CALIFORNIA

In California, Assembly Bill 1025, which requires all employers to provide lactation accommodation for employees, was signed by Governor Davis and added to the Labor Code effective January 1, 2002. [Cal. Labor Code §§ 1030 through 1033] The new law requires employers to provide a reasonable amount of break time to accommodate an employee desiring to express breast milk for the employee's infant child. The break time shall, if possible, run concurrently with any break time already provided to the employee. Break time for an employee that does not run concurrently with a rest time authorized for the employee by the applicable IWC Wage Order shall be unpaid.

The California law also addresses privacy concerns by requiring employers to make reasonable efforts to provide an employee with the use of a room or other location, other than a toilet stall, in close proximity to the employee's work area, for the employee to express milk in private. The room or location may include the place where the employee normally works if it otherwise meets the requirements of the provision. [Cal. Labor Code § 1031]

An employer that violates any provision of this new law is subject to a civil penalty in the amount of $100 for each violation. If inspection or investigation by the Labor Commissioner determines that a violation of this law has occurred, a citation may be issued. [Cal. Labor Code § 1033]

The California law provides for a narrow exception to the new requirements. An employer is not required to provide break time under the law if to do so would seriously disrupt the operations of the employer. It is likely that this provision will be construed in a way that is consistent with the "undue hardship" exception to reasonable accommodation requirements for persons with disabilities. Thus, employers should take care not to assume that any disruption caused by compliance with the law will be accepted as "serious."

CONNECTICUT

The Connecticut legislature has enacted a statute that prohibits any person from restricting or limiting the right of a mother to breastfeed her child. The law further prohibits discrimination by a place of public accommodation in the form of limiting a woman's breastfeeding of her child in public. Fines of not less than $25 nor more than $100, and penalties of imprisonment for not more than 30 days, may be imposed for violations of this law. In 2001, a new law was enacted that provides that employees can express breast milk or breastfeed at work during meal or break periods, and that employers must make reasonable efforts to provide a room or other location near the work area (not a toilet stall) to express milk in private as long as providing such a place would not impose an undue hardship on the operations of the employer. Discriminating against or taking any adverse action against breastfeeding mothers for exercising their rights under this law is also prohibited. [Conn. Gen. Stat. Ann. §§ 46a-64, 53-34b]

DELAWARE

Delaware law provides simply that a mother is "entitled to breast-feed her child in any location of a place of public accommodation wherein the mother is otherwise permitted." [Del. Code Ann. tit. 31, § 310]

FLORIDA

The Florida legislature has stated that it is the public policy of the state to encourage the interests of maternal and child health. More specifically, the legislature has enacted a statute that provides that a woman has a right to breastfeed in any place she has a right to be, even if there is some exposure of the breast. Although Florida does not specifically require employers to accommodate breastfeeding, the legislature set up a project to look at the feasibility of breastfeeding guidelines for employers and encourages employers to accommodate employees. [Fla. Stat. Ann. §§ 383.015, 800.02 through 800.04, 827.071, 847.001]

GEORGIA

The Georgia legislature has enacted a law stating that an employer may provide reasonable unpaid break time each day to an employee who needs to express breast milk for her infant child. The employer may make reasonable efforts to provide a room or other location (in close proximity to the work area), other than a toilet stall, where the employee can express her milk in privacy. These provisions suggest that they are not mandatory. The statute further states, however, that "the break time shall, if possible, run concurrently with any break time already provided to the employee." This provision appears to be mandatory, for it is followed by a provision that states that "[a]n employer is not required to provide break time under this Code section if to do so would unduly disrupt the operations of the employer." [Ga. Code Ann. § 34-1-6(b)]

HAWAII

Legislation in Hawaii specifically prohibits the following: to refuse to hire or employ, to bar or discharge from employment, or to withhold pay from, demote, or penalize a lactating employee because an employee breastfeeds or expresses milk at the workplace. [Haw. Rev. Stat. Ann. § 378-2(7)]

ILLINOIS

In 2001, the Illinois legislature enacted a statute requiring employers to accommodate breastfeeding mothers when they return to work. Specifically, the statute requires an employer to provide reasonable unpaid break time each day to an employee who needs to express breast milk for her infant child. It requires an employer to make reasonable efforts to provide a room or other location, in close proximity to the work area, other than a toilet stall, where the employee can express her milk in privacy. [2001 Ill. Laws 68 (July 12, 2001)]

IOWA

The State of Iowa has enacted a provision stating simply that "a woman may breast-feed the woman's own child in any public place where the woman's presence is otherwise authorized." [Iowa Code Ann. § 135.30A]

KENTUCKY

In 2002, the Kentucky House of Representatives passed HB 351, which contains a number of provisions intended to encourage and protect the practice of breastfeeding. The bill would provide that a mother may breastfeed her baby in any location, public or private, where the mother is otherwise authorized to be. In addition, businesses or agencies would be permitted under the bill to use the designation "mother-friendly" in promotional materials if they institute a supportive worksite breastfeeding policy addressing:

(a) Work schedule flexibility, including scheduling breaks and work patterns to provide time for the expressing of milk;
(b) The provision of accessible locations allowing privacy;
(c) Access nearby to a clean, safe water source, and a sink for washing hands and rinsing out any needed breast-pumping equipment; and
(d) Access to hygienic storage alternatives in the workplace for the mother's breastmilk.

LOUISIANA

In 2001, Louisiana enacted a number of pro-breastfeeding provisions. Act 576 provides that a mother may breastfeed her baby in any place of public accommodation and prohibits "any direct or indirect act or practice of exclusion, distinction, restriction, segregation, limitation, refusal, denial, or any other act or practice of differentiation or preference in the treatment of a mother breastfeeding her baby." Act 576 further clarifies that a mother breastfeeding her baby in any location, public or private, where the mother is otherwise authorized to be, does not violate any provision of law. [La. Rev. Stat. Ann. § 51:2247.1]

MAINE

In 2001, Maine enacted a provision that states that "[n]otwithstanding any other provision of law, a mother may breast-feed her baby in any location, public or private, where the mother is otherwise authorized to be." [Me. Rev. Stat. Ann. tit. 5, § 4634]

MINNESOTA

Minnesota has legislation that requires employers to accommodate breastfeeding mothers when they return to work. An employer must provide reasonable unpaid break time each day to an employee who needs to express breast milk for her infant child. The break time must, if possible, run concurrently with any break time already provided to the employee. An employer is not required to provide break time under this provision if to do so would unduly disrupt the operations of the employer. The employer must make reasonable efforts to provide a room or other location, in close proximity to the work area, other than a toilet stall, where the employee can express her milk in privacy. The employer will be held harmless if reasonable effort has been made. [Minn. Stat. Ann. §181.939]

NEVADA

Nevada law states that "a mother may breast feed her child in any public or private location where the mother is otherwise authorized to be, irrespective of whether the nipple of the mother's breast is uncovered during or incidental to the breast feeding." [Nev. Rev. Stat. Ann. § 201.232]

NEW MEXICO

New Mexico law provides that a mother may breastfeed her child in any location, public or private, where the mother is otherwise authorized to be present. [N.M. Stat. Ann. § 28-20-1]

NEW YORK

New York law does not impose any specific requirements on employers regarding breastfeeding, nor does it have any legislation that applies specifically to the workplace. New York has, however, enacted an amendment to its Civil Rights Law that provides as follows: "Notwithstanding any other provision of law, a mother may breast feed her baby in any location, public or private, where the mother is otherwise authorized to be, irrespective of whether or not the nipple of the mother's breast is covered during or incidental to the breast feeding." [N.Y. Civ. Rights Law § 79-e]

Under consideration by New York legislators in 2002 was the Nursing Mothers in the Workplace Act (SB 5832). If enacted, the legislation will require employers with more than five employees to provide, for at least two years after childbirth, reasonable unpaid break time (not to exceed 20 minutes or three breaks per eight-hour period) or to permit employees to use paid break or meal time during work hours, so that employees may express breast milk for nursing infants. Employers would also be required under the legislation to provide private accommodations suitable for the purpose of expressing milk, in close proximity to the work area, excluding bathroom stalls or storage areas. Furthermore, discrimination of any sort would be prohibited with respect to employees who choose to express milk in the workplace.

NORTH CAROLINA

North Carolina law provides that "a woman may breast feed in any public or private location where she is otherwise authorized to be." [N.C. Gen. Stat. § 14-109.9]

TENNESSEE

Tennessee requires employers to provide reasonable unpaid break time each day to an employee who needs to express breast milk for that employee's infant child. The break time shall, if possible, run concurrently with any break time already provided to the employee. An employer shall not be required to provide break time under this section if to do so would unduly disrupt the operations of the employer. The employer is required to make reasonable efforts to provide a room or other location in close proximity to the work area, other than a toilet stall, where the employee can express breast milk in privacy. Unlike a number of state statutes, Tennessee's law contains a provision designed to protect employers. Under this provision, the employer will be held harmless if reasonable effort has been made to comply with the provisions set out above. [Tenn. Code Ann. § 50-1-305]

TEXAS

The Texas legislature has specifically recognized the benefits of breastfeeding. It has also enacted provisions that state that women have a right to breastfeed in public. In addition, the legislature has established standards for employers to advertise themselves as "mother friendly" if they develop breastfeeding support policies and has established a demonstration project to determine the feasibility of breastfeeding support policies for all state employees. [Tex. Lab. Code Ann. §§ 165.001–165.005, 165.031–165.034]

VIRGINIA

The Virginia General Assembly passed two pieces of pertinent legislation in 2002. House Joint Resolution No. 145 encourages employers to "recognize the benefits of breast-feeding and set aside appropriate space for such activities," and to provide "reasonable unpaid break time each day" for employees to breast-feed or express milk for infant children. More significantly, legislators also enacted a provision (HB 1264) prohibiting employers from discharging employees on the basis of "lactation," defined as "a condition that may result in the feeding of a child directly from the breast or the expressing of milk from the breast." The enactment provides for a cause of action against an employer who violates the provision. Up to 12 months of back pay may generally be awarded to a successful claimant, plus attorney's fees in an amount not to exceed 25 percent of the back pay awarded. Other damages and reinstatement are not available remedies. It remains to be seen whether Virginia Governor Mark Warner will sign HB 1264.

WASHINGTON

Legislation in Washington encourages employers to accommodate breastfeeding mothers and creates an incentive program for employers by permitting them to advertise that they are "infant friendly" if they provide lactation support for their employees. In order to qualify for the designation, the employer must submit a policy that provides for the following:

(a) Flexible work scheduling, including scheduling breaks and permitting work patterns that provide time for expression of breast milk;

(b) A convenient, sanitary, safe, and private location, other than a restroom, allowing privacy for breastfeeding or expressing breast milk;

(c) A convenient, clean, and safe water source with facilities for washing hands and rinsing breast-pumping equipment located in the private location specified in (b) of this subsection; and

(d) A convenient hygienic refrigerator in the workplace for the mother's breast milk.

[Wash. Rev. Code Ann. § 43.70.640]

WISCONSIN

Legislation was considered in 2001 by Wisconsin legislators that would have created an income tax and franchise tax credit for businesses that construct or equip a facility for an employee to pump and store breast milk during the employee's working hours. The credit was to be granted in an amount equal to 50 percent of the amount paid or incurred by a business for such purposes, not to exceed $10,000 in a taxable year. The legislation, including the tax credit provision, Assembly Bill 124, failed to pass during the 2001 session, but a similar provision may be brought up again for further consideration.

WYOMING

House Joint Resolution HJ0011 was introduced during the 2002 session of the Wyoming Legislature. The resolution recognized the importance of breastfeeding, encouraged breastfeeding "in all situations," congratulated public and private sector employers that accommodate breastfeeding mothers, and indicated the Legislature's support for "the right of a woman to breastfeed in any location where she has the right to be with her child." Legislators failed to adopt the resolution during the brief 2002 budget session.

[f] Recent Decisions on the ADA's Coverage of Carpal Tunnel Syndrome

The U.S. Supreme Court has issued a ruling that will have an impact on the growing number of claims being filed under the Americans with Disabilities Act (ADA) based on repetitive motion injuries. In *Toyota Motor Manufacturing, Kentucky, Inc. v. Williams*,[41] the Court held that the Sixth Circuit did not apply the proper standard in determining that an employee was disabled under the ADA because it analyzed only a limited class of manual tasks and failed to ask whether the employee's impairments prevented or restricted her from performing tasks that are of central importance to most people's daily lives.

Although the headlines in the press generally asserted that the Court's decision constituted a new restriction on the applicability of the ADA, it would be more accurate to characterize it as a refusal to expand the coverage of the ADA. Under the Court's decision, employees with carpal tunnel syndrome are not necessarily excluded from the protections of the ADA. The Court made it clear, however, that employees with carpal tunnel syndrome must meet the same standard applicable to employees with other disabilities, and that this standard does not allow courts to create subclasses of substantial life activities in analyzing whether an individual is covered by the ADA.

In the case before the Supreme Court, the employee, Williams, claimed that she was disabled from performing her automobile assembly line job by carpal tunnel syndrome and related impairments. Williams sued her former employer for failing to provide her with a reasonable accommodation as required by the ADA. The district court granted summary judgment to the employer, holding that Williams's impairment did not qualify as a "disability" under the ADA because it had not "substantially limit[ed]" any "major life activit[y],"[42] and that there was no evidence that Williams had a record of a substantially limiting impairment or that her employer regarded her as having such an impairment.

The Sixth Circuit reversed the decision, finding that the impairments substantially limited Williams in the major life activity of performing manual tasks. According to the Supreme Court, the Sixth Circuit applied an improper standard in reaching this conclusion.

First, in determining what an individual must prove to demonstrate a substantial limitation in the major life activity of performing manual tasks, the court failed to properly apply the ADA's disability definition. "Substantially" in the phrase "substantially limits" suggests "considerably" or "to a large degree," and thus clearly precludes impairments that interfere in only a minor way with performing manual tasks. Moreover, because "major" means important, "major life activities" refers to those activities that are of central importance to daily life. To be substantially limited in the specific major life activity of performing manual tasks, the Court reasoned, an individual must have an impairment that prevents or severely restricts the individual from doing activities that are of central importance to most people's daily lives. The impairment's impact must also be permanent or long-term. The Supreme Court held that it was insufficient for individuals attempting to prove disability status under this test merely to submit evidence of a medical diagnosis of an impairment. Instead, the ADA requires them to offer evidence that the extent of the limitation caused by their impairment in terms of their own experience is substantial. In other words, there must be some individualized assessment of the impact of the disability. Such an individualized assessment of the effect of an impairment is particularly necessary when the impairment is one such as carpal tunnel syndrome, in which symptoms vary widely from person to person.

Second, the Supreme Court held that the Sixth Circuit erred in suggesting that, in order to prove a substantial limitation in the major life activity of performing manual tasks, a plaintiff must show that his or her manual disability involves a "class" of manual activities, and that those activities affect the ability to perform tasks at work. On this point, the Court noted that nothing in the ADA's text, the Court's opinions, or the regulations suggests that a class-based framework should apply outside the context of the major life activity of working. While the Sixth Circuit addressed the different major life activity of performing manual tasks, its analysis erroneously circumvented the Supreme Court's prior rulings by focusing on Williams's inability to perform manual tasks associated only with her job. Under the Court's holding, the central inquiry must be whether the claimant is unable to perform the variety of tasks central to most people's daily lives. The Supreme Court also rejected the Sixth Circuit's assertion that the question of whether an impairment constitutes a disability is to be answered only by analyzing the impairment's effect in the workplace. That the ADA's "disability" definition applies not only to the portion of the ADA dealing with employment, but also to the other provisions dealing with public

---

41. 122 S.Ct. 681 (2002).

42. 42 U.S.C. § 12102(2)(A).

transportation and public accommodations, demonstrates that the definition is intended to cover individuals with disabling impairments regardless of whether they have any connection to a workplace. Moreover, because the manual tasks unique to any particular job are not necessarily important parts of most people's lives, occupation-specific tasks may have only limited relevance to the manual-task inquiry.

In the case before it, the Supreme Court found that repetitive work with hands and arms extended at or above shoulder levels for extended periods, the manual task on which the Sixth Circuit relied, was not an important part of most people's daily lives. Household chores, bathing, and brushing one's teeth, in contrast, are among the types of manual tasks of central importance to people's daily lives, so the Sixth Circuit should not have disregarded Williams's ability to perform these activities.

Not surprisingly, reaction to the Court's decision has been mixed. The National Association of Manufacturers and the U.S. Chamber of Commerce, which both filed amicus briefs on behalf of Toyota, applauded the ruling. According to these organizations, had the Sixth Circuit's decision become the law of the land there would have been a substantial increase in ADA claims and litigation. Advocates for employees and unions generally regarded the decision as negative, in that it refused to uphold the Sixth Circuit's standard, which would have brought many more employees under the coverage of the ADA. Even some employee advocates acknowledged, however, that the Sixth Circuit decision had not been followed by other circuits, and most legal experts were not surprised by the Supreme Court's decision.

In fact, the Sixth Circuit's decision in *Williams* arguably constituted a departure from prior precedent in that circuit. In a 1997 case, which also involved an assembly line worker for Toyota, the Sixth Circuit had held that the employee was not covered by the ADA because she could not show that her impairment restricted her from a broad class of jobs.[43] The fact that the employee was restricted from a narrow range of assembly line manufacturing positions that required repetitive motion or lifting over 10 pounds was not sufficient to constitute a substantial limitation in the major life activity of working. The Eighth Circuit Court of Appeals had applied

similar reasoning to hold that an employee with carpal tunnel syndrome was not covered by the ADA.[44]

Thus, the headlines in the press notwithstanding, the Supreme Court's decision in *Williams* did not represent a major departure from prior precedent. The fact that the Court's decision was unanimous also indicates that the Justices did not view the decision as involving a particularly close or controversial issue.

Although the Supreme Court's decision is not a departure from established law, there have been some groundbreaking decisions regarding the ADA and carpal tunnel syndrome. These groundbreaking decisions have come not from the Supreme Court, however, but from the federal Seventh and Eighth Circuit Courts of Appeals. These courts have held that not only is carpal tunnel syndrome (or any other cumulative trauma disorder) not necessarily a disability covered by the ADA, but also employers can actively screen employees using tests that determine whether an individual is susceptible to carpal tunnel syndrome or other cumulative trauma disorder.

These courts have upheld the use of nerve conduction tests to screen workers who may be prone to developing such a condition in certain jobs. In the case from the Seventh Circuit,[45] an employer required applicants for certain positions to undergo nerve conduction tests to help identify individuals susceptible to cumulative trauma disorders such as carpal tunnel syndrome. The Equal Employment Opportunity Commission (EEOC) brought suit under the ADA against the employer on behalf of 72 applicants rejected on the basis of abnormal test results, claiming that the company had regarded the applicants as disabled. The district court granted summary judgment to the employer, and the Seventh Circuit affirmed, holding that the EEOC could not show that the employer regarded the applicants as unable to perform a broad range of jobs without statistical evidence relating to the local labor market. Similarly, in the case from the Eighth Circuit, the court held that an employer did not regard employees as disabled merely because the employer required nerve conduction tests and denied assembly line jobs to workers thought to be susceptible to carpal tunnel syndrome.[46]

---

43. McKay v. Toyota Motor Mfg., U.S.A., Inc., 110 F.3d 369 (6th Cir. 1997).

44. Wooten v. Farmland Foods, 58 F.3d 382 (8th Cir. 1995).

45. EEOC v. Rockwell Int'l Corp., 243 F.3d 1012 (7th Cir. 2001).

46. EEOC v. Woodbridge Corp., 263 F.3d 812 (8th Cir. 2001).

As these decisions indicate, an individual with carpal tunnel syndrome may, but does not necessarily, come within the definition of a person with a disability under the ADA. In a recent California case involving a transit operator who suffered from carpal tunnel syndrome, the court raised this point, although it was not directly at issue in the case. In the case, *Rowe v. City & County of San Francisco*,[47] the defendant sought summary judgment, based on its assertion that the interactive process of seeking an accommodation had broken down because of the plaintiff's bad faith. The court denied summary judgment but warned both parties to be mindful of the *Williams* decision while preparing for trial and specifically cited the *Williams* language requiring a plaintiff to meet the burden of showing that she cannot perform a variety of tasks, not merely the tasks required for her specific job. If carpal tunnel syndrome does not preclude an individual from performing a broad class of jobs, the individual will not be regarded as substantially limited in the life activity of working and will have to show that he or she is substantially limited in some other major life activity. Furthermore, as the cases from the Seventh and Eighth Circuits indicate, an employer may, under some circumstances, screen out employees susceptible to developing carpal tunnel syndrome or other cumulative trauma disorders without violating the ADA.

[g] Nebraska Limits Public Policy Exception to At-Will Rule

Although the trend had been to expand the public policy exception to the at-will rule (see § 4.3[d] of this Guide), a recent case from the Supreme Court of Nebraska reflects a growing backlash in which courts have limited or refused to expand the public policy exception. In *Malone v. American Business Information*,[48] the court held that the state's Wage Payment and Collection Act did not provide a basis for a claim of wrongful discharge in violation of public policy.

Generally, under Nebraska law, the only exceptions to the employment at-will rule are situations where a statute, a contract, or the "very clear mandate of public policy" has been violated. At-will employee Armeda Malone sued her employer after being terminated, allegedly in retaliation for having demanded payment of wages due her. The Nebraska Wage Payment and Collec-

tion Act requires employers to pay all wages owed at regular, designated intervals.

Malone's demand for payment of her unpaid wages under the Act in question and her subsequent discharge provided the basis for the plaintiff's claim of wrongful discharge in violation of public policy.

The Supreme Court of Nebraska held that the Wage Payment and Collection Act did not represent a "very clear mandate of public policy" justifying an exception to the employment-at-will rule. According to the court, the Act did not clearly establish an important public policy that would support such a claim. The statute, the court noted, did not contain a specific provision restricting an employer's right to discharge an at-will employee, nor did it provide criminal penalties.

In other recent decisions, courts have followed similar logic to that applied in *Malone*. In *Eckhardt v. Yerkes Regional Primate Center*,[49] the court found that employees who were discharged following their documentation and reporting of a transfer process for monkeys that presented a public health danger did not state an exception to the at-will employment rule. The court explained that, because the state legislature had not specifically created a public policy exception that would allow recovery on a claim of wrongful termination for whistleblowing in these circumstances, the case had been properly dismissed. In another case, the Supreme Court of Virginia found that a plaintiff who argued that she was wrongfully dismissed in violation of state public policy when her employer fired her for failing to drop criminal charges against a fellow employee had failed to state an exception to the at-will rule.[50]

However, all courts have not headed in this direction. The Minnesota Supreme Court found that plaintiffs discharged for questioning whether another employee was entitled to vacation pay under wage and hour laws had stated a claim for wrongful termination. The court stated that the whistleblower statute protects reports of a violation or suspected violation of any federal or state law and that there is no additional requirement that the report of a violation or suspected violation of law implicate public policy.[51]

---

47. No. C 00-03676 BZ (N.D. Cal. Feb. 13, 2002).

48. 634 N.W.2d 788 (Neb. 2001).

49. No. A01A2533 (Ga. App. Feb. 22, 2002) .

50. Rowan v. Tractor Supply Co., No. 011732 (Va. Mar. 1, 2002).

51. Anderson-Johanningmeier v. Mid-Minnesota Women's Center, Inc., No. C0-00-164 (Minn. Jan. 3, 2002).

[h] Ergonomics and the Repeal of the Federal Standard

The imposition of ergonomics standards represents a radical transformation in workplace safety regulation. Whereas the focus of occupational safety enforcement has traditionally been in manufacturing and construction, workplace safety compliance is now an important consideration for every employer, and citations for violations will become common for computer, clerical, and other office jobs. On November 13, 2000, the federal Occupational Safety and Health Administration (OSHA) published a final ergonomics standard. Although Congress rescinded the federal ergonomics regulation in 2001, employers should not conclude that they can ignore ergonomics issues. First, it should be noted that new federal standards may be on the way. Second, many states are taking an active role in ergonomics regulation. Finally, many employers have concluded that ergonomics policies, even if not required, are an important tool for mitigating the costs associated with employee absenteeism and workers' compensation claims.

Defined as the scientific study of human work, *ergonomics* focuses on the physical and mental capabilities and limits of the worker as he or she interacts with tools, equipment, work methods, tasks, and the working environment. OSHA maintains that ergonomic standards are necessary to prevent work-related musculoskeletal disorders (MSDs) or repetitive motion injuries (RMIs) that occur when there is a poor fit between the required task and the worker. As discussed in section 4.2[c] of the *State by State Guide to Workplace Safety Regulation* (Panel/Aspen Publishers, 2001), the ergonomic standards generated substantial opposition from Congress and business groups, which contend that OSHA has overstated the benefits of such programs and underestimated the potential costs to employers.

Although the final rule incorporated some changes intended to address concerns raised during public hearings on the rule, the changes made to the most controversial aspects of the federal standard were not enough to win support from business groups. The federal standard may have been repealed for now, but the salient issues in the battle over the federal standard are still relevant. Even congressional critics of the federal standard concede that workplace ergonomics is an issue that is here to stay. As Sen. Mike Enzi (R-Wyo.) stated in his floor statement introducing the resolution to kill the standard, "[t]his vote is not about whether we should have ergonomics protection. We should." In Enzi's view, OSHA's rush to publish a final standard and the agency's failure to allay employers' concerns produced a flawed rule. Echoing Enzi's statements, Sens. John Breaux and Mary Landrieu of Louisiana, who also voted to rescind the ergonomics standard, announced on March 13, 2001, that they will push for legislation that protects workers without putting too heavy a burden on businesses. Secretary of Labor Elaine Chao has stated that she "intends to pursue a comprehensive approach to ergonomics, which may include new rulemaking" that "addresses the concerns levied against the current standard."

The U.S. Department of Labor (DOL) had been set to announce a new plan of action on ergonomics issues in September 2001. In July 2001, the DOL conducted forums regarding ergonomics in Virginia, Illinois, and California. Public comment was received, and a review of written comments and witness testimony was conducted. by the DOL. The announcement was postponed, however, following the events of September 11. On January 28, 2002, the DOL issued a statement delaying presentation of new ergonomics standards and did not set a new target date for enacting standards.

Even before a final regulation was in place, OSHA took the position that it could address ergonomics issues under what is referred to as the General Duty Clause of the Occupational Safety and Health Act. The General Duty Clause is a broadly worded statutory provision that requires employers to provide work environments free from recognized hazards likely to cause death or serious physical harm. OSHA claims that the proposed ergonomic standard does not create any new duties for employers, beyond that which they already have under the General Duty Clause or other OSHA standards. The new standards, OSHA argues, simply create a more defined framework for employers to use in meeting these obligations. Whether congressional action rescinding OSHA's formal ergonomics standard also prevents OSHA from addressing ergonomic issues under the General Duty Clause is likely to be the subject of debate, and perhaps litigation. For now, however, employers should be aware of the possibility that a recognized ergonomic hazard could result in a citation for a violation of the General Duty Clause.

Although workplace safety is often thought of as a federal issue, 24 states, Puerto Rico, and the Virgin Islands have their own workplace safety laws and enforcement agencies. Each statute in these jurisdictions contains a general duty clause similar to that of the federal statute. Consequently, state workplace safety agencies may also take the position that they can address ergonomics issues and may cite employers for related safety violations, under the state's analogous general duty clauses. Indeed, at least nine states have already issued citations to employers for ergonomics-related violations.

Furthermore, states that promulgate and administer their own workplace safety laws are free to adopt additional or more stringent standards (the only limitation on this power is that their standards must be at least as effective as the federal standards). A number of states have used this power to create their own ergonomics standards or ergonomics programs. Since the repeal of the federal ergonomics standard, a number of states have indicated that they are considering the adoption of state standards.[52]

Apart from the statutory and regulatory compliance issues, a growing number of employers have recognized that the formulation and implementation of ergonomics policies is justified by considerations solely by virtue of their potentially positive effect on a company's bottom line. Specifically, many employers have found that addressing potential ergonomic hazards before they result in MSDs or RMIs can reduce costs associated with lost worker productivity and workers' compensation claims.

Once considered a novel concept, carpal tunnel syndrome is now a common basis for a workers' compensation claim. Furthermore, many states specifically recognize carpal tunnel syndrome and other MSDs or RMIs as being covered by the states' workers' compensation statute. Table I sets out the specific provisions for coverage of MSDs and RMIs under state workers' compensation statutes and discusses other related provisions of state law.

---

52. For specific coverage of state ergonomic standards, *see* Buckley, *State by State Guide to Workplace Safety Regulation* (New York: Panel/Aspen Publishers, 2001).

Table I

COVERAGE OF REPETITIVE MOTION INJURIES: STATE WORKERS' COMPENSATION STATUTES

	Does Definition of Injury Discuss Repetitive Motion Injuries?	Other	Citations to Authority
AL	Yes. The definition of injury includes physical injury caused either by carpal tunnel syndrome disorder or by other cumulative trauma disorder if either disorder arises out of and in the course of the employment.	—	Ala. Code Ann. § 25-5-1.
AR	Yes. The definition covers injuries caused by rapid repetitive motion. Carpal tunnel syndrome is specifically categorized as a compensable injury falling within this definition.	—	Ark. Code Ann. § 11-9-102.
CA	Yes. Definition provides that an injury may be cumulative, occurring as repetitive traumatic activities extending over a period of time, the combined effect of which causes any disability or need for medical treatment.	Statute provides that the date of injury in cases of cumulative injuries is the date when the employee first suffered disability and either knew or should have known that the disability was caused by the employment. In a case involving cumulative injury, the employee and employer or insurance carrier may enter into a compromise and release agreement settling either all or any part of the employee's claim. Liability for cumulative injury claims is limited to those employers that employed the employee during a period of one year immediately preceding either the date of injury or the last date on which the employee was employed in an occupation exposing the employee to the hazards of the occupational disease or cumulative injury, whichever occurs first.	Cal. Lab. Code §§ 3208.1, 5005, 5303, 5412, 5500.5.
CT	Yes. Injury includes an injury to an employee that is causally connected with the employment and is the direct result of repetitive trauma or repetitive acts incident to the employment.	—	Conn. Gen. Stat. Ann. § 31-275.
KY	Yes. Injury includes cumulative trauma arising out of the course of employment.	—	Ky. Rev. Stat. Ann. § 342.0011.
MN	—	Labor commissioner is to set rules for treatment of injuries, including criteria for diagnosis and treatment of upper-extremity repetitive trauma injuries.	Minn. Stat. Ann. § 176.83.
MO	Yes. Definition states that ordinary, gradual deterioration or progressive degeneration of the body caused by aging shall not be compensable, *except where* the deterioration or degeneration follows as an incident of employment.	For repetitive motion injuries, if the exposure to the repetitive motion that is found to be the cause of the injury is for a period of less than 3 months and the evidence demonstrates that the exposure to the repetitive motion with a prior employer was the substantial contributing factor to the injury, the prior employer shall be liable for such occupational disease.	Mo. Ann. Stat. §§ 287.020, 287.063, 287.067.
MT	No. Definition states that an injury must occur as a result of a specific event on a single day.	—	Mont. Code Ann. § 39-71-119.

(Table continues.)

Table I

STATE BY STATE GUIDE TO HUMAN RESOURCES LAW

xlviii

Table I *(cont'd)*

COVERAGE OF REPETITIVE MOTION INJURIES: STATE WORKERS' COMPENSATION STATUTES

	Does Definition of Injury Discuss Repetitive Motion Injuries?	*Other*	*Citations to Authority*
OK	Statute defines *cumulative trauma* as an injury resulting from employment activities that are repetitive in nature and engaged in over a period of time.	For cumulative trauma, there is a rebuttable presumption that injury from cumulative trauma does not arise out of the course of employment unless oral or written notice is given by the employee to the employer within 2 years of the employee's separation from employment. The presumption must be overcome by a preponderance of the evidence.	Okla. Stat. Ann. tit. 85, §§ 3, 24.2.
TX	No, but repetitive motion disorders are included under occupational disease.	—	Tex. Lab. Code Ann. § 401.011.

[i] Scope of Safe Harbor Protection for Employee in Drug Rehabilitation Program

The Ninth Circuit has addressed a vexing question for employers: the scope of the Americans with Disabilities Act's (ADA's) so-called safe-harbor provision,[53] which extends ADA protections to an individual "participating in a supervised rehabilitation program, and . . . no longer engaging in" the illegal use of drugs. In a ruling that gives employers much-needed guidance in this area, the court held that the "safe harbor" provision applies only to employees who have refrained from using drugs for a significant period of time.[54] Because the California courts,[55] and the courts of many other states, use federal court decisions concerning the ADA to interpret analogous provisions of state fair employment laws, this decision may be influential in the interpretation of both state and federal law.

In *Brown v. Lucky Stores, Inc.,* Karen Brown was terminated from her position with Lucky Stores and then sued her employer, claiming that she was terminated because of her alcoholism in violation of the ADA, the Rehabilitation Act, and California's Fair Employment and Housing Act (FEHA). Brown was employed as a checker at Lucky Stores when, early on the morning of November 10, 1996, she was arrested for drunk driving, possession of methamphetamine, and being under the influence of an illegal controlled substance. Brown remained incarcerated until November 15, when she appeared in court and was convicted of driving under the influence of intoxicants and possession of methamphetamine. The court conditioned suspension of her sentence on her participation in a round-the-clock 90-day drug and alcohol rehabilitation program, Sunrise House. Brown attended the program from November 15, 1996, to February 12, 1997.

On the day of her arrest, Brown contacted Rebecca Caldeira, her sister-in-law, and asked her to inform John Hunt, Brown's manager at Lucky Stores, that she was in jail and could not make it to work that day. Caldeira called Hunt on November 10 to inform him of Brown's incarceration and asked if Brown would be fired. Hunt replied that he did not know.

Because she was incarcerated on November 10 and 11 and was required to attend round-the-clock rehabilitation at Sunrise House on November 16, Brown did not report to work for her assigned shifts on those days. Lucky Stores discharged Brown for abandoning her job. It relied on a provision of the collective bargaining agreement (CBA) governing Brown's terms of employment, which authorizes discharge of an employee for "improper conduct," and a company policy providing that an employee who misses three consecutive shifts for an unauthorized reason will be terminated from employment.

Brown argued that her absence from work on November 16 was protected by the ADA. Section 12114(a) of the statute specifies that an employee or applicant "currently engaging in the use of illegal drugs" is not covered by the ADA, while Section 12114(b) clarifies that subsection (a) does not apply to an individual who "has successfully completed a supervised drug rehabilitation program and is no longer engaging in the illegal use of drugs, or has otherwise been rehabilitated successfully and is no longer engaging in such use,"[56] nor to one who "is participating in a supervised rehabilitation program and is no longer engaging in such use."[57] Referring to the legislative history of the ADA, the court noted that mere participation in a rehabilitation program is not enough to trigger the protections of Section 12114(b); refraining from illegal use of drugs also is essential. Furthermore, employers are entitled to seek reasonable assurances that no illegal use of drugs is occurring or has occurred recently enough so that continuing use would be a real and ongoing problem.[58]

Addressing the case before it, the Ninth Circuit Court of Appeals held that Brown's continuing use of drugs and alcohol was clearly an ongoing problem at least until November 10, as demonstrated by her incarceration for driving while intoxicated and possession of methamphetamine. Because she had not refrained from the use of drugs and alcohol for a sufficient length of time, she was not entitled to the protections of the ADA's safe-harbor provision.

The court also rejected Brown's claim that Lucky Stores had a duty to provide a reasonable accommodation for her disability by excusing her absence from her

---

53. 42 U.S.C. § 12114(b)(2).

54. Brown v. Lucky Stores, Inc., 246 F.3d 1182 (9th Cir. 2001).

55. Bradley v. Harcourt, Brace & Co., 104 F.3d 267, 271 (9th Cir. 1996) (applying the same analysis to FEHA and ADA claims). See § 2.6 of this Guide for coverage of other states.

---

56. 42 U.S.C. § 12114(b)(1).

57. 42 U.S.C. § 12114(b)(2).

58. H.R. Conf. Rep. No. 101-596, at 64 (1990), *reprinted in* 1990 U.S.C.C.A.N. 565, 573; *see also* Zenor v. El Paso Healthcare Sys., Ltd., 176 F.3d 847, 857–58 (5th Cir. 1999); Shafer v. Preston Mem'l Hosp. Corp., 107 F.3d 274, 280 (4th Cir. 1997).

November 16 shift in order to attend the rehabilitation program.[59] The court found that neither Brown nor her sister-in-law asked for an accommodation, and that Brown testified that she never believed she needed rehabilitation while working for Lucky Stores. That, coupled with the absence of evidence that she ever requested an accommodation, led the court to conclude that Lucky Stores was under no affirmative obligation to provide an accommodation for her.

[j] Discrimination Against Younger Employees

The federal Age Discrimination in Employment Act (ADEA) protects individuals who are 40 years of age or older from employment discrimination based on age, and most state fair employment statutes contain similar prohibitions against age discrimination. While it is clear that these statutes prohibit employers from favoring younger workers over older workers because of age, there is some controversy regarding whether these statutes also prohibit favoring older workers over younger ones. The Equal Employment Opportunity Commission (EEOC) has taken the position that the ADEA prohibits age discrimination against the younger of two workers in the protected age range in favor of the older person.[60] A number of courts have also interpreted the ADEA and analogous state fair employment statutes to prohibit discrimination against younger workers.

A federal district court in Mississippi has held that reverse discrimination suits are permitted under the ADEA.[61] In *Mississippi Power & Light Co. v. Local Union No. 605,*[62] a provision in a collective bargaining agreement permitted an employer to transfer disabled employees unless they were between 60 and 65 years old and had been employed for at least 30 years. Citing the EEOC's regulation, the court held that this provision violated the ADEA because it allowed the privilege of employment to be doled out to one subset of the protected group (those between 60 and 65 years of age) while denying the privilege to other persons within the protected group (those between ages 40 and 59).

Unlike the ADEA, many state antidiscrimination statutes do not limit prohibitions against age discrimination to persons over 40.[63] That is, unlike the ADEA, which protects persons only once they have attained age 40, these statutes simply prohibit age discrimination in employment without specifying any minimum age requirement. Several state court cases have held that because the state's antidiscrimination statute does not specify a minimum age a plaintiff must reach to enjoy the statute's protections, no legislative intent to foreclose a reverse age discrimination action can be gleaned from the statute.

For example, in *Bergen Commercial Bank v. Sisler,*[64] the plaintiff, a former vice president for credit card operations at the defendant bank, sued his former employer for age discrimination, alleging that he was fired shortly after certain high-ranking bank officials discovered that he was only 35 years old. A lower court first dismissed the case, holding that New Jersey's Law Against Discrimination (LAD)[65] protected only more "mature" employees and applicants. On appeal, however, the New Jersey Supreme Court reinstated the plaintiff's claim and allowed it to go forward.

The New Jersey Supreme Court first noted that nowhere in the LAD's text did it state that the Act protected individuals from age discrimination only once they attained a certain age. Then, applying what it termed normal methods of divining legislative intent, the court determined that had the legislature wanted to preclude reverse age discrimination suits under the LAD, it would have said so; or, at the least, it would have specified some minimum age for coverage under the statute. The court also determined that the omission of any language setting out minimum age requirements indicated that the legislature was motivated by a desire to end all use of age-based stereotyping in employment matters.

Similarly, in *Zanni v. Medaphis Physician Services Corp.,*[66] the Michigan Court of Appeals ruled that a 31-year-old woman could maintain a cause of action for wrongful discharge under the age discrimination provi-

59. *See* 29 C.F.R. pt. 1630, app. at 371 ("[A]n employer . . . may, in appropriate circumstances, have to consider the provision of leave to an employee with a disability as a reasonable accommodation unless the provision of leave would impose an undue hardship.").

60. *See* 29 C.F.R. § 1625.2(a).

61. *See* Mississippi Power & Light Co. v. Local Union No. 605, 945 F. Supp. 980 (S.D. Miss. 1996).

62. 945 F. Supp. 980 (S.D. Miss. 1996).

63. For further information on who is covered by state age discrimination prohibitions, see Tables 2.3-1 Part A and 2.5-1.

64. 723 A.2d 944 (N.J. 1999).

65. *See* N.J. Stat. Ann. §§ 10:5-1–10:5-42 (West 1999).

66. 240 Mich. App. 472, 612 N.W.2d 845 (2000), *overruling* Zoppi v. Chrysler Corp., 520 N.W.2d 378 (Mich. Ct. App. 1994).

sion of the Michigan Civil Rights Act (CRA).[67] The plaintiff in *Zanni* alleged that her supervisor told her that she sounded too young on the telephone, and that the business's clients preferred to work with older executives. The employer shortly thereafter terminated the plaintiff, citing as justification the fact that she allegedly had lost two sales accounts. In her suit, the plaintiff alleged that older employees who lost the same number of accounts were not terminated. She also introduced evidence indicating that her replacement was older than 31 years of age.

Initially, both a circuit court and a three-judge panel dismissed the plaintiff's claim and granted summary judgment to the defendant employer. The full court of appeals vacated the panel's decision, however, and granted the plaintiff the right to proceed to trial on the suit's merits. Because the CRA provided no basis to limit its protection to any particular group (like New Jersey's LAD, it does not specify a minimum age potential plaintiffs must attain), the court determined that the legislature had intended to prohibit any age-based discrimination in employment.

Likewise, in *Ogden v. Bureau of Labor*,[68] the Supreme Court of Oregon affirmed that portion of an appellate court's holding which extended the state's antidiscrimination provisions to plaintiffs under the age of 40. In *Ogden*, a 30-year-old plaintiff alleged that she was not hired as a beautician on the basis of her age. Recognizing that the defendant's clientele, which averaged between 80 and 95 years of age, might prefer an older beautician, the court nonetheless noted that there was nothing to suggest that a younger, otherwise qualified beautician would hamper the defendant's business operations. Moreover, the court observed that the purpose of the state's employment discrimination statute[69] is to discourage the use of categories in employment decisions that ignore the individual characteristics of particular workers and applicants. Accordingly, the court ruled that the claim could go forward.

As previously noted, however, prohibitions against age discrimination are traditionally viewed as protecting older employees. In *Hamilton v. Caterpillar, Inc.*,[70] the defendant employer, Caterpillar, announced the closing of two of its plants. In so doing, Caterpillar extended

early retirement benefits to employees age 50 and over who had at least 10 years of experience with the company. Employees between the ages of 40 and 50 brought a class-action suit alleging that this early retirement plan violated the ADEA. Citing the EEOC's position, the employees asserted that it was unlawful for an employer to discriminate by giving preference to older workers within the protected age group over younger employees also protected by the ADEA.

The Seventh Circuit rejected this claim. Parsing the ADEA's legislative history, the court criticized the EEOC's position regarding the issue. Finding that Congress did not intend to prohibit reverse age discrimination when it passed the ADEA, the Seventh Circuit refused to allow the class's suit to go forward.

At least two other federal district courts have also held[71] that a reverse age discrimination claim is not viable under the ADEA. Rejecting the EEOC's position, the Northern District of Indiana held that nothing in the Act's legislative history supported the plaintiff's contention that the ADEA was intended to insulate younger members of the protected class from discrimination in favor of older, also-protected employees. In addition, the Southern District of New York dismissed a retiree's claim that a pension plan that provided greater benefits to older employees with fewer years of service violated the ADEA. The judge stated that no court has held that the ADEA allows reverse discrimination claims, and moreover, the plaintiff's claim would fail because the ADEA specifically authorizes early retirement plans that set minimum age requirements.[72]

Thus, while reverse age discrimination suits may continue to be somewhat novel under the federal ADEA, they appear to be gaining acceptance in those states with potentially broader age discrimination prohibitions.

[k] EEOC Guidelines on Disability-Related Inquiries and Medical Examinations of Employees

The EEOC has issued Enforcement Guidance on Disability-Related Inquiries and Medical Examinations of Employees Under the Americans with Disabilities Act (ADA). The guidance explains when it is permissible for employers to make disability-related inquiries or require medical examinations of current employees.

---

67. *See* Mich. Comp. Laws §§ 37.2101 *et seq.* (2000); Mich. Stat. Ann. § 3.548(101) (Law. Co-op. 2000).

68. 699 P.2d 189 (Or. 1985).

69. *See* Or. Rev. Stat. §§ 659.030 *et seq.* (2000).

70. 966 F.2d 1226 (7th Cir. 1992).

71. *See* Wehrly v. American Motor Sales Corp., 678 F. Supp. 1366 (N.D. Ind. 1988).

72. Greer v. PBGC, No. 00 Civ. 1272 (S.D.N.Y. Feb. 14, 2001).

The guidance states that disability-related inquiries and medical examinations of employees must be "job-related and consistent with business necessity." This essentially means that the inquiry or examination has to be closely related to the requirements of the job. Included in the guidance are examples of the kinds of questions that are and are not "disability related" and examples of tests and procedures that generally are and are not "medical."

Examples of disability-related inquiries include the following:

- Asking an employee whether he or she has (or ever had) a disability or how he or she became disabled or inquiring about the nature or severity of an employee's disability
- Asking an employee to provide medical documentation regarding his or her disability
- Asking an employee's co-worker, family member, doctor, or another person about an employee's disability
- Asking about an employee's genetic information
- Asking about an employee's prior workers' compensation history
- Asking an employee whether he or she currently is taking any prescription drugs or medications or whether he or she has taken any such drugs or medications in the past, or monitoring an employee's taking of such drugs or medications
- Asking an employee a broad question about his or her impairments that is likely to elicit information about a disability (e.g., What impairments do you have?)

A "medical examination" is defined under the guidance as a procedure or test that seeks information about an individual's physical or mental impairments or health. Factors that should be considered to determine whether a test (or procedure) is a medical examination include (1) whether the test is administered by a health care professional; (2) whether the test is interpreted by a health care professional; (3) whether the test is designed to reveal an impairment of physical or mental health; (4) whether the test is invasive; (5) whether the test measures an employee's performance of a task or measures his or her physiological responses to performing the task; (6) whether the test normally is given in a medical setting; and (7) whether medical equipment is used. In many cases, a combination of factors will be relevant in determining whether a test or procedure is a medical examination. In other cases, one factor may be enough to determine that a test or procedure is medical.

Examples of covered medical examinations cited by the guidance include the following:

- Vision tests conducted and analyzed by an ophthalmologist or optometrist
- Blood, urine, and breath analyses to check for alcohol use
- Blood, urine, saliva, and hair analyses to detect disease or genetic markers (e.g., for conditions such as sickle-cell trait, breast cancer, or Huntington's disease)
- Blood pressure screening and cholesterol testing
- Nerve conduction tests (i.e., tests that screen for possible nerve damage and susceptibility to injury, such as carpal tunnel syndrome)
- Range-of-motion tests that measure muscle strength and motor function
- Pulmonary function tests (i.e., tests that measure the capacity of the lungs to hold air and to move air in and out)
- Psychological tests that are designed to identify a mental disorder or impairment
- Diagnostic procedures such as X rays, computerized axial tomography (CAT) scans, and magnetic resonance imaging (MRI)

Examples of procedures and tests employers may require that generally are not considered medical examinations include the following:

- Tests to determine the current illegal use of drugs
- Physical agility tests, which measure an employee's ability to perform actual or simulated job tasks, and physical fitness tests, which measure an employee's performance of physical tasks, such as running or lifting, as long as these tests do not include examinations that could be considered medical (e.g., measuring heart rate or blood pressure)
- Tests that evaluate an employee's ability to read labels or distinguish objects as part of a demonstration of the ability to perform actual job functions
- Psychological tests that measure personality traits such as honesty, preferences, and habits
- Polygraph examinations

The guidance also defines what the term "job-related and consistent with business necessity" means and addresses situations in which an employer would meet the general standard for asking an employee a disability-related question or requiring a medical examination. Other acceptable inquiries and examinations of employees, such as inquiries and examinations required by federal law and those that are part of voluntary wellness and health screening programs, as well as invitations to voluntarily self-identify as persons with disabilities for affirmative action purposes, also are addressed.

[1] Domestic Partner Benefits

The issue of whether domestic partners of workers are entitled to the same benefits as the spouses of married workers continues to be a hot topic in legislatures, governmental agencies, the courts, and the private sector. Recent court decisions on same-sex marriage in Hawaii and Vermont, and recent legislation in California, have served to keep the issue in the spotlight. In recent years, companies have begun extending benefits, such as health insurance, to domestic partners of employees. Hundreds of companies, municipalities, colleges and universities, and other organizations currently allow employees to obtain benefits for domestic partners. One 1996 study found that 10 percent of firms extended such benefits. Some companies extend the benefits to both same-sex and opposite-sex domestic partners, although other companies include only one of these classifications.

The number of employers providing benefits to the domestic partners of employees may increase in light of recent indications from the Internal Revenue Service (IRS) that the payment of benefits to domestic partners may receive favorable tax treatment. In two private letter rulings, the IRS has indicated that payments for benefits to the domestic partners of employees may be entitled to favorable tax treatment if the domestic partner qualifies as a dependent under Section 152(a)(9) of the Internal Revenue Code (Code).[73] Under Code Section 152(a)(9), a dependent is an individual who resides with the taxpayer as a member of the household and who receives over half of his or her support from the taxpayer.

A domestic partner who is not related to the employee in one of the relationships specified in Code Sections 152(a)(1) through 152(a)(8) may qualify as a dependent of the employee if the following requirements of Code Sections 152(a)(9) and 152(b)(5) are met:

1. The domestic partner receives more than half of his or her support for the calendar year from the employee;
2. The domestic partner has the home of the employee as his or her principal abode and is a member of the employee's household; and
3. The relationship between the employee and the domestic partner does not violate local law.[74]

Recent guidance from the IRS suggests that with respect to same-sex domestic partners who do not qualify as dependents, payments for premiums attributable to the employee are not included as income to the employee, but payments for premiums attributable to the domestic partner of an employee are included. The amount included in the employee's income is determined not by the amount of the premium but by the amount of the fair market value of the coverage provided. If the employee pays for part of the premium for the employee's nondependent domestic partner, the excess of the fair market value of the coverage provided to the domestic partner over the amount paid by the employee for such coverage is includible in the gross income of the employee.[75]

Generally, the decision whether to extend benefits to domestic partners is made by the individual firm. In some jurisdictions, however, such benefits may be mandated by legislation or judicial decision.

Legislation passed in San Francisco in late 1996 requires firms doing business with the city to offer benefits to domestic partners. To the extent that they wish to bid on city contracts, private employers are therefore affected by the legislation. Other cities, including Los Angeles, have considered such legislation. A bill that would require domestic partner benefits for firms contracting for state or local government work throughout California has been introduced in the California State Senate.

In a court challenge by the airline industry, however, the San Francisco legislation passed in 1996 was found to be partially preempted by the Employee Retirement Income Security Act of 1974 (ERISA). In 1998, the U.S. District Court for the Northern District of California, in the case of *Air Transport Association of America v. City & County of San Francisco*,[76] determined that the San Francisco domestic partner ordinance had a direct connection with ERISA plans because it mandated "employee benefit structures" for city contractors.

---

73. Ltr. Rul. 9717018 (Apr. 25, 1997); Ltr. Rul. 9231062 (July 31, 1992). Note that these private letter rulings are not binding precedent; they do, however, indicate the position taken by the IRS with respect to specific taxpayers.

74. Ltr. Rul. 9850011 (Dec. 11, 1998).

75. Id.

76. 992 F. Supp. 1149 (N.D. Cal. 1998).

Therefore, ERISA preempted the ordinance, but only to the extent that the ordinance addressed ERISA benefits under ERISA plans. In other words, ERISA did not preempt the ordinance with respect to non-ERISA benefits, such as travel benefits or moving expenses.

In *Air Transport,* the court further held that, regardless of semantics, an employer establishes an ERISA plan when it makes a commitment to pay benefits systematically and to undertake various obligations relating to such benefits. Even though employers may establish separate plans to provide benefits for domestic partners, these plans would nonetheless constitute an "employee welfare benefit plan" and would not be exempt from ERISA coverage. Finally, the court held that the San Francisco ordinance, with its nationwide reach, impermissibly regulated out-of-state conduct that was not related to contracts with the city.

On September 11, 2001, however, a panel of the Ninth Circuit Court of Appeals voted 2 to 1 to overturn the district court's decision in *Air Transport.*[77] The panel ruled that the San Francisco ordinance was not, after all, preempted by ERISA. As a result of the ruling, it appears that airlines doing business with San Francisco International Airport will be forced to offer domestic partner benefits to homosexual and heterosexual domestic partners. Only months before, the Ninth Circuit had upheld provisions of the same ordinance in another case, but interpreted the domestic partner law such that it would apply only to local employees and directly involved nonlocal employees of businesses contracting with the city.[78]

In addition to the San Francisco ordinance, a number of other municipalities have passed provisions that seek to require private employers or municipal contractors to provide certain domestic partner benefits. Davis, California, requires all employers operating in the city to offer "family care leave" and "bereavement leave" to employees with domestic partners if they are offered to married employees. Sacramento, California, requires private employers that operate within Sacramento to provide "unpaid related person leave" (such as "family care leave" or "bereavement leave") to married employees. Broward County, Florida, offers a bidding preference in the amount of 1 percent to those private employers that offer employment benefits to employees with domestic

partners at the same level as it does to married employees. Seattle, Washington, requires those private employers holding contracts with the city that have an estimated value of $33,000 or more to extend benefits to employees with domestic partners at the same level as it does for married employees. However, to the extent that the cost of providing employment benefits to the domestic partners of employees exceeds the cost of providing those same benefits to the spouses of employees (or vice versa), the employee is required to make up the difference.

In other local developments, in November 2001 voters in Houston, Texas, the nation's fourth-largest city, passed Proposition 2, amending the city charter to prohibit the city from offering benefits to gay domestic partners. At the same time, a similar city charter amendment failed in Kalamazoo, Michigan. Also in 2001, voters in three Michigan cities, including Kalamazoo, opted not to disallow antidiscrimination measures protecting homosexuals.

Municipal domestic partner benefits vary from jurisdiction to jurisdiction. The most important differences relate to coverage. Specifically, some ordinances require that domestic partner benefits be provided only for municipal government employees. Others go further, demanding that private contractors that wish to do business with local government must guarantee similar benefits to their employees as well. Still others may go further, purporting to require compliance by all private businesses within the jurisdiction. Ordinances also vary in a number of other respects, including whether or not opposite sex domestic partners are covered. Thus, some mandate benefits only for homosexual domestic partners, while others would extend these benefits to cohabiting heterosexuals.

Municipal domestic partnership ordinances commonly require those wishing to receive benefits to register as domestic partners. For instance, Atlanta, Georgia, recently began providing health and dental benefits to registered domestic partners of city employees. Domestic partners may register by filing a "Declaration of Domestic Partnership." Benefits are provided only to "dependent" domestic partners, as defined by the ordinance, and domestic partners of city employees must file an "Affidavit of Financial Reliance" to receive benefits. City sick leave, funeral leave, and annual leave may also apply with respect to registered domestic partners.[79]

---

77. Air Transport Ass'n of Am. v. City & County of San Francisco, 266 F.3d 1064 (9th Cir. 2001).

78. S.D. Myers, Inc., v. City & County of San Francisco, 253 F.3d 461 (9th Cir. 2000).

---

79. Atlanta, Ga., Code of Ordinances § 2-858.

The availability of benefits may also depend on how domestic partnerships are defined, which also varies by jurisdiction. Again, Atlanta provides an example of the kinds of requirements found in such ordinances. There, domestic partnership is defined as "two people of the opposite or same gender who live together in the mutual interdependence of a single home and have signed a declaration of domestic partnership," attesting that

1. They share the same primary, regular and permanent residence and have lived together for the previous six months;

Note. Documentation must be submitted verifying joint residency. Domestic partners must share the same primary, regular and permanent residence. It is not necessary that the legal right to possess the residence be in both names. Domestic partners do not cease to live together if one leaves the shared residence for a period not to exceed one year but intends to return. Whether or not the relationship is sexual is not relevant for the purposes of determining eligibility.

2. They have a committed personal relationship with each other that is mutually interdependent and intended to be lifelong;
3. They agree to be jointly obligated and responsible for the necessities of life for each other;

Note. "Necessities of life" means the cost of basic food, shelter, clothing, and medical care. The individuals need not contribute equally or jointly to the cost of these expenses as long as they agree that both are responsible and obligated for the cost.

4. They are not married to anyone or legally separated from anyone;
5. They are 18 years of age or older;
6. They are competent to enter into a contract;
7. They are not related by blood closer than would bar marriage in the state;
8. They are each other's sole domestic partner;
9. They agree to file a termination of domestic partnership within 30 days if any of the facts set out in this definition change; and
10. Any prior domestic partnership in which their domestic partner participated with a third party was terminated not less than six months prior to the date of such affidavit, and, if such earlier domestic partnership had been acknowledged under provisions of this section, that notice of termination of such earlier domestic partnership was provided to the city in writing to the business license division of the department of fi-

nance not less than six months prior to the date of said affidavit. If the prior domestic partnership was terminated by the death of the partner, there shall be no waiting period.[80]

To qualify for benefits as a domestic partner of a city employee in Chicago, Illinois, the partner and the employee must file an "Affidavit of Domestic Partnership," certifying that

1. They are one another's sole domestic partner, responsible for one another's common welfare;
2. Neither is married;
3. They are not related by blood closer than would bar marriage in the state;
4. Both are 18 or older, of the same sex, and reside together; and
5. Two of the following apply:
   a. They have resided together for 12 months before filing,
   b. They have common or joint ownership of a residence,
   c. They have at least two of the following:
      • Joint ownership of a motor vehicle
      • Joint credit account
      • Joint checking account
      • A residential lease identifying both as tenants
   d. The city employee declares that the domestic partner is the primary beneficiary of his or her will.[81]

The Atlanta and Chicago provisions discussed above apply to the domestic partnerships of city employees. As mentioned above, however, some localities have sought to impose domestic partnership benefits on the private businesses with which they conduct business.

The Code of the City of Berkeley, California, for example, provides that contractors may not discriminate in providing "bereavement leave, family medical leave, health benefits, membership or membership discounts, moving expenses, pensions and retirement benefits or travel benefits" or in the provision of any other benefits "between employees with domestic partners and employees with spouses, and/or between the domestic partners and spouses of such employees. . . ." Contractors may, however, require employees whose domestic partner benefits are more costly than marital benefits to pay the difference, provide a cash equivalent (under certain

80. Atlanta, Ga., Code of Ordinances § 94-131.
81. Chicago, Ill., Code of Ordinances § 2-152-072.

circumstances) in lieu of domestic partner benefits, or opt not to provide benefits to either employees' spouses or employees' domestic partners.[82]

Ordinances mandating domestic partner benefits in the public and/or private sectors remain highly controversial, but have nevertheless been enacted by hundreds of jurisdictions nationwide. Because municipal domestic partner benefits ordinances can vary in the ways mentioned previously, and in numerous other respects, it is important for employers that find themselves in jurisdictions having such ordinances to review these provisions closely.

In July 1997, legislation was passed in Hawaii that could require employers to extend health coverage to the domestic partners and dependents of employees. The legislation essentially grants rights normally recognized only in favor of married couples to unmarried couples who register with the state as reciprocal beneficiaries.[83] Employers that offer family health care coverage would be required to extend such benefits to registered partners. A group of employers in Hawaii has brought suit to block enforcement of the legislation.

On October 2, 1999, the Governor of California signed into law Assembly Bill 26, a law providing for the official registration of adult same-sex domestic partners. The new law also provides for registration of opposite-sex partners over the age of 62. This registry is to be compiled and administered by the state Secretary of State. In order to be eligible, same-sex partners and opposite-sex partners over the age of 62 must share a common residence.

The 1999 law also contains provisions dealing with the dissolution or termination of a domestic partnership. For instance, an individual who has filed a Declaration of Domestic Partnership is prohibited from filing a new declaration until at least six months has elapsed from the date that a Notice of Termination of Domestic Partnership was filed with the Secretary of State in connection with the most recent domestic partnership, except where the previous domestic partnership ended because one of the partners died or married.

Under the California law, the Secretary of State is required to prepare forms for the registration and termination of domestic partnerships and to distribute these forms to each county clerk. The law also empowers the Secretary of State to pass regulations imposing fees to recoup costs associated with these forms' creation, distribution, and administration.

The 1999 law preempts, on or after July 1, 2000, any local ordinance or law that provides for the creation of a domestic partnership, except that localities may retain or adopt policies or laws that offer rights to domestic partners within the jurisdiction and impose duties that are in addition to those imposed by the new statewide law.

Legislation passed in 2001 by the California General Assembly builds upon the 1999 measure by providing much more comprehensive benefits to domestic partners. Among the sweeping new provisions in the act are (1) the right to unemployment benefits for persons who leave their jobs to follow a domestic partner, (2) the right to claim disability benefits on behalf of a domestic partner, and (3) the right to use sick leave to care for an unhealthy domestic partner or child of a partner. Other radical new marriage-like rights for domestic partners included in the measure deal with the adoption of a domestic partner's child as a "stepparent," inheritance rights, medical decision making, tax filing as spouses, and the right to bring certain claims when a domestic partner is negligently killed. Insurance companies offering group health benefits are also required by the act to offer employers plans that cover domestic partners on the same terms as other dependents. The new law became effective January 1, 2002.

The preexisting Public Employees' Medical and Hospital Care Act authorizes the Board of Administration of the Public Employees' Retirement System to provide health benefits plan coverage to state and local public employees and annuitants and their family members. The 1999 law authorized state and local employers to offer health care coverage and other benefits to domestic partners who have presented a certificate of eligibility or a Declaration of Domestic Partnership to the Board. The 2001 legislation makes domestic partners, and children of domestic partners, eligible for continued health coverage upon the death of the employee or annuitant if the domestic partner is receiving a beneficiary allowance, as specified. It also prohibits surviving domestic partners from enrolling additional family members in a health benefits plan.

On March 22, 2002, the Minnesota House of Representatives voted to adopt a state employee contract agreement that does not include domestic partner provisions. Governor Ventura had been negotiating with state employee labor unions to provide labor contracts that include domestic partner benefits. Despite Ventura's support for the domestic partnership proposal, the con-

---

82. Berkeley, Calif., Code of Ordinances § 13.29.040.

83. Haw. Rev. Stat. Ann. §§ 572C-3–572C-7 (1999).

tract negotiations stalled last fall, resulting in a two-week strike by state employees. An interim contract was agreed to, bringing the employees back to work while awaiting legislative approval in the 2002 legislative session. Senate ratification of the contract is anticipated, because rejecting the contract might lead to another employee strike.

In an interesting development based on a local ordinance, on March 1, 2002, the Columbus (Ohio) Community Relations Commission ruled that the city had violated its antidiscrimination ordinance in denying health insurance benefits to domestic partners of city employees. Under the Columbus ordinance, employers may not discriminate on the basis of "sexual orientation" in employment decisions. In 1997, a city employee filed a complaint with the Commission after his partner was denied health insurance coverage. The Commission conducted its own investigation of the case and last summer hired a hearing officer in the case. The hearing officer found that the city was required to allow coverage of domestic partners of homosexuals. The outcome of this case could potentially apply to all city employees in Columbus.

The issue has also been raised in the judicial forum, with some interesting results.

The Virginia Supreme Court recently ruled that Arlington County, Virginia, exceeded its authority in making its self-funded health insurance benefits available to the unmarried domestic partners of county employees.[84] The members of the court were in agreement on the result but differed as to reasons for it. According to the majority, Arlington County acted unlawfully by violating the "Dillon Rule," which limits local government powers to those expressly granted by the state legislature. The Chief Justice and two others agreed that the Dillon Rule had been violated but argued that the county had erred more fundamentally by recognizing common-law marriages and "same-sex unions" in conferring the benefits. According to these justices, the county's attempt to legislate in the area of domestic relations, a prerogative belonging exclusively to the state legislature, and the recognition of common-law marriage and homosexual unions, violated the public policy of the Commonwealth of Virginia.

The Supreme Court of Vermont recently addressed a suit by three same-sex couples who alleged that denying them marriage licenses for which they had applied violated the Vermont Constitution. The court noted that the U.S. Supreme Court and lower federal courts have held that distinctions based on sexual orientation do not trigger any heightened scrutiny under the federal Equal Protection Clause. Thus, under the U.S. Constitution, a legislative distinction based on sexual orientation will be upheld as long as there is a rational basis for the distinction. After a lengthy discussion of the history of the Common Benefits Clause of the Vermont Constitution, and distinguishing that clause from the federal Equal Protection Clause, the court concluded that the state must extend to same-sex couples the common benefit, protection, and security that Vermont law provides opposite-sex married couples.[85]

Significantly, the court did not conclude that same-sex couples were entitled to marriage licenses and did not order that the plaintiffs who brought the case be issued marriage licenses. Rather, the court left to the Vermont legislature the task of crafting an appropriate means of addressing the constitutional mandate recognized by the court. The court noted that this constitutional mandate could be met by adopting statutory schemes similar to those of other jurisdictions, including "domestic partnership" or "registered partnership" acts.

In the wake of the Vermont Supreme Court decision, a bill was introduced that would recognize "civil unions" between same-sex partners. On April 26, 2000, Vermont Governor Howard Dean signed HB 847. The law specifically states that same-sex marriages are not valid in the state, but it creates a process for same-sex couples to register for "civil unions" and grants to such couples many legal rights and economic benefits that Vermont currently extends to married people. On December 26, 2001, Vermont's Supreme Court rejected a challenge to the civil unions law.[86] One of the claims was from the town clerks, who had argued that the law is unconstitutional because it forces them to violate their religious beliefs that homosexuality is wrong by issuing civil union licenses to couples. The justices did not rule directly on the claim that the law violates the town clerks' religious beliefs. But the opinion described as "highly questionable" the "proposition that a public official . . . can retain public office while refusing to perform a generally applicable duty of that office on religious grounds." Also, the court said the law accommodates the town clerks' concerns by explicitly permitting them to

---

84. Arlington County v. White, 259 Va. 708, 528 S.E.2d 706 (2000).

85. Baker v. State, 744 A.2d 864 (Vt. 1999).

86. Brady v. Dean, 2001 WL 1673775 (Vt. Sup. Ct., Dec., 26, 2001).

appoint an assistant to issue the licenses. In addition to the continuing controversy in Vermont, bills that would ban the recognition of a same-sex civil union or other same-sex relationship have been introduced in Colorado, New Hampshire, Oklahoma, and Texas. On February 8, 2002, the Connecticut legislature proposed legislation giving same-sex couples marital benefits. House Bill 5001 would amend the current marriage statutes to state that the registrar may issue a marriage license to any two persons, regardless of the sex of the persons. The legislation would also delete from current law the statement that marriage in Connecticut is limited to a marriage between a man and a woman.

As previously referred to, a similar statutory scheme has been adopted in Hawaii and, on a more limited basis, in California. In Hawaii, legislation allowing certain benefits for "reciprocal beneficiaries" was passed after a 1993 ruling by the Hawaii Supreme Court, which held that the state's failure to recognize gay marriages amounted to gender discrimination under the state's constitution.[87] In 1998, voters in Hawaii overwhelmingly approved an amendment to the state constitution that effectively gave the legislature the authority to withhold state recognition of same-sex marriages.[88] The legislature subsequently passed a statute that provides that a valid marriage "shall be only between a man and a woman."[89] A challenge to the statute was rejected by the Hawaii Supreme Court as moot in light of the constitutional amendment approved by the voters.[90] Eight states (California, Connecticut, Delaware, Massachusetts, New York, Oregon, Vermont, and Washington) now offer domestic partner benefits to employees of the state and their partners. Two of the states—Delaware and Massachusetts—provide only bereavement leave and family sick leave, while the benefits provided to employees of the other states are more extensive.

Effective January 1, 2002, a new state law provides that group insurers and health maintenance organizations (HMOs) in Maine are required to offer domestic partner benefits under the same terms and conditions as for husbands and wives of health plan members. The statute does not require employers offering group health benefits to offer such coverage but does require insurers and HMOs to provide such benefits as an option to Maine employers. Domestic partners are defined under the statute as mentally competent adults who are legally domiciled with a health plan member for at least one year. A domestic partner must be the sole partner of the plan member and must not be legally married or separated from another person. Health plan members may not enroll a new domestic partner for one year after terminating a domestic partnership. Under the statute, policyholders and their domestic partners may be required by insurers to sign affidavits and provide documentation.

District of Columbia employees will soon be able to purchase health benefits for same- and opposite-sex domestic partners if an appropriations bill passed by Congress is signed into law. Included in the legislation is a provision that would permit the district to fund its domestic partner benefits program, which was created in 1992. Under the 1992 measure, city employees can, at their own expense, purchase health insurance for a registered domestic partner. The program also provides for the use of sick leave by domestic partners to care for one another, domestic partner bereavement leave, and visitation rights for domestic partners at hospitals within the district.

The Oregon Court of Appeals held that the denial of health and life insurance benefits to the unmarried domestic partners of Oregon Health Sciences University's homosexual employees violated Article I, Section 20, of the Oregon Constitution.[91] The court ruled that the denial of domestic partner benefits did not violate Oregon's fair employment practices act, which prohibits discrimination in employment on the basis of the sex of an employee or the sex of any other person with whom the employee associates. The university maintained that it determined insurance on the basis of marital status, not sexual orientation, and that the unintentional effect on homosexuals did not violate either the fair employment practices act or the state constitution. The court disagreed, holding that Article I, Section 20, of the Oregon Constitution, which prohibits granting privileges or immunities not equally belonging to all citizens, applied whether the effect was intended or not. Therefore, the court held that the university could not refuse to provide the same benefits to the lesbian partners of its employees that it provided to the married partners of employees.

In several cases, a denial of domestic partner benefits has been challenged as a violation of a state prohibition

87. Baehr v. Lewin, 74 Haw. 645, 852 P.2d 44 (1993).

88. Haw. Const. art. 1, § 23.

89. Haw. Rev. Stat. Ann. § 572-1 (1999).

90. Baehr v. Miike, 92 Haw. 634, 994 P.2d 566 (Table) (1999).

91. Tanner v. Oregon Health Sciences Univ., 157 Or. App. 502, 971 P.2d 435 (1998).

against discrimination based on marital status. In early 1997 this issue was addressed in a significant opinion from the Alaska Supreme Court.[92] In the Alaska case, two employees of the University of Alaska requested health insurance benefits for their same-sex domestic partners, and the university refused. The employees claimed that the denial violated the Alaska Human Rights Act, which bars discrimination in employment on the basis of marital status. The university admitted that the denial was discriminatory but denied that the Act was violated.

Although the Alaska Human Rights Act was amended during the course of the litigation to provide that an employer could, without violating the Act, provide greater health and retirement benefits on the basis of marital status, the court found that the question was not moot, because of potential recovery of back benefits. The court decided that the policy of the university did in fact violate the Alaska Human Rights Act.

In a New Jersey case involving the same issue, the court reached a different conclusion.[93] The New Jersey Superior Court found that Rutgers University's denial of health insurance to same-sex domestic partners did not violate the New Jersey Law Against Discrimination, nor did it violate rights to equal protection under the state constitution. The court also found that an executive order banning discrimination on the basis of sexual orientation was not violated by the refusal to extend benefits. As of the time of this writing, the plaintiffs intended to appeal the case to the New Jersey Supreme Court.

Currently, marital status is a protected classification under the fair employment laws of 26 jurisdictions (Alaska, California, Connecticut, Delaware, District of Columbia, Florida, Hawaii, Illinois, Kentucky, Maryland, Massachusetts, Michigan, Minnesota, Montana, Nebraska, New Hampshire, New Jersey, New Mexico, New York, North Dakota, Oklahoma, Oregon, South Dakota, Virginia, Washington, and Wisconsin). Given the prevalence of such laws, it is likely that there will be further litigation over whether these statutes prohibit the denial of benefits to domestic partners.

---

92. University of Alaska v. Tumeo, 933 P.2d 1147 (Alaska 1997).

93. Rutgers Council of AAUP Chapters v. Rutgers Univ., 298 N.J. Super. 442, 689 A.2d 828 (App. Div. 1997).

2

Fair Employment Practices

Tables in Part 2 cover protected classifications under fair employment practice (FEP) statutes, compliance with FEP statutes, exceptions to compliance, fair employment commission powers and procedures, appeal of commission rulings, remedies available for violations, additional FEP laws, affirmative action requirements, and federal guidelines and precedent in state FEP enforcement.

§ 2.6 The Role of Federal Guidelines and Precedent in State Fair Employment Practice Enforcement

This section discusses the substantive regulations regarding enforcement of federal fair employment practice (FEP) laws within the jurisdiction of the Equal Employment Opportunity Commission (EEOC). These guidelines contain detailed information regarding the EEOC's interpretation of these laws and are regarded as persuasive authority by the federal courts.

[a] The Importance of Federal Precedent

In construing their FEP statutes, state courts often look to federal precedent in this area, including the EEOC guidelines.[1]

State courts are not bound to follow the EEOC regulations, and they sometimes do deviate from them.[2]

Apprenticeship Programs. One point on which there has been a significant divergence between the EEOC guidelines and state FEP laws and decisions interpreting those laws is the exemption of apprenticeship programs from prohibitions against age discrimination. Since 1969, when the Department of Labor (DOL) was responsible for administering the Age Discrimination in Employment Act (ADEA), the EEOC regulations had recognized an exemption for "bona fide apprenticeship programs." The reason for this exemption was that the traditional limitation of apprenticeship programs to younger people was "in recognition of the fact that apprenticeship is an extension of the educational process to prepare young men and women for skilled employment." About half the state FEP laws contain such an exemption, while the other half prohibit age discrimination in apprenticeship programs. In June 1996, the EEOC eliminated the exemption. The rule revised prohibits age discrimination in apprenticeship programs subject to the ADEA.[3]

Although there are some other points of divergence between state law and the EEOC regulations (see Table 2.6-1 and Exhibits 2.6-1 and 2.6-2), most state courts regard the regulations as persuasive authority in constru-

---

§ 2.6

1. *See, e.g.,* Harrison v. Chance, 244 Mont. 215, 797 P.2d 200 1990) (federal precedent is helpful and appropriate in construing Montana Civil Rights Act); Byrd v. Richardson-Greenshields Sec., Inc., 552 So. 2d 1099 (Fla. 1989) (federal precedent is persuasive in interpreting Florida Human Rights Act); Radtke v. Everett, 189 Mich. App. 346, 471 N.W.2d 660 (1991) (when reviewing claims under state civil rights act, court may look to federal precedent, including EEOC guidelines); Board of Directors, Green Hills Country Club v. Illinois Human Rights Comm'n, 162 Ill. App. 3d 216, 514 N.E.2d 1227 (1987) (citing EEOC regulations and federal case law, and stating that while federal decisions are not controlling they provide relevant and helpful precedents); *see also* Vainio v. Brookshire, 258 Mont. 273, 852 P.2d 596 (1993); Syndex Corp. v. Dean, 820 S.W.2d 869 (Tex. App. 1991); Kerans v. Porter Paint Co., 61 Ohio St. 3d 486, 575 N.E.2d 428 (1991).

2. *See* Jenson v. Siemson, 118 Idaho 1, 794 P.2d 271 (1990) (court would decline to judicially apply federal guidelines to Idaho case; adopting federal guidelines would be a matter for the legislature or Department of Employment).

3. 29 C.F.R. § 1625.21.

ing similar provisions of state law. Table 2.6-1 sets out state court holdings regarding the applicability of specific substantive EEOC regulations to state FEP laws.

[b] Rescission of EEOC Guidelines on Employer Liability for Harassment

In 1999, in light of recent pronouncements from the U.S. Supreme Court, the EEOC rescinded its longstanding regulations regarding employer liability for harassment. Until replacement regulations are finalized, the EEOC's position on employer liability is set out in an Enforcement Guidance on these Supreme Court decisions.[4] Subsection [i] of "Trends and Controversies in Human Resources Law" discusses these Supreme Court decisions, the EEOC Guidance, what employment actions are considered "tangible" for purposes of strict employer liability, and how an employer must prevent, investigate, and remedy harassment in order to avoid liability.

[c] Final Regulations Promulgated by the EEOC

Regulations Covering Waivers of Age Discrimination Claims. The EEOC has promulgated regulatory guidance on Title II of the Older Workers Benefit Protection Act of 1990 (OWBPA), which amended the ADEA to permit knowing and voluntary unsupervised waivers of rights and claims arising under the ADEA. Representatives of both the employer and the employee communities have strongly demonstrated their interest in obtaining additional guidance in this area. As part of the development of a regulation on waivers under the ADEA, the EEOC engaged in a regulatory negotiation and obtained a consensus recommendation to the Commission. The Commissioners approved the recommendation unanimously on October 9, 1996. The final regulations, published in June 1998, resolved a number of issues that had arisen in the context of assessing the validity of ADEA waivers.[5]

In the regulations, the EEOC rejected the position that a material error will invalidate a waiver agreement only if an employee proves that the error was intentional and that he or she reasonably relied on the misinformation. The EEOC took the position that the question of materiality of an error should be judged by traditional standards without regard to intent, and that reliance is not an element of proof either in the statute or in the regulation. The EEOC also rejected the suggestion that the regulation require "substantial" consideration (i.e., a substantial monetary payment) as a condition of a valid waiver. In the EEOC's view, any requirement regarding the amount of the payment would be contrary to the language of the ADEA itself, which requires only "consideration in addition to anything of value to which the individual already is entitled," not "substantial" consideration.

The importance of strict adherence to the requirements of the OWBPA cannot be overemphasized. In *Oubre v. Entergy Operations, Inc.*,[6] the Supreme Court held that an employer's failure to adhere to the applicable requirements not only invalidated the waiver but also allowed a former employee to bring suit under the ADEA without first giving back the money received in exchange for executing the waiver. Although the EEOC's 1998 regulation regarding the validity of waivers under the ADEA was approved in its final form before the Supreme Court's decision in *Oubre,* the EEOC indicated that any requirement in a waiver agreement that the employee tender back any amount paid prior to instituting a lawsuit would be void (see below).

EEOC Regulation on "Tender Back" of Payments in Connection with Waivers. On December 11, 2000, the EEOC published a final rule prohibiting the return, or "tender back," of payments made in connection with challenges to waivers under the ADEA.[7] The new rule addresses the Supreme Court's decision in *Oubre* and related issues regarding waivers.

The regulation provides that an employer may not require an employee to return, or "tender back," severance pay or other benefits in order to challenge a waiver as inconsistent with the ADEA. In addition, the rule prohibits the imposition of other financial penalties against an employee simply for challenging a waiver in court. It does, however, protect an employer's ability to recover attorneys' fees if a challenge is filed in bad faith. The rule also sets out standards regarding when an employer may obtain restitution of funds it has paid an employee and what an employer's duties are when a waiver is challenged.

---

4. EEOC Enforcement Guidance: Vicarious Employer Liability for Unlawful Harassment by Supervisors (June 18, 1999).

5. 29 C.F.R. § 1625.22.

---

6. 522 U.S. 422 (1998).

7. 65 Fed. Reg. 77,437–77,447 (2000) (codified at 29 C.F.R. § 1625.23).

Table 2.6-1 PART 2—FAIR EMPLOYMENT PRACTICES 2-4

Table 2.6-1

STATE DECISIONS ON APPLICABILITY OF EEOC GUIDELINES AND FEDERAL PRECEDENT

(See also text at § 2.6.)

KEY: An em dash (—) indicates no explicit decision.
A "Yes" indicates state court decision relying on EEOC regulation or federal precedent.
A "No" indicates state court decision rejecting applicability of EEOC regulation or federal precedent.

	Guidelines Held Generally Applicable	Age	Disability	Equal Pay	National Origin	Race	Religion	Sex	Other
AL	—	Yes.	—	—	—	—	—	—	—
AK	—	—	—	—	—	—	Yes.	Yes.	—
AZ	—	—	Yes.	—	—	—	—	—	—
CA	—	Yes.	Yes, but definition of persons with disabilities is broader under state law.	—	—	—	—	Yes.[1]	—
CO	—	Yes.	Yes.[2]	—	—	—	—	—	—
CT	—	Yes.	Yes.	—	—	Yes.	—	Yes, for pregnancy discrimination.	Continuing violation theory. Federal definition of employer applied.
DC	—	—	Yes.	—	—	—	—	—	—
FL	Yes.	—	Yes.	—	—	—	—	Yes.	Federal definition of employer applied.
HI	—	Yes.	—	—	—	—	—	Yes.	Applies federal collateral source rule.
IL	Yes.	Yes.	—	—	—	—	—	Yes.	—
ID	No.	—	Yes.	—	—	—	—	—	—
IA	Yes.	Yes.	Yes.[3]	—	—	—	—	—	—
KS	—	Yes.	—	—	—	Yes.	—	—	—
KY	—	—	—	—	—	Yes.	—	Yes.	—
LA	—	—	Yes.	—	—	—	—	—	—

State									Comments
ME	—	—	—	—	—	—	Yes.	—	—
MA	Yes.	Yes.[4]	Yes. Unlike federal courts construing the Americans with Disabilities Act, courts construing Massachusetts law are not required to consider mitigating or corrective measures in determining whether an individual is a person with a disability	Yes.	—	—	—	Yes.[5]	Applies federal proof scheme in mixed-motive cases. Federal rule regarding continuing violation in sexual harassment cases does not apply to state law claims.
MI	Yes.	—	Yes.	—	—	Yes.	No.	No, with regard to definition of sexual harassment and burden of proof with respect to employer liability in sexual harassment cases.	—
MN	—	—	Yes.	—	Yes.	—	—	Yes.[6]	—
MO	—	Yes.	Yes.	Yes.	—	Yes.	—	Yes.	Arbitral decision pursuant to collective bargaining agreement does not preclude discrimination suit.
MT	Yes.	—	Yes.	—	—	—	—	—	—
NE	—	—	—	—	—	—	—	Yes.	EEOC Compliance Manual definition of employer applied.
NJ	Yes.	—	Yes.	—	—	Yes.	—	Yes.[7]	Federal precedent applied to retaliation claim. Exhaustion of administrative remedies not required for suit. Federal proof scheme for discrimination cases applies to cases under New Jersey's Conscientious Employee Protection Act.
NY	—	Yes.	Yes.[8]	—	EEOC guideline on English-only policies not applied to the extent that it could be interpreted to create a presumption of discrimination.	Yes.	—	Yes.	Interagency agreement creates automatic dual filing of administrative charge with EEOC and state agency. Persons with "ownership interest" may be held liable as individuals.

(Table continues.)

Table 2.6-1 (cont'd)
STATE DECISIONS ON APPLICABILITY OF EEOC GUIDELINES AND FEDERAL PRECEDENT

(See also text at § 2.6.)

KEY: An em dash (—) indicates no explicit decision.
A "Yes" indicates state court decision relying on EEOC regulation or federal precedent.
A "No" indicates state court decision rejecting applicability of EEOC regulation or federal precedent.

	Guidelines Held Generally Applicable	Age	Disability	Equal Pay	National Origin	Race	Religion	Sex	Other
ND	—	—	—	—	—	—	—	Yes.	—
OH	Yes.	Yes.	Yes.	—	—	—	—	Yes.	Federal analysis of circumstantial versus direct evidence methods of proof applied. Federal precedent on causal connection required for retaliation claim applied. Applies federal standard in same-sex harassment cases. Applies federal proof scheme in mixed-motive cases.
OK	—	—	—	—	—	Yes.	—	Yes.	—
OR	—	—	Yes.	—	—	—	—	Yes.	Applies federal standard for defining prevailing party status for purposes of award of attorneys' fees.
PA	—	Yes.	—	—	—	Yes.	—	—	Judicial action limited to scope of administrative charge. Follows federal precedent for same-sex harassment cases.
PR	—	No.	Yes.	—	—	—	—	Yes.	—
TN	—	Yes.	Yes.	—	Yes.	Yes.	—	—	—
TX	Yes.	—	Yes.	—	—	—	—	—	—
VT	—	—	Yes.	—	—	—	—	Yes.	—

					Federal rule on effect of after-discovered evidence applied. Applies federal proof scheme in mixed-motive cases.
WA	—	—	Yes.	—	Yes.[9]
WV	No.	—	—	—	Yes.
WI	—	—	—	No.	Yes.

1. Federal precedent does not apply, however, to hostile work environment or employer liability for supervising harassment, on which California and federal law may differ.
2. Colorado court was persuaded by public policy underlying the ADEA in striking down state disability statute.
3. Iowa court declined to adopt the undue hardship standard for reasonable accommodation in the EEOC guidelines and maintained a *de minimis* standard. Additionally, Iowa law allows for consideration of mitigating effects of medicine or assistive devices in determining whether an impairment substantially limits a major life activity.
4. Pretext-plus standard under federal law does not apply to Massachusetts antidiscrimination statute; thus, plaintiff's burden to prove pretext under state law is lighter.
5. Federal precedent does not apply, however, to claims of same-sex harassment, on which Massachusetts law and federal law may differ.
6. Minnesota does not apply same definition of sexual harassment as federal courts and the EEOC.
7. New Jersey and federal courts interpreting New Jersey law have noted that the New Jersey Law Against Discrimination is in some respects broader and more flexible than federal law. Further, at least one New Jersey court has adopted a "reasonable woman standard" for sexual harassment rather than the "reasonable person standard" applied under federal law.
8. No reasonable accommodation required for private employers under New York law; claimant not required to show substantial limitation of normal activities to state a claim.
9. Federal precedent does not apply, however, to strict liability of employer for sexual harassment by supervisor. Note, however, that the EEOC has rescinded its regulations regarding employer liability for sexual harassment in light of recent Supreme Court precedent. For further discussion of the EEOC's current position, see subsection [i] of "Trends and Controversies" in Human Resources Law.

Exhibit 2.6-1

STATE DECISIONS RELYING ON EEOC GUIDELINES OR FEDERAL PRECEDENT

(See also text at § 2.6.)

Age Discrimination

ALABAMA

Because the purposes and prohibitions of the federal and state statutes are manifestly the same, federal principles apply to state statute. An employee at a mortgage company who was denied promotions alleged age discrimination under the ADEA and the Alabama Age Discrimination in Employment Act. The plaintiff attempted to proceed on the basis of direct evidence of discriminatory intent, but statements by the employer that the plaintiff "was getting real old" and that, on account of her age, she might "have to stop staying up so late and partying at night" reflected a general bias only. Under a circumstantial evidence approach, however, the age discrimination cause of action withstood a motion for summary judgment. [*Bonham v. Regions Mortgage, Inc.*, 129 F. Supp. 2d 1315 (M.D. Ala. 2001)]

CALIFORNIA

Same standard for proof of pretext applied in age discrimination suits. A terminated employee brought suit against a real estate company for age discrimination under the ADEA and the California antidiscrimination statute. In affirming a lower court's grant of summary judgment, the appellate court applied the general burden-shifting analysis outlined in *McDonnell Douglas* to the employee's state claims. Following federal precedent, the court held that the employee, who was hired as a regional communications director, failed to show that the proffered reasons for terminating him—that the position was being restructured to focus more on external communications and he lacked requisite skills—were a pretext for discrimination. [*Horn v. Cushman & Wakefield Western, Inc.*, 72 Cal. App. 4th 798, 85 Cal. Rptr. 2d 459 (Cal. Ct. App. 1999)]

COLORADO

Public policy underlying ADEA. A claimant who was denied permanent total disability benefits brought an action challenging the state statute disqualifying employees 65 or older from receiving workers' compensation for permanent total disability. In striking down the state disability statute, the court was persuaded by the expression of public policy underlying the ADEA and referred to federal precedent to address the legality of the state statute. [*Romero v. Industrial Claims Appeals Office*, 902 P.2d 896 (Colo.Ct. App. 1995)]

CONNECTICUT

No inference of age discrimination based on comments of co-workers. A former bus driver brought action against his former employer alleging, *inter alia*, age and disability discrimination under the ADA, the ADEA, and the state antidiscrimination statute. With respect to the age discrimination claim, the court applied federal precedent to the state claim and held that where an employee hears co-workers commenting on the employer's history of terminating older employees, the evidence is insufficient to raise the inference that the employer discharged the employee based on considerations of age. The court granted summary judgment to the defendant on the claims of age and disability discrimination under both state and federal law. [*Williams v. H.N.S. Management Co.*, 56 F. Supp. 2d 215 (D. Conn. 1999)]

Federal standard for prima facie case of age discrimination applied to an age discrimination claim under the Connecticut Fair Employment Practices Act (CFEPA). An anesthesiologist who was denied a request for a half-time position made out a prima facie case of age discrimination under the ADEA and the CFEPA. The employer's hiring of two younger doctors to replace the workload of the plaintiff, who had been on leave, and two other senior doctors, who had gone to half-time status, gave rise to an inference of age discrimination. [*Shaw v. Greenwich Anesthesiology Associates, P.C.*, 137 F. Supp. 2d 48 (D. Conn. 2001)]

Federal pretext analysis used.   In a case involving a female professor who brought a claim under the state FEP law for age and sex discrimination after her college employer failed to grant her tenure, the court used the federal burden-shifting analysis. [*Craine v. Trinity College*, 791 A.2d 518 (Conn. 2002)]

HAWAII

Same actor inference applicable to state discrimination claim.   In attempting to establish pretext in the final step of the *McDonnell Douglas* framework, some federal courts have required plaintiffs to overcome the "same actor inference." Under this concept, if the same actor is responsible for both the hiring and the firing of a discrimination plaintiff and both actions occur within a short period of time, there arises a strong inference that there was no discriminatory motive. In a termination case brought under the Hawaii Employment Discrimination Law, the court adopted the same actor inference, but held that it is merely a permissive inference that is supplemental to other evidentiary or policy considerations. [*Shoppe v. Gucci America, Inc.*, 94 Haw. 368, 14 P.3d 1049 (2000)]

IOWA

No inference of age discrimination raised by supervisor's comments.   A former employee brought an action for age discrimination under the ADEA and the Iowa Civil Rights Act (ICRA). The court held that discrimination claims brought under the ICRA are analyzed in the same manner as their federal law counterparts. Upholding a lower court's grant of summary judgment to the employer, the court held that evidence that the employee was transferred to a new job for which he lacked experience, that he was referred to with an age-related epithet by a supervisor, and that he was repeatedly offered early retirement was not sufficient to raise an inference of age discrimination under either the ADEA and the ICRA. [*Montgomery v. John Deere & Co.*, 169 F.3d 556 (8th Cir. 1999)]

KANSAS

Court relies on federal precedent in age discrimination claim.   Following his termination, a construction company employee sued his employer under the ADEA and the Kansas Age Discrimination in Employment Act (KADEA). The court held that the analysis of the ADEA claim applied equally to the KADEA claim, and thus followed federal precedent in interpreting the KADEA. [*Elkins v. Bayer Construction Co.*, 68 F. Supp. 2d 1249 (D. Kan. 1999)]

MASSACHUSETTS

Retention of younger employees, the inference of discrimination, and the insufficiency of a theory of disparate impact in an age discrimination suit.   An employer moved for summary judgment in a suit brought by a former employee alleging age discrimination in violation of the Massachusetts antidiscrimination statute. The court asserted that, in the absence of overt acts of age discrimination, Massachusetts courts applying the state statute analyze age discrimination cases that allege disparate treatment under the the same three-stage burden-shifting analysis applied in federal age discrimination cases. Accordingly, the court held that a supervisor's sporadic and temporary redelegation of a former employee's essential duties to younger employees, who had never performed those duties before, constituted "retention" of the younger employees in the same position. The court also found that stray remarks made by the employer to an employee may properly constitute evidence of a discriminatory intent for the jury to consider in combination with other evidence in the action. Finally, the court followed federal precedent in determining that an age discrimination claim under the Massachusetts antidiscrimination statute cannot be grounded solely on a theory of disparate impact. [*Flebotte v. Dow Jones & Co.*, 51 F. Supp. 2d 36 (D. Mass. 1999)]

Age discrimination claims cannot be grounded solely on a theory of disparate impact.   A former employee who was downgraded with a salary reduction brought an age discrimination claim under the ADEA and the Massachusetts Anti-Discrimination Act (MADA). In analyzing the employee's disparate impact claim under the ADEA, the court noted that such a claim is based not on proof of intentional discrimination, as is a disparate treatment claim, but rather on proof that the employer utilized employment practices that were facially neutral in their treatment of different groups but fell more harshly on one group than another and could not be legitimated by business necessity. The court asserted that since intentional discrimination is a prerequisite to liability under the ADEA, claims that an adverse employment decision may have had a disparate impact on an older employee may not be made under the ADEA. In the absence of Massachusetts case law on point, the court held that claims under the MADA could not be grounded solely on a theory of disparate impact either. [*Mullin v. Raytheon Co.*, 164 F.3d 696 (1st Cir. 1999)]

MISSOURI

Application of federal precedent to age discrimination claim.   A former employee brought an action for age discrimination under the ADEA and the Missouri Human Rights Act (MHRA). The court applied the same analysis to the employee's ADEA and MHRA claims, thus following federal precedent in evaluating the employee's prima facie case. Finding the evidence sufficient to establish that the employer inten-

Exhibit 2.6-1 PART 2—FAIR EMPLOYMENT PRACTICES 2-10

tionally discriminated against the employee on account of age, the Eighth Circuit affirmed a lower court's judgment as a matter of law for the employee. [*Morse v. Southern Union Co.,* 174 F.3d 917 (8th Cir. 1999)]

NEW YORK

Burden-shifting analysis in age discrimination claim. An employee sued an employer and its president for age discrimination under the ADEA, the New York State Human Rights Law (NYSHRL), and the New York City Human Rights Law (NYCHRL). The court applied the *McDonnell Douglas* burden-shifting analysis to the employee's NYSHRL and NYCHRL claims, thus following federal precedent in interpreting the applicable state law. [*Abramowitz v. Inta-Boro Acres Inc.,* 64 F. Supp. 2d 166 (E.D.N.Y. 1999); *see also Morris v. Northrop Grumman Corp.,* 37 F. Supp. 2d 556 (E.D.N.Y. 1999); *Brink v. Union Carbide Corp.,* 41 F. Supp. 2d 406 (S.D.N.Y. 1999)]

Stating a claim for age discrimination based on demeaning comments. A female employee filed a complaint under Title VII and New York State law, alleging discrimination on the basis of age and sex. In granting the employer's motion to dismiss the complaint, the court followed federal guidelines in holding that where a complaint does not cite specific examples of demeaning age-based comment, the complaint fails to state a claim for age discrimination under New York State law. A supervisor's statement that the employee should "get on board or quit" was not sufficient, according to the court. [*Gregory v. Daly,* 78 F. Supp. 2d 48 (N.D.N.Y. 1999)]

No direct cause of action by a spouse and no loss of consortium claim. An employee brought an action against her former employer alleging age discrimination in violation of the ADEA and the NYSHRL. The employee's husband appealed the denial of a motion to intervene. In affirming the lower court's denial to the husband's motion to intervene, the Second Circuit held that neither the ADEA nor the NYSHRL affords a direct cause of action to a nonemployee for discrimination against a spouse. The court further held that neither statute provides for a claim of a loss of consortium. [*Moss v. Stinnes Corp.,* 169 F.3d 784 (2d Cir. 1999)]

OHIO

Requirement that employee be qualified for position; impact of statements by co-workers in assessing whether an employer harbors or tolerates age bias. An employer motioned for summary judgment in a suit brought by a former employee under the ADEA and the Ohio discrimination statute, alleging discrimination on the basis of age. At the outset, the court stated that an employee claiming discrimination under the ADEA and the Ohio statute must show the same

elements under both statutes to make out a prima facie case of age discrimination. Following federal precedent in interpreting the state claim, the court held that where an employee finds normal tasks difficult and consistently fails to maintain customer files and account information according to company standards, the employee is not "qualified" for the position— here, a regional manager at a rent-to-own home furnishings company—from which he was discharged. In granting the defendant-employer's motion for summary judgment, the court stated further that comments by a co-worker that the employee "was a bit long in the tooth" did not support the employee's claim that the employer tolerated or harbored age bias, especially when there was no evidence that the co-worker was involved in the decision to terminate the employee. [*Brown v. Renter's Choice, Inc.,* 55 F. Supp. 2d 788 (N.D. Ohio 1999)]

PENNSYLVANIA

Assessing a claim of pretext and the role of the jury in an age discrimination claim. A widow of a former employee sued an employer for age discrimination under the ADEA and the Pennsylvania Human Relations Act (PHRA). Following the *McDonnell Douglas* framework for analysis in examining the state claim, the court held that for a plaintiff's pretext argument to work the plaintiff need only show that there were "weaknesses, implausibilities, inconsistencies, incoherences, or contradictions in the employer's proffered legitimate reason for its action" such that a rational factfinder could reasonably find them unworthy of credibility. Finding that the employee satisfied the requirement, the court denied the employer's motion for summary judgment, asserting that whether the employer's proffered reason was pretext should be decided by a jury. [*Tumolo v. Triangle Pacific Corp.,* 49 F. Supp. 2d 798 (E.D. Pa. 1999)]

Same standards applied in age discrimination suit. A defendant-employer moved for summary judgment in an age discrimination suit brought by a former employee under the ADEA and the PHRA. The court noted that since Pennsylvania courts use the *McDonnell Douglas* burden-shifting analysis in deciding PHRA claims, the analysis of the ADEA claim would apply equally to both the federal and the state claims, a denial of a claim under the ADEA precluding a claim brought under the PHRA. Accordingly, the court held that where a police department was disbanded and a former police chief's former position was itself terminated, the former police chief could not establish a prima facie case under the ADEA or the PHRA. The court further held that the relevant question under the ADEA and hence the PHRA is not whether the employer made the best, or even a sound decision; rather, it is whether the real reason is discrimination. In light of the foregoing concerns, the court granted summary judgment to the employer. [*Martel v. Great Bend Borough,* 40 F. Supp. 2d 261 (M.D. Pa. 1999)]

TENNESSEE

Standard for admissibility of direct evidence of age discrimination. A meat department manager at a grocery store was allowed to use as evidence a chart he created showing the ages of meat department managers employed by the grocery chain, even without evidence of the number of older persons potentially available for the position. As to the claims under the ADEA as well as the Tennessee Human Rights Act, the chart was admissible when coupled with direct evidence of discrimination consisting of a supervisor's statement that the employer was attempting to terminate older employees and hire younger ones who could be trained in the company "way." [*Watson v. Food Lion, Inc.*, 147 F. Supp. 2d 883 (E.D. Tenn. 2000)]

WASHINGTON

Court applies federal standard for showing of pretext. A former employee at a computer training institute challenged her termination on the ground that it was discrimination based on her age, race, and disability. The court found that no trier of fact could have reasonably concluded that the employee's age was more likely than not a substantial factor in the termination. As had the U.S. Supreme Court in a federal case under the ADEA [*Reeves v. Sanderson Plumbing Products, Inc.*, 530 U.S. 133 (2000)], the court rejected a pretext-plus standard of liability under which a showing that the employer's proffered reason for the challenged action was pretextual was never by itself adequate to prove employment discrimination. It held that a prima facie case, plus evidence sufficient to show pretext, will ordinarily, but not always, suffice to show discrimination. [*Hill v. BCTI Income Fund-I*, 144 Wash. 2d 172, 23 P.3d 440 (2001)]

Disability or Handicap

ARIZONA

Burden of proof of undue hardship. In a disability discrimination case, the court stated that because of the similarity between federal and state laws it regarded as persuasive federal cases citing to the EEOC guidelines' burden of proof of undue hardship. [*Francini v. Phoenix Newspapers, Inc.*, 937 P.2d 1382 (Ariz. Ct. App. June 27, 1996)]

CALIFORNIA

Coverage of mental disability. Suit was brought under the California Fair Employment and Housing Act (CFEHA) by a woman alleging that she was discharged because of mental disability. In the absence of controlling state law, the court considered decisions interpreting federal law, as well as the EEOC guidelines, because the state antidiscrimination law's disability provisions are based on the ADA and other federal law. [*Brundage v. County of Los Angeles Office of Assessor*, 66 Cal. Rptr. 2d 830 (Cal. App. 4th 228 1997)]

What is necessary to "reasonably accommodate" a disabled employee is best determined through a flexible, interactive process involving both employer and employee. In a case brought by a former employee under the CFEHA, the court relied on the EEOC regulations in finding a continuing violation for the entire course of the employer's unlawful conduct because the employee sought an accommodation. [*Richards v. CHZM Hill, Inc.*, 111 Cal. Rptr. 2d 87 (Ct. App. 2001)]

CONNECTICUT

Definition of *substantially limited* and the inference of discrimination. A former bus driver brought action against his former employer alleging, *inter alia*, disability discrimination under the ADA and the state antidiscrimination statute. The district court looked to the EEOC guidelines for a definition of what it means for a person to be "substantially limited," adding that an impairment that disqualifies a person from a narrow range of jobs is not a substantial limitation. Based on these holdings, the court granted summary judgment to the defendant on the claims of age and disability discrimination under both state and federal law. [*Williams v. H.N.S. Management Co.*, 56 F. Supp. 2d 215 (D. Conn. 1999)]

DELAWARE

Alcoholism as a disability. The court cited federal regulations and the EEOC Technical Assistance Manual for the proposition of alcoholism as a disability in case under state workers' compensation law. Court found that an agreement providing that employee would be terminated if admitted to a rehabilitation program void as a violation of public policy. [*Sann v. Renal Care Centers Corp.*, 1995 WL 161458 (Del. Super. Ct. Mar. 28, 1995)]

DISTRICT OF COLUMBIA

Definitions of *major life activity* and *substantial limitation*. The plaintiff had problems attending work as a result of stress, depression, and post-traumatic stress disorder due to too much work and a poor work environment. After he was suspended, he alleged a violation of the District of Columbia Human Rights Act (DCHRA). The court cited to the federal ADA regulations at 29 CFR Section 1630.2(i) in holding that working is in fact a major life activity. The court then found that the plaintiff was not disabled because he could have worked at another job. This finding was based on a review of 29 CFR Section 1630.2(j)(3)(i), which states that the inability to perform a single particular job does not mean that the plaintiff suffers from a substantial limitation in the major life area of working. [*Woodland v. District Council 20*, 777 A.2d 795 (D.C. 2001)]

Exhibit 2.6-1   PART 2—FAIR EMPLOYMENT PRACTICES   2-12

FLORIDA

Defining *disability*. An employee appealed from an order of the Florida Commission on Human Rights dismissing his complaint against his employer in which he alleged employment discrimination based on disability. The court adopted the federal definition of "disability" in construing the state claim. [*Brand v. Florida Power Corp.*, 633 So. 2d 504 (Fla. Dist. Ct. App. 1994)]

IDAHO

State law patterned after federal law. In action under the ADA and the Idaho Human Rights Act, court stated that when it had not had occasion to determine the standards applicable to state claims patterned on federal law, it might look to relevant federal law for guidance. Court referred to pertinent provisions of the EEOC guidelines. [*Stanbury v. Blue Cross of Idaho Health Service*, 128 Idaho 682, 918 P.2d 266 (1996)]

ILLINOIS

Applying *Sutton* and EEOC guidelines in determining whether severe depression is substantially limiting. A police officer who was diagnosed with severe depression and was prescribed Prozac was placed in the department's "Personnel Concerns Program" (PCP) after a blood test revealed Prozac in his blood. The officer sued under the ADA, alleging that he was placed in the PCP (a program for officers with disciplinary problems) solely because he was taking Prozac. The court applied the U.S. Supreme Court ruling in *Sutton v. United Airlines* [527 U.S. 471 (1999)] as well as the EEOC guidelines in holding that the officer was not substantially limited in a major life activity. Although the officer had severe depression, he was able to perform his job while on Prozac. Thus, he was not actually disabled under the ADA. The officer's claim for intentional infliction of emotional distress based on statements made by fellow employees about his mental condition was preempted by the Illinois Human Rights Act. [*Krocka v. City of Chicago*, 203 F.3d 507 (7th Cir. 2000)]

IOWA

Defining *substantially limited* and *major life activity*. An employee sued under the ADA and the Iowa Civil Rights Act (ICRA) claiming disability discrimination. The issue before the court was whether the employee was disabled within the meaning of the ADA and the ICRA. Given the common purpose and similarity in terminology of the ADA's and ICRA's prohibition on disability discrimination, the court looked to the ADA and federal regulations in developing standards under the ICRA for disability discrimination claims. The court followed the EEOC position that a court should first determine whether an individual is substantially limited in a major life activity other than working before proceeding to determine whether an individual is substantially limited in working. [*Bearshield v. John Morrell & Co.*, 570 N.W.2d 915 (Iowa 1997)]

LOUISIANA

Defining *qualified handicapped person*. In a disability discrimination action under state law, the court noted that the EEOC regulations were consistent with the Louisiana Civil Rights for Handicapped Persons Act regarding its definition of "qualified handicapped person." The regulations defined "qualified handicapped person" as one who with reasonable accommodation could perform the essential functions of the position. The court cited the regulations and other federal authority in deciding a claim brought under the Act. [*Riddle v. Louisiana Power & Light Co.*, 654 So. 2d 698 (La. Ct. App. 1995)]

Definition of *substantially limits*. The plaintiff employee was fired after yelling at his supervisor. He brought an action under the Louisiana Human Rights Act (LHRA), claiming that he suffered from a disability, attention deficit hyperactivity disorder (ADHD), which substantially limited his ability to learn. The LHRA states that a person is disabled if he suffers from "a physical or mental impairment that substantially limits one or more major life activities." The court stated that because the LHRA is similar in scope to the ADA, it is proper to consider federal ADA cases in interpreting the LHRA. The court examined the federal regulations at 29 CFR Sections 1630.2(j)(1) and (2) and federal case law in making the determination of whether the plaintiff was significantly restricted in the duration, manner, and conditions under which he could learn, as compared to the average person in the general population. [*Hook v. Georgia Gulf Corp.*, 788 So.2d 47 (La. App. 1 Cir. 2001)]

MASSACHUSETTS

Coverage of temporary disabilities. Former employee brought action against former employer alleging that her termination was discrimination on the basis of her handicap. The issue in the case was whether knee injury from which employee fully recovered in a month and from which she had no residual disability was a handicap within the meaning of the statute. Because of the similarity between state and federal statutes, state court followed the EEOC's regulation interpreting the ADA. Court held that temporary disabilities not resulting in permanent injuries are not disabilities under state antidiscrimination law. [*Hallgren v. Integrated Financial Corp.*, 679 N.E.2d 259 (Mass. App. Ct. 1997)]

Definition of *essential function*. Former executive director of law firm who was suffering from multiple sclerosis brought handicap discrimination suit under Massachusetts discrimination law. Court stated that federal guidelines can be used to guide court in interpreting whether a certain function is an "essential function." [*Labonte v. Hutchins & Wheeler*, 678 N.E.2d 853 (Mass. 1997)]

Definition of *disability*. An employee brought an action under the ADA and the Massachusetts antidiscrimination statute. The focus of the case was whether the plaintiff, who suffered a cognitive impairment following chemotherapy, was substantially limited in her ability to work. The court stated that the definition of the term "handicap" under Massachusetts law is virtually identical to that of "disability" in the ADA. Therefore, the court found, it was appropriate to examine the regulations defining disability at 29 CFR Sections 1630.2(j)(3)(ii)(B) and (C) for both the plaintiff's federal and state law claims. [*Whitney v. Greenberg, Rosenblatt, Kule & Bitsoli*, 258 F.3d 30 (1st Cir. 2001)]

MICHIGAN

Balancing state statutory obligations. A restaurant owner suspended a waitress until she underwent testing to determine whether she was infected with AIDS. The waitress brought an action under the Michigan Handicappers' Civil Rights Act (MHCRA) and the Public Health Code. The court looked to the EEOC regulations for guidance in balancing the employer's state statutory obligations not to discriminate against employees versus its obligation to provide a safe environment for diners. [*Sanchez v. Lagoudakis*, 581 N.W.2d 257 (Mich. 1998) (after remand)]

Definition of *direct threat* **in a disability discrimination claim.** A former assistant fire chief sued the township, the fire department, and individual defendants for disability discrimination under the ADA and the MHCRA. The court held that MHCRA claims "essentially track" federal disability discrimination law. In analyzing both the federal and the state claims, the court looked to the EEOC guidelines for factors to consider in deciding whether the employee's disability—here, heart attack–related medical disabilities—posed a "direct threat" to the safety of others in the workplace, and hence whether the employee was entitled to protection under the ADA. [*Hamlin v. Charter Township of Flint*, 165 F.3d 426 (6th Cir. 1999)]

Applying *Sutton* **in determining** *substantial limitation*. A truck driver was fired for refusing to make an out-of-town delivery because he would have run out of his blood pressure medication before his return. He sued under the ADA and the Michigan Elliot-Larsen Civil Rights Act. The court applied the U.S. Supreme Court's holding in *Sutton v. United Airlines* [527 U.S. 471 (1999)] that "[t]he use or nonuse of a corrective device does not determine whether an individual is disabled; that determination depends on whether the limitations an individual with an impairment actually faces are in fact substantially limiting." The Sixth Circuit held that because the truck driver could successfully perform his duties when using his blood pressure medication, he was not substantially limited in working. The fact that he failed to get his prescription refilled in a timely manner did not render him disabled under the ADA or Michigan law. [*Hein v. All America Plywood, Inc.*, 232 F.3d 482 (6th Cir. 2000)]

MINNESOTA

Definition of *qualified disabled person* **and the statutory duty to accommodate.** A former police officer brought an action against the city under the Minnesota Human Rights Act (MHRA). He averred that he was a "qualified disabled person" and that, since the city did not accommodate him by reassigning him to a different position, he had been discriminated against based on his disability. The appellate court looked to the ADA for an articulation of the prima facie case. Furthermore, in defining "qualified disabled person," the court adhered to federal precedent, determining that where a plaintiff represents to a long-term disability carrier that he or she is totally disabled and continues to collect benefits, the plaintiff cannot bring suit under the MHRA. It was also held, in accordance with federal precedent, that the MHRA did not require the city to find the employee a different job if he could not perform the duties of the job he was hired to perform with reasonable accommodation. The court therefore upheld a district court's grant of summary judgment to the city. [*Lang v. City of Maplewood*, 574 N.W.2d 451 (Minn. Ct. App. 1998)]

Applying EEOC guidelines in defining *major life activity*. A banker with fibromyalgia sued her employer for disability discrimination and failure to provide reasonable accommodation under the MHRA. The appellate court applied the *McDonnell Douglas* framework in analyzing her claim and also looked to the EEOC regulations in determining whether her disability impairs a "major life activity." The court held that her condition, a chronic pain illness, impaired her ability to work and the evidence created a presumption of discriminatory discharge. [*Hoover v. Norwest Private Mortgage Banking, Inc.*, 605 N.W.2d 757 (Minn. Ct. App. 2000)]

The inability to perform essential functions bars disability discrimination claim. A former employer moved for summary judgment in a disability and age discrimination suit brought by a former employee under the ADA, the ADEA, and the MHRA. In granting the motion, the court held that the *McDonnell Douglas* framework for analysis, and hence federal precedent, applies to MHRA claims. The court found that medical certification statements stating that the employee was unable to perform her job because of the severity of her disability were sufficient evidence to show that the employee was unable to perform the "essential functions" of her job, with or without reasonable accommodation. [*Graham v. Rosemount, Inc.*, 40 F. Supp. 2d 1093 (D. Minn. 1999)]

MISSOURI

Ability to attend work on a regular basis is an essential function of position. A former employee with a wrist disease brought an action against his former employer under the ADA and the Missouri Human Rights Act (MHRA). The court analyzed the MHRA claim with the tools outlined in *McDonnell Douglas*, thus adhering to federal precedent. More specifically, the court held that where an employee has excessive absences unrelated to a disability, the employee is unable to perform the "essential functions" of his position, because he or she is unable to attend work on a regular basis. The court further held that an employee's indefinite leave of absence is not a reasonable request for accommodation under the ADA or the MHRA, since it does not enable a disabled person to work and the cost to the employer to pay both the absent worker and the replacement is an undue burden. [*Kinnaman v. Ford Motor Co.,* 2000 WL 19246 (E.D. Mo. Jan. 10, 2000)]

MONTANA

Defining *disability* **and** *substantially limits.* Employee brought suit under the Montana Human Rights Act (MHRA) claiming disability discrimination. State court applied EEOC regulations interpreting the ADA to the state Act in determining that genuine issues of material fact existed as to whether employee was disabled. [*Reeves v. Dairy Queen, Inc.,* 953 P.2d 703 (Mont. 1998)] In an employee disability discrimination action under the MHRA, the court cited the EEOC's Technical Assistance Manual and regulations on the meaning of "disability" and "substantially limits" in construing those terms under the MHRA. [*Walker v. Montana Power Co.,* 924 P.2d 1339 (Mont. 1996)]

NEW JERSEY

EEOC guidelines applied in defining *physical or mental impairment.* Former law enforcement officer brought suit under the New Jersey Law Against Discrimination and the ADA claiming disability discrimination. The former officer alleged he was "impaired" in two ways: (1) his involvement with illegal drug activity and (2) his perceived mental impairment after a psychological evaluation. The court applied the EEOC guidelines in defining "physical or mental impairment" under the ADA and held that neither of the former officer's allegations was severe enough to rise to the level of an impairment under the ADA or under New Jersey law. [*Santiago v. City of Vineland,* 107 F. Supp. 2d 512 (D.N.J. 2000)]

Definition of *reasonable accommodation.* An employee injured his eye at work and could not continue with his job as a crane operator because he had lost binocular vision. He experienced difficulty at work following the accident and claimed his employer kept moving him from job to job, without regard to his physical limitations. The employee claimed the employer violated the New Jersey Law Against Discrimination (NJLAD). The court stated that it is well-settled in New Jersey that courts should look to federal cases as a key source for interpretation and authority for the NJLAD. The court looked to federal case law and cited to the federal regulations at 29 CFR Section 1630.2(o)(3) to find that reasonable accommodation under the NJLAD requires an interactive process between employer and employee. [*Jones v. Aluminum Shapes, Inc.,* 772 A.2d 34 (N.J. Super. A.D. 2001)]

NEW YORK

EEOC guidelines applied in defining *substantial limitation* **and** *major life activity.* A former employee brought an action against his former employee alleging, *inter alia,* discrimination on the basis of disability in violation of the ADA, the New York State Human Rights Law (NYSHRL), and the New York State Executive Law. In analyzing the employee's prima facie case in accordance with federal precedent, the court looked to the EEOC guidelines to define "major life activities," which are defined as "functions such as caring for oneself, performing manual tasks, walking, seeing, hearing, speaking, breathing, learning, and working." Additionally, the court used the EEOC guidelines to assess whether a "major life activity" had been "substantially limited" by the disability at issue. [*Francis v. Chemical Banking Corp.,* 62 F. Supp. 2d 948, 961–62 (E.D.N.Y. 1999)]

EEOC guidelines applied in defining *substantial limitation.* A former police officer brought a disability discrimination suit under the ADA and the NYSHRL when he was prohibited from returning to road patrol after suffering from an eye injury that left him nearly blind in one eye. The court applied the EEOC guidelines regarding the term "substantially limits" and held that the police officer was not disabled. Even though he suffered from a 15 percent impairment in his total visual system, his overall vision was 20/20 and thus he was not "unable to perform a major life activity that the average person in the general population can perform." [*Ditullio v. Village of Massena,* 81 F. Supp. 2d 397 (N.D.N.Y. 2000)]

Definition of *reasonable accommodation* **and the employer's duty in EEOC guidelines applied.** A nurse sued her hospital-employer, alleging that she was discharged on the basis of her age, race, and disability, under the ADA and New York state law. The court held that the procedure for demonstrating both age and race discrimination under New York law follows the *McDonnell Douglas* order of proof for claims brought under Title VII. One issue before the court was whether a lower court erred in failing to instruct the jury that an employer's offer of an inferior position does not constitute "reasonable accommodation" when jobs comparable to the employee's former position are vacant. In reversing the jury's verdict with respect to the age discrimination action and remanding the case, the court of appeals looked to the EEOC guidelines to determine whether an employer who utilizes reassignment as a means of reasonable accommodation has adequately fulfilled its duty. [*Norville v. Staten Island University Hospital,* 196 F.3d 89 (2d Cir. 1999)]

OHIO

Coverage of drug use. Court applied the definition of "current drug use" in the EEOC's ADA Technical Assistance Manual to interpret the state's civil rights statute regarding claim of discrimination on account of drug addiction. Court noted that state statute prohibiting handicapped discrimination is patterned after the ADA. [*Starr v. Delta Airlines, Inc.*, 1995 WL 763647 (Ohio Ct. App. Dec. 29, 1995)]

Defining *disability, major life activity,* and *substantially limits*. Firefighter brought action alleging that he was discriminated against on the basis of a handicap, his visual impairment. In interpreting the Ohio handicap discrimination law, court looked to cases and regulations interpreting the ADA for guidance. The court followed analogous federal laws and regulations to define *disability* under the Ohio statute. [*Columbus Civil Service Commission v. McGlone*, 697 N.E.2d 204 (Ohio 1998)]

EEOC guidelines applied in defining *regarded as being disabled*. A former employee who was demoted and eventually terminated after having surgery for a brain hematoma sued his employer under the state nondiscrimination statutes for disability discrimination. The court applied the EEOC guidelines in determining whether, under state law, the employee was regarded as having "a physical impairment that substantially limited one or more of his major life activities." The court held that the employee provided direct evidence that his employer regarded him as having a neurological impairment that substantially limited his ability to work in a broad range of jobs within the company. [*McIntosh v. Stanley-Bostich, Inc.*, 82 F. Supp. 2d 775 (S.D. Ohio 2000)]

Definitions of *mental impairment, substantially limits,* and *major life activity*. In this case brought under the Ohio antidiscrimination law, the court found it appropriate to use the federal regulatory definitions of "mental impairment," "substantially limits," and "major life activity" for purposes of defining similar terms in the Ohio law. The court concluded that the plaintiff's depression did not substantially limit him in any major life activities. [*Swanson v. University of Cincinnati*, 268 F.3d 307 (6th Cir. 2001)]

OREGON

Perceived disability and the admissibility of evidence of alleged employer hostility toward employees with medical problems. A former employee appealed a jury verdict in a suit for discrimination on the basis of disability brought under the ADA and Oregon law. In analyzing the state claims, the court followed federal precedent. Affirming a lower court's verdict, the court of appeals held that although the plaintiff did in fact suffer from multiple impairments, she was not entitled to a jury instruction addressing perceived disability that may occur when the employee suffers no impairment—despite the plaintiff's contention that the jury might not have believed her claims of de facto impairments. The court also held that the trial court did not err in refusing to allow evidence that the employer was hostile toward people with medical problems, since such testimony would reflect hostility to a group that is not clearly defined and not clearly protected under the law, and thus would be prejudicial. [*Beachy v. Boise Cascade Corp.*, 191 F.3d 1010 (9th Cir. 1999)]

TENNESSEE

Federal standard applied in determining whether employee is qualified. A terminated employee who had Bell's Palsy successfully sued his former employer under the Tennessee Handicap Discrimination Act. On the initial inquiry as to whether the plaintiff was qualified for the position he formerly occupied, the court looked to the ADA and the federal precedent in *Southeastern Community College v. Davis* [442 U.S. 397 (1979)]. Further, the court stated that analysis of the qualifications of an individual alleging discrimination should focus on the time frame during which the employment decision was made. [*Barnes v. Goodyear Tire & Rubber Co.*, 48 S.W.3d 698 (Tenn. 2000)]

Definition of *substantially limiting* and the assessment of whether an employee is qualified. An employer moved for summary judgment in a suit for disability and age discrimination brought under the ADA, the ADEA, and the Tennessee Human Rights Act (THRA). The federal district court held that the analysis of the ADA and ADEA claims applied equally to the analogous claims brought under the THRA. As for the disability claims, the court held that excessive absenteeism of a former employee with foot problems was a legitimate nondisability-based reason for the employer's decision to discharge the employee. The court, moreover, looked to the EEOC regulations for a definition of what it means for a disability to be "substantially limiting." As for the age discrimination claim, the court held that an employee's foot problems, which rendered him unable to work for 100 days out of a two-year period, were sufficient to show that the employee was not qualified for the position from which he was discharged. Based on the foregoing considerations, the court granted the defendant's motion for summary judgment. [*Gann v. Chevron Chemical Co.*, 52 F. Supp. 2d 834 (E.D. Tenn. 1999)]

TEXAS

Defining *disability, major life activity,* and *substantially limits*. In a disability discrimination case, the court cited the EEOC guidelines on the meaning of various terms in the ADA to interpret the Texas Commission on Human Rights Act (TCHRA). Court stated that where purpose of the state law is to execute the policies of the federal law, court will look to federal regulations. [*Primeaux v. Conoco, Inc.*, 961 S.W. 2d 401 (Tex. App. 1997)] Employee who was terminated after not attending a training session brought action under the TCHRA. Employee claimed that she was disabled and that her disability was the sole reason she was discharged. Court followed analogous federal laws and regulations to define "disability." Employee was unable to prove the existence of a genuine issue of material fact on the question of whether she was disabled. Court held that employee's diabetes did not render her disabled under state act. [*Hearne v. Amwest Savings Ass'n*, 951 S.W.2d 950 (Tex. App. 1997)] Terminated employee with lower back

Exhibit 2.6-1   PART 2—FAIR EMPLOYMENT PRACTICES   2-16

injury brought suit against employer alleging discrimination based on employee's disability in violation of the TCHRA. Appellate court followed the EEOC regulations that provide guidance on the meaning of certain terms of the ADA. Court looked to regulations to define "major life activity" and "substantially limits." Court ruled that the determination of whether an individual is disabled is fact intensive and reversed and remanded trial court's ruling of summary judgment for employer. [*Primeaux v. Conoco, Inc.*, 961 S.W.2d 401 (Tex. App. 1997)] Employer sought summary judgment in action brought by former employee alleging discrimination on account of his diabetes. In determining whether diabetes was a disability under the TCHRA, the court referred to the EEOC regulations to define "major life activity." Court ruled that evidence presented by former employee raised an issue of material fact as to whether his diabetes substantially limited a major life activity and that summary judgment on that ground was not proper. [*Norwood v. Litwin Engineers & Constructors, Inc.*, 962 S.W.2d 220 (Tex. App. 1998)]

Applying *Sutton* and EEOC regulations to interpret meaning of *major life activities*. A terminated employee sued under the TCHRA claiming, *inter alia,* disability discrimination. The TCHRA's definition of "disability" mirrors the ADA's, and the court looked to the Supreme Court's opinion in *Sutton v. United Airlines* [527 U.S. 471 (1999)] and the EEOC regulations to interpret the meaning of "major life activities." The court held that the employee's loss of a kneecap and subsequent surgery did not constitute a "disability" under the TCHRA because the activities that the employee could not perform (crawling, squatting, climbing ladders, and kneeling) are not "major life activities." [*Garcia v. Allen,* 28 S.W.3d 587 (Tex. App. 2000)]

VERMONT

Defining *substantially limits*. An employee brought a disability discrimination action under the Vermont Fair Employment Practices Act. Noting that state and federal statutes employed identical language, the court applied the EEOC regulations in determining whether the employee's disability was substantially limiting. [*Potvin v. Champlain Cable Corp.*, 687 A.2d 95 (Vt. 1996)]

Equal Pay

MASSACHUSETTS

Meaning of *wages*. Female cafeteria workers of public school system filed a complaint under the Massachusetts Equal Pay Act (MEPA). For purpose of construing "wages" under the MEPA, the court looked to the EEOC guidelines. [*Jancey v. School Committee of Everett*, 421 Mass. 482, 658 N.E.2d 162 (1995)]

National Origin

MINNESOTA

The inference of discrimination in a national origin discrimination suit. A defendant-employer moved for summary judgment in a case brought by a former employee—a Korean registered nurse—under Title VII and the Minnesota Human Rights Act (MHRA), in which the employee alleged that she had been discriminated against based on her national origin. The court stated that in the absence of direct evidence Minnesota courts analyze the MHRA using the burden-shifting framework set out in *McDonnell Douglas.* In granting the employer's motion for summary judgment, the court asserted that the employer's proffered reason for terminating the employee (that she had missed a patient appointment and that she had a history of other employment problems) was not pretext under Title VII and the MHRA. The court assessed that though the nurse's failure to come to the appointment might have been due to a scheduling error and other employees were terminated only after missing multiple appointments, there was scant evidence that other employees were similarly situated or had histories of serious violations, as did the employee at issue. It was also held that the employer's failure to go through policy-based steps for terminating an employee did not raise an inference of discrimination, since no other comparable employees were afforded the benefit of the policy. [*Thompson v. Olsten Kimberly Qualitycare, Inc.*, 33 F. Supp. 2d 806 (D. Minn. 1999)]

WASHINGTON

Discrimination based on linguistic characteristics. Bank employee brought national origin discrimination claim based on accent discrimination. Court stated that it would look to relevant federal cases and regulations because state courts had yet to address a national origin discrimination claim based on accent discrimination. Court followed the EEOC regulation stating that national origin discrimination includes discrimination against an employee because he shares the "linguistic characteristics of a national origin group." [*Xieng v. People's National Bank of Washington*, 63 Wash. App. 572, 821 P.2d 520 (1991)]

Racial Discrimination

CONNECTICUT

The inference of racial discrimination and the assessment of pretext. A former employee brought suit against a former employer and supervisor alleging racial discrimination in violation of Title VII, Section 1981, and the Connecticut Fair Employment Practices Act (CFEPA). The court stated that the legal standards used to analyze Title VII liability apply to race discrimination claims brought under the CFEPA. Accordingly, in granting the defendant's motion for summary judgment, the court stated that where a supervisor gives a black employee who had above average sales a low rating, thereby denying the employee certain financial incentives, the evidence is insufficient to give rise to an inference of unlawful racial discrimination. Furthermore, even though the employee had received positive ratings in the past, the evidence is not sufficient to establish that a poor sales evaluation was a pretext for racial discrimination. [*Zephyr v. Ortho McNeil Pharmaceutical,* 62 F. Supp. 2d 599 (D. Conn. 1999)]

KANSAS

Same standards applied in a racial discrimination suit. The Board of Public Utilities moved for summary judgment and to dismiss for failure to state a claim in a suit brought by a former mechanic who alleged racial discrimination and retaliation under Title VII and the Kansas Act Against Discrimination (KAAD). The court announced that the exhaustion of administrative remedies requirement applies to cases brought under both Title VII and the KAAD and that the requirement in both cases is a jurisdictional one. The court went on to apply its analysis of the employee's claims under Title VII to the claims under the KAAD, thus following federal precedent in interpreting the applicable state provisions. In granting the employer's motions, the court held that the Board's proffered reason for promoting a white mechanic to supervisor rather than the plaintiff—that the white mechanic had prior supervisory experience and was the most qualified—was legitimate and thus not a pretext for discrimination. As for the retaliation claims, the court adhered to federal precedent when holding that for an employment action to be considered "adverse" the alleged retaliatory act must have affected the terms and conditions of employment. [*Smith v. Board of Public Utilities,* 38 F. Supp. 2d 1272 (D. Kan. 1999)]

KENTUCKY

State law prohibiting racial discrimination mirrors federal law. An African-American employee who was fired after making a death threat to his co-workers after being subject to racial slurs sued under the Kentucky Civil Rights Act (KCRA) for racial discrimination. Because the KCRA mirrors federal law, the court looked to federal precedent and determined that the employee did not proffer sufficient evidence to prove a hostile work environment. The evidence consisted merely of a racial slur in 1974 by an unknown co-worker, a racially offensive and obscene cartoon that was circulated around the office, one racist joke, and one racist reference by his supervisor. [*Smith v. Leggett Wire Co.,* 220 F.3d 752 (6th Cir. 2000)]

MICHIGAN

Federal analysis applied to state race discrimination claim. An employee who was denied a promotion allegedly because of her race sued under Michigan's Elliott-Larson Civil

Rights Act. Employing the same *McDonnell Douglas* test as is used in cases brought under federal law, the court reinstated a trial court decision for the employer. The plaintiff had stated a prima facie case, but was unable to show that the reasons given for the decision—the respective qualifications of the candidates—were a pretext for discrimination. [*Hazle v. Ford Motor Co.,* 628 N.W.2d 515 (Mich. 2001)]

Same evidentiary burdens in racial discrimination and retaliation cases. An African-American employee sued a former employer for racial discrimination and retaliation in violation of Title VII and Michigan's Elliott-Larson Civil Rights Act. The court noted that a plaintiff asserting claims under Elliott-Larson must satisfy the same evidentiary burden as that imposed under Title VII. Following federal precedent, then, the court granted the defendant's motion for summary judgment, asserting that the employer had proffered a legitimate nondiscriminatory reason for reducing the employee's salary and for failing to promote him. [*Hollowell v. Michigan Consolidated Gas Co.,* 50 F. Supp. 2d 695 (E.D. Mich. 1999)]

MISSOURI

Employees must be similarly situated under state or federal law for purposes of disparate discipline claim. When an employee who was discharged alleged race discrimination, the employer responded that he was fired for inadequate performance and for falsifying documentation that was to be completed as part of his job. Under both Title VII and the Missouri Human Rights Act (MHRA), employees are similarly situated for purposes of raising an inference of race discrimination if they are involved in or are accused of the same or similar conduct and are disciplined in different ways. The plaintiff's case was unsuccessful because he was not similarly situated with a white employee with whom he sought to compare himself. [*Evans v. Siegel-Robert, Inc.,* 139 F. Supp. 2d 1120 (E.D. Mo. 2001)]

***McDonnell Douglas* analysis applies to claims of race discrimination under state law.** In a race discrimination and retaliation suit brought under Title VII and the MHRA, an employee appealed the district court's grant of summary judgment to the employer, based on the preclusive effect of a prior arbitral decision. In reversing the district court, the court of appeals emphasized that in analyzing claims under the MHRA the *McDonnell Douglas* framework is implicated. [*Bell v. Conopco, Inc.,* 186 F.3d 1099 (8th Cir. 1999)]

NEW JERSEY

Supporting the inference of reverse discrimination. A white male municipal housing authority employee brought an action against his former employer alleging reverse discrimination based on his gender and race in violation of Title VII and the New Jersey Law Against Discrimination (NJLAD). The federal district court noted that the prima facie elements of employment discrimination are the same for claims under Title

Exhibit 2.6-1   PART 2—FAIR EMPLOYMENT PRACTICES   2-18

VII and the NJLAD and that the *McDonnell Douglas* burden-shifting standard applies to the NJLAD as well. The court held that employer denied white male employee's request to take a municipal finance course, even though three black employees from another department were allowed to take the course, the evidence was insufficient to support an inference of reverse discrimination. The court therefore granted the employer's motion for summary judgment. [*Murphy v. Housing Authority, Atlantic City,* 32 F. Supp. 2d 753 (D.N.J. 1999)]

NEW YORK

Same analytical framework in both federal and state law. Black former employees brought action against their former employer, alleging racial discrimination under Title VII, Section 1981, and the New York State Human Rights Law (NYSHRL). The court stated that discrimination claims brought under the NYSHRL are governed by federal precedent, namely the burden-shifting analytical framework set forth in *McDonnell Douglas Corp. v. Green* [411 U.S. 792 (1973)] and later refined in *Texas Department of Community Affairs v. Burdine* [450 U.S. 248 (1981)]. [*Hines v. Hillside Children's Center,* 73 F. Supp. 2d 308 (W.D.N.Y. 1999); *see also Francis v. Chemical Banking Corp.,* 62 F. Supp. 2d 948 (E.D.N.Y. 1999) (same standards of proof governing an employment discrimination claim); *Brinson v. New York City Transit Authority,* 60 F. Supp. 2d 23 (E.D.N.Y. 1999); *Berkowitz v. County of Orange,* 120 F. Supp. 2d 386 (S.D.N.Y. 2000)]

PENNSYLVANIA

Same standards applied in a race discrimination claim. An African-American former employee filed a complaint alleging racial discrimination under Title VII, the Pennsylvania Human Relations Act (PHRA), and Section 1981. The court applied Title VII standards, as set out in federal precedent, to all elements of the employee's PHRA claim. [*Bullock v. Children's Hospital of Philadelphia,* 71 F. Supp. 2d 482 (E.D. Pa. 1999); *see also Harris v. Smithkline Beecham,* 27 F. Supp. 2d 569 (E.D. Pa. 1998) (applying same standard to Title VII, Section 1981, PHRA, and ADEA claims); *Clark v. Pennsylvania,* 885 F. Supp. 694 (E.D. Pa. 1995); *Violanti v. Emery Worldwide A-CF Co.,* 847 F. Supp. 1251 (M.D. Pa. 1994)]

TENNESSEE

Federal burden-shifting standard applied in state race discrimination case. According to a federal appellate court that ruled against a race discrimination action brought under state and federal law, such claims under the Tennessee Human Rights Act are governed by the same burden-shifting standards as are used for claims under Title VII. The employer had refused to allow the plaintiff to return to his position after 20 months of disability leave because a physician's report indicated that mental disorders prevented a return to the stress of a work environment. This proffered reason was not shown to be a pretext for race discrimination. [*Wade v. Knoxville Utilities Board,* 259 F.3d 452 (6th Cir. 2001)]

TEXAS

Employee unable to make out claim of race discrimination under either federal or state standards. A demoted nurse was unable to state a prima facie case of race or age discrimination when a court used the same burden-shifting analysis for her claims under Title VII, the ADA, and the Texas Commission on Human Rights Act. [*Evans v. City of Houston,* 246 F.3d 344 (5th Cir. 2001)]

Religion

ALASKA

Similarities between federal and state law. Noting the similarities between federal and state antidiscrimination laws, the Alaska Supreme Court remarked that the state commission's regulations on religious discrimination incorporate the EEOC regulations. [*Bald v. RCA Alascom,* 569 P.2d 1328 (Alaska 1977)]

MAINE

State law analogous to federal law. Employee brought religious discrimination action under the Maine Human Rights Act (MHRA). The court commented that the state law was intended to be analogous to the federal statute and that it bears strong similarities of language to the federal law. The court looked to federal regulations and decisions by federal courts to interpret the MHRA. [*Maine Human Rights Commission v. Local 1361, United Paperworkers International Union,* 383 A.2d 369 (Me. 1978)]

Sex Discrimination

ALASKA

Hostile work environment sexual harassment. In holding that the state antidiscrimination statute encompassed a sex discrimination claim of hostile work environment harassment, the court relied on federal precedent, including the EEOC guidelines. The court emphasized, however, that Title VII precedent was not binding on its interpretation of the state statute and was followed only where it had persuasive force. [*French v. Jadon, Inc.,* 911 P.2d 20 (Alaska 1996)]

CALIFORNIA

Hostile work environment sexual harassment. An employee brought an action against a former employer alleging sex discrimination. In considering the sex discrimination claim under state statutory and common law, the court relied on the EEOC guidelines in determining whether a plaintiff states a cause of action for sexual discrimination based on a romantic relationship between an employer and a fellow employee. [*Proksel v. Gattis*, 41 Cal. App. 4th (626), 49 Cal. Rptr. 2d 322 (Cal. Ct. App. 1996)]

Employer liability for sexual harassment by nonsupervisory employee. California courts have looked to federal authority interpreting Title VII to determine the meaning of analogous provisions of the California Fair Employment and Housing Act (CFEHA). Under federal case law and the EEOC guidelines an employer is not liable for sexual harassment by a nonsupervisory employee unless the employer knew or should have known of the harassment and failed to take immediate and appropriate corrective action. Employer liability for co-worker harassment is judged under a negligence standard. [*Carrisales v. Department of Corrections*, 77 Cal. Rptr. 2d 517 (Cal. Ct. App. 1998)]

Same-sex harassment and retaliation claim governed by federal law but distinguishable on facts. A former employee sued for sexual harassment and retaliatory termination under the CFEHA. He allegedly was subjected to ongoing same-sex harassment by a supervisor and then was terminated when he complained to a company official. The retaliation claim survived a summary judgment motion because of evidence that the officials with knowledge of the employee's complaints terminated him soon after the last of the complaints was made. This distinguished the case from the facts in *Clark County School District v. Breeden* [121 S. Ct. 1508 (2001)], a Title VII case in which the U.S. Supreme Court ruled that a 20-month delay was not sufficiently close temporal proximity between the employer's knowledge of protected activity and the adverse employment action for such proximity to be sufficient evidence of causality. The Court in *Breeden* also held that a single, isolated incident consisting of an offensive statement had not constituted actionable sexual harassment under federal law. In a meeting attended by Breeden and two male employees to review reports on job applicants, the male employees had read aloud and laughed about a sexually oriented comment that one of the applicants had made to a co-worker. No reasonable person could have believed that the single incident in *Breeden* violated Title VII's standard. [*Valdex v. Clayton Industries, Inc.*, 88 Cal. App. 4th 1162, 107 Cal. Rptr. 2d 15 (2001)]

CONNECTICUT

Continuing violation **in a pregnancy discrimination suit.** A former director of physical therapy for a corporation sued the corporation and shareholders, alleging, *inter alia*, discrimination based on pregnancy in violation of Title VII and the Connecticut Fair Employment Practices Act (CFEPA). In partially granting the defendant's motion to dismiss, the court held that federal law regarding exhaustion of administrative remedies as the prerequisite to a suit under Title VII was applicable to the CFEPA. The court further noted that a mere allegation of ongoing discriminatory practice was sufficient to withstand a motion to dismiss based on the tardiness of a claim of

discrimination under Title VII and the CFEPA. That the employee was progressively denied employment benefits and ultimately terminated after disclosing she was pregnant, the court asserted, was sufficient to state a claim of continuing violation, thus precluding a claim that the statute of limitations had run on the federal and state claims. [*Maloney v. Connecticut Orthopedics, P.C.*, 47 F. Supp. 2d 244 (D. Conn. 1999)]

FLORIDA

The *totality of the circumstances* **in assessing sexual harassment.** A female former employee brought suit for sexual harassment under Title VII and the Florida Civil Rights Act (FCRA). The federal district court stated that because the FCRA is modeled after Title VII, the FCRA is subject to Title VII analysis as set out in federal precedent. The court looked to the EEOC guidelines in stating that the trier of fact must determine the existence of sexual harassment by examining the totality of the circumstances. [*Scelta v. Delicatessen Support Service, Inc.*, 57 F. Supp. 2d 1327 (M.D. Fla. 1999)]

HAWAII

Bona fide occupational qualification **defense.** An employer appealed a lower court's affirmance of an administrative decision in a sex discrimination suit brought under the Hawaii Revised Statutes and the Hawaii Administrative Rules. The court noted that federal precedent, *viz.*, the *McDonnell Douglas* framework for developing evidence in discrimination suits, continues to be useful in interpreting the analogous Hawaii statutes; it added, however, that federal courts' interpretation of Title VII cases is not binding on Hawaii courts. Nevertheless, the court relied on federal precedent in interpreting the meaning and applicability of the bona fide occupational qualification defense. The court therefore upheld a lower court's affirmance of the administrative judgment for the employee. [*Sam Teague, Ltd. v. Hawaii Civil Rights Commission*, 89 Haw. 269, 971 P.2d 1104 (1999)]

ILLINOIS

Defining *sexual harassment*. In considering a claim of sex discrimination, the court held that the definition of "sexual harassment" set forth in the EEOC guidelines is virtually identical to the one adopted by Illinois General Assembly in the Human Rights Act. [*Geise v. Phoenix Co. of Chicago, Inc.*, 159 Ill. 2d 507, 639 N.E.2d 1273 (1994)]

Prohibited sexual harassment. Firefighter disciplined by Board of Fire Commissioners for sexually harassing co-employee brought action appealing Board's actions. Court noted that the prohibition of sexual harassment found in the Illinois Human Rights Act (IHRA) was closely paralleled that found in Title VII and the accompanying EEOC guidelines and that therefore examination of federal law was appropriate. How-

Exhibit 2.6-1   PART 2—FAIR EMPLOYMENT PRACTICES   2-20

ever, the IHRA need not be applied in lockstep with the Supreme Court's construction of Title VII. Court looked to federal courts and the EEOC guidelines in determining what constituted prohibited sexual harassment. [*Trayling v. Board of Fire & Police Commissioners of Village of Bensonville*, 273 Ill. App. 3d 1, 652 N.E.2d 386 (1995)]

KENTUCKY

Hostile work environment sexual harassment. An employee filed a sexual harassment suit against his supervisor. Because the Kentucky statute is similar to Title VII, the court held that the state statute would be interpreted consistently with the interpretation given to Title VII. The court followed the EEOC guidelines, stating that in evaluating whether a hostile work environment exists the court must examine the totality of circumstances. [*Hall v. Transit Authority of Lexington–Fayette Urban County Government*, 883 S.W.2d 884 (Ky. Ct. App. 1994)]

MASSACHUSETTS

Allocation of burdens. The Massachusetts Supreme Court stated that in mixed-motive sexual harassment cases it follows the U.S. Supreme Court's allocation of the burden of proof in *Price Waterhouse v. Hopkins* [490 U.S. 228 (1989)]. Thus, the plaintiff must first prove by a preponderance of the evidence that the proscribed factor played a motivating part in the adverse employment decision. Then the burden of persuasion shifts to the defendant to prove that it would have made the same decision even without an illegitimate motive. [*Wynn & Wynn, P.C. v. Massachusetts Commission Against Discrimination*, 431 Mass. 655, 729 N.E.2d 1068 (2000)]

MINNESOTA

Sexual harassment by nonemployees. Employee brought sexual harassment suit under the Minnesota Human Rights Act (MHRA). In ruling that the MHRA allows an employee to bring an action against an employer for sexual harassment when the harassing party is a nonemployee, the court considered federal precedent, including the EEOC guidelines. [*Costilla v. State*, 571 N.W.2d 587 (Minn. Ct. App. 1997)]

MISSOURI

Constructive discharge harassment claims not precluded by plaintiff's ability to perform well at work despite harassment. A defendant-employer moved for judgment in a suit brought by a former employee, which alleged sexual harassment in violation of Title VII and the Missouri Human Rights Act (MHRA). In partially granting the motion, the court applied federal precedent in interpreting the state law claim, which turned on whether or not the employee had been constructively discharged. The court ruled that evidence of verbal and physical conduct visited upon the female employee was

sufficient to support a jury's determination that the sexual harassment was so severe and pervasive that it altered the conditions of employment by creating a hostile work environment, and that although the employee performed well at work this performance could have been achieved while enduring a hostile work environment. [*Gray v. Tyson Foods, Inc.*, 46 F. Supp. 2d 948 (W.D. Mo. 1999)]

NEBRASKA

Defining *employer* for purposes of state act. Employee filed complaint charging employer with employment discrimination on the basis of her gender. Issue raised on appeal was whether employer was an "employer" under the Nebraska Fair Employment Practice Act (NFEPA). Court applied position of EEOC in its Compliance Manual in defining "employer" for purposes of Title VII, noting that the NFEPA was patterned after federal law. [*Bluff's Vision Clinic, P.C. v. Krzyzanowski*, 543 N.W.2d 761 (Neb. Ct. App.), *aff'd*, 555 N.W.2d 556 (Neb. 1996)]

NEW YORK

Failure to establish *Faragher/Ellerth* defense. In a state sexual harassment suit, the defendants sought to use the *Faragher/Ellerth* defense, arguing that they were sufficiently elevated within the corporate hierarchy to be considered "corporate proxies." The court assumed that the *Faragher/Ellerth* defense applied to sexual harassment claims brought under state law but held that the defense did not apply. The defendant was the president, treasurer, and 50 percent owner of the corporation. His wife was the vice president, secretary, and other 50 percent owner. The court held that based on these facts the defendants failed to establish that they were corporate proxies. [*Randall v. Tod-Nik Audiology, Inc.*, 270 A.D.2d 38, 704 N.Y.S.2d 228 (App. Div. 2000)]

Quid pro quo sexual harassment. A female employee sued her employer for sexual harassment under the New York Human Rights Law (NYSHRL) and Title VII. The employee alleged, *inter alia*, that she was subject to unwelcome sexual advances and that her negative reaction to those advances was the basis for her employer's denying permission for restroom breaks. The court applied the EEOC guidelines regarding quid pro quo sexual harassment, and held that the employee stated sufficient facts to support a finding of quid pro quo sexual harassment. [*Turner v. Olympic Regional Development Authority*, 89 F. Supp. 2d 241 (N.D.N.Y. 2000)]

Federal precedent regarding employer liability for sexual harassment applies to state claim. A former manager of a music store failed in her sexual harassment action under the NYSHRL when her employer showed that she made inadequate use of harassment procedures by waiting almost a year to make a complaint, although fear of reprisal was unwarranted. The principles applicable to employer liability for the harassment were taken from federal precedents. [*O'Dell v.*

Trans World Entertainment Corp., 153 F. Supp. 2d 378 (S.D.N.Y. 2001)]

Sufficiency of evidence for a hostile work environment claim. A former employee brought an action under the ADEA, Title VII, and the NYSHRL, alleging both age and sex discrimination. The Second Circuit noted that New York courts follow the same standard of proof for claims brought under the NYSHRL as for those brought under Title VII and the ADEA. Accordingly, the court held that where a female employee is continually threatened with being fired and replaced with "young and sexy" hires, a reasonable juror could conclude that the discriminatory conduct is sufficiently severe to create a hostile working environment on account of sex. The court therefore remanded the hostile work environment on account of sex claim under both Title VII and the NYSHRL and affirmed a lower court's judgment for the employer with respect to the age discrimination claim. [*Leopold v. Baccarat, Inc.*, 174 F.3d 261 (2d Cir. 1999)]

NORTH DAKOTA

Court relies on federal precedent in assessing requisite severity of sexual harassment. A former employee sued his employer under the North Dakota Human Rights Act after being terminated, claiming that he had suffered sexual harassment and retaliatory discharge. In recognizing the first claim of sexual harassment under the North Dakota law, the state supreme court looked to federal precedent to determine whether the plaintiff stated a claim of sexual harassment. Plaintiff's allegations were based primarily on a number of cards and E-mails sent him by his female supervisor. After reviewing the five elements of a sexual harassment claim articulated by federal courts under federal law, including the requirement that the plaintiff state that the harassment was severe enough to affect a term, condition, or privilege of employment, the North Dakota Supreme Court held that reasonable persons could only conclude that the conduct alleged by the plaintiff was insufficient to rise to a level of actionable harassment under the law. Agreeing with federal law that isolated incidents of teasing, offhand remarks, gender-related jokes, or vulgar language are insufficient to alter the conditions of employment, the court held that the conduct alleged was likewise insufficient to affect the conditions of employment and granted summary judgment on the plaintiff's claim. [*Opp v. Source One Management, Inc.*, 591 N.W.2d 101 (N.D. 1999)]

NEW JERSEY

Bona fide occupational qualifications. In a sex discrimination case under New Jersey Law Against Discrimination (NJLAD) in which the defense of a bona fide occupational qualification (BFOQ) was raised, the court stated that New Jersey courts have traditionally looked to federal law for guidance in the field of employment discrimination. The court cited Title VII's BFOQ provision, noting that it was virtually identical to the state provision, and applied the relevant EEOC guidelines on discrimination because of sex. [*Spragg v. Shore Care*, 293 N.J. Super. 33, 679 A.2d 685 (App. Div. 1996)]

Hostile work environment sexual harassment. Former employee filed complaint of hostile work environment sexual harassment under the NJLAD. The court observed that the New Jersey Supreme Court has noted that in construing the NJLAD federal precedent governing Title VII is a key source of interpretive authority. The court applied relevant EEOC regulations to the NJLAD. [*Woods-Pirozzi v. Nabisco Foods*, 290 N.J. Super. 252, 675 A.2d 684 (App. Div. 1996)]

Plaintiff's burden in a sex discrimination claim. A former employee brought an action against an employer for gender discrimination under the NJLAD. The court emphasized that in analyzing employment discrimination under the NJLAD the *McDonnell Douglas* burden-shifting framework is applied. The precise issue before the court was whether a lower court's jury interrogatories were correctly articulated. The interrogatories required the employer, at the second stage of the *McDonnell Douglas* test, to prove by a preponderance of the evidence that there was a legitimate nondiscriminatory reason for discharging the employee. The court held that federal precedent requires a defendant-employer not to *prove* a nondiscriminatory reason but merely to *produce* a plausible one. Moreover, the court held that, given that the *McDonnell Douglas* framework itself arose in the context of a pretrial motion and that there has been much "confusion" that results when the first two stages of the *McDonnell Douglas* test go to the jury, courts should resolve the first two stages as matters of law. [*Mogull v. CB Commercial Real Estate Group, Inc.*, 2000 WL 175277 (N.J. Feb. 16, 2000)]

Same standards applied where there is only circumstantial evidence in a sex discrimination suit. An employee brought an action alleging, *inter alia,* gender discrimination under both Title VII and the NJLAD. The court stated that where a case involves discrimination claims based on circumstantial rather than direct evidence, the burden-shifting analysis of *McDonnell Douglas* applies to both the state and the federal claims. In interpreting the state claims according to federal precedent, the court granted the employer's motion for summary judgment, asserting that the employee had failed to meet her burden of proving that the employer's proffered legitimate reasons for discharging the employee were mere pretext for discrimination. [*Lemke v. International Total Services, Inc.*, 56 F. Supp. 2d 472 (D.N.J. 1999)]

Jury charge predicated on federal law suffices for state claims of sex discrimination. A female police sergeant brought a sex discrimination suit against the police department, a police chief, a police captain, and a male sergeant under Title VII and the NJLAD. The police department appealed a jury verdict rendered against it, arguing, *inter alia,* that the trial court erred in its charge to the jury on the hostile

Exhibit 2.6-1 PART 2—FAIR EMPLOYMENT PRACTICES 2-22

work environment claim, mixing different concepts from Title VII and the NJLAD. Specifically, they contended that the charge on the NJLAD claim did not square with a multi-factor test articulated in New Jersey state precedent. In holding that the jury charge on hostile work environment was not errone-ous, the court asserted that the charge properly apprised the jury of the issues and law under the NJLAD. The court pre-dicted that the New Jersey Supreme Court would find many of the factors in the charge relevant and useful for deliberations in a hostile work environment sexual harassment suit, despite the fact that the charge was derived chiefly from Title VII precedent. The court cited to New Jersey precedent, which suggests that New Jersey courts find Title VII law valuable in interpreting the NJLAD. The court noted, however, that the NJLAD is a remedial statute "in some respects broader and more flexible than Title VII, indicating that there might be room for a divergence between federal law and New Jersey law in the future with respect to sex discrimination claims." [*Hurley v. Atlantic City Police Department,* 174 F.3d 95 (3d Cir. 1999)]

NEW YORK

Sexual harassment by employer. Former employee brought action alleging supervisor had intimate relationship with fe-male employee and attempted to remove plaintiff and replace him with female employee. Court noted consistency of claim of sexual favoritism under New York State Human Rights Law (NYSHRL) and Title VII. Court applied federal court deci-sions and EEOC regulations to determine types of sexual harassment that would constitute a violation under the NYSHRL. [*Nicolo v. Citibank New York State,* 147 Misc. 2d 111, 554 N.Y.S.2d 795 (Sup. Ct. 1990)]

Virtually identical standards governing employer liability for sex discrimination and retaliation. A female municipal employee brought suit against the city, alleging sex discrimi-nation and retaliation in violation of Title VII, Section 1983, and the NYSHRL. The court stated that its analysis of the Title VII and Section 1983 claims would equally apply to the em-ployee's state law cause of action, as "the standards governing liability under the [NYSHRL] are virtually identical to those applied to Title VII and [Section] 1983 claims." [*Brennan v. City of White Plains,* 67 F. Supp. 2d 362, 372 (S.D.N.Y. 1999); *see also Clark v. New York State Electric & Gas Corp.,* 67 F. Supp. 2d 63, 71 n.5 (N.D.N.Y. 1999); *Marks v. New York University,* 61 F. Supp. 2d 81 (S.D.N.Y. 1999) (*McDonnell Douglas* burden-shifting analysis applies equally to NYSHRL with respect to both age and sex discrimination claims); *Gumbs v. Hall,* 51 F. Supp. 2d 275 (W.D.N.Y.) (following federal precedent in a constructive discharge claim); *Funk v. F & K Supply, Inc.,* 43 F. Supp. 2d 205 (N.D.N.Y. 1999) (applying federal precedent in interpreting sexual harassment hostile work environment claims under state law)]

The insufficiency of *pretext* in itself. A former employee brought an action for sex discrimination under Title VII and New York state law. The federal district court held that the evidentiary burdens for establishing sex discrimination under New York state law are identical to those under Title VII. The court then proceeded to interpret the state law claims in light of federal precedent relating to the *McDonnell Douglas* frame-work for analysis. The court noted in particular that a finding that an employer's stated reason for discharging the employee was a "pretext" is not sufficient to compel a finding of discrim-ination in circumstances where there are not only many possi-ble reasons for a false explanation but also concrete facts that make these alternatives plausible enough to compel the con-clusion that illegal discrimination was no more likely the motivating force than the alternatives. [*Greenbaum v. Handels-banken,* 67 F. Supp. 2d 228 (S.D.N.Y. 1999)]

Applying EEOC guidelines to quid pro quo harassment. A female employee sued her employer for sexual harassment under the NYSHRL and Title VII. The employee alleged, *inter alia*, that she was subject to unwelcome sexual advances and that her negative reaction to those advances was the basis for her employer's denying permission for restroom breaks. The court applied the EEOC guidelines regarding quid pro quo sexual harassment, and held that the employee stated sufficient facts to support a finding of quid pro quo sexual harassment. [*Turner v. Olympic Regional Development Authority,* 89 F. Supp. 2d 241 (N.D.N.Y. 2000)]

Applying federal employer liability standards in state sex-ual harassment case. In a state sexual harassment suit, the defendants sought to use the *Faragher/Ellerth* defense, arguing that they were sufficiently elevated within the corporate hier-archy to be considered "corporate proxies." The court assumed that the *Faragher/Ellerth* defense applied to sexual harassment claims brought under state law, but held that the defense did not apply. The defendant was the president, treasurer, and 50 percent owner of the corporation. His wife was the vice-president, secretary, and other 50 percent owner. The court held that based on these facts the defendants failed to establish that they were not corporate proxies. [*Randall v. Tod-Nik Audiology, Inc.,* 270 A.D.2d 38, 704 N.Y.S.2d 228 (2000)]

Federal standard of proof for sex discrimination applied to claim under NYSHRL. A female chef who was forced to resign survived summary judgment on her sex discrimination claim under state and federal law. The standard of proof for such claims is the same under the NYSHRL and Title VII, and triable issues existed on whether the alleged inability of the chef to get along with the staff was a pretext for discrimination. [*Ramos v. Marriott International, Inc.,* 134 F. Supp. 2d 328 (S.D.N.Y. 2001)]

OHIO

Quid pro quo sexual harassment. In determining whether quid pro quo sexual harassment creates liability in the absence of any effect on the terms and conditions of employment, the court looked to federal decisions and the EEOC guidelines to interpret state law provision analogous to Title VII. The court stated that while the EEOC guidelines are not binding, they are persuasive authority on analogous federal law. It followed the EEOC guidelines and held that the plaintiff must suffer an actual effect on his terms of employment rather than suffer mere threats. [*Schmitz v. Bob Evans Farms, Inc.*, 697 N.E.2d 1037 (Ohio Ct. App. 1997)]

Same-sex sexual harassment. A male employee brought a suit for sexual harassment under state law, alleging that his supervisor made a graphic sexual proposition during work hours. The court applied the U.S. Supreme Court's interpretation of Title VII in *Oncale v. Sundowner Offshore Service, Inc.* [523 U.S. 75 (1998)] and interpreted the state sex discrimination statute to also prohibit same-sex sexual harassment. However, the court held that the supervisor's conduct toward the employee was personal and not gender-based, and that therefore the harassment, although severe, was not a discriminatory practice under state statute. [*Hampel v. Food Ingredients Specialties*, 729 N.E.2d 726 (Ohio 2000)]

Cases interpreting federal precedent generally applicable to state substantive standard for sexual harassment claim. In ruling that summary judgment for the employer was precluded by a material fact issue as to whether the employee viewed various gestures and comments directed at her by a supervisor as sexual harassment, the court observed that decisions interpreting and applying Title VII generally are applicable to cases involving Ohio's employment discrimination statute. [*Brentlinger v. Highlights for Children*, 142 Ohio App. 3d 25, 753 N.E.2d 937 (2001)]

OKLAHOMA

Hostile work environment sexual harassment. In action alleging hostile work environment sexual harassment, court stated that one of the expressed purposes of Oklahoma's antidiscrimination statute was to implement the provisions of Title VII in the state of Oklahoma. Courts must therefore interpret state's antidiscrimination statute together with Title VII to determine an employee's rights under state law. [*Marshall v. OK Rental & Leasing, Inc.*, 939 P.2d 1116 (Okla. 1997)]

OREGON

Fringe benefits. Female employee brought action under state statute alleging sex discrimination against employer. Court, noting that the state version of the Pregnancy Discrimination Act is modeled on the federal statute, applied EEOC regulations in finding that employer's insurance plan, which gave benefits to the pregnant wives of terminated male employees but not to terminated female employees who were pregnant, violated state antidiscrimination laws. [*Hillesland v. Paccar, Inc.*, 722 P.2d 1239 (Or. Ct. App. 1986)]

PENNSYLVANIA

Definition of *employee supervisor* and the assessment of *hostile work environment* in a sex discrimination claim. A female postal worker brought an action for sex discrimination and resultant hostile work environment under Title VII and the Pennsylvania Human Rights Act (PHRA). The court analyzed the federal and state claims in exactly the same way, using tools afforded by federal precedent. Accordingly, the court held that a hostile work environment exists where by a totality of the circumstances it is shown that conditions are severe enough to affect the working conditions of a female employee. Moreover, the court used the EEOC guidelines in defining an "employee supervisor." After finding that the employee had not provided evidence sufficient to find that the defendant had authority to hire, fire, reassign, demote, or institute a tangible adverse employment action against the employee, the court granted the defendant's motion for summary judgment. [*Kent v. Henderson*, 77 F. Supp. 2d 628 (E.D. Pa. 1999); *see also Pittman v. Continental Airlines, Inc.*, 35 F. Supp. 2d 434 (E.D. Pa. 1999) (federal precedent applies to hostile work environment sex discrimination claims brought under the PHRA)]

PUERTO RICO

EEOC guidelines and federal precedent apply to sexual harassment claim. An employer-defendant moved for summary judgment in a sexual harassment suit brought by a former employee under Title VII and Puerto Rico law. The court noted that Puerto Rico's Anti-Sexual Harassment Statute, Law No. 17, justifies causes of action that are nearly identical to the EEOC's guidelines for Title VII sex discrimination actions (quid pro quo and hostile work environment), and that since the court found genuine issues of material fact with respect to the employee's quid pro quo and hostile work environment claims, thus denying summary judgment on those claims, summary judgment was also inappropriate as to the alleged violations of Law No. 17. [*Ruiz v. Caribbean Restaurants, Inc.*, 54 F. Supp. 2d 97 (D.P.R. 1999)]

TEXAS

Interpretation of *employer* and *adverse employment action.* A discharged female employee brought an action against her former employer and supervisor alleging, *inter alia,* sexual discrimination and retaliation under the Texas Commission on Human Rights Act (TCHRA). Following the Texas legislature's expressed legislative intent, the court interpreted the TCHRA in a manner consistent with federal laws prohibiting employment discrimination. Specifically, the court used fed-

Exhibit 2.6-1   PART 2—FAIR EMPLOYMENT PRACTICES   2-24

eral precedent to interpret the meanings of such terms as "employer," "continuing violation," and "adverse employment action." [*Martin v. Kroger Co.,* 65 F. Supp. 2d 516 (S.D. Tex. 1999)]

Same-sex harassment as sexual harassment. A former employee claimed he was forced out of his job due to same-sex sexual harassment and brought an action under the Texas FEP law, the Texas Commission for Human Rights Act (TCHRA). The court found that because the TCHRA was modeled on the federal Title VII law, the court should look to federal precedent in deciding whether the case could go forward. The court ultimately determined that because same-sex sexual harassment is actionable under Title VII, it should be actionable under the TCHRA. [*Dillard Dept. Stores, Inc. v. Gozales,* 2002 WL 358517 (Tex. App.—El Paso, Mar. 7, 2002)]

VERMONT

Reliance on federal precedent in articulating the prima facie case in sex discrimination and retaliation claims. A female packaging employee brought gender discrimination claims against her employer and plant manager under Title VII and the Vermont Fair Employment Practices Act. The federal district court adhered to the *McDonnell Douglas* framework for analysis and its progeny in holding that the employee could satisfy the fourth element of the prima facie case by offering evidence that she was treated less favorably than male employees "in circumstances from which a gender-based motive could be inferred." The court also followed federal precedent in determining whether the employee had shown that the employer's alleged reasons for discharge were "pretext." Last, with regard to the employee's retaliation claim, the court relied on federal precedent to assess whether there had been a causal connection between the discriminatory treatment and the protected activity. [*Forant v. Cabot Creamery Cooperative, Inc.,* 74 F. Supp. 2d 415 (D. Vt. 1999)]

WISCONSIN

Hostile work environment. Given the identical purposes of the Wisconsin Fair Employment Act and Title VII, the court stated it was appropriate to consider federal decisions. In drawing the line between conduct that is sexual harassment and conduct that is not, the court followed EEOC regulations and federal decisions stating that the cumulative effects of all the incidents must be considered in deciding whether the work environment was reasonably perceived as hostile. [*Kannenberg v. Lirc,* 213 Wis. 2d 373, 571 N.W.2d 165 (Wis. Ct. App. 1997)]

WEST VIRGINIA

Quid pro quo harassment. In case alleging sexual harassment by foreman, court adopted the EEOC's definition of quid pro quo harassment. [*Westmoreland Coal Co. v. West Virginia Human Rights Commission,* 181 W. Va. 368, 382 S.E.2d 562 (1989)]

Hostile work environment sexual harassment. Female supervisor brought action against former employer alleging sexual harassment retaliatory discharge under the West Virginia Human Rights Act (WVHRA). Court held that EEOC regulations and WVHRA regulations concur that co-workers and customers can cause a hostile environment and that a different result was not warranted under the WVHRA when hostile work environment was created by subordinate. [*Hanlon v. Chambers,* 195 W. Va. 99, 464 S.E.2d 741 (1995)]

Other Issues and Procedures

CONNECTICUT

Continuing violations theory. A former director of physical therapy for a corporation sued the corporation and shareholders, alleging, *inter alia,* discrimination based on pregnancy in violation of Title VII and the Connecticut Fair Employment Practices Act (CFEPA). In partially granting the defendant's motion to dismiss, the court held that federal law regarding exhaustion of administrative remedies as the prerequisite to a suit under Title VII was applicable to the CFEPA. The court further noted that a mere allegation of ongoing discriminatory practice was sufficient to withstand a motion to dismiss based on the tardiness of a claim of discrimination under Title VII and the CFEPA. That the employee was progressively denied employment benefits and ultimately terminated after disclosing she was pregnant, the court asserted, was sufficient to state a claim of continuing violation, thus precluding a claim that the statute of limitations had run out on the federal and state claims. [*Maloney v. Connecticut Orthopedics, P.C.,* 47 F. Supp. 2d 244 (D. Conn. 1999)]

Definition of *employer* for purposes of liability. A police officer, a single parent, claimed that he was transferred to a less desirable work location because he was not available to work unscheduled shifts. In addition, he claimed that other retaliation, including verbal abuse, had occurred. He argued that single mothers were not similarly required to work unscheduled shifts. In the case, brought under the Connecticut antidiscrimination law, the court looked to federal case law authority to help it determine that individuals who are not employers may not be held liable under the state FEP law. [*Perodeau v. City of Hartford,* 2002 WL 414248, 259 Conn. 729 (Mar. 26, 2002)]

FLORIDA

Definition of *employer* in a sex discrimination suit. A female former employee brought suit for sexual harassment under Title VII and the Florida Civil Rights Act (FCRA). The court stated that because the FCRA is modeled after Title VII, the FCRA is subject to Title VII analysis as set out in federal precedent. The court looked to Title VII for the definition of "employer," which is defined as "a person engaged in an industry affecting commerce who has 15 or more employees for each working day in each of the 20 or more calendar weeks in the current or preceding calendar year, and any agent of such a person." [42 U.S.C. § 2000e-2] In determining whether an "employer" can consist of multiple alleged "employers," the court looked to four factors enunciated in federal precedent: (1) common management, (2) centralized control of labor relations, (3) common financial control, and (4) interrelation of operations. [*Scelta v. Delicatessen Support Service, Inc.,* 57 F. Supp. 2d 1327 (M.D. Fla. 1999)]

HAWAII

Applying federal precedent regarding collateral source rule. An employer appealed a lower court's affirmance of an administrative decision in a sex discrimination suit brought under the Hawaii Revised Statutes and the Hawaii Administrative Rules. In applying the "collateral source rule," the court heeded federal precedent in holding that unemployment benefits should not, as a matter of law, be deducted from awards of back pay under Hawaii's employment discrimination law. The court therefore upheld a lower court's affirmance of the administrative judgment for the employee. [*Sam Teague, Ltd. v. Hawaii Civil Rights Commission,* 89 Haw. 269, 971 P.2d 1104 (1999)]

MISSOURI

Arbitral decision does not preclude judicial claim of race discrimination. In a race discrimination and retaliation suit brought under Title VII and the Missouri Human Rights Act (MHRA), an employee appealed the federal district court's grant of summary judgment to the employer. The employer contended that the district court need not have reached the merits of the case because of a previous arbitral decision pursuant to a collective bargaining agreement rendered in the employer's favor. The employer maintained that the arbitral decision barred the employee's action under Title VII and the MHRA. Following federal precedent, the Eighth Circuit ruled that the arbitrator's decision did not preclude a judicial claim under Title VII and the MHRA. In reversing the district court's grant of summary judgment, the court of appeals emphasized that in analyzing claims under the MHRA the *McDonnell Douglas* framework is implicated. [*Bell v. Conopco, Inc.,* 186 F.3d 1099 (8th Cir. 1999)]

NEW JERSEY

Improper grant of summary judgment in retaliation case. A teacher brought an action against the Board of Education and its members under the Conscientious Employment Protection Act (CEPA), a New Jersey statute. She alleged that the Board and its members retaliated against her by withholding her salary increment after she testified before a public body, which was looking into whether the Board and its members had violated the law by failing to provide a disabled child with an appropriate education. The appellate court held that the analytical framework applied in a retaliatory discharge case under the CEPA is similar to that applied to violations of Title VII. The court reversed the trial court's grant of summary judgment to the defendant-employer. In so doing, the court argued that federal precedent demands that if there is evidence sufficient to enable a rational fact finder to conclude that an employer's proffered reason for discharging the employee is "pretext," summary judgment on the issue is improper. [*Kolb v. Burns,* 320 N.J. Super. 467, 727 A.2d 525 (App. Div. 1999)]

NEW YORK

Interagency agreements and dual filing of administrative charge. In a suit by a former employee alleging sexual and racial discrimination under Title VII and New York law, the court found that under an interagency agreement the filing of a sexual harassment charge with the EEOC also constituted a filing with the New York State Division of Human Rights (NYSDHR). The court therefore held that the employer-defendant's claim that failure to file charges with the NYSDHR barred a sexual harassment suit was precluded, even though the alleged victim noted on the charge that she wanted the charge filed only with the EEOC. [*Cooper v. Wyeth Ayerst Lederle,* 34 F. Supp. 2d 197 (S.D.N.Y. 1999)]

OHIO

Substantive and procedural differences between cases involving direct evidence and those involving circumstantial evidence. An African-American former employee brought an action against his former employer alleging racial discrimination under Title VII and the applicable Ohio state antidiscrimination law. In denying the employer-defendant's motion for summary judgment, the court held that where circumstantial evidence of discrimination is at issue the evidentiary standards applicable to an employment discrimination claim under Title VII are applicable to the Ohio state claim as well. The court emphasized, however, that where there is direct evidence of racially based employment discrimination, the analysis based on circumstantial evidence does not apply; instead, the case must proceed to trial for a determination of whether the proffered direct evidence is credible, and if it is, the burden shifts to the defendant to show that the plaintiff would have been terminated notwithstanding the defendant's discriminatory motivation. The court cited to federal precedent in articulating the distinction between the different procedures required for direct and circumstantial cases of discrimination. [*Yetts v. ITW-Nifco, Inc.,* 50 F. Supp. 2d 776 (S.D. Ohio 1999)]

Establishing a causal connection in retaliation claims. A former employee brought an action for discrimination and retaliation based on sex and age in violation of Title VII, the ADEA, and Ohio state law. The court relied on federal precedent in holding that where a leave of absence for surgery would be necessary regardless of whether an employee was laterally transferred to a new position as a result of retaliatory motives, a causal connection between the medical leave and the transfer was not established and, hence, back pay should not be awarded. The court also relied on federal precedent when it emphasized that the most critical factor in determining reasonableness when calculating an award for attorneys' fees is the degree of success obtained: the court maintained that where an employee is awarded only nominal damages, the employee is not entitled to an award for attorneys' fees. [*Virostek v. Liberty T.P. Police Department/Trustees*, 55 F. Supp. 2d 758 (N.D. Ohio 1999)]

Federal pretext analysis applied. The Ohio appellate court noted that Ohio courts rely on federal law construing Title VII in order to resolve discrimination cases brought under the Ohio FEP law. Specifically, the court cited to the federal burden-shifting analysis. [*Alcorn v. Auto Systems Centers, Inc.*, 2002 WL 360129 (Ohio App., 2 Dist., Mar. 8, 2002)]

OREGON

Defining *prevailing party* **for award of attorneys' fees.** A truck driver who sued for employment discrimination sought to recover back pay. Although the jury found that the defendant engaged in discrimination, it did not award back pay. The truck driver sought attorneys' fees on the ground that she was a "prevailing party." The court looked to federal law for guidance, and, in particular, the U.S. Supreme Court's ruling in *Hensley v. Eckerhar* [461 U.S. 424 (1983)]. *Hensley* held that plaintiffs are considered a "prevailing party" for purposes of attorneys' fees if "they succeed on any significant issue in litigation which achieves some of the benefit the parties sought in bringing suit." The court adopted this definition and held that the truck driver was not a prevailing party under the applicable state statute, which was enacted prior to *Hensley*. The truck driver received none of the relief she sought other than a bare finding that the defendant acted improperly, and thus was not entitled to attorneys' fees. [*Siverly v. Young & Morgan Trucking Co.*, 17 P.3d 579, 172 Or. App. 282 (2001)]

PENNSYLVANIA

Claim of retaliation within scope of reasonable agency investigation. In an amended complaint, an employee filed an action for racial discrimination and retaliation under Title VII and the Pennsylvania Human Relations Act (PHRA). The court held that PHRA claims are interpreted in accordance with their Title VII counterparts. Applying federal precedent, the court determined that the documents that the employee filed with the Pennsylvania Human Relations Commission (PHRC) provided facts that should have led the agency to investigate the charge of retaliatory termination that the employee was seeking to litigate. The court therefore reversed a lower court's dismissal of the employee's claim for failure to exhaust state administrative remedies with respect to the claim of retaliation, holding that a dismissal of that sort would penalize a charging party for mere technical shortcomings. [*Bailey v. Storlazzi*, 729 A.2d 1206, 1211 n.6, 1217 (Pa. Super. Ct. 1999)]

Claim of discriminatory discharge not within the scope of administrative charge alleging harassment, discriminatory discipline, and retaliation. A former employee brought a judicial action for discriminatory termination based on national origin, age, and religion in violation of the ADEA, Title VII, and the PHRA. Following federal precedent relating to EEOC procedures, the court held that the scope of a judicial complaint filed at a state agency—here the PHRC—is not limited to the four corners of the administrative charge; rather, the parameters of subsequent private actions in courts are defined by the scope of the investigation, which can reasonably be expected to grow out of a charge of discrimination. In granting the employer's motion for summary judgment, however, the court held that the employee's claims could not reasonably be expected to grow out of his charge to the PHRC, which alleged harassment, discriminatory discipline, and retaliation, and thus that the exhaustion requirements for the employee's discrimination claim had not been met. [*Galvis v. HGO Services*, 49 F. Supp. 2d 445 (E.D. Pa. 1999)]

TEXAS

Triggering limitations period for state discrimination suits. An employee brought suit against her employer for age and disability discrimination under Texas law. The federal district court held that her claims were time barred because she did not file her suit in state court within 60 days after receiving her "right to sue" letter from the EEOC. The Fifth Circuit reversed, holding that her claim was not time barred. The court held that the scope of the EEOC's "agency relationship" for the Texas Commission on Human Rights was not so broad that it could notify a complainant of her "right to file a civil action" under state law by issuing a federal "right to sue" letter. Thus, the state "right to file a civil action" letter was not interchangeable with the federal "right to sue" letter and would not trigger the 60-day limitations period. In its holding, the court abrogated the holdings of *Dean v. Xerox Corp.* [1997 WL 756574 (N.D. Tex. Nov. 25, 1997)], *Battee v. Eckerd Drugs, Inc.* [1997 WL 34091 (N.D. Tex. June 12, 1997)], and *James v. Texas Department of Human Services* [818 F. Supp. 987 (N.D. Tex. 1993)]. [*Vielma v. Eureka Co.*, 218 F.3d 458 (5th Cir. 2000)]

WASHINGTON

After-discovered evidence. A hospital appealed a jury verdict in a sex discrimination suit brought by a former employee under the Washington discrimination statute. Generally, the court noted, "Washington courts traditionally look to federal precedent for guidance in employment discrimination" claims. The court adhered to the U.S. Supreme Court's decision in *McKennon v. Nashville Banner Publishing Co.* [513 U.S. 352 (1995)], holding that after-discovered evidence of an employee's misconduct—here, a prior drug conviction—is admissible and may affect an award given to the employee, and that before an employer can rely on after-discovered evidence of wrongdoing and thus seek to limit the damage award it must first show that the wrongdoing was "of such severity that the employee would have been terminated on those grounds alone once the employer discovered the wrongdoing." [*Janson v. North Valley Hospital,* 93 Wash. App. 892, 971 P.2d 67 (1999)]

Need for circumstantial proof. In this case, involving an employee who was fired and claimed the firing was due to age discrimination, the court cited to federal law in noting that direct, smoking-gun evidence of discriminatory animus is rare, and that there is seldom any eyewitness testimony as to the employer's mental process. [*Post v. Coronet Industries, Inc.,* 2002 WL 384510 (Wash. App. Div. 3, Mar. 12, 2002)]

Federal pretext analysis applied. In this case (which involved a contractor discrimination claim under Washington state law), the court noted that Washington antidiscrimination law follows the federal burden-shifting analysis. [*Elcon Corp. v. City of Tacoma*, 2002 WL 368603 (Wash. App. Div 2, Mar. 8, 2002)]

Exhibit 2.6-2
STATE DECISIONS NOT FOLLOWING EEOC GUIDELINES OR FEDERAL PRECEDENT

(See also text at § 2.6.)

Age Discrimination

MASSACHUSETTS

Plaintiff's burden is lighter in state age discrimination claim. In an age discrimination suit brought by a former employee under the ADEA and the Massachusetts Anti-Discrimination Act (MADA), the employee—an older executive—appealed a lower court's grant of summary judgment to the employer. In analyzing the state claim, the court noted that under the MADA, in the third phase of a disparate treatment claim, an employee must establish a trialworthy question as to the pretextuality of the employer's explanation for an adverse employment action—a somewhat lighter burden than what the court asserted the federal standard to be, *viz.,* the "pretext-plus age animus" standard. [*Mullin v. Raytheon Co.,* 164 F.3d 696 (1st Cir. 1999)]

PUERTO RICO

Burden shifting and the definition of *just cause* in age discrimination claims. A former employee brought an action alleging he was terminated in violation of the ADEA and the Puerto Rico antidiscrimination laws, specifically Puerto Rico Law No. 100. While noting that Law No. 100 and the ADEA are similar in some respects, the federal district court pointed out a substantial difference: under Law No. 100, when a prima facie case is set forth and hence a rebuttable presumption of discrimination established, not only is the burden of production shifted from the employee to the employer, as is the case under the ADEA, but the burden of persuasion is as well. The result is that, in order to rebut the Law No.100 presumption, the employer must prove by a preponderance of the evidence that the challenged discharge was not motivated by a discriminatory age animus. Moreover, for the purposes of determining whether the employer lacked "just cause" under a Law No. 100 claim, the court declined to look at federal precedent, looking instead to Puerto Rico Law No. 80, which defines and gives examples of what would and would not constitute "just cause." The court did, however, note that the Law No. 100 plaintiff is in the same situation as an ADEA plaintiff after the defendant has articulated a legitimate, nondiscriminatory reason for its actions; that is, the burden is on the plaintiff to show that, even if the dismissal could be justified, it was nevertheless in violation of the law, because it was "motivated by discriminatory animus instead of or in addition to the legitimate reasons for dismissal." [*Soto v. Corporation of Bishop of Church of Jesus Christ,* 73 F. Supp. 2d 116, 130–31 (D.P.R. 1999); *see also Guillermety Mendez v. Puerto Rican Cement Co.,* 56 F. Supp. 2d 176 (D.P.R. 1999) (holding that, in age discrimination claims, federal and Puerto Rico statutes differ on proof required to show discrimination; Puerto Rico law establishes rebuttable presumption that the employer has engaged in unlawful discrimination unless the employer can show that it had just cause for the discharge); *Cardona Jimenez v. Bancomerico de Puerto Rico,* 174 F.3d 36 (1st Cir. 1999)]

Heavier burden on employer in age discrimination suit. An employer-defendant motioned for summary judgment in a sexual harassment suit brought by a former employee under Title VII and the Puerto Rico law. The court noted that under Puerto Rico Law No. 100, upon a satisfactory showing of a prima facie case by an employee, not only does the burden of production shift to the defendant, as is the case under Title VII, but also the burden of persuasion shifts. Thus, under Law No. 100, the employer must prove by a preponderance of the evidence that the challenged action was not motivated by a discriminatory age animus. [*Ruiz v. Caribbean Restaurants, Inc.,* 54 F. Supp. 2d 97 (D.P.R. 1999)]

WEST VIRGINIA

Disparate impact claim. A university professor brought an age discrimination suit under the West Virginia Human Rights Act (WVHRA) seeking to have the court follow the majority of federal courts and apply a disparate impact theory in his age discrimination claims arising under the ADEA. In view of the language of the WVHRA, the court held that it was not necessary to consider the federal statute or regulations, because the disparate impact theory applies to all claims under the state statute, including claims of age-based discrimination. [*West Virginia University/West Virginia Board of Regents v. Decker*, 191 W. Va. 567, 447 S.E.2d 259 (1994)]

Disability or Handicap

CALIFORNIA

Amended definition of disability does not require plaintiff to show "substantial" limitation, although prior definition applied to employee's claim. A foreman on a golf course maintenance crew brought a claim of disability discrimination under the California Fair Employment and Housing Act (CFEHA) based on his termination in 1997. The trial court held that the plaintiff could not state a claim under the CFEHA because his back condition did not constitute a protected physical disability. The appellate court noted that, as a result of amendments to the CFEHA enacted in 2000, the definition of disabled persons was enlarged to include defined conditions that cause *any* limitation that makes a major life activity *difficult*, not just those that constitute a "substantial limitation," as defined under previous state law. Although the court recognized that the amended definition created a difference between state and federal law, it held that the 2000 amendments were not retroactive to the plaintiff's claim, which arose in 1997. Applying the "substantial limitation" test, the court affirmed the trial court's dismissal of the plaintiff's claim. [*Colmenares v. Braemar Country Club, Inc.*, 89 Cal. App. 4th 778, 107 Cal. Rptr. 2d 719 (Ct. App. 2001)]

IOWA

Reasonable accommodation. An employee brought a disability discrimination action after his employer reassigned him to a lower-paying position after discovering that the employee was legally blind in one eye. The state court declined to adopt the undue hardship standard for reasonable accommodation expressed in the EEOC guidelines and maintained the *de minimis* standard developed under Iowa case law. [*Courtney v. American National Can Co.* 537 N.W.2d 681 (Iowa 1995)]

Mitigating factors considered in determining existence of impairment. An employee brought a claim under the Iowa Civil Rights Act (ICRA) alleging discrimination in employment based on mental disability. To define terms in the ICRA, the court was guided by the definitions provided in the EEOC regulations issued to implement the ADA. In determining whether the employee was substantially limited in a major life activity, however, the court rejected the EEOC's interpretation regarding the consideration of mitigating measures. The Court stated that EEOC's guidance was in direct conflict with the

ICRA. [*Fuller v. Iowa Department of Human Services*, 576 N.W.2d 324 (Iowa 1998)]

MASSACHUSETTS

Mitigating measures not considered under state law in determining disability. A former police officer with a severe hearing impairment from birth could correct it to within normal limits with hearing aids. Massachusetts's highest court answered a question certified to it by a federal district court by ruling that the state antidiscrimination statute did not require consideration of mitigating or corrective measures in determining whether an employee was disabled. The court relied on guidance from the Massachusetts Commission Against Discrimination and its reading of the state law as extending coverage to persons with significant, but correctable, impairments. Given the differences between the state statute and the ADA, the court stated that "it is not appropriate to follow the federal jurisprudence in this case." [*Dahill v. Police Department of Boston*, 434 Mass. 233, 748 N.E.2d 956 (2001)]

Definition of *reasonable accommodation*. A security guard suffered several accidents at work that caused injury sufficient to lead to his missing work. He filed workers' compensation and disability claims. He was eventually terminated, ostensibly for his attendance problems. He argued that the real reason for his dismissal was retaliation for filing the workers' compensation and disability claims and brought an action under the Massachusetts antidiscrimination statute. He argued that the employer failed to engage in an interactive process to determine an appropriate accommodation and cited to 29 CFR Section 1630.2(o)(3). The court, however, rejected the plaintiff's argument and found that the interactive process requirement does not exist for claims brought under the Massachusetts statute and should not be adopted from the federal law. [*Sullivan v. Raytheon Co.*, 262 F.3d 41 (1st Cir. 2001)]

MICHIGAN

Mitigating factors considered in determining existence of impairment. An employee brought a claim against his employer under the Michigan Handicappers' Civil Rights Act (MHCRA). In determining whether the employee met the MHCRA's definition of "handicap," the court looked to federal court decisions and the EEOC guidelines. The court followed the reasoning of federal courts that had rejected the EEOC's position regarding the consideration of mitigating factors and held that the EEOC's position in this regard contravened the plain language of the MHCRA. [*Chmielewski v. Xermac, Inc.*, 580 N.W.2d 817 (Mich. 1998)]

NEW YORK

Definitions of *substantially limiting* and *disability* and the requirement of reasonable accommodations different under state law. A former employee brought an action against his former employer and supervisor alleging disability

Exhibit 2.6-2   PART 2—FAIR EMPLOYMENT PRACTICES   2-30

discrimination and retaliation under the ADA and the New York State Human Rights Law (NYSHRL). In interpreting the state law claims, the court distinguished between the definition of disability under the NYSHRL and that under the ADA. In contrast to the ADA, the NYSHRL does not require that an individual show a substantial limitation of his or her normal activities to state a claim; rather, under the NYSHRL, an individual need show only that his or her impairment is "demonstrable by medically accepted techniques." The court further noted that the New York State Administrative Code defines "disability" even more broadly than do both the ADA and the NYSHRL: the Code states that a disability can be a "physical, medical, mental, or psychological impairment, or a history or record of such impairment." Finally, the court emphasized that, in contrast to federal law, the NYSHRL does not require an employer to provide "reasonable accommodations" for an employee's disability, and that therefore complaints about the lack of reasonable accommodations are not protected activities under the NYSHRL. [*Sacay v. Research Foundation of City University of New York,* 44 F. Supp. 2d 505 (E.D.N.Y. 1999)]

OREGON

Although substantive state law applied to state disability discrimination claim, burden-shifting analysis was federal procedural law and had to be applied when claim was removed to federal court. On the basis of diversity jurisdiction, a former employee's disability discrimination claim brought under an Oregon statute was removed to federal court. There, the court was faced with a difference between state and federal law on what the plaintiff must show to overcome a summary judgment motion. Under Oregon law, an employment discrimination plaintiff need only adduce a prima facie case. Under federal law, the burden-shifting analysis from *McDonnell Douglas* applies. Ruling that the burden-shifting analysis was federal procedural law, the Ninth Circuit used that analysis rather than the Oregon standard. The plaintiff made out a prima facie case, but failed to raise a fact issue as to whether the reason given for her termination was pretextual. [*Snead v. Metropolitan Property & Casualty Insurance Co.,* 237 F.3d 1080 (9th Cir. 2001)]

National Origin

NEW YORK

Disparate treatment claim. An employee who was hired by a hospital as a Spanish-speaking patient representative alleged that she was fired for violating an English-only policy. In her claim against the hospital for national origin discrimination, she relied on an EEOC regulation that stated that an English-only rule applied "only at certain times" is permissible only if the employer can show that such a rule is justified by business necessity. [29 C.F.R. § 1606.7] The court held that the EEOC

guidelines were inconsistent with the plain language of Title VII to the extent that they could be interpreted to create a presumption of discrimination and allow a plaintiff to circumvent his or her burden of proving discriminatory intent. The employee could not satisfy her burden merely by showing that she was terminated for violating an English-only policy; she would also need to show that she was intentionally discriminated against on the basis of her national origin. [*Velasquez v. Goldwater Memorial Hospital,* 88 F. Supp. 2d 257 (S.D.N.Y. 2000)]

Court refuses to follow EEOC regulations on English-only rules. An employee who was hired by a hospital as a Spanish-speaking patient representative alleged she was fired for violating an English-only policy. In her claim against the hospital for national origin discrimination, she relied on an EEOC regulation that stated that an English-only rule applied "only at certain times" is permissible only if the employer can show that such a rule is justified by business necessity. [29 C.F.R. § 1606.7] The court held that the EEOC guideline was inconsistent with the plain language of Title VII to the extent that it could be interpreted to create a presumption of discrimination and allow a plaintiff to circumvent his or her burden of proving discriminatory intent. The employee could not satisfy her burden merely by showing that she was terminated for violating an English-only policy; she would also need to show that she was intentionally discriminated against on the basis of her national origin. [*Velasquez v. Goldwater Memorial Hospital,* 88 F. Supp. 2d 257 (S.D.N.Y. 2000)]

Racial Discrimination

IOWA

Contrary to federal law, individual supervisors could be liable under state law prohibiting race discrimination. An employee claiming race discrimination regarding a hostile work environment and a demotion sued under Title VII and the Iowa Civil Rights Act (ICRA). As a matter of law, neither claim could be asserted under Title VII against supervisors in their individual capacities. By contrast, the ICRA allows discrimination claims against supervisors individually, and such claims by the plaintiffs survived summary judgment. [*McGregory v. Crest/Hughes Technologies,* 149 F. Supp. 2d 1079 (S.D. Iowa 2001)]

MASSACHUSETTS

Employee's burden is lighter in race discrimination claim. Former employees brought an action against an employer under federal and state antidiscrimination statutes for refusal to hire based on race. In analyzing the claims, the court noted that the *McDonnell Douglas* framework applies to disparate treatment claims brought under the Massachusetts statute but that the plaintiff's burden is lighter in one way: while federal law requires a showing of pretext plus racial animus, the Massachusetts courts appear, at the third step of the analysis, to require a claimant to show only pretext. The First Circuit therefore reversed a lower court's grant of summary judgment to the employer with respect to both the federal and the state claims, asserting that there were general issues of material fact as to whether the employer's stated reasons for discharging the employee were pretext. [*Fernandez v. Costa Bros. Masonry, Inc.*, 199 F.3d 572 (1st Cir. 1999)]

Religion

MICHIGAN

Reasonable accommodation. An employee who was terminated after refusing to work on her Sabbath brought religious discrimination action under the Michigan Fair Employment Practices Act (MFEPA). The employee asked the court to adopt the EEOC guidelines requiring reasonable accommodation for religious needs as a proper construction of the MFEPA. The court held, however, that there was no basis for construing the MFEPA to impose the duty or reasonable accommodation as enunciated by the EEOC. [*Michigan Department of Civil Rights v. General Motors Corp.*, 412 Mich. 610, 317 N.W.2d 16 (1982)]

WISCONSIN

Religious holiday. The court held that the Wisconsin Fair Employment Act, unlike Title VII, does not require employers to accommodate employees' observance of religious holidays. [*American Motors v. Department of Industry, Labor, & Human Relations*, 305 N.W.2d 62 (Wis. 1981)]

Sex Discrimination

CALIFORNIA

Strict liability of employers for sexual harassment by supervisors. Sales agents brought action under the California Fair Employment and Housing Act alleging sexual harassment. The 1980 EEOC final guidelines state that employers are strictly liable for all sexual harassment conduct committed by their supervisors. The California legislature codified the EEOC regulations. In a 1986 brief the EEOC disavowed its previous position and adopted the new position that an employer is not liable for supervisor harassment when the theory of liability is hostile work environment. The court stated that the standard in California was clear and rejected arguments based on current federal case law and regulations. [*Lai v. Prudential Insurance Co. of America*, 62 Cal. App. 4th 220, 72 Cal. Rptr. 2d 551 (Cal. Ct. App. 1998)]

Affirmative defense of *Faragher* and *Ellerth* does not apply to actions involving sexual harassment by a supervisor brought under the California Fair Employment and Housing Act (CFEHA). In a decision which departs from a prior decision of the federal Ninth Circuit Court of Appeals inter-

preting the CFEHA, the court held that distinctions between the CFEHA and Title VII prevented application of the *Faragher* and *Ellerth* defense to claims under the CFEHA. The court noted that while Title VII does not specifically address an employer's liability for supervisor harassment, the CFEHA does. On this point, California law provides: "Harassment of an employee . . . by an employee other than an agent or supervisor shall be unlawful if the entity, or its agents or supervisors, knows or should have known of this conduct and fails to take immediate and appropriate corrective action. An entity shall take all reasonable steps to prevent harassment from occurring. Loss of tangible job benefits shall not be necessary in order to establish harassment." The court concluded that, under this language, "harassment by a nonsupervisory coworker is unlawful only if the employer knew, or should have known, of the harassment and failed to correct it. No such limitation exists for harassment by a supervisor or agent." Thus, the court held that employers are vicariously liable for harassment by supervisors and enjoy no defense to such harassment. [Dept. of Health Services v. Superior Court (McGinnis), 94 Cal. App. 4th 14, 113 Cal. Rptr. 2d 878 (2001)]

MASSACHUSETTS

Same-sex harassment. Former employee brought sexual harassment and retaliation charges against former employer. Issue in case was whether state discrimination law applied to same-sex sexual harassment, even when the perpetrator of the harassment was a heterosexual. Relying on federal case law, defendant argued that sexual harassment was actionable only as a form of sex discrimination and, therefore, the only form of sexual harassment that was prohibited by state law was sexual harassment perpetrated by a homosexual. Court ignored federal regulations in finding that state law included a prohibition against nondiscriminatory sexual harassment. Court held that any conduct of a sexual nature that is found to interfere unreasonably with an employee's work performance through the creation of sexually offensive work environment can be sexual harassment under state law. [*Melnychenko v. 84 Lumber Co.*, 676 N.E.2d 45 (Mass. 1997)]

Court declines to adopt federal precedent on continuing violation doctrine in sexual harassment case. Noting that it frequently does not follow the reasoning of federal appellate decisions on Title VII when construing the Massachusetts counterpart to Title VII, the Supreme Judicial Court of Massachusetts declined to adopt the federal precedent on application of the continuing violation doctrine to claims of hostile work environment sexual harassment. The federal standard denied recovery for conduct outside the limitations period if, when the conduct occurred, the employee had notice that she had an actionable claim. The Massachusetts test, more favorable to the plaintiff, allows litigation of otherwise time-barred acts of harassment unless the plaintiff's delay was objectively unreasonable. [*Cuddyer v. Stop & Shop Supermarket Co.*, 434 Mass. 521, 750 N.E.2d 928 (2001)]

Exhibit 2.6-2   PART 2—FAIR EMPLOYMENT PRACTICES   2-32

MICHIGAN

Hostile work environment sexual harassment. A plaintiff who was subjected to comments involving pregnancy and child rearing brought a claim of hostile work environment sexual harassment. The court observed that it often turns to federal precedent interpreting Title VII for guidance when interpreting the Michigan Civil Rights Act (MCRA), although federal precedent is not binding. However, while the definition of sexual harassment under the MCRA strongly paralleled the relevant EEOC guidelines, the court held that the difference between the MCRA definition and federal case law interpreting Title VII foreclosed its reliance on Title VII precedents to interpret sexual harassment under the MCRA. [*Koester v. City of Novi*, 213 Mich. App. 653, 540 N.W.2d 765 (1995)]

Quid pro quo harassment. Unlike its federal counterpart, which does not explicitly define "sexual harassment," the MCRA requires an employee alleging quid pro quo sexual harassment to show either that submission to or rejection of a sexual advance was "made a term or condition either explicitly or implicitly to obtain employment" or that it was used as a factor in decisions affecting his or her employment. The Michigan Court of Appeals held that an employee who had been raped by her supervisor, and who subsequently felt compelled to resign, did not meet either of these definitions of quid pro quo harassment. While acknowledging the difference between state and federal law, the Michigan Supreme Court reversed that decision, holding that the supervisor's decision to rape the employee was a "decision affecting . . . employment." [*Champion v. Nationwide Securities, Inc.*, 450 Mich. 702, 545 N.W.2d 596 (1996)]

Court follows state precedent in allocating burden of proof. Although the U.S. Supreme Court in *Faragher* and *Ellerth* shifted the burden of proof from the employee to the employer regarding whether the employer should be held vicariously liable for the actions of a supervisor, the Michigan Supreme Court decided to follow state precedent instead and ruled in favor of the employer. The court noted that the allocation of the burden in *Faragher* and *Ellerth* conflicted with state precedents, which place the burden on the employee to "prove that the employer failed to take prompt and adequate remedial action" to deal with the creation of a hostile work environment by a supervisor. [*Chambers v. Trettco, Inc.*, 463 Mich. 297, 614 N.W.2d 910 (2000)]

MINNESOTA

Definition of *sexual harassment* requires that employer know or should know of harassment. An employee brought an action under Title VII and the Minnesota Human Rights Act (MHRA) alleging hostile work environment based on a single severe act of sexual harassment. The Eighth Circuit declined to follow federal precedent, including the Supreme Court's decisions in *Faragher* and *Ellerth*, when defining "sexual harassment" for the purposes of the MHRA claim; instead, it

adhered to the plain language of the Minnesota statute, which defines sexual harassment as requiring proof that "the employer knows or should know of the harassment and fails to take timely and appropriate action." Although the court remanded the Title VII claim for further proceedings to determine whether a single act of harassment was sufficient under *Faragher* and *Ellerth*, it upheld a grant of summary judgment for the employer with respect to the state law claim, reasoning that such a single act of harassment could not be brought under the MHRA's definition of "sexual harassment." [*Todd v. Ortho Biotech, Inc.*, 175 F.3d 595 (8th Cir. 1999)]

PUERTO RICO

Heavier burden on employer in age discrimination suit. An employer-defendant motioned for summary judgment in a sexual harassment suit brought by a former employee under Title VII and Puerto Rico law. The court noted that under Puerto Rico Law No. 100, upon a satisfactory showing of a prima facie case by an employee, not only does the burden of production shift to the defendant, as is the case under Title VII, but also the burden of persuasion shifts. Thus, under Law No. 100, the employer must prove by a preponderance of the evidence that the challenged action was not motivated by a discriminatory age animus. [*Ruiz v. Caribbean Restaurants, Inc.*, 54 F. Supp. 2d 97 (D.P.R. 1999)]

WASHINGTON

Strict liability of employers for sexual harassment by supervisors. Two female employees brought a hostile work environment sexual harassment suit against their employer. The court refused to follow the EEOC guidelines regarding strict liability of an employer for sexual harassment by a supervisor in applying the Washington Law Against Discrimination (WLAD), noting that the interpretations of Title VII, while instructive, were not binding on the court. [*Glasgow v. Georgia-Pacific Corp.*, 693 P.2d 708 (Wash. 1985)] Employee brought action against employer alleging sexual discrimination based on actions of supervisor. Court rejected EEOC guidelines regarding strict liability of employer for sexual harassment by supervisor in applying the WLAD, noting that interpretations of Title VII, while instructive, were not binding on the court. [*Henderson v. Pennwalt Corp.*, 704 P.2d 1256 (Wash. Ct. App. 1985)]

Other Issues and Procedures

MISSOURI

Exhaustion of administrative remedies is jurisdictional. A female professor brought an action against her employer, a university, for discriminatory denial of tenure under Title VII and the Missouri Human Rights Act (MHRA). The court asserted that, unlike the exhaustion of administrative remedies requirement under Title VII, the exhaustion requirement for the MHRA is jurisdictional. As the employee failed to file an administrative complaint within the time period required by state law (180 days), yet within the time period required by federal law (300 days), the court entertained only the federal claim, dismissing the state claim for want of jurisdiction. [*Tapp v. St. Louis University,* 78 F. Supp. 2d 1002 (E.D. Mo. 2000)]

NEW JERSEY

Exhaustion of administrative remedies not required. In a gender discrimination suit under the New Jersey Law Against Discrimination (NJLAD) and Title VII, the court emphasized that the administrative requirements for an NJLAD claim differ greatly from the procedural requirements under Title VII—namely, under New Jersey law, exhaustion of administrative remedies is not required. [*Lemke v. International Total Services, Inc.,* 56 F. Supp. 2d 472 (D.N.J. 1999)]

NEW YORK

Liability of individuals under state law. A former employee brought an action against his former employer and supervisor, alleging disability discrimination and retaliation under the ADA and the New York State Human Rights Law (NYSHRL). In interpreting the state claims, the court distinguished between the definition of disability under the NYSHRL and the definitions under Title VII and the ADA: unlike Title VII and the ADA, the NYSHRL imposes liability for discriminatory acts on individuals who have any "ownership interest" in the defendant company or have power to make personnel decisions, adding that some district courts have interpreted Section 296(6) of the New York State Executive Law as holding individuals liable for aiding, abetting, or inciting discrimination. [*Sacay v. Research Foundation of City University of New York,* 44 F. Supp. 2d 505 (E.D.N.Y. 1999)]

10

State Workers' Compensation Laws

Tables in Part 10 cover state workers' compensation laws, including employers covered, insurance requirements, coverage of minors, and covered benefits. Also included are tables covering notice, recordkeeping, and reporting requirements.

Origins of Workers' Compensation and Interplay with Other Laws

Workers' compensation laws were first introduced by a few states in 1912, in response to an increased focus on workplace injuries by unions and by federal and state governments. Since then, workers' compensation laws have been passed by all states and the federal government. The objective of these laws is to provide universal coverage and compensation for work-related injuries and diseases. Although all state laws share the same basic purpose, they differ in the method of providing coverage, the specified individuals entitled to compensation, and a host of specific issues related to covered injuries, illnesses, and health care services.

Every state has enacted its own workers' compensation act, in response to a multitude of negligence suits brought by injured workers against their employers. These acts guarantee compensation and medical care to employees injured in the course of employment, but under these no-fault statutory regimes employees lose the right to sue their employers for injuries suffered on the job.

Changes in state workers' compensation acts are made regularly. In the course of a typical state legislative session, numerous pieces of legislation proposing to amend the workers' compensation laws will be considered. In fact, it is not at all uncommon for multiple pieces of such legislation to be enacted in a single session.

In California, for example, legislative battles have been fought regularly in recent years over workers' compensation reform, putting business interests against organized labor and certain attorney organizations. Last year, California saw legislation that would have dramatically increased benefits vetoed for the third straight year. Similar legislation was approved, however, on February 15, 2002. The American Insurance Association estimated that the bill would raise the workers' compensation costs of that state's employers, already high by national standards, by over $3.5 billion. At the same time, several other less significant pieces of workers' compensation legislation were successfully enacted in California in 2001, putting in place additional presumptions of compensability and otherwise making benefits available to specific categories of beneficiaries.

Tables 10.1-1 through 10.12-1 include legislative changes made around the country through the first part of 2002.

[a] Basic Components of State Workers' Compensation Laws

The primary method of providing coverage for workers' compensation claims is through private insurance purchased by the employer. A small minority of states require that employers insure in monopolistic state funds. A larger minority of states give employers the option of purchasing insurance from either a state fund or private insurance companies. The majority of states also allow large companies to self-insure for workers' compensation coverage.

Coverage under state workers' compensation laws is either elective or compulsory. Under a compulsory law, each covered employer is required to accept the provisions of the workers' compensation law and to provide specified benefits. Under an elective law, the employer may accept or reject the act, but if the act is rejected the employer loses certain defenses that workers' compensation law provides. Chief among these defenses is the exclusivity of workers' compensation relief, under which employers are given the benefit of the limited liability associated with workers' compensation and are shielded from larger damage awards that could be obtained under state tort or negligence law.

Discussion of other components of state workers' compensation laws can be found in the introduction to each section in Part 10.

[b] Interplay Between ADA, FMLA, and State Workers' Compensation Laws

A troubling conflict for employers arises in connection with the interplay between the Americans with Disabilities Act (ADA) and state workers' compensation statutes. It is possible, for example, for a person to be considered "permanently and totally disabled" for purposes of a state workers' compensation statute yet come within the definition of a "qualified individual with a disability" under the ADA.

Under the typical workers' compensation law, an employer is not required to consider whether a worker can perform a job's "essential functions" or to provide a reasonable accommodation. An injured worker may therefore be legally entitled to receive workers' compensation benefits and also may be able to demand that he or she be employed through reasonable accommodation of his or her disability.

Under disability discrimination laws, however, an injured worker will be protected if he or she has a physical or mental impairment that substantially limits major life activities, such as caring for oneself, performing manual tasks, walking, seeing, hearing, speaking, breathing, learning, or working in a job requiring heavy labor. An employer's obligation of reasonable accommodation may include job restructuring, part-time or modified work schedules, provision or modification of equipment, and, if necessary, reassignment to a vacant position. Thus, an employer that tells an injured worker that he or she may not return to work until he or she is 100 percent recovered may be in violation of the ADA. In such a situation, therefore, it is in the employer's best interest to attempt accommodation if possible, and the Equal Employment Opportunity Commission (EEOC) has taken the position that failure to make reasonable accommodation in this situation may violate the ADA.[1]

On September 3, 1996, the EEOC issued an Enforcement Guidance on Workers' Compensation and the ADA.[2] This notice provides guidance on many of the issues that have entrapped employers and injured employees.

As noted above, under the typical workers' compensation law, an injured worker may be legally entitled to receive workers' compensation benefits and also may be able to demand that he or she be employed through reasonable accommodation of his or her disability. As a threshold matter, however, the employee must demonstrate that he or she is disabled. Under the ADA, a "disability" is defined as

1. A physical or mental impairment that substantially limits a major life activity;
2. A record of such an impairment; or
3. Being regarded as having such an impairment.

The guidance makes clear that not every person with an occupational injury is a person with a disability under the ADA.

Impairments resulting from occupational injury will not come within the first portion of the ADA's definition of disability if they are not severe enough to substantially limit a major life activity, or if they are only temporary, nonchronic injuries and have little or no long-term impact. The mere filing of a workers' compensation claim does not, by itself, establish a record of impairment sufficient to come within the second portion of the definition. With respect to the third portion of the ADA definition—when a person with an occupational injury is considered to have a disability—the guidance states as follows:

> A person with an occupational injury has a disability under the "regarded as" portion of the ADA definition if he/she: (1) has an impairment that does not substantially limit a major life activity but is treated by an employer as if it were substantially limiting, (2) has an impairment that substantially limits a major life activity because of the attitude of others towards the impairment, or (3) has no impairment but is treated as having a substantially limiting impairment.[3]

Two examples given by the EEOC illustrate the potential conflict:

Example 1. An employer has a "sack-handler" position that requires the employee to pick up 50-pound sacks from a loading dock and carry them to the storage room. The employee who holds this position is disabled by a work-related back impairment and requests an accommodation. The employer analyzes the job and finds that the essential function of the position is to *move* the

---

1. EEOC Technical Assistance Manual §§ 3.8, 9.2 (1992).
2. Notice No. 915.002 (Sept. 3, 1996).

---

3. EEOC Enforcement Guidance No. 915.002, at 3.

sacks from the loading dock to the storage room, not necessarily to lift and carry the sacks. After consulting with the employee to determine his exact physical abilities and limitations, it is determined, with medical documentation, that the employee can lift 50-pound sacks to waist level, but cannot carry them to the storage room. A number of potential accommodations may be instituted, including the use of a dolly, a handtruck, or a cart.

Example 2. A construction worker falls from a ladder and breaks a leg; the leg heals normally within a few months. Although this worker may be awarded workers' compensation benefits for the injury, he would not be considered a person with a disability under the ADA because the impairment did not "substantially limit" a major life activity, since the injury healed within a short period and had little or no long-term impact. However, if the worker's leg took significantly longer to heal than is usual for this type of injury and during that period the worker could not walk, he would be considered to have a disability under the ADA. Or, if the injury caused a permanent limp, the worker might be considered disabled under the ADA if the limp substantially limited his walking as compared to the average person in the general population. If so, the employer could not refuse to make reasonable accommodation.

In one case in which this conflict was presented, the Tenth Circuit Court of Appeals held that an employee was not the victim of discrimination despite not being allowed to return to work after a work-related injury. He had permanent partial disabilities to his feet, and medical opinions were inconsistent (one opinion stated that he could not return to work at all; the other, that he could return to work only with restrictions on time spent standing). The court held that the employee could not be considered to be handicapped or disabled because he failed to demonstrate a significant restriction in his ability to perform a class of jobs, rather than just the particular job in question.[4]

In another case, a U.S. district court held that an employer violated the Rehabilitation Act by summarily discharging an employee who sustained a back injury at work that restricted her ability to walk, sit, stand, drive, care for her home, and engage in recreational activities.[5] The employee was, in the court's view, a person with a disability and was qualified to perform her job as a receptionist-clerk with reasonable accommodation. The employer's failure to allow the employee to continue working with accommodations, such as providing her with a wooden straight-backed chair, allowing her to use the elevator, and allowing for regular breaks, violated the Rehabilitation Act.

States have split on how they treat the interplay between their workers' compensation statutes and their disability discrimination statutes. For example, some courts have held that the remedy for disability discrimination related to injuries that occurred on the job is exclusive to the workers' compensation statute.[6] Other courts have taken the opposite approach, allowing remedies under both the workers' compensation statute and the statute prohibiting disability discrimination.[7]

In addition to issues related to incumbent employees, the interplay between the ADA and state workers' compensation laws may present problems with respect to applicants for employment. It should be noted, for example, that an employer may be prohibited from even inquiring into an applicant's workers' compensation history. An employer is prohibited under the ADA from asking an applicant for employment who has not yet been extended a formal job offer if he or she has ever filed for workers' compensation insurance. Under the ADA, an employer is not allowed to screen out applicants with disabilities on the basis that such an applicant might be more likely to sustain an injury on the job and cause the employer additional workers' compensation costs. There is an exception to this rule if the employee poses a direct threat to himself or herself or to others, but this is a narrow exception that must be supported by objective medical evidence specifically related to the individual employee.

After making a conditional job offer, an employer may inquire about a person's workers' compensation history in a medical inquiry or examination that is required of all applicants in the same job category. However, an employer may not require an applicant to have a medical examination because a response to a medical inquiry indicated a medical problem, unless all appli-

---

4. Bolton v. Scrivner, Inc., 36 F.3d 939 (10th Cir. 1994).

5. Perez v. Philadelphia Hous. Auth., 677 F. Supp. 357 (E.D. Pa. 1987), *aff'd*, 841 F.2d 1120 (3d Cir. 1988).

6. Usher v. American Airlines, 20 Cal. App. 4th 1520, 25 Cal. Rptr. 2d 335 (1993); Karst v. FC Hayer Co., 447 N.W.2d 180 (Minn. 1989).

7. Cox v. Glazer Steel Corp., 606 So. 2d 518 (La. 1992) (stating that the Civil Rights Act for Handicapped Persons provides a distinct statutory remedy for the handicapped not within the scope of the workers' compensation law, and its application is not barred by that law); King v. Bangor Fed. Credit Union, 568 A.2d 507 (Me. 1989).

cants in the same job category are required to have the examination.

There is also substantial overlap, as well as some potential conflicts, between the ADA, the Family and Medical Leave Act (FMLA), and state workers' compensation laws. An FMLA "serious health condition" is not necessarily an ADA "disability." Some FMLA "serious health conditions" may also be ADA disabilities (e.g., most cancers and serious strokes). Other "serious health conditions," however, may not be ADA disabilities (e.g., pregnancy or a routine broken leg or hernia). This is because the condition is not an impairment (e.g., pregnancy) or because the impairment is not substantially limiting (e.g., a routine broken leg or hernia).

An issue arises regarding workers' compensation leave and the FMLA requirement that, to be eligible for FMLA leave, an employee must have worked 1,250 hours. For the FMLA, "hours" means actual hours worked, but state law on this point may vary. For purposes of the New Jersey Family and Medical Leave Law, for example, a court has held that regular hours for which an employee is paid workers' compensation benefits as a result of temporary disability must be counted as "base hours" toward the 1,000-hour New Jersey requirement for determining whether a person is an "employee" under the FMLA.[8]

Finally, an interesting question arises regarding the effect of state workers' compensation "exclusive remedy" provisions and the FMLA. As adverted to in subsection [a], most states provide that the remedies available under the workers' compensation statute are the only remedies available to an employee who suffers a workplace injury. Thus, a Wisconsin court held that a former employee who settled her workers' compensation claim was estopped from arguing that her injury was not work-related, and she therefore lost her FMLA claim under the exclusive remedy provision of the Workers' Compensation Act.[9]

---

8. Kenny v. Meadowview Nursing & Convalescent Ctr., 308 N.J. Super. 565, 706 A.2d 295 (Super. Ct. A.D. 1998).

9. Finnell v. Department of Industry, Labor & Human Relations, 188 Wis. 2d 187, 519 N.W.2d 731 (Wis. Ct. App. 1994).

§ 10.1 Covered Employers and Exceptions to Employee Coverage

To qualify for coverage under the state acts, a worker must be an employee; independent contractors do not qualify. Certain categories of employees, including domestic, agricultural, and casual employees, are widely exempted from coverage under the state acts. Fourteen states (Alabama, Arkansas, Delaware, Georgia, Indiana, Iowa, Nevada, North Carolina, North Dakota, Oklahoma, Rhode Island, Virginia, West Virginia, and Wisconsin) exclude all three categories of workers. Twelve other states (Kentucky, Louisiana, Maine, Mississippi, Missouri, Nebraska, New Mexico, New York, South Dakota, Tennessee, Texas, and Utah) expressly exclude only domestic and agricultural workers. Half of the state workers' compensation acts exempt real estate agents or brokers from their coverage.

Table 10.1-1 shows the coverage of various state workers' compensation acts, including whether public and private employers are covered by a given state law, which categories of workers are exempt from the law, and which employees may elect coverage or opt not to be covered by a state act.

[a] Disqualifying Events and Conduct

In addition to the general exceptions to coverage set out in Table 10.1-1, employees may be disqualified from receiving workers' compensation based on certain events or conduct. Almost every state, for example, dis-

qualifies claimants who deliberately attempt to injure or kill themselves on the job. Similarly, 27 states and the District of Columbia specifically disqualify claimants who are injured in an effort to intentionally injure or kill another. Some conduct-related provisions also deal with the behavior of persons other than the injured employee. For example, many states disallow compensation for employees who are assaulted by third parties for personal, non-employment-related reasons. Nineteen states deny or reduce compensation in certain situations where an injury was caused by the claimant's failure to utilize appropriate safety appliances. Employees who violate rules or regulations, or who are injured as a result of illegal acts, are also barred from receiving compensation in many states. Nearly every state has enacted statutory provisions denying compensation, under certain circumstances, where injury or death is caused by the employee's intoxication from alcohol and/or controlled substances.

A variety of other provisions disqualifying workers on the basis of disfavored conduct have also been enacted in the various states. Even where no specific statutory exception applies, many states have catch-all exceptions for employee misconduct, willful negligence, and the like, which may bar compensation in a given situation. Table 10.1-2 (Parts A, B, and C) covers the events and conduct that disqualify claimants from receiving workers' compensation benefits.

Table 10.1-1　　　　PART 10—STATE WORKERS' COMPENSATION LAWS　　　　10-8

Table 10.1-1
COVERED EMPLOYERS
AND EXCEPTIONS TO EMPLOYEE COVERAGE

(See also text at § 10.1.)

	Is Coverage Compulsory for Employment?			
	Public	**Private**	**Exceptions**	**Other Provisions**	**Citations to Authority**
AL	Yes, applicable to municipalities with populations greater than 2,000, but not to cities with populations of 250,000 or more; also applies to boards of education and public 2-year colleges.	Yes.	Casual workers, domestic and agricultural workers, employers with fewer than 5 employees; licensed real estate agents.	—	Ala. Code §§ 25-5-1, 25-5-13, 25-5-50.
AK	Yes.	Yes.	Part-time babysitters, cleaning persons, harvest help, entertainers and sports officials employed on a contractual basis, commercial fishermen, certain taxi drivers.	Sole proprietors and partners may elect coverage; corporate executives may waive coverage.	Alaska Stat. §§ 23.30.230, 23.30.239, 23.30.240, 23.30.395.
AZ	Yes.	Yes.	Domestic servants, independent contractors if relationship evidenced by a written agreement, licensed real estate agents, motion picture employers when working within the state for 8 months or less.	Employers of domestic servants may elect coverage.	Ariz. Rev. Stat. Ann. §§ 23-902, 23-909, 23-910.
AR	No, except for officers and employees of public schools, county and municipal officials, employees, and volunteer firefighters.	Yes, for all employers of 3 or more workers.	Domestic servants in private homes; gardening, maintenance, or repair workers; agricultural workers; the state and its subdivisions; nonprofit religious or charitable organizations; newspaper sellers; real estate agents.	Sole proprietors or partners may elect coverage.	Ark. Code Ann. §§ 6-17-1401, 11-9-102, 14-26-101.
CA	Yes.	Yes.	Volunteers for nonprofit organizations, recreational camps, and voluntary ski patrolmen; domestic workers who worked fewer than 52 hours or earned less than $100 in the 90 days immediately preceding the injury; student athletes; any person employed by his or her parent, spouse, or child.	Employees not otherwise covered may be covered if employer and employee jointly elect coverage. Sole proprietors and partners are covered.	Cal. Lab. Code §§ 3300, 3351, 3352, 4150.

	Covered	Exclusions/Exceptions	Elections	Statute
CO	Yes.	Part-time domestic servants, part-time repair and maintenance employees, advisors of charitable or religious organizations receiving less than $750 a year, commissioned real estate agents, ski area volunteers, casual laborers who earn no more than $2,000 a year.	Public officials who receive no compensation may be excluded from the act. Corporate officers may reject coverage. Exempt employers may elect coverage.	Colo. Rev. Stat. Ann. §§ 8-40-202, 8-40-203, 8-40-302, 8-41-202.
CT	Yes.	Casual employees, domestic workers regularly employed 26 or fewer hours a week, corporate officers who elect to be excluded from coverage.	Elected or appointed municipal officials may be covered upon vote of the municipal governing body. Corporate officers may opt out. Sole proprietors or business partners may elect coverage.	Conn. Gen. Stat. Ann. § 31-275.
DE	No.	Domestic servants or casual laborers earning less than $750 in any 3-month period from a single household, farm workers, licensed real estate salespersons paid on commission, sole proprietors and partners. Immediate family members of a sole proprietor or partner may be exempt by electing to be exempt in writing.	Exempt employers may elect coverage. State and subdivisions may elect coverage, as may volunteer fire and ambulance companies. Corporate executive officers may opt out of coverage.	Del. Code Ann. tit. 19, §§ 2306–2316.
DC	Yes.	Secretaries, stenographers, or others employed in the office of any member of Congress; licensed real estate agents; independent contractors.	—	D.C. Code Ann. §§ 36-301, 36-303.
FL	Yes, for employers of 4 or more.	Independent contractors, real estate salespersons, musical and theatrical performers, owner-operators of motor vehicles under contract with a motor carrier, casual laborers, volunteers for nonprofit agencies, certain professional horse-training jockeys, taxicab and limousine drivers, agricultural laborers performing work on a farm in the employ of a bona fide farmer, professional athletes.	Sole proprietors and partners who work full time for the business or partnership may elect to be included. Excluded employees may elect coverage. Officers of corporations may opt out.	Fla. Stat. Ann. §§ 440.02, 440.04.

(Table continues.)

Table 10.1-1 (cont'd)
COVERED EMPLOYERS
AND EXCEPTIONS TO EMPLOYEE COVERAGE

(See also text at § 10.1.)

	Is Coverage Compulsory for Employment?		Exceptions	Other Provisions	Citations to Authority
	Public	Private			
GA	Yes.	Yes, for employers with 3 or more employees.	Owner-operators, inmates working through a work release program, farm laborers, domestic servants, licensed real estate agents, independent contractors, common carriers by railroad engaged in interstate commerce.	Employers with fewer than 3 employees, farm employers, owners, and sole proprietors may elect coverage. Corporate officers may elect to be exempt.	Ga. Code Ann. §§ 34-9-1–34-9-5, 34-9-120, 34-9-121.
HI	Yes, for public board members, reserve police officers, volunteer firefighters, and certain other public employees.	Yes.	Real estate salespersons working on commission; volunteers for religious, charitable, or nonprofit organizations; enrolled students who work in return for board, lodging, or tuition; religious personnel in the exercise of their duties; part-time domestic workers who have earned less than $225 per quarter in the last 12 months.	Exempt employers may elect to provide coverage.	Haw. Rev. Stat. Ann. §§ 386-1, 386-4, 386-181.
ID	Yes.	Yes.	Domestic servants, casual employees, partners or sole proprietors, corporate officers owning at least 10% of stock in corporation, pilots of crop dusting planes, real estate salespersons, volunteer ski patrollers, officials at student athletic contests.	Exempt employers may elect to provide coverage.	Idaho Code §§ 72-201–72-213.
IL	Yes.	Yes, for enumerated hazardous businesses.	Real estate brokers, salespersons paid by commission only, employees of certain agricultural businesses.	Sole proprietors and partners in businesses may elect coverage, as may any otherwise exempt employer.	820 Ill. Comp. Stat. Ann. 305/1, 305/3.
IN	Yes.	Yes.	Railroad employees, casual laborers, farm or agricultural employees, domestic servants.	Exempt employers may choose coverage.	Ind. Code Ann. §§ 22-3-2-2, 22-3-2-9, 22-3-7-34.

State			Exceptions to coverage	Elective coverage	Statute
IA	Yes.	Yes.	Domestic and casual workers earning less than $1,500 a year, agricultural workers, regular members of the employer's household, employers with a payroll of less than $2,500 a year.	Corporate officers may waive coverage. Partners and sole proprietors may elect coverage.	Iowa Code Ann. §§ 85.1, 85.1A.
KS	Yes.	Yes.	Agricultural workers, workers for employers whose total gross payroll is less than $20,000 for all employees, firefighters who are members of a firemen's relief association, real estate agents working as independent contractors, volunteers for religious and charitable organizations.	Exempt employers may elect coverage.	Kan. Stat. Ann. §§ 44-505, 44-508.
KY	Yes.	Yes.	Domestic servants who work for an employer with fewer than 2 workers for 40 hours per week, workers employed no more than 20 consecutive weeks to do maintenance and repair around the employer's home, agricultural workers.	Exempt employers may elect coverage.	Ky. Rev. Stat. Ann. §§ 342.630–342.660.
LA	Yes, except for certain officials and sheriff's deputies.	Yes.	Domestic workers and agricultural workers for private, unincorporated farms; crew members of crop dusting planes acting as independent contractors; real estate salespersons; certain landmen; musicians and performers rendering services pursuant to a performance contract; uncompensated officers and board members of nonprofit, religious, and charitable institutions.	Officers of corporations and members of limited liability companies who own at least 10% of the stock or interest therein, partners, and sole proprietors may elect not to be covered. Exempt employees may elect coverage.	La. Rev. Stat. Ann. §§ 23:1034, 23:1035, 23:1035.1, 23:1045–23:1047, 23:1048.
ME	Yes.	Yes.	Domestic, aquacultural, and agricultural workers; certain wood harvesters; real estate brokers, salespersons paid by commission. Exemption for agricultural and aquacultural employees requires, among other things, that employers maintain medical payment coverage of $25,000.	Exempt employers may elect coverage. Sole proprietors and partners may elect coverage.	Me. Rev. Stat. Ann. tit. 39-A, § 102.

(Table continues.)

Table 10.1-1 PART 10—STATE WORKERS' COMPENSATION LAWS 10-12

Table 10.1-1 *(cont'd)*
COVERED EMPLOYERS
AND EXCEPTIONS TO EMPLOYEE COVERAGE

(See also text at § 10.1.)

	Is Coverage Compulsory for Employment?		Exceptions	Other Provisions	Citations to Authority
	Public	Private			
MD	Yes.	Yes.	Casual employees, a person performing maintenance who works no more than 30 consecutive workdays (1) at the private home of the employer or (2) for an employer with no other covered employee, domestic servants earning less than $750 in a quarter from a given household, real estate salespersons, certain tractor owner-operators.	Individuals not covered, including partners in a partnership and sole proprietors, can elect coverage. Corporate or limited liability company officers owning 20% of the corporation or company may elect to be excluded from coverage under certain circumstances.	Md. Code Ann., Lab. & Empl. §§ 9-201, 9-204–9-223, 9-227, 9-402–9-404.
MA	Yes. Commonwealth, counties, cities, and districts having the power to tax may elect coverage.	Yes.	Masters and seamen on vessels engaged in interstate or foreign commerce, professional athletes whose contracts provide for payment during disability, real estate salespersons receiving commissions only, direct salespersons of consumer products, taxi operators, employees not in the usual course of the employer's business.	Coverage is elective for employers of seasonal, casual, or part-time domestic servants.	Mass. Gen. Laws Ann. ch. 152, §§ 1, 25A, 69.
MI	Yes.	Yes, for all private employers with 3 or more employees, or all private employers who have employed fewer than 3 workers for 35 or more hours per week for 13 weeks or longer in the last year.	Domestics who worked fewer than 35 hours per week for 13 weeks or longer during the preceding year; real estate salespersons and brokers 75% of whose compensation is related to sales and who have written agreement that they are not employees.	Exempted employers may voluntarily assume coverage.	Mich. Comp. Laws Ann. §§ 418:111, 418:115, 418:118, 418:119, 418:121, 418:151, 418:611; Mich. Stat. Ann. §§ 17.237(111), 17.237(115), 17.237(118), 17.237(119), 17.237(121), 17.237(151), 17.237(611).

State		Exclusions	Election	Statutory References
MN	Yes.	Railroad workers; persons employed on family farms; sole proprietors; executive officers of closely held corporations having fewer than 22,800 hours of payroll in the preceding calendar year, if the individual owns at least 25% of the corporation's stock; casual employees; independent contractors; domestic workers earning less than $1,000 in cash in 3-month period from a single household.	Certain exempt workers may elect coverage.	Minn. Stat. Ann. §§ 176.021, 176.041, 176.051.
MS	Yes.	Nonprofit charitable, fraternal, cultural, or religious entities; domestic servants; farmers and farm labor except for commercial farming; independent contractors; newspaper vendors.	Exempt employers may elect coverage. Sole proprietors, partners in partnerships, and employees owning 15% or more of stock in a corporation may also elect to be exempt.	Miss. Code Ann. §§ 71-3-3, 71-3-5.
MO	Yes, for employers of 5 or more workers. Construction employers are covered with only 1 worker. *Note:* A worker who is a member of the employer's family within the 3rd degree of affinity or consanguinity is counted in determining the total number of employees of such employer.	Farm labor, domestic servants, occasional labor for a private household, real estate agents and direct sellers, inmates or patients, volunteers of tax-exempt organizations who are unpaid, referees or other sports officials not otherwise employed by the sponsoring school.	Partners, sole proprietors, and other exempt employers may elect coverage.	Mo. Rev. Stat. §§ 287.030, 287.035, 287.090.
MT	Yes.	Domestic workers, casual employment, dependent family members, sole proprietors and partners, real estate agents, employees covered by federal law, direct sellers, railroad workers, officials at amateur school sports events, direct sellers, newspaper delivery persons and freelance correspondents, cosmetologists, independent contractors.	Exempt employers may elect coverage. Sole proprietors and partners who operate as independent contractors are covered by the statute, but may apply for an exemption.	Mont. Code Ann. §§ 39-71-117, 39-71-118, 39-71-120, 39-71-401.
NE	Yes.	Domestic workers, agricultural laborers.	Employers of exempt employees, sole proprietors, and partners may elect coverage. Executive officers owning 25% or more of stock in a corporation may waive coverage.	Neb. Rev. Stat. §§ 48-106, 48-115.

(Table continues.)

Table 10.1-1   PART 10—STATE WORKERS' COMPENSATION LAWS   10-14

Table 10.1-1 *(cont'd)*

COVERED EMPLOYERS
AND EXCEPTIONS TO EMPLOYEE COVERAGE

(See also text at § 10.1.)

	Is Coverage Compulsory for Employment?		Exceptions	Other Provisions	Citations to Authority
	Public	Private			
NV	Yes.	Yes.	Casual employees, theatrical and stage employees and certain musicians, domestic workers and farm labor, voluntary ski patrol persons, clergy, licensed real estate brokers.	Employers of excluded workers may elect coverage. Real estate salespersons may elect coverage.	Nev. Rev. Stat. Ann. §§ 616A.110, 616A.220, 616B.656.
NH	Yes.	Yes.	Railroad employees covered by federal law, direct sellers, real estate brokers and agents.	Employers not subject to the law, including sole proprietors and partners, may elect coverage.	N.H. Rev. Stat. Ann. §§ 281-A:2, 281-A:3.
NJ	Yes.	Yes.	Longshoremen protected by federal law, casual workers.	—	N.J. Stat. Ann. §§ 34:15-7, 34:15-9, 34:15-36, 34:15-43, 34:15-70 *et seq.*
NM	Yes.	Yes, for all employers of 3 or more workers.	Domestic servants, agricultural workers, real estate salespersons.	Exempt employers may elect coverage under the act. Executive officers owning 10% or more of a business and sole proprietors may elect not to be covered.	N.M. Stat. Ann. §§ 52-1-3, 52-1-3.1, 52-1-6, 52-1-7, 52-1-15, 52-1-16.
NY	Yes, if worker is employed by state, or if worker is employed by municipal corporation or subdivision of the state and is engaged in an enumerated hazardous operation.	Yes.	Domestic servants; certain corporate executives owning all outstanding stock in the corporation; sole proprietors; partners; agricultural workers; babysitters; licensed real estate brokers; certain volunteers; teachers or nonmanual workers for educational, charitable, or religious institutions.	Exempt employers, sole proprietors, and partners may elect coverage.	N.Y. Work. Comp. Law §§ 2, 3.
NC	Yes.	Yes, for employers of 3 or more workers and employers whose work involves the use of radiation.	Agricultural workers (unless 10 or more full-time nonseasonal workers are regularly employed), certain sawmill and logging operators, domestic workers, casual employees, volunteer ski patrol persons.	Corporate executives may opt out of coverage. Sole proprietors and partners may elect to be covered by the statute.	N.C. Gen. Stat. § 97-2.

			Exceptions / Exclusions	Elections	Citation
ND	Yes.	Yes, for all hazardous employment.	Independent contractors, casual employees, real estate brokers, directors of business corporations not actually employed by corporation, newspaper delivery persons, agricultural workers, domestic workers, railroad workers covered by federal law, clergy or employees of religious organizations, spouses or children of the employer dwelling in the employer's household.	Employers not covered by the act may voluntarily secure coverage.	N.D. Cent. Code §§ 65-01-02, 65-04-01 *et seq.*, 65-07-01.
OH	Yes.	Yes.	Household and casual workers who have earned less than $160 in a calendar quarter from a single employer, duly ordained ministers, officers of family farm corporations. Police and firefighters eligible to participate in pension funds established by municipalities are not covered.	Exempt employers may elect coverage, as may sole proprietors and partners.	Ohio Rev. Code Ann. §§ 4123.01, 4123.02.
OK	Yes.	Yes.	Domestic servants and casual workers if employer has payroll less than $10,000 per year, workers covered by federal law, agricultural workers for employer with gross annual payroll less than $100,000, licensed real estate salespersons, employers with 5 or fewer employees all related by blood or marriage to employer.	Sole proprietors, partners, and stockholder-employees holding at least 10% ownership in corporation may opt for coverage.	Okla. Stat. Ann. tit. 85, §§ 2.1, 2.6, 2b, 3.
OR	Yes.	Yes.	Domestic servants in private homes, gardeners and maintenance persons around private homes, casual employees, railroad workers in interstate commerce, workers of a city having a population greater than 200,000 that has established an equivalent system of compensation, corporate officers who are also directors and who have a substantial ownership interest in the corporation, sole proprietors, partners not engaged in providing construction services, newspaper carriers, certain amateur athletes, volunteer ski patrol persons, golf caddies, real estate salespersons.	Employers of exempt workers may elect coverage, as may sole proprietors and partners. Statute specifically excludes one who has withdrawn from the workforce during the period for which benefits are sought.	Or. Rev. Stat. §§ 656.005, 656.027, 656.037, 656.039, 656.128.

(Table continues.)

Table 10.1-1 (cont'd)

COVERED EMPLOYERS
AND EXCEPTIONS TO EMPLOYEE COVERAGE

(See also text at § 10.1.)

	Is Coverage Compulsory for Employment?		Exceptions	Other Provisions	Citations to Authority
	Public	Private			
PA	Yes, except elected state officials.	Yes.	Casual workers, domestic workers, licensed real estate and insurance salespersons.	Executives of corporations, including nonprofit corporations, who serve without pay may opt out of coverage. Employers of domestic workers may elect coverage.	Pa. Stat. Ann. tit. 77, §§ 21, 22, 676.
RI	Yes, for state employment and for the city of Providence; elective for other public employment.	Yes, for all employers of 4 or more workers.	Agricultural and domestic workers, casual employees, real estate agents.	Exempt employers may elect coverage.	R.I. Gen. Laws §§ 28-29-5, 28-29-6, 28-29-7–28-29-7.2, 28-29-8, 28-31-1, 28-31-1.1.
SC	Yes, except for elected and appointed officials.	Yes, for employers of 4 or more workers regularly employed. Employers with total annual payrolls of less than $300,000 are exempt.	Railroad workers, casual employees, workers for state and county fair associations, agricultural workers, sellers of agricultural products, licensed real estate salespersons.	Sole proprietors and partners may elect coverage. Agricultural employers also may elect coverage.	S.C. Code Ann. §§ 42-1-130, 42-1-150, 42-1-350–42-1-375.
SD	Yes, for state and political subdivisions, and municipalities, but not for elected or appointed county, municipal, or school district officials unless those entities elect to be covered.	Yes.	Domestic servants, including babysitters, who work fewer than 20 hours in a calendar week and fewer than 6 weeks in a 13-week period; agricultural workers; workfare participants; employees covered by federal compensation laws.	Executive officers of nonprofit charitable, religious, or educational corporations may be covered by election.	S.D. Codified Laws §§ 62-1-2, 62-1-3, 62-1-8, 62-3-4, 62-3-15.
TN	No, but coverage is elective.	Yes, for employers of 5 or more workers and all employers engaged in the mining of coal.	Domestic servants, casual workers, agricultural workers, common carriers involved in interstate business, volunteer ski patrol persons.	Sole proprietors and partners who devote full time to the proprietorship or partnership, and employers of fewer than 5 workers, may elect coverage.	Tenn. Code Ann. §§ 50-6-102, 50-6-106.
TX	Yes, for state employees.	No, elective.	Domestic and casual workers engaged in employment incidental to a personal residence, employees covered by federal compensation laws, farm or ranch employees.	Exempted employers may elect coverage.	Tex. Lab. Code Ann. §§ 406.002, 406.091, 406.126, 501.001 et seq.

State			Exceptions	Elective Coverage	Citation
UT	Yes.	Yes.	Agricultural workers who are related to the owner of the farm, or who work for a farm with 5 or fewer full-time employees for 13 weeks or less during the year; domestic workers who are employed fewer than 40 hours a week for any one employer; real estate salespersons.	Partners and sole proprietors may elect coverage. Corporate directors and officers may opt out of coverage.	Utah Code Ann. §§ 34A-2-103, 34A-2-104.
VT	Yes.	Yes.	Casual employees, amateur athletes, agricultural workers for employer whose annual payroll is less than $2,000 a year, workers in connection with a private dwelling, sole proprietors, partners, real estate salespeople.	Agricultural employees, sole proprietors, and partners may elect coverage.	Vt. Stat. Ann. tit. 21, §§ 601, 616.
VA	Yes, except for elected or appointed commonwealth officers.	Yes, for employers of 3 or more workers and for all coal mine operators.	Railroad workers; casual employees; agricultural workers (unless employer regularly employs 2 or more workers); domestic workers; licensed real estate agents; taxi drivers; sports officials performing services for an entity sponsoring an interscholastic, intercollegiate, or charitable athletic contest.	Exempt employers may elect coverage. Sole proprietors and partners may elect coverage.	Va. Code Ann. § 65.2-101.
WA	Yes.	Yes.	Domestic workers for a home with fewer than 2 employees regularly employed, workers who perform gardening or maintenance around a private home, sole proprietors and partners, jockeys, corporate officers who are also directors and shareholders, musicians or entertainers employed on casual basis, newspaper carriers, insurance agents.	Exempt employers may elect coverage.	Wash. Rev. Code Ann. §§ 51.12.010, 51.12.020, 51.12.110.
WV	Yes.	Yes.	Domestic workers, agricultural workers of employers employing 5 or fewer full-time workers, casual employees, employees of churches, workers for organized professional sports activities, municipal volunteers.	Sole proprietors and partners may opt out of coverage.	W. Va. Code §§ 23-2-1–23-2-1d.

(Table continues.)

Table 10.1-1 *(cont'd)*
COVERED EMPLOYERS
AND EXCEPTIONS TO EMPLOYEE COVERAGE

(See also text at § 10.1.)

	Is Coverage Compulsory for Employment?				
	Public	*Private*	*Exceptions*	*Other Provisions*	*Citations to Authority*
WI	Yes.	Yes, for employers of 3 or more workers, and those with fewer who have paid wages of $500 or more in every calendar quarter for services performed in the state.	Certain farm workers, domestic servants, casual employees.	Exempt employers may elect coverage.	Wis. Stat. Ann. §§ 102.04, 102.05, 102.07.
WY	Yes, for extra-hazardous employers as enumerated in statute.	Yes, for extra-hazardous employers as enumerated in statute.	Casual laborers, sole proprietors or partners, officers of corporations, independent contractors, professional athletes, federal employees, employees of private households, volunteers, elected officials except for sheriffs.	Exempt employers may elect coverage.	Wyo. Stat. Ann. §§ 27-14-102, 27-14-108.

Table 10.1-2 Part A

DISQUALIFYING EVENTS OR CONDUCT

(See also text at § 10.1.)

	Injury/Death Purposely Self-inflicted	Intent to Cause Injury/Death of Another	Assault, Physical Altercations	Willful Negligence, Reckless Indifference, or Wilful Self-Exposure	Horseplay	Citations to Authority
AL	Yes.	Yes.	No specific statutory provision.	Yes, for willful negligence.	No specific statutory provision.	Ala. Code §§ 25-5-32, 25-5-51.
AK	Compensation is not permitted for injuries proximately caused by the employee's willful intent to kill any person, which would presumably include purposely self-inflicted injuries.	Yes.	Injuries caused by the willful act of a third party directed against an employee because of the employment are compensable.	No specific statutory provision.	No specific statutory provision.	Alaska Stat. §§ 23.30.235, 23.30.395.
AZ	Yes.	No specific statutory provision.	Injuries caused by the willful act of a third party directed against an employee because of the employment are compensable.	No compensation is permitted for occupational disease due to willful self-exposure. Willful self-exposure includes failure of an employee or applicant to indicate truthfully in writing in answer to an inquiry made by the employer (1) the place, duration, and nature of previous employment; (2) whether or not the employee or applicant had previously been disabled, laid off, or compensated due to a physical disability; and (3) full information about the previous status of the employee's health, previous medical and hospital attention, and direct and continuous exposure to active pulmonary tuberculosis.	No specific statutory provision.	Ariz. Rev. Stat. §§ 23-901, 23-901.04, 23-1021.

(Table continues.)

Table 10.1-2 Part A *(cont'd)*

DISQUALIFYING EVENTS OR CONDUCT

(See also text at § 10.1.)

	Injury/Death Purposely Self-inflicted	Intent to Cause Injury/Death of Another	Assault, Physical Altercations	Willful Negligence, Reckless Indifference, or Wilful Self-Exposure	Horseplay	Citations to Authority
AR	Yes.	No specific statutory provision.	Injuries to active participants in assaults or combats which are the result of non-employment-related animus, and which amount to a deviation from customary duties, are not compensable.	No specific statutory provision.	Injuries caused by horseplay are not compensable, except with regard to innocent victims.	Ark. Code Ann. §§ 11-9-102, 11-9-401.
CA	Yes.	No specific statutory provision.	No compensation permitted for injuries due to an altercation in which the injured employee was the initial physical aggressor.	No specific statutory provision.	No specific statutory provision.	Cal. Labor Code § 3600.
CO	Yes.	To be compensable, an injurious event must occur "without the will or design of the person whose mere act causes it."	No specific statutory provision, but see entry in third column.	No specific statutory provision.	No specific statutory provision.	Colo. Rev. Stat. §§ 8-40-201, 8-41-301.
CT	No specific statutory provision, but compensable injuries must be accidental.	No specific statutory provision.	No specific statutory provision.	No specific statutory provision.	No specific statutory provision.	Conn. Gen. Stat. Ann. § 31-275.
DE	Yes.	Yes.	Injury is not compensable if caused by the willful act of another employee directed against the employee for personal reasons and not as an employee or because of the employee's employment.	Yes, for deliberate and reckless indifference to danger.	No specific statutory provision.	Del. Code Ann. tit. 19, §§ 2301, 2353.
DC	Yes, where injury is occasioned solely thereby.	Yes, where injury is occasioned solely thereby.	No specific statutory provision.	No specific statutory provision.	No specific statutory provision.	D.C. Code Ann. § 32-1503.
FL	Yes.	Yes.	No specific statutory provision.	No specific statutory provision.	No specific statutory provision.	Fla. Stat. Ann. § 440.09.

State						Citation
GA	Yes.	Yes.	Injuries caused by the willful act of a third person directed at the employee for personal reasons are not compensable.	No specific statutory provision.	No specific statutory provision.	Ga. Code Ann. §§ 34-9-1, 34-9-17.
HI	Yes.	Yes.	No compensation is allowed for an injury due to the employee's engaging in an unprovoked non-work-related physical altercation, except in self defense. Injuries due to the willful act of a third person directed against an employee because of the employee's employment are compensable.	No specific statutory provision.	No specific statutory provision.	Haw. Rev. Stat. § 386-3.
ID	Yes.	Yes.	No specific statutory provision.	No specific statutory provision.	No specific statutory provision.	Idaho Code § 72-208.
IL	No specific statutory provision.	No specific statutory provision.	No specific statutory provision.	No specific statutory provision.	No specific statutory provision.	—
IN	Yes.	No specific statutory provision.	No specific statutory provision.	No specific statutory provision.	No specific statutory provision.	Ind. Code Ann. §§ 22-3-2-8, 22-3-7-21.
IA	Yes.	Yes.	No compensation for injury caused by the willful act of a third party directed against the employee for personal reasons.	No specific statutory provision.	No specific statutory provision.	Iowa Code Ann. § 85.16.
KS	Yes.	No specific statutory provision.	No specific statutory provision.	No specific statutory provision.	No specific statutory provision.	Kan. Stat. Ann. § 44-501.
KY	Yes.	Yes.	No specific statutory provision.	No specific statutory provision.	No specific statutory provision.	Ky. Rev. Stat. Ann. § 342.610.
LA	Yes.	Yes.	No compensation for the initial physical aggressor in an unprovoked physical altercation, unless excessive force was used in retaliation against the initial aggressor.	No specific statutory provision.	No specific statutory provision.	La. Rev. Stat. Ann. § 23:1081.
ME	Yes.	Yes.	No specific statutory provision.	No specific statutory provision.	No specific statutory provision.	Me. Rev. Stat. Ann. tit. 39-A, § 202.
MD	Yes.	Yes.	Injuries are compensable if caused by a willful or negligent act of a third person directed against a covered employee in the course of the employee's employment.	No specific statutory provision.	No specific statutory provision.	Md. Code Ann. Lab. & Empl. §§ 9-101, 9-506.

(Table continues.)

Table 10.1-2 Part A   PART 10—STATE WORKERS' COMPENSATION LAWS   10-22

Table 10.1-2 Part A *(cont'd)*

DISQUALIFYING EVENTS OR CONDUCT

(See also text at § 10.1.)

	Injury/Death Purposely Self-inflicted	Intent to Cause Injury/Death of Another	Assault, Physical Altercations	Willful Negligence, Reckless Indifference, or Willful Self-Exposure	Horseplay	Citations to Authority
MA	Dependents may recover for death by suicide of the employee, if it is shown by the weight of the evidence that, due to injury, the employee was of such unsoundness of mind as to make him or her irresponsible for his or her act of suicide.	No specific statutory provision.	No specific statutory provision.	No specific statutory provision.	No specific statutory provision.	Mass. Gen. Laws Ann. ch. 152, § 26A.
MI	No specific statutory provision.	No specific statutory provision.	No specific statutory provision.	No specific statutory provision.	No specific statutory provision.	—
MN	Yes.	No specific statutory provision.	Injuries caused by the act of a third person or fellow employee intended to injure the employee due to personal reasons, and not directed against the employee as an employee or because of the employment, are not compensable.	Willful negligence of the injured employee is a defense in a court action, which may be brought where the employer fails to insure or self-insure against liability for injured employees and dependents.	No specific statutory provision.	Minn. Stat. Ann. §§ 176.011, 176.021, 176.031.
MS	Yes.	Yes.	Injuries caused by the willful act of a third person directed at an employee because of his employment while so employed and working on the job are compensable.	No specific statutory provision.	No specific statutory provision.	Miss. Code Ann. §§ 71-3-3, 71-3-7.
MO	Yes.	No specific statutory provision.	Compensation is payable for injury or death of an employee due to unprovoked violence or assault against the employee by any person.	No specific statutory provision.	No specific statutory provision.	Mo. Rev. Stat. § 287.120.

MT	No specific statutory provision.	No specific statutory provision.	Injury caused by the deliberate act of a fellow employee or employer, specifically and actually intended to cause injury to the employee, is compensable.	No specific statutory provision.	No specific statutory provision.	Mont. Code Ann. § 39-71-413.
NE	No specific statutory provision. However, no compensation is permitted where injury is caused by willful negligence, which includes a "deliberate act."	No specific statutory provision.	No specific statutory provision.	Yes, for willful negligence, which consists of a deliberate act, such conduct as evidences reckless indifference to safety, or intoxication at the time of the accident.	No specific statutory provision.	Neb. Rev. Stat. §§ 48-102, 48-110, 48-127, 48-151.
NV	Yes.	Yes.	No specific statutory provision.	No compensation for occupational disease due wholly or in part to willful self-exposure.	No specific statutory provision.	Nev. Rev. Stat. §§ 616C.230, 617.400.
NH	Yes.	Yes.	No specific statutory provision.	No specific statutory provision.	No specific statutory provision.	N.H. Rev. Stat. Ann. § 281-A:2.
NJ	No specific statutory provision. However, no compensation is permitted for an injury due to willful negligence, including a deliberate act or deliberate failure to act.	No specific statutory provision.	No specific statutory provision.	Yes, for willful negligence. Willful negligence consists of (1) a deliberate act or deliberate failure to act, (2) such conduct as evidences reckless indifference to safety, (3) intoxication, operating as the proximate cause of injury, or (4) unlawful use of a controlled dangerous substance. No compensation is permitted for workers with occupational diseases due to willful self-exposure to a known hazard.	An injury is compensable if it results from horseplay or skylarking on the part of a fellow employee, if the horseplay or skylarking was not instigated or taken part in by the injured employee.	N.J. Stat. Ann. §§ 34:15-1, 34:15-7.1, 34:15-30, 34:15-36.
NM	Yes.	Yes.	No specific statutory provision.	Yes, for willful negligence or willful self-exposure. Willful self-exposure includes certain misrepresentations or omissions regarding past employment, disability, layoffs, or compensation due to disability, previous health status or medical and hospital attention, and exposure to active pulmonary tuberculosis.	No specific statutory provision.	N.M. Stat. Ann. §§ 52-1-11, 52-3-7, 52-3-8, 52-3-45.
NY	Yes.	Yes.	No specific statutory provision.	No specific statutory provision.	No specific statutory provision.	N.Y. Work. Comp. Law § 10.
NC	Yes.	Yes.	No specific statutory provision.	No specific statutory provision.	No specific statutory provision.	N.C. Gen. Stat. § 97-12.

(Table continues.)

Table 10.1-2 Part A   PART 10—STATE WORKERS' COMPENSATION LAWS   10-24

Table 10.1-2 Part A *(cont'd)*

DISQUALIFYING EVENTS OR CONDUCT

(See also text at § 10.1.)

	Injury/Death Purposely Self-inflicted	Intent to Cause Injury/Death of Another	Assault, Physical Altercations	Willful Negligence, Reckless Indifference, or Willful Self-Exposure	Horseplay	Citations to Authority
ND	Yes.	Yes.	An injury that arises out of an altercation in which the injured employee is an aggressor is not compensable, except for public safety employees, including law enforcement officers or private security personnel who are required to engage in altercations as part of their job duties. An injury caused by the willful act of a third person directed against an employee because of the employee's employment is compensable.	No specific statutory provision.	No specific statutory provision.	N.D. Cent. Code § 65-01-02.
OH	Yes.	No specific statutory provision.	No specific statutory provision.	No specific statutory provision.	No specific statutory provision.	Ohio Rev. Code Ann. §§ 4123.46, 4123.54.
OK	Yes.	Yes.	No specific statutory provision.	No specific statutory provision.	Except for innocent victims, no compensation is allowed for injuries due to prank, horseplay, or similar willful or intentional behavior.	Okla. Stat. tit. 85, § 11.
OR	Yes.	Yes.	Injuries to any active participant in assaults or combats that are not connected to the job assignment, and that amount to a deviation from customary duties, are not compensable.	No specific statutory provision.	No specific statutory provision.	Or. Rev. Stat. §§ 656.005, 656.156.

State					Citation
PA	Yes.	No specific statutory provision.	No compensation for an injury caused by an act of a third person intended to injure the employee for personal reasons, and not directed against him or her as an employee or because of his or her employment.	Yes, for injury caused by an employee's reckless indifference to danger.	77 Pa. Const. Stat. §§ 201, 301.
RI	Yes.	Yes.	No specific statutory provision.	No specific statutory provision.	R.I. Gen. Laws § 28-33-2.
SC	Yes.	Yes.	No specific statutory provision.	No specific statutory provision.	S.C. Code Ann. §§ 42-9-60, 42-11-100
SD	Yes.	No specific statutory provision.	No specific statutory provision.	No compensation for occupational disease due to willful self-exposure. Willful self-exposure is conclusively presumed where one fails to respond truthfully in writing to an employer's inquiry regarding the place, duration and nature of previous employment; previous disability, layoff, or compensation due to any physical disability; or previous health status, medical or hospital attention, or exposure to tuberculosis.	S.D. Cod. Laws Ann. §§ 62-4-37, 62-8-22, 62-8-23.
TN	Yes.	No specific statutory provision.	No specific statutory provision.	No specific statutory provision.	Tenn. Code Ann. § 50-6-110.
TX	Yes.	Yes, for willful intent to unlawfully injure another person.	Injury is not compensable if it arose out of an act of a third person, was intended to injure the employee for personal reasons, and was not directed at the employee as an employee or because of the employment.	Yes, if the employee's horseplay was a producing cause of the injury.	Tex. Lab. Code Ann. § 406.032.
UT	Yes.	No specific statutory provision.	An injury is compensable if caused by the willful act of a third person directed against an employee because of the employee's employment.	No specific statutory provision.	Utah Code Ann. §§ 34A-2-102, 34A-2-401.
VT	Yes.	Yes.	No specific statutory provision.	No specific statutory provision.	Vt. Stat. Ann. tit. 21, § 649.
VA	Yes.	Yes.	No specific statutory provision.	No specific statutory provision.	Va. Code Ann. § 65.2-306.

(Table continues.)

Table 10.1-2 Part A *(cont'd)*

DISQUALIFYING EVENTS OR CONDUCT

(See also text at § 10.1.)

	Injury/Death Purposely Self-inflicted	Intent to Cause Injury/Death of Another	Assault, Physical Altercations	Willful Negligence, Reckless Indifference, or Willful Self-Exposure	Horseplay	Citations to Authority
WA	Yes.	No specific statutory provision.	If injury or death to a worker results from the deliberate intention of a beneficiary of that worker to produce the injury or death, or as a consequence of a beneficiary of that worker engaging in the attempt to commit, or the commission of, a felony, the beneficiary shall not receive any payment under this title.	No specific statutory provision.	No specific statutory provision.	Wash. Rev. Code Ann. § 51.32.020.
WV	Yes.	No specific statutory provision.	No specific statutory provision.	No specific statutory provision.	No specific statutory provision.	W. Va. Code § 23-4-2.
WI	Yes.	No specific statutory provision.	No specific statutory provision.	No specific statutory provision.	No specific statutory provision.	Wis. Stat. Ann. § 102.03.
WY	Yes.	Yes.	No specific statutory provision.	Yes, for injury due solely to the culpable negligence of the injured employee.	No specific statutory provision.	Wyo. Stat. Ann. § 27-14-102.

Table 10.1-2 Part B

DISQUALIFYING EVENTS OR CONDUCT

(See also text at § 10.1.)

	Failure to Use Safety Appliance	Illegal Acts	Violation of Rule or Regulation	Willful Misconduct	Other	Citations to Authority
AL	Yes, for willful failure or willful refusal to use safety appliances provided by the employer.	No specific statutory provision.	No specific statutory provision.	Yes.	No compensation is allowed where the employee knowingly and falsely misrepresented his or her physical or mental condition in writing, if the condition is aggravated or reinjured in the course of employment. Employer must provide written notice that misrepresentations regarding preexisting physical or mental conditions may void workers' compensation benefits.	Ala. Code §§ 25-5-32, 25-5-51.
AK	No specific statutory provision.	No specific statutory provision.	No specific statutory provision.	No specific statutory provision.	Employee who knowingly makes a false statement in writing as to his or her physical condition, in response to a medical inquiry or in a medical examination, after a conditional offer of employment may not receive benefits if (1) the employer relied on the false representation and such reliance was a substantial factor in the hiring and (2) there was a causal connection between the false representation and the employee's injury.	Alaska Stat. § 23.30.022.
AZ	No specific statutory provision.	No specific statutory provision.	Yes. No compensation for occupational disease caused by disobedience of a reasonable rule or regulation adopted by the employer, if it has been and is kept posted in conspicuous places in and about the premises of the employer, or otherwise brought to the attention of the employee.	Yes, for occupational disease.	—	Ariz. Rev. Stat. § 23-901.04.

(Table continues.)

Table 10.1-2 Part B *(cont'd)*

DISQUALIFYING EVENTS OR CONDUCT

(See also text at § 10.1.)

	Failure to Use Safety Appliance	Illegal Acts	Violation of Rule or Regulation	Willful Misconduct	Other	Citations to Authority
AR	No specific statutory provision.	No specific statutory provision.	No specific statutory provision.	No specific statutory provision.	Compensation is not payable for an occupational disease if the employee, at the time of entering into employment, falsely represented himself or herself in writing as not having previously been disabled, laid off, or compensated, in damages or otherwise, because of the disease.	Ark. Code Ann. § 11-9-601.
CA	No specific statutory provision.	An injured employee may not be compensated for injuries caused by the employee's commission of a felony or certain misdemeanors.	No specific statutory provision.	Where the injury is caused by serious and willful misconduct of the employee, the compensation will be reduced by one-half, except where the injury results in death, or permanent disability of 70% or over, or where the injured employee is under 16 at the time of injury. The reduction also does not apply to an injury caused by an employer's failure to comply with a provision of law or safety order of the Division of Occupational Safety and Health, with reference to the safety of places of employment.	—	Cal. Labor Code §§ 3600, 4551.

						Citation
CO	No specific statutory provision.	Compensation is reduced by 50% if the employee willfully fails to use safety devices provided by the employer.	No specific statutory provision.	Compensation is reduced by 50% if the injury results from the employee's willful failure to obey any reasonable rule adopted by the employer for the safety of the employee.	No specific statutory provision.	Where an employee willfully misleads an employer concerning his or her physical ability to perform the job, and is subsequently injured on the job as a result of the physical ability about which the employee willfully misled the employer, a 50% reduction applies.
CT	No specific statutory provision.	No specific statutory provision.	No specific statutory provision.	No specific statutory provision.	No specific statutory provision.	—
DE	Yes, for willful failure or refusal to use a reasonable safety appliance provided for the employee.	No specific statutory provision.	No compensation where injury is due to the employee's willful failure or refusal to perform a duty required by statute.	No specific statutory provision.	No compensation where an injured employee refuses employment suitable to the employee's capacity, unless such refusal is found to be justifiable.	Del. Code Ann. tit. 19, § 2353.
DC	No specific statutory provision.	No specific statutory provision.	No specific statutory provision.	No specific statutory provision.	No specific statutory provision.	—
FL	Compensation is reduced by 25% where injury is caused by employee's knowing refusal to use a safety appliance required by law or provided by the employer.	No specific statutory provision.	Compensation is reduced by 25% where injury is caused by employee's knowing refusal to observe a safety rule required by statute and brought to the employee's knowledge prior to the accident. No compensation is allowed where an employee knowingly or intentionally makes a false statement or otherwise commits insurance fraud for the purpose of securing workers' compensation benefits.	Compensation is reduced by 25% where injury is caused by employee's knowing refusal to observe a safety rule required by statute or regulation and brought to the employee's knowledge prior to the accident.	Employees injured deviating from the course of employment, including leaving the premises, are ineligible for benefits unless the deviation or act is expressly approved by the employer or is in response to an emergency and designed to save life or property. Compensation is also barred if it is determined that the employee knowingly or intentionally makes a false statement or otherwise commits insurance fraud for the purpose of securing workers' compensation benefits.	Fla. Stat. Ann. §§ 440.09, 440.092, 440.105.
GA	Yes, for willful failure or refusal to use a safety appliance.	No specific statutory provision. However, willful failure or refusal to perform a duty required by statute is a disqualifying factor.	Yes.	No specific statutory provision.	—	Ga. Code Ann. § 34-9-17.

(Table continues.)

Table 10.1-2 Part B   PART 10—STATE WORKERS' COMPENSATION LAWS   10-30

Table 10.1-2 Part B *(cont'd)*

DISQUALIFYING EVENTS OR CONDUCT

(See also text at § 10.1.)

	Failure to Use Safety Appliance	Illegal Acts	Violation of Rule or Regulation	Willful Misconduct	Other	Citations to Authority
HI	No specific statutory provision.	No specific statutory provision.	No specific statutory provision.	No specific statutory provision.	No specific statutory provision.	—
ID	No specific statutory provision.	No specific statutory provision.	No specific statutory provision.	No specific statutory provision.	The commission may order the suspension or reduction of compensation of an injured employee who persists in unsanitary or unreasonable practices that tend to imperil or retard recovery. No compensation is allowed for occupational disease if the employee falsely represented himself or herself to the employer in writing as not having previously been disabled, laid off, or compensated because of such disease.	Idaho Code §§ 72-435, 72-441, 72-1366.
IL	No specific statutory provision.	No specific statutory provision.	No specific statutory provision.	No specific statutory provision.	An employee who persists in unsanitary or injurious practices that tend to imperil or retard his or her recovery may be subject to reduction or suspension of compensation.	820 Ill. Comp. Stat. Ann. 305/19.
IN	Yes.	Yes.	Yes, for knowing failure to obey a reasonable written or printed rule of the employer which has been posted in a conspicuous position in the place of work.	No specific statutory provision.	—	Ind. Code Ann. §§ 22-3-2-8, 22-3-7-21.
IA	No specific statutory provision.	No specific statutory provision.	No specific statutory provision.	No specific statutory provision.	No specific statutory provision.	—

State					
KS	Yes, for failure to use a guard or protection against accident required by statute and provided for the employee, or a reasonable and proper guard or protection voluntarily furnished to the employee by the employer.	No specific statutory provision.	No specific statutory provision.	No compensation for occupational disease if the employee fraudulently represented to the employer in writing that the employee had not previously been disabled, laid off, or compensated because of such disease.	Kan. Stat. Ann. §§ 44-501, 44-503.
KY	Compensation is reduced by 15% if an accident is caused in any degree by the intentional failure of the employee to use any safety appliance furnished by the employer.	No specific statutory provision.	Compensation is reduced by 15% if an accident is caused in any degree by the intentional failure of the employee to obey a lawful and reasonable order or administrative regulation of the commissioner, or the employer, intended for the safety of employees or the public.	Compensation is not payable if the employee knowingly, willfully, and falsely represented to his or her employer, in writing, his or her physical condition or medical history, if (1) the employer's reliance upon the false representation was a substantial factor in the hiring and (2) there is a causal connection between the false representation and the injury. Similar provisions apply in cases of representations by employees suffering from an occupational disease.	Ky. Rev. Stat. Ann. §§ 342.165, 342.316.
LA	No specific statutory provision.	No specific statutory provision.	No specific statutory provision.	—	—
ME	No specific statutory provision.	No specific statutory provision.	No specific statutory provision.	—	—
MD	No specific statutory provision.	No specific statutory provision.	Yes.	No compensation for occupational disease if the affected employee falsely represented in writing to the employer that the employee had not been disabled, laid off, or compensated due to the occupational disease.	Md. Code Ann. Lab. & Empl. §§ 9-502, 9-506.
MA	No specific statutory provision.	No specific statutory provision.	No specific statutory provision.	An injury received due to serious and willful misconduct is not compensable, but compensation is not barred to dependents if the injury results in death.	Where an employee knowingly and willfully made a false representation as to his or her physical condition and the employer relied upon the misrepresentation in hiring the employee, and the employee knew or should have known that it was unlikely he or she could fulfill the duties of the job without incurring a serious injury, no compensa-	Mass. Gen. Laws Ann. ch. 152, §§ 27, 27A.

(Table continues.)

(cont'd)

Table 10.1-2 Part B   PART 10—STATE WORKERS' COMPENSATION LAWS   10-32

Table 10.1-2 Part B *(cont'd)*

DISQUALIFYING EVENTS OR CONDUCT

(See also text at § 10.1.)

	Failure to Use Safety Appliance	Illegal Acts	Violation of Rule or Regulation	Willful Misconduct	Other	Citations to Authority
MA *(cont'd)*					tion is payable if an injury related to the condition misrepresented occurs. The right to compensation is restored, however, if an employee who rectifies any such misrepresentation prior to the injury is thereafter retained.	
MI	No specific statutory provision.	No specific statutory provision.	No specific statutory provision.	Compensation is barred for an employee injured by reason of his or her intentional and willful misconduct.	No compensation is payable for occupational disease if the employee willfully and falsely represented in writing that he or she had not previously suffered from the disease which is the cause of the disability or death. Benefits may also be forfeited by refusal of a bona fide employment offer without good and reasonable cause.	Mich. Comp. Laws §§ 418.301, 418.305, 418.431.
MN	No specific statutory provision.	No specific statutory provision.	No specific statutory provision.	No specific statutory provision.	—	—
MS	No specific statutory provision.	No specific statutory provision.	No specific statutory provision.	No specific statutory provision.	—	—
MO	Willful failure of the employee to use safety devices provided by the employer will result in the reduction of compensation and death benefit by 15% if the employer had, prior to the injury, made a diligent effort to cause his or her employees to use the safety device or devices.	No specific statutory provision.	For injury caused by an employee's failure to obey any reasonable, conspicuously posted rule adopted by the employer for the safety of employees, the compensation and death benefit is reduced by 15%, provided that the employee had actual knowledge of the rule and the employer had, prior to the injury, made a diligent effort to cause the employees to obey the rule.	No specific statutory provision.	—	Mo. Rev. Stat. § 287.120.

State					Citation
MT	No specific statutory provision.	No specific statutory provision.	No specific statutory provision.	No compensation is payable for an occupational disease if the employee knowingly and falsely represented himself or herself in writing as not having previously been disabled, laid off, or compensated due to such disease. Compensation for occupational disease may also be suspended or reduced where a claimant persists in unsanitary or injurious practices tending to imperil or retard recovery.	Mont. Code Ann. §§ 39-72-404, 39-72-714.
NE	No specific statutory provision, but conduct evidencing reckless indifference to safety may bar compensation.	No specific statutory provision.	No specific statutory provision.	—	Neb. Rev. Stat. §§ 48-127, 48-151.
NV	No specific statutory provision.	No specific statutory provision.	Yes, for occupational diseases.	Where an employee has knowingly misrepresented or concealed a material fact to obtain any benefits or payments, the amount obtained by the misrepresentation or concealment may be deducted therefrom. No compensation may be awarded on account of a disease suffered by an employee who knowingly and falsely represented himself or herself as not having previously suffered from the disease. If an employee persists in an unsanitary or injurious practice that imperils or retards his or her recovery, his or her compensation may be reduced or suspended.	Nev. Rev. Stat. §§ 616C.225, 616C.230, 617.400, 617.402.
NH	No specific statutory provision.	No specific statutory provision.	Yes, if injury was caused in whole or in part by the employee's serious and willful misconduct.	—	N.H. Rev. Stat. Ann. § 281-A:2.
NJ	No compensation is permitted for occupational diseases if, despite repeated warnings, the employee willfully failed to properly and effectively utilize a reasonable *(cont'd)*	No specific statutory provision.	No specific statutory provision.	—	N.J. Stat. Ann. §§ 34:15-30, 34:15-35.22.

(Table continues.)

Table 10.1-2 Part B   PART 10—STATE WORKERS' COMPENSATION LAWS   10-34

Table 10.1-2 Part B *(cont'd)*

DISQUALIFYING EVENTS OR CONDUCT

(See also text at § 10.1.)

	Failure to Use Safety Appliance	*Illegal Acts*	*Violation of Rule or Regulation*	*Willful Misconduct*	*Other*	*Citations to Authority*
NJ *(cont'd)*	and proper guard or personal protective device required and furnished by the employer, unless imminent danger or need for immediate action did not allow for appropriate use thereof. Moreover, compensation is specifically barred for hearing loss due to hazardous noise where, despite repeated warnings, an employee willfully failed to properly and effectively utilize a suitable protective device or devices provided by the employer.					
NM	Compensation is reduced by 10% if an injury or death results from the employee's failure to use a safety device provided by the employer.	Compensation is reduced by 10% if an injury or death results from the employee's failure to observe statutory regulations appertaining to the safe conduct of his or her employment.	No compensation for injury or death due to willful disobedience to an employer's reasonable rules and regulations, if such rules and regulations are conspicuously posted or otherwise brought to the attention of the employee. Compensation is reduced by 10% if an injury or death results from the employee's failure to observe statutory regulations appertaining to the safe conduct of his or her employment.	Yes.	Compensation is not payable, under certain conditions, when a worker knowingly and willfully conceals information or makes a false representation of his or her medical condition in response to an employer's written questionnaire. This provision does not apply unless the written questionnaire clearly and conspicuously discloses that the worker will be deprived of compensation for such concealment or misrepresentation.	N.M. Stat. Ann. §§ 52-1-10, 52-3-45, 52-3-45.3.
NY	No specific statutory provision.	No specific statutory provision.	No specific statutory provision.	No specific statutory provision.	No specific statutory provision.	—

					Citation
NC	Compensation is reduced by 10% where injury or death is caused by the employee's willful failure to use a safety appliance.	Compensation is reduced by 10% where injury or death is caused by the employee's willful failure to perform a statutory duty.	No specific statutory provision.	No compensation for asbestosis and/or silicosis where an employee falsely represented himself or herself in writing as not having previously been disabled or laid off because of asbestosis or silicosis.	N.C. Gen. Stat. §§ 97-12, 97-52.
ND	No specific statutory provision.	Yes, for injuries arising from an illegal act by the employee.	No specific statutory provision.	No specific statutory provision.	N.D. Cent. Code § 65-01-02.
OH	No specific statutory provision.	No specific statutory provision.	No specific statutory provision.	No compensation for occupational disease where the employee wilfully and falsely represented himself or herself as not having previously suffered from such disease.	Ohio Rev. Code Ann. § 4123.70.
OK	Yes, for injury resulting directly from the injured employee's wilfull failure to use a guard or protection against accident furnished for use pursuant to any statute or by order of the Commissioner of Labor.	No specific statutory provision.	No specific statutory provision.	—	Okla. Stat. tit. 85, § 11.
OR	No specific statutory provision.	No specific statutory provision.	No specific statutory provision.	—	Or. Rev. Stat. § 656.005.
PA	No specific statutory provision.	Yes, if injury was caused thereby.	No specific statutory provision.	—	77 Pa. Const. Stat. §§ 301, 1401.
RI	No specific statutory provision.	No specific statutory provision.	No specific statutory provision.	No compensation for occupational disease if the employee wilfully and falsely represents in writing that he or she has not previously had the disease that is the cause of the disability or death.	R.I. Gen. Laws § 28-34-7.
SC	No compensation for disability from occupational disease caused by the employee's refusal to use a safety appliance provided by, and regularly required to be used by, the employer.	No compensation for disability from occupational disease caused by the employee's refusal to obey a safety rule or regulation adopted and regularly enforced by the employer. Also, an employee is not compensated where the employee refuses to accept suitable employment when ordered to do so by the commission.	No specific statutory provision.	No compensation for occupational disease where the employee wilfully and falsely represents in writing that he or she has not previously suffered from the disease that is the cause of disability or death.	S.C. Code Ann. §§ 42-11-80, 42-11-100.

(Table continues.)

Table 10.1-2 Part B   PART 10—STATE WORKERS' COMPENSATION LAWS   10-36

Table 10.1-2 Part B *(cont'd)*

DISQUALIFYING EVENTS OR CONDUCT

(See also text at § 10.1.)

	Failure to Use Safety Appliance	Illegal Acts	Violation of Rule or Regulation	Willful Misconduct	Other	Citations to Authority
SD	Yes, for willful failure or refusal to use a safety appliance furnished by the employer. No compensation is payable for occupational hearing loss due to excessive noise if the employee fails to regularly use employer-provided protection devices capable of preventing loss of hearing from excessive noise. Nor may an employee be compensated for occupational disease due to willful failure to use protective and safety devices provided by the employer.	Yes, for willful failure or refusal to perform a duty required by statute.	Compensation prohibited for occupational disease where caused by the employee's disobedience to reasonable regulations adopted by the employer, which have been and are kept posted in conspicuous places in and about the premises of the employer, or have otherwise been brought to the attention of the employee.	Yes.	No compensation is allowed where an employee intentionally and willfully made a false representation as to his or her physical condition, if the employer substantially and justifiably relied on the false representation in the hiring of the employee and a causal connection existed between the false representation and the injury.	S.D. Cod. Laws Ann. §§ 62-4-37, 62-4-46, 62-8-22, 62-8-23, 62-9-8.
TN	Yes, for willful failure or refusal to use a safety appliance.	No compensation for injury or death due to willful failure or refusal to perform a duty required by law.	No specific statutory provision.	Yes.	—	Tenn. Code Ann. § 50-6-110.
TX	No specific statutory provision.	No specific statutory provision.	No specific statutory provision.	No specific statutory provision.	—	—
UT	Except in case of injury resulting in death, compensation is reduced by 15% when injury is caused by the willful failure of the employee to use safety devices when provided by the employer.	No specific statutory provision.	Except in case of injury resulting in death, compensation is reduced by 15% when injury is caused by the willful failure of the employee to obey any order or reasonable rule adopted by the employer for the safety of the employee.	No specific statutory provision.	—	Utah Code Ann. § 34A-2-302.
VT	Yes, if provided for the employee's use.	No specific statutory provision.	No specific statutory provision.	No specific statutory provision.	—	Vt. Stat. Ann. tit. 21, § 649.

State					Citation
VA	Yes.	No compensation where injury or death is due to the employee's willful failure or refusal to perform a duty required by statute.	No compensation where injury or death is caused by the employee's willful breach of any reasonable rule or regulation adopted by the employer and brought, prior to the accident, to the knowledge of the employee.	Yes.	Va. Code Ann. § 65.2-306.
WA	No specific statutory provision.	No compensation is payable if injury or death results while the worker is engaged in the attempt to commit, or the commission of, a felony.	No specific statutory provision.	—	Wash. Rev. Code Ann. § 51.32.020.
WV	No specific statutory provision.	No specific statutory provision.	No specific statutory provision.	—	—
WI	For injury due to failure to use adequately maintained safety devices provided in accord with any statute, rule, or order of the department, and the use of which is reasonably enforced by the employer, compensation and death benefits shall be reduced by 15%, but total reduction may not exceed $15,000.	For injury due to failure to obey any reasonable rule adopted and reasonably enforced by the employer for the safety of the employee and of which the employee has notice, compensation and death benefits shall be reduced by 15%, but total reduction may not exceed $15,000.	No specific statutory provision.	—	Wis. Stat. Ann. § 102.58.
WY	No specific statutory provision.	No specific statutory provision.	No specific statutory provision.	An injured employee who knowingly engages or persists in an unsanitary or injurious practice that tends to imperil or retard the employee's recovery forfeits the right to compensation.	Wyo. Stat. Ann. § 27-14-407.

Table 10.1-2 Part C

DISQUALIFYING EVENTS OR CONDUCT

(See also text at § 10.1.)

	Intoxication	Use of Controlled Substances	Refusal to Take Drug Test	Refusal of Medical Exam	Refusal of Reasonable Treatment	Citations to Authority
AL	Yes.	Yes.	Yes.	No specific statutory provision.	No specific statutory provision.	Ala. Code § 25-5-51.
AK	Yes.	Yes. Injuries proximately caused by the employee's being under the influence of drugs are not compensable, unless the drugs were taken as prescribed by the employee's physician.	No specific statutory provision.	No specific statutory provision.	No specific statutory provision.	Alaska Stat. § 23.30.235.
AZ	Yes, if intoxication is a substantial contributing cause of the employee's personal injury or death, unless the employer had actual knowledge of, and permitted or condoned, the employee's use of alcohol.	Yes, if the unlawful use thereof was a substantial contributing cause of the employee's personal injury or death, unless the employer had actual knowledge of, and permitted or condoned, the employee's unlawful use of drugs.	Where an employer has a certified drug and alcohol testing program, an employee's failure to pass, refusal to cooperate with, or refusal to take such a test, if requested within 24 hours after the employer learns of the injury, is a bar to compensation, unless the employee proves (1) that the alcohol or drug use was not a contributing factor to the injury or death, (2) that the alcohol impairment test indicated a blood alcohol level lower than the legal limit for operating a motor vehicle, or (3) that the drug or alcohol test in question utilized cutoff levels below those prescribed for transportation workplace drug and alcohol testing programs under 49 C.F.R. part 40. The foregoing is inapplicable where the	No specific statutory provision.	No specific statutory provision.	Ariz. Rev. Stat. §§ 23-901.04, 23-1021.

State						Citation
AR	Injuries substantially occasioned by the use of alcohol are not compensable. The presence of alcohol creates a rebuttable presumption that the injury was substantially occasioned by the use thereof.	Injuries substantially occasioned by the use of illegal drugs, or the use of prescription drugs in contravention of physician's orders, are not compensable. The presence of such creates a rebuttable presumption that the injury was substantially occasioned by the use thereof.	employer had actual knowledge of, and permitted or condoned, the employee's unlawful use of drugs.		No specific statutory provision.	Ark. Code Ann. §§ 11-9-102, 11-9-601.
CA	Yes.	Yes, for unlawful use.	All employees are deemed to have implicitly consented to reasonable and responsible testing by properly trained medical or law enforcement personnel for the presence of alcohol, illegal drugs, or prescription drugs used in contravention of physician's orders.	No specific statutory provision.	No specific statutory provision.	Cal. Labor Code § 3600.
CO	50% reduction in nonmedical benefits where injury results from the presence in the worker's system, during working hours, of a blood alcohol level at or above .10%	50% reduction in nonmedical benefits where injury results from the presence in the worker's system, during working hours, of controlled substances not medically prescribed.	No specific statutory provision, but statute clearly contemplates the use of drug tests.	No specific statutory provision.	No specific statutory provision.	Colo. Rev. Stat. § 8-42-112.5.
CT	Disability or death due to consumption of alcohol is not a compensable injury.	Yes, except for drugs prescribed in the course of medical treatment or in a program of research operated under the direction of a physician or pharmacologist.	No specific statutory provision.	No specific statutory provision.	No specific statutory provision.	Conn. Gen. Stat. Ann. § 31-275.
DE	Yes.	No compensation for injury due to employee's "intoxication."	No specific statutory provision.	Yes.	Refusal of reasonable surgical, medical, and hospital services, medicines, and supplies results in forfeiture of compensation for any injury or any increase in incapacity resulting therefrom. Refusal to accept rehabilitation services ordered by the board results in loss of compensation for each week of the period of refusal.	Del. Code Ann. tit. 19, §§ 2343, 2353.
DC	Yes, where injury is occasioned solely thereby.	Injuries occasioned solely by employee's "intoxication" are not compensable.	No specific statutory provision.	No specific statutory provision.	No specific statutory provision.	D.C. Code Ann. § 32-1503.

(Table continues.)

Table 10.1-2 Part C   PART 10—STATE WORKERS' COMPENSATION LAWS   10-40

Table 10.1-2 Part C *(cont'd)*

DISQUALIFYING EVENTS OR CONDUCT

(See also text at § 10.1.)

	Intoxication	Use of Controlled Substances	Refusal to Take Drug Test	Refusal of Medical Exam	Refusal of Reasonable Treatment	Citations to Authority
FL	Yes, if injury was primarily caused thereby.	Yes, if injury was primarily caused thereby.	Where an injured worker refuses to submit to a drug test, a presumption arises, in the absence of clear and convincing evidence to the contrary, that the injury was caused primarily by the influence of drugs.	No specific statutory provision.	No specific statutory provision.	Fla. Stat. Ann. § 440.09.
GA	Yes.	Yes, except for substances lawfully prescribed by a physician and taken in accordance therewith.	Unjustifiable refusal to submit to a drug or alcohol test gives rise to a presumption that the injury was caused by the effects of alcohol or drugs.	No specific statutory provision.	No specific statutory provision.	Ga. Code Ann. § 34-9-17.
HI	Yes.	No compensation for injuries caused by an employee's "intoxication."	No specific statutory provision.	No specific statutory provision.	No specific statutory provision.	Haw. Rev. Stat. § 386-3.
ID	Yes, if intoxication is a reasonable and substantial cause of an injury, except where the intoxicants were furnished by the employer or supervisor knowingly permitted the employee to remain at work while intoxicated.	Yes, except when used as prescribed by a physician.	No specific statutory provision, but employers may require a drug or alcohol test as a condition of hiring or continued employment.	No specific statutory provision, but the commission may order the suspension or reduction of compensation of an injured employee who persists in unsanitary or unreasonable practices that tend to imperil or retard recovery.	No specific statutory provision, but the commission may order the suspension or reduction of compensation of an injured employee who persists in unsanitary or unreasonable practices that tend to imperil or retard recovery.	Idaho Code §§ 72-208, 72-435, 72-1702.
IL	No specific statutory provision.	No specific statutory provision.	No specific statutory provision.	Refusal to submit to or unnecessarily obstructing an examination will result in a	Refusal to submit to medical, surgical, or hospital treatment that is reasonably essential to promote recovery may result in	820 Ill. Comp. Stat. Ann. 305/8, 305/12, 305/19.

IN	Yes.	No compensation for injury or death due to the employee's "intoxication."	No specific statutory provision.	No specific statutory provision.	temporary suspension of compensation until such examination takes place.	reduction or suspension of compensation. However, when an employer and employee so agree in writing, no reduction or suspension of compensation shall apply when an employee relies in good faith on treatment by prayer or spiritual means alone, in accordance with the tenets and practice of a recognized church or religious denomination, by a duly accredited practitioner thereof. If it is found that a doctor selected by the employee is rendering improper or inadequate care and the employee is ordered to select another doctor certified or qualified in the appropriate medical field but refuses to do so, the employer may be relieved of the obligation to pay the doctor's charges from the date of refusal to the date of compliance.	Ind. Code Ann. §§ 22-3-2-8, 22-3-7-21.
IA	Yes, if intoxication was a substantial factor in the injury.	Yes, for narcotic, depressant, stimulant, hallucinogenic, or hypnotic drugs not prescribed by an authorized medical practitioner, if such substances were a substantial factor in the injury.	No specific statutory provision.	No specific statutory provision.	No specific statutory provision.	No specific statutory provision.	Iowa Code Ann. § 85.16.
KS	Yes, where the injury, disability, or death was contributed to by the employee's use or consumption of alcohol. It is conclusively presumed that the employee was impaired due to alcohol if it is shown that at the time of the injury the employee had an alcohol concentration of .04% or more. For occupational disease, compensation is barred if disablement is due solely to intoxication.	Yes, where the injury, disability, or death was contributed to by the employee's use or consumption of any drugs, chemicals, or any other compounds or substances, including, but not limited to, those available without a prescription, prescription drugs or medications, any form or type of narcotic drugs, marijuana, stimulants, depressants, or hallucinogens. For drugs available without a *(cont'd)*	Refusal to submit to a chemical test is not admissible to prove impairment unless there was probable cause to believe that the employee used, possessed, or was impaired by a drug or alcohol while working. The results of a chemical test may be used as evidence if certain conditions are met.	No specific statutory provision.	No specific statutory provision.	No specific statutory provision.	Kan. Stat. Ann. § 44-501.

(Table continues.)

Table 10.1-2 Part C   PART 10—STATE WORKERS' COMPENSATION LAWS   10-42

Table 10.1-2 Part C (cont'd)

DISQUALIFYING EVENTS OR CONDUCT

(See also text at § 10.1.)

	Intoxication	Use of Controlled Substances	Refusal to Take Drug Test	Refusal of Medical Exam	Refusal of Reasonable Treatment	Citations to Authority
KS (cont'd)		prescription, compensation will not be denied if taken in therapeutic doses and if there were no prior incidences of the employee's impairment at work due to use of such drugs in the previous 24 months.				
KY	Yes, if intoxication is voluntary.	Yes. Intoxication includes a disturbance of mental or physical capacities resulting from the introduction of substances into the body.	No specific statutory provision.	If an employee refuses to submit himself to or in any way obstructs the examination, no compensation is payable for the period during which the refusal or obstruction continues.	No specific statutory provision.	Ky. Rev. Stat. Ann. §§ 342.205, 342.610, 501.010.
LA	Yes, unless the employee's intoxication resulted from activities that were in pursuit of the employer's interests or in which the employer procured the intoxicating beverage and encouraged its use during the employee's work hours. If there was, at the time of the accident, 0.05% or less of alcohol in the employee's blood, it shall be presumed that the employee was not intoxicated. A blood alcohol level between 0.05% and 0.10% gives rise to no presumption, but may be considered along with other	Yes, unless the employee's use thereof resulted from activities that were in pursuit of the employer's interests or in which the employer procured the substance and encouraged its use during the employee's work hours.	Refusal to submit to drug or alcohol test results in presumption that the employee was intoxicated.	No specific statutory provision.	No specific statutory provision.	La. Rev. Stat. Ann. § 23:1081.

State					Citation
	evidence. Where the level is 0.10% or higher, it is presumed that the employee was intoxicated. (*Note*: Effective 9/30/2003, 0.08% will be substituted for 0.10% with respect to the foregoing.) However, where an injured worker later presumed or found to have been intoxicated receives emergency care following an accident, the employer is responsible for the reasonable medical care provided the worker only until the worker is stabilized and ready for discharge from the acute care facility.				
ME	Yes, unless the employer knew at the time of the injury that the employee was intoxicated or that the employee was in the habit at that time of becoming intoxicated while on duty.	No specific statutory provision, but statute generally excludes compensation for injury due to "intoxication."	No specific statutory provision.	No specific statutory provision.	Me. Rev. Stat. Ann. 39-A, § 202.
MD	Yes, if injury, hernia, or occupational disease was caused solely thereby. Only medical benefits may be received where injury, hernia, or occupational disease was primarily caused by intoxication.	Yes, if the injury, hernia, or occupational disease was caused solely due to a depressant, hallucinogenic, hypnotic, narcotic, or stimulant drug, or other drug that makes the covered employee incapable of satisfactory job performance, unless it was taken pursuant to the prescription of a physician. No compensation is permitted, other than medical benefits, if the primary cause was the effect of a controlled dangerous substance, unless the use thereof was by prescription and was not excessive or abusive.	No specific statutory provision.	No specific statutory provision.	Md. Code Ann. Lab. & Empl. § 9-506.
MA	No specific statutory provision.	No specific statutory provision.	No specific statutory provision.	No specific statutory provision.	—
MI	No specific statutory provision.	No specific statutory provision.	No specific statutory provision.	No specific statutory provision.	—
MN	Yes, if the injury is proximately caused thereby.	Statute indicates that compensation is not payable where injury is proximately caused by "intoxication."	No specific statutory provision.	No specific statutory provision.	Minn. Stat. Ann. § 176.021.

(*Table continues.*)

Table 10.1-2 Part C *(cont'd)*

DISQUALIFYING EVENTS OR CONDUCT

(See also text at § 10.1.)

	Intoxication	Use of Controlled Substances	Refusal to Take Drug Test	Refusal of Medical Exam	Refusal of Reasonable Treatment	Citations to Authority
MS	Yes, if the injury was proximately caused thereby.	Statute indicates that compensation is not payable where injury is proximately caused by "intoxication."	No specific statutory provision.	No specific statutory provision.	No specific statutory provision.	Miss. Code Ann. § 71-3-7.
MO	Compensation and death benefit reduced by 15% for violation of a reasonable, conspicuously posted rule or policy adopted by an employer regarding the use of alcohol in the workplace if the injury was sustained in conjunction with the use thereof, provided that the employee had actual knowledge of the rule or policy and the employer had, prior to the injury, made a diligent effort to inform the employee of the requirement to obey the rule or policy. However, if the use of alcohol in violation of the rule or policy is the proximate cause of the injury, then no compensation is payable, unless (1) the employer had actual knowledge of the employee's use of the alcohol and failed to take any recuperative or disciplinary action or (2) the employee is authorized by the employer to use alcohol as part of the employment.	Compensation and death benefit reduced by 15% for violation of a reasonable, conspicuously posted rule or policy adopted by an employer regarding the use of nonprescribed controlled drugs in the workplace if the injury was sustained in conjunction with the use thereof, provided that the employee had actual knowledge of the rule or policy and the employer had, prior to the injury, made a diligent effort to inform the employee of the requirement to obey the rule or policy. However, if the use of nonprescribed controlled drugs in violation of the rule or policy is the proximate cause of the injury, then no compensation is payable, unless (1) the employer had actual knowledge of the employee's use thereof and failed to take any recuperative or disciplinary action or (2) the employee is authorized by the employer to use nonprescribed controlled drugs as part of the employment.	No specific statutory provision.	No specific statutory provision.	No specific statutory provision.	Mo. Rev. Stat. § 287.120.

MT	No specific statutory provision.	No specific statutory provision.	No specific statutory provision.	Failure or refusal to submit to, or any obstruction of, an examination, after a written request, will result in suspension of the right to compensation.	Compensation may be suspended or reduced where a claimant with an occupational disease refuses to submit to medical or surgical treatment as is reasonably essential to promote the claimant's recovery.
NE	Yes, if intoxication is without the consent, knowledge, or acquiescence of the employer or the employer's agent.	Yes, if employee is under the influence of a controlled substance not prescribed by a physician.	No specific statutory provision.	No specific statutory provision.	No specific statutory provision.
NV	Yes, if injury is proximately caused thereby. Proximate causation by intoxication is presumed if the employee was intoxicated at the time of the injury.	Yes, if injury is proximately caused thereby. Proximate causation is presumed if the employee had any amount of a controlled substance, excluding marijuana when lawfully used for medicinal purposes, in his or her system at the time of the injury and did not have a current and lawful prescription for the substance.	No specific statutory provision.	No specific statutory provision.	No compensation is payable for the death, disability, or treatment if the death is caused by, or insofar as the disability is aggravated, caused or continued by, an unreasonable refusal or neglect to submit to or to follow any competent and reasonable surgical treatment or medical aid. If an employee refuses to submit to such medical or surgical treatment that is necessary to promote recovery, the employee's compensation may be reduced or suspended. Compensation *must* be suspended, moreover, if (1) the employee is unable to undergo treatment, testing, or examination for the industrial injury solely because of a condition or injury that did not arise out of and in the course of his or her employment and (2) it is within the ability of the employee to correct the nonindustrial condition or injury. The compensation must be suspended until the injured employee is able to resume treatment, testing, or examination for the industrial injury.

Citations:
- **MT** — Mont. Code Ann. §§ 39-71-605, 39-72-714.
- **NE** — Neb. Rev. Stat. §§48-102, 48-127, 48-151.
- **NV** — Nev. Rev. Stat. § 616C.230.

(Table continues.)

Table 10.1-2 Part C   PART 10—STATE WORKERS' COMPENSATION LAWS   10-46

Table 10.1-2 Part C *(cont'd)*

DISQUALIFYING EVENTS OR CONDUCT

(See also text at § 10.1.)

	Intoxication	Use of Controlled Substances	Refusal to Take Drug Test	Refusal of Medical Exam	Refusal of Reasonable Treatment	Citations to Authority
NH	Yes, if injury is caused in whole or in part thereby, unless the employer knew of the intoxication.	Yes, if injury is caused in whole or in part thereby, except for an employee's use of a controlled drug in accordance with a prescription authorizing the use of such drug.	No specific statutory provision.	No specific statutory provision.	No specific statutory provision.	N.H. Rev. Stat. Ann. §§ 281-A:2, 281-A:14.
NJ	Yes, if the employee's injury is proximately caused thereby.	Yes, for unlawful use thereof.	No specific statutory provision.	No specific statutory provision.	No specific statutory provision.	N.J. Stat. Ann. §§ 34:15-1, 34:15-36.
NM	Yes, if the injury was occasioned thereby. Compensation is reduced by 10% where injury or death was not occasioned by intoxication, but where voluntary intoxication was a contributing cause.	Compensation is not permitted for an injury occasioned solely by the employee's being under the influence of a depressant, stimulant, or hallucinogenic drug, or a narcotic drug, unless dispensed upon the prescription of a licensed practitioner or administered by one authorized to do so. Where such drug use was not the sole cause, compensation will be reduced by 10% if the drug use was a contributing cause of injury or death.	No specific statutory provision.	No specific statutory provision.	No specific statutory provision.	N.M. Stat. Ann. §§ 52-1-11, 52-1-12, 52-1-12.1.
NY	No compensation when an injury was solely occasioned by the injured employee's intoxication from alcohol while on duty.	No compensation when an injury was solely occasioned by the employee's intoxication from a controlled substance while on duty.	No specific statutory provision.	No specific statutory provision.	No specific statutory provision.	N.Y. Work. Comp. Law § 10.
NC	Yes, if injury or death is proximately caused thereby, unless the intoxicant was provided by the employer or the employee's supervisor.	Yes, where the controlled substance was not by prescription.	No specific statutory provision.	No specific statutory provision.	No specific statutory provision.	N.C. Gen. Stat. § 97-12.
ND	Yes.	Yes, if caused by the illegal use thereof.	No specific statutory provision.	No specific statutory provision.	No specific statutory provision.	N.D. Cent. Code § 65-01-02.

State					Citation
OH	Yes, if injury or death was proximately caused thereby.	Yes, if injury or death was proximately caused by the employee's being under the influence thereof, unless the substance was prescribed by a physician.	Where the employee refuses to a requested drug test, there is a rebuttable presumption that the employee was intoxicated or under the influence of a nonprescription controlled substance.	No specific statutory provision.	Ohio Rev. Code Ann. § 4123.54.
OK	Yes, for an injury resulting directly from the use or abuse thereof, but only when the use or abuse rendered the employee incapable of acting in the manner in which an ordinarily prudent and cautious person, in full possession of his or her faculties and using reasonable care, would have acted at the time of the injury.	Yes, for an injury resulting directly from the use or abuse of illegal drugs or chemicals or the abuse of prescription drugs. Compensation is disallowed, however, only when the use or abuse rendered the employee incapable of acting in the manner in which an ordinarily prudent and cautious person, in full possession of his or her faculties and using reasonable care, would have acted at the time of the injury.	No specific statutory provision.	No specific statutory provision.	Okla. Stat. tit. 85, § 11.
OR	No compensation for an injury the major contributing cause of which is the injured worker's consumption of alcoholic beverages, unless the employer permitted, encouraged, or had actual knowledge of such consumption.	No compensation for an injury the major contributing cause of which is the injured worker's unlawful consumption of any controlled substance, unless the employer permitted, encouraged, or had actual knowledge of such consumption.	No specific statutory provision.	No specific statutory provision.	Or. Rev. Stat. § 656.005.
PA	Yes, if the injury would not have occurred but for the employee's intoxication.	Yes, if injury was caused by use of illegal drugs.	No specific statutory provision.	No specific statutory provision.	77 Pa. Cons. Stat. §§ 201, 301.
RI	Yes, if the injury or death resulted therefrom.	Yes, if the injury or death resulted from the unlawful use thereof.	No specific statutory provision.	No specific statutory provision.	R.I. Gen. Laws § 28-33-2.
SC	Yes, if injury or death was occasioned thereby.	No specific statutory provision, but compensation is not permitted for injury or death occasioned by an employee's "intoxication."	No specific statutory provision.	No specific statutory provision.	S.C. Code Ann. §§ 42-9-60, 42-11-100.
SD	Yes.	Yes, for illegal use of any schedule I or schedule II drug.	Failure or refusal to submit to medical or X-ray examination when requested so to do by the employer at the employer's expense constitutes *(cont'd)*	No specific statutory provision.	S.D. Cod. Laws Ann. §§ 62-4-37, 62-8-22, 62-8-23.

(Table continues.)

Table 10.1-2 Part C *(cont'd)*

DISQUALIFYING EVENTS OR CONDUCT

(See also text at § 10.1.)

	Intoxication	Use of Controlled Substances	Refusal to Take Drug Test	Refusal of Medical Exam	Refusal of Reasonable Treatment	Citations to Authority
SD *(cont'd)*				willful self-exposure, which is a bar to compensation for occupational disease.		
TN	Yes, if injury or death was due to intoxication. There is a rebuttable presumption that alcohol was the proximate cause of the injury where the employee has a blood alcohol level of .10 % or higher for non-safety-sensitive positions, or .04 % for safety-sensitive positions. However, the foregoing does not apply if, before the accident, the employer had actual knowledge of and acquiesced in the employee's presence at the workplace while under the influence of alcohol.	Yes, if injury or death was due to illegal drugs. There is a rebuttable presumption that such drug use was the proximate cause of the injury if the injured employee has a positive confirmation of use of a drug. However, the foregoing does not apply if, before the accident, the employer had actual knowledge of and acquiesced in the employee's presence at the workplace while under the influence of such drug.	If the injured worker refuses to submit to a drug test, it is presumed, absent a preponderance of evidence to the contrary, that the proximate cause of the injury was the influence of drugs.	No specific statutory provision.	No specific statutory provision.	Tenn. Code Ann. § 50-6-110.
TX	Yes, if the injury occurred while the employee was in a state of intoxication. An employee is intoxicated who has a blood alcohol level of .08 % or higher or who does not have the normal use of mental or physical faculties resulting from the voluntary introduction into the body of an alcoholic beverage.	Yes, if the injury occurred while the employee was in a state of intoxication. An employee is intoxicated who does not have the normal use of mental or physical faculties resulting from the voluntary introduction into the body of a controlled substance or controlled substance analogue, a dangerous drug, an abusable glue or aerosol paint, or any similar substance, the use of which is regulated under state law. Intoxication does	No specific statutory provision.	No specific statutory provision.	No specific statutory provision.	Tex. Lab. Code Ann. §§ 401.013, 406.032.

UT	No compensation for disability where the major contributing cause of injury is the employee's intoxication from alcohol with a blood or breath alcohol concentration of .08 %, unless the employer permitted, encouraged, or had actual knowledge thereof.	not include the effects of a substance taken by prescription, or inhaled or absorbed as an incident to the employee's work. No compensation for disability where the major contributing cause of injury is the employee's use of a controlled substance that the employee did not obtain under a valid prescription, or intentional abuse of a prescribed substance, unless the employer permitted, encouraged, or had actual knowledge thereof.	No specific statutory provision.	No specific statutory provision.	Utah Code Ann. § 34A-2-302.
VT	No compensation for an injury caused by or during the employee's intoxication.	No specific statutory provision, but compensation is disallowed for injuries caused by or during an employee's "intoxication."	No specific statutory provision.	No specific statutory provision.	Vt. Stat. Ann. tit. 21, § 649.
VA	Yes, if injury or death is caused thereby. There is a rebuttable presumption that the employee was intoxicated at the time of the injury or death if a test indicates a blood alcohol concentration of .08% or greater.	Yes, if the injury or death is caused by the employee's use of a nonprescribed controlled substance. There is a rebuttable presumption that the employee was using a nonprescribed controlled substance at the time of the injury or death if the employee tests positive for such a substance according to a certified laboratory.	No specific statutory provision.	No specific statutory provision.	Va. Code Ann. § 65.2-306.
WA	No specific statutory provision.	No specific statutory provision.	No specific statutory provision.	No specific statutory provision.	—
WV	Yes, if the injury or death is caused thereby.	No specific statutory provision, but injury or death is not compensable where caused by "intoxication."	No specific statutory provision.	No specific statutory provision.	W. Va. Code § 23-4-2.
WI	For injury due to intoxication of the employee by alcoholic beverages, compensation and death benefits shall be reduced by 15%, but total reduction may not exceed $15,000.	For injury due to use of a controlled substance or a controlled substance analog, compensation and death benefits shall be reduced by 15%, but total reduction may not exceed $15,000.	No specific statutory provision.	No specific statutory provision.	Wis. Stat. Ann. § 102.58.

(Table continues.)

Table 10.1-2 Part C *(cont'd)*

DISQUALIFYING EVENTS OR CONDUCT

(See also text at § 10.1.)

	Intoxication	Use of Controlled Substances	Refusal to Take Drug Test	Refusal of Medical Exam	Refusal of Reasonable Treatment	Citations to Authority
WY	Yes, for injuries caused thereby.	Yes, for injury caused by an employee's being under the influence of a controlled substance, except any prescribed drug taken as directed by an authorized health care provider.	No specific statutory provision.	No specific statutory provision.	No compensation for an injured employee who refuses to submit to medical or surgical treatment reasonably essential to promote the employee's recovery.	Wyo. Stat. Ann. §§ 27-14-102, 27-14-407.

§ 10.2 Workers' Compensation Insurance Requirements

In virtually every state, the workers' compensation laws require employers to insure against possible liability, with either a private carrier, a state fund, or self-insurance. In states in which self-insurance for workers' compensation is permitted, the employer must demonstrate its financial ability to handle the potentially costly claims that may be filed. Employers that fail to insure can be subject to heavy fines. For example, in Connecticut, an employer that fails to insure may be subject to fines of up to $50,000,[1] and employers in Arkansas, Iowa, Louisiana, Maine, and West Virginia are subject to maximum fines of $10,000.[2] Illinois passed a law in 2001 requiring a minimum fine of $10,000 and making certain corporate officers and directors, partners, and limited liability company members personally liable under certain circumstances.[3] Employers that fail to insure may also face criminal penalties and may be enjoined from conducting business.

Table 10.2-1 indicates whether employers are required to insure and whether they may self-insure, and sets out the penalties for failure to insure.

§ 10.2

1. Conn. Gen. Stat. Ann. § 31-288 (1999).

2. Ark. Code Ann. § 11-9-406 (1999); Iowa Code Ann. § 87.21 (1996); La. Rev. Stat. Ann. § 23:1172 (Supp. 1999); Me. Rev. Stat. Ann. tit. 39-A, § 324 (Supp. 1999); W. Va. Code § 23-1-16 (Supp. 1999).

3. 820 Ill. Comp. Stat. Ann. 305/4.

Table 10.2-1   PART 10—STATE WORKERS' COMPENSATION LAWS   10-52

Table 10.2-1
WORKERS' COMPENSATION INSURANCE REQUIREMENTS

(See also text at § 10.2.)

	Is Insurance Required?	Is Self-Insurance Permitted?	Penalties for Failure to Secure Coverage	Citations to Authority
AL	Yes.	Yes.	An employer that fails to secure compensation is guilty of a misdemeanor and subject to fines of at least $100 but no more than $1,000, and is liable for 2 times the amount of compensation otherwise payable for the death or injury of an employee. A court of competent jurisdiction is also authorized to impose civil penalties against noncompliant employers of up to $100 per day.	Ala. Code § 25-5-8.
AK	Yes.	Yes.	An employer that fails to either insure or obtain a certificate of self-insurance is liable for a fine of $10,000 and for imprisonment for up to 1 year. For a corporate employer, all those who had authority to insure and the person actively in charge of the business are subject to the penalties and are personally, jointly, and severally liable for payment of compensation or benefits. Employer is barred from asserting certain defenses, and may be subject to an order preventing use of employee labor until the employer comes into compliance.	Alaska Stat. §§ 23.30.075, 23.30.080, 23.30.090.
AZ	Yes.	Yes.	An employer that fails to secure compensation is liable to repay the state fund and a penalty of 10% of the amount expended by the state or $500, whichever is greater, as well as attorneys' fees. The employer may be subject to an injunction preventing the employer from operating the business until it is in compliance. In addition, an employer is subject to a civil penalty of $500 if a noncompensable claim is awarded against the employer at a time when it was uninsured.	Ariz. Rev. Stat. Ann. §§ 23-907, 23-961, 23-961.01.
AR	Yes.	Yes.	An employer that fails to secure payment of compensation is subject to a fine of up to $10,000, and may also be subject to a fine of $1,000 per day of violation. Such failure may constitute a class D felony. Failure to comply with the law or to pay civil penalties may result in an injunction preventing the employer from doing business.	Ark. Code Ann. §§ 11-9-404, 11-9-406.
CA	Yes.	Yes.	An employer that fails to secure coverage is subject to a stop order prohibiting the use of employee labor until the employer is in compliance. The failure to observe a stop order is a misdemeanor punishable by 60 days of imprisonment or a fine of up to $10,000, or both.	Cal. Lab. Code §§ 3710.1, 3710.2.
CO	Yes.	Yes.	Employers that fail to insure are subject to an injunction preventing them from continuing business operations while in default or fines of up to $500 per day not in compliance. An employer that does not pay an award against it arising from its failure to insure is liable for an additional 50% of the award or $1,000, whichever is greater, and attorneys' fees.	Colo. Rev. Stat. Ann. §§ 8-43-408, 8-43-409, 8-44-101.

State				
CT	Yes.	Yes.	An employer found not to be in compliance will be assessed a civil penalty of at least $500 per employee or $5,000, whichever is less, up to a maximum of $50,000. An additional penalty of $100 per day will be assessed for each day that the employer fails to comply.	Conn. Gen. Stat. Ann. §§ 31-284, 31-285, 31-288.
DE	Yes.	Yes.	Employers that fail to insure are subject to a civil penalty of $1 per day for each employee but at least $25 per day of noncompliance, up to $2,500. Employer is barred from asserting certain defenses and may be enjoined from doing business.	Del. Code Ann. tit. 19, §§ 2371–2374.
DC	No specific statutory provision.	No specific statutory provision.	—	—
FL	Yes.	Yes.	State may issue stop-work order on business and seek injunction; once imposed, a stop-work order will be lifted only when the employer furnishes proof of insurance or self-insurance and pays penalties of $100 per day of noncompliance. Employer is liable for a penalty of twice the amount of premiums the employer would have paid during period it failed to insure in the last 3 years or $1,000, whichever is greater.	Fla. Stat. Ann. §§ 440.03, 440.09, 440.107.
GA	Yes.	Yes.	Civil penalties of at least $500 and no more than $5,000 may be assessed, plus the cost of collection and attorneys' fees.	Ga. Code Ann. §§ 34-9-18, 34-9-120, 34-9-121, 34-9-150 et seq.
HI	Yes.	Yes.	An employer that fails to secure coverage is liable for a fine of $10 per employee or $250, whichever is higher, for each day of noncompliance. An employer in default for 30 days is subject to an injunction preventing it from operating its business.	Haw. Rev. Stat. Ann. §§ 386-121, 386-123.
ID	Yes.	Yes.	An employer that fails to secure payment of compensation is guilty of a misdemeanor, and corporate officers are personally, jointly, and severally liable; the employer is also liable for civil fines of $2 per employee per day or $25 per day of noncompliance, whichever is greater. An employer that fails a second time to secure compensation within 3 years of a previous violation is liable in addition for a fine of $500, and for a fine of $1,000 for a third or any subsequent failure to secure compensation.	Idaho Code §§ 72-301, 72-319.
IL	Yes, for certain enumerated businesses.	Yes, individual and group.	Knowing and willful failure to insure is punishable by penalties of up to $500 per day. The minimum penalty is $10,000. Penalties may be assessed personally and individually against corporate officers and directors, partners of an employer partnership, or members of an employer limited liability company, after a finding of a knowing and willful refusal or failure to comply. A construction employer that is required by statute to make premium payments based on the site of its work and that fails to do so is liable for penalties of $1,000 for each day it failed to pay up to a maximum of $50,000 per project.	820 Ill. Comp. Stat. Ann. 305/4, 305/4a.
IN	Yes.	Yes.	Violation may result in a maximum fine of $10,000 or in double the compensation called for by law; employer may be enjoined from doing business until it obtains insurance. If employer is found to have been in bad faith, claimant may be awarded from $500 to $20,000.	Ind. Code §§ 22-3-2-2, 22-3-2-5, 22-3-4-12.1, 22-3-4-13, 22-3-7-34.
IA	Yes.	Yes.	An employer that violates the self-insurance requirements is subject to a fine of $1,000 per violation per employee, and a maximum of $10,000 in any single proceeding against one employer. An employer that violates insurance requirements generally is guilty of a class D misdemeanor. Such an employer may not assert certain defenses in an action by an employee, and certain presumptions will apply against the employer in such an action.	Iowa Code Ann. § 85.21.

(Table continues.)

Table 10.2-1　　　　　　　　　　PART 10—STATE WORKERS' COMPENSATION LAWS　　　　　　　　　　10-54

Table 10.2-1 (cont'd)
WORKERS' COMPENSATION INSURANCE REQUIREMENTS

(See also text at § 10.2.)

	Is Insurance Required?	Is Self-Insurance Permitted?	Penalties for Failure to Secure Coverage	Citations to Authority
KS	Yes.	Yes.	Failure to secure compensation is a class A misdemeanor, and is subject to a civil fine of twice the annual premium the employer would have paid for insurance, or $25,000, whichever is greater.	Kan. Stat. Ann. § 44-532.
KY	Yes.	Yes.	An employer may be fined from $100 to $1,000 for each offense, with each employee and each day of failing to comply constituting a separate offense; employers that have committed fraud are subject to fines of up to $10,000 for each offense; employer may be temporarily or permanently enjoined from doing business.	Ky. Rev. Stat. Ann. §§ 342.335, 342.340, 342.402, 342.990.
LA	Yes.	Yes.	Failure to secure coverage may result in civil fine of $250 per employee for first offense and maximum of $500 per employee for second offense, with $10,000 maximum civil penalty for all related violations. Employer may also be subject to an injunction preventing the conduct of business until coverage is acquired. An additional 50% of the amount of weekly compensation for which it would have been liable, and criminal fines up to $10,000 or imprisonment for 1 year or both, may be assessed if employer has failed to provide security. An employer that willfully misrepresented having coverage can be liable for up to 10 years in prison and up to $10,000.	La. Rev. Stat. Ann. §§ 23:1168–23:1172.2, 23:1191 et seq.
ME	Yes.	Yes.	An employer that fails to secure coverage may be subject to class D criminal charges; a $10,000 civil penalty or 108% of the premium that should have been paid, whichever is larger; and revocation of the employer's business license. Such an employer may not avail itself of defenses provided under the act.	Me. Rev. Stat. Ann. tit. 39-A, §§ 324(3), 401, 403, 404.
MD	Yes.	Yes.	An employer that fails to secure compensation will be ordered to do so, and an employer that fails to comply with such an order is liable to the state for a penalty equal to the premiums for 6 months of insurance with the Injured Workers Insurance Fund. A self-insured employer that fails to secure payment of compensation is guilty of a misdemeanor and, on conviction, is subject to a maximum fine of $5,000 or 1 year in prison, or both.	Md. Code Ann., Lab. & Empl. §§ 9-201, 9-401 et seq., 9-1107.
MA	Yes.	Yes.	Failure to insure results in a stop-work order against the employer, which is effective until the employer presents satisfactory proof of insurance and pays fines of $100 for each day of noncompliance. Employers also may be subject to criminal penalties of up to $1,500 in fines and up to 1 year of imprisonment.	Mass. Gen. Laws Ann. ch. 152, §§ 25A, 25C.

MI	Yes.	Yes.	An employer that fails to secure compensation is guilty of a misdemeanor and subject to a maximum fine of $1,000 or imprisonment for not more than 6 months, or both; each day's failure is a separate offense. Also, the employer may be liable for a maximum civil fine of $1,000 for each day of noncompliance and subject to an injunction preventing the employer from employing any worker until coverage is obtained. An employer found to have willfully violated notice provisions on numerous occasions regarding its coverage may be subject to a $750 civil fine.	Mich. Comp. Laws §§ 418:611, 418:641, 418:645; Mich. Stat. Ann. §§ 17.237(611), 17.237(641), 17.237(645).
MN	Yes.	Yes.	An employer that fails to insure may be subject to a penalty of $1,000 per employee per week of noncompliance, and to an order that it refrain from employing any person while not in compliance. An employer that willfully and intentionally violates the law is guilty of a gross misdemeanor. Self-insurers that violate rules regarding securing of compensation are subject to a civil penalty of $10,000 per offense.	Minn. Stat. Ann. § 176.181.
MS	Yes.	Yes.	An employer that fails to secure the payment of compensation is guilty of a misdemeanor and subject to a maximum criminal fine of $1,000 or imprisonment for up to 1 year, or both; corporate officers (president, secretary, treasurer) are severally liable. Employers may also be subject to a maximum civil penalty of $10,000. A person who willfully makes false statements to withhold benefits is guilty of a felony and may be subject to a maximum fine of $5,000 or double the value of the fraud, or imprisonment for up to 3 years, or both fine and imprisonment.	Miss. Code Ann. §§ 71-3-69, 71-3-83.
MO	Yes.	Yes.	Employers that knowingly fail to insure their liability are guilty of a class A misdemeanor and liable for a penalty of twice the amount of their annual premium or $25,000, whichever is greater. Late payments are punishable by an additional 10% of that amount.	Mo. Rev. Stat. §§ 287.128, 287.280.
MT	Yes.	Yes.	An uninsured employer will be ordered to cease operations until it becomes insured. An employer that does not comply with such an order is guilty of a misdemeanor. Such an employer is also prevented from asserting certain defenses in a suit brought by an injured employee. An uninsured employer may be required to pay a penalty of either double the premium amount the employer would have paid had it been insured or $200, whichever is greater.	Mont. Code Ann. §§ 39-71-401, 39-71-403, 39-71-406, 39-71-507, 39-71-2101 *et seq.*, 39-71-2201 *et seq.*, 39-71-2311 *et seq.*
NE	Yes.	Yes.	An employer that fails to insure is liable for damages to an injured worker or his or her heirs. An employer that willfully fails to secure compensation is guilty of a class I misdemeanor; with respect to corporations, officers are individually criminally liable. The employer may also be enjoined from doing business in the state.	Neb. Rev. Stat. Ann. §§ 48-145, 48-145.01.
NV	Yes.	Yes.	An employer that fails to insure may be subject to fines between $1,000 and $50,000 and 1 to 5 years of imprisonment.	Nev. Rev. Stat. Ann. §§ 616B.300 *et seq.*, 616B.612, 616D.120.
NH	Yes.	Yes.	An employer that fails to secure payment of compensation is liable for a civil penalty of up to $2,500, plus $100 per employee for each day of noncompliance. Such an employer may also be enjoined from conducting business and is guilty of a misdemeanor.	N.H. Rev. Stat. Ann. §§ 281-A:5, 281-A:5-a, 281-A:7.

(Table continues.)

Table 10.2-1 *(cont'd)*

WORKERS' COMPENSATION INSURANCE REQUIREMENTS

(See also text at § 10.2.)

	Is Insurance Required?	Is Self-Insurance Permitted?	Penalties for Failure to Secure Coverage	Citations to Authority
NJ	Yes.	Yes.	An employer that fails to provide required protection may be subject to criminal penalties, and an employer that willfully fails to comply will be guilty of a crime of the fourth degree. If the employer fails to comply for at least 10 days to provide coverage, it is subject to a fine of up to $1,000; if the employer fails to provide coverage for over 20 days, it is subject to up to an additional $1,000, and to the same amount for every 10-day period of noncompliance thereafter.	N.J. Stat. Ann. §§ 34:15-77, 34:15-79.
NM	Yes.	Yes.	Any person who violates the act or any rule enacted under it is subject to a fine of $25 to $1,000 per occurrence. Persons violating the group self-insurance requirements are subject to maximum fines of $1,000 for each violation, up to $10,000. Such an employer may be subject to a cease and desist order regarding the noncompliance, and failure to abide by the order may result in penalties of up to $10,000 per occurrence and up to $100,000 in the aggregate.	N.M. Stat. Ann. §§ 52-1-4, 52-1-61, 52-5-4.1, 52-6-21, 52-6-22.
NY	Yes.	Yes.	Failure to secure payment of compensation constitutes a misdemeanor, punishable by fines ranging from $500 to $2,500, or imprisonment for 1 year, or both. For a second conviction within 5 years, employer is subject to additional fines of $1,000 to $5,000; upon a third conviction, employer is subject to fines of up to $7,500. Where an employer has failed for at least 10 consecutive days to secure compensation, the employer may be fined an additional $250 for each 10-day period or up to 2% of payroll during the period of noncompliance. Where employer is a corporation, the president, secretary, and treasurer thereof are liable for any failure to secure the payment of compensation.	N.Y. Work. Comp. Law §§ 50, 52.
NC	Yes.	Yes.	An employer that refuses or neglects to secure the payment of compensation is subject to a penalty of $1 per employee for each day of noncompliance, with a $50 minimum and a $100 maximum penalty. An employer that negligently fails to secure compensation is guilty of a class 1 misdemeanor; an employer that willfully fails to secure compensation is guilty of a class H felony.	N.C. Gen. Stat. §§ 58-47-60 *et seq.*, 97-9, 97-93, 97-94.
ND	Yes.	No.	Failure to secure insurance coverage constitutes a class A misdemeanor, which is punishable by a $500 fine, 1 year of imprisonment, or both, and the employer may be enjoined from employing uninsured workers. An employer that willfully fails to secure compensation is fined $2,000 plus 10 times the difference between the premium paid and the amount that should have been paid. Where the employer is a corporation or limited liability company, officers of the entity are individually liable for any failure to secure workers' compensation coverage.	N.D. Cent. Code § 65-01-05.

State	Required	Penalties	Citations
OH	Yes, with fund administered by state.	An employer that has failed to pay its premium into the state fund may be enjoined from doing business, and the amount owed will be filed as a lien against the employer. An officer of a firm that fails to comply with the law is guilty of a minor misdemeanor and subject to a fine of up to $100, or, if the violation is willful, is guilty of a 2nd-degree misdemeanor and subject to a maximum fine of $750 or up to 90 days in jail, or both.	Ohio Rev. Code Ann. §§ 4123.35, 4123.75, 4123.79.
OK	Yes.	An employer that fails to secure coverage is liable for a civil penalty of $250 per employee for a first offense, unless the employer secures coverage within 30 days of receipt of notice of noncompliance. If such coverage is secured, the employer is liable for $75 per employee. A maximum fine of $1,000 per employee, or $10,000 for all related violations, may be assessed for subsequent violations. Employer also is subject to a cease and desist order. An employer that willfully fails to provide coverage is guilty of a misdemeanor and subject to a maximum criminal fine of $1,000 or 6 months in jail, or both. Late payments are subject to a 15% penalty.	Okla. Stat. Ann. tit. 85, §§ 61, 63.1, 63.3.
OR	Yes.	Actions may be brought against noncomplying employers without benefit of certain defenses. Noncomplying employers may also be subject to a civil penalty of $1,000 or twice the premium the employer would have paid during the period of noncompliance, whichever is greater. A person who continues to violate the law after an order declaring such a violation has become final is subject to additional daily fines of $250. Additional fines of up to $5,000 may be imposed if a worker suffers a compensable injury at a time when the employer is not insured. Officers and directors of corporate employers not complying with the act are jointly and severally liable for civil penalties.	Or. Rev. Stat. §§ 656.017, 656.020, 656.735.
PA	Yes.	An employer that fails to secure compensation is guilty of a 3rd-degree misdemeanor. An employer that intentionally fails to comply will be guilty of a 3rd-degree felony. Each noncompliant day constitutes a separate violation. A judge may, in addition to imposing fines and imprisonment, require an employer to pay restitution to any injured employee(s).	Pa. Stat. Ann. tit. 77, § 501.
RI	Yes.	An employer that knowingly fails to comply with the insurance requirements may be liable to suit by an injured employee without benefit of defenses provided in the act; the employer is also guilty of a misdemeanor and subject to fines of at least $500 for each day of noncompliance, up to a maximum fine of $1,000, or to imprisonment of up to 1 year, or both. Administrative penalties also may be imposed. Corporate officers are personally, jointly, and severally liable.	R.I. Gen. Laws §§ 28-36-1, 28-36-15.
SC	Yes.	An employer that fails to secure payment will be fined 10¢ for each employee at time insurance comes due, and between $1 and $50 for each day of noncompliance; an employer that willfully fails to secure compensation is guilty of a misdemeanor and subject to a fine of $100 to $1,000 or imprisonment for 30 days to 6 months, or both.	S.C. Code Ann. §§ 42-5-10, 42-5-20, 42-5-40, 42-5-45.
SD	Yes.	An employer that fails to obtain coverage is subject to suit by an injured employee without benefit of the defenses provided by the act; if an employee elects to pursue remedies under the act against a noncomplying employer, he or she may obtain the measure of benefits permitted by the act as well as twice any other compensation allowable under the act.	S.D. Codified Laws §§ 62-3-11, 62-5-1–62-5-5, 62-5-7.

(Table continues.)

Table 10.2-1 (cont'd)
WORKERS' COMPENSATION
INSURANCE REQUIREMENTS

(See also text at § 10.2.)

	Is Insurance Required?	Is Self-Insurance Permitted?	Penalties for Failure to Secure Coverage	Citations to Authority
TN	Yes.	Yes.	An employer that willfully refuses or neglects to comply with insurance requirements is subject to a penalty of 3 times the average yearly workers' compensation insurance premium in the state, up to a maximum of $100,000. For subsequent failure to comply, employer will be prevented from doing business until the employer complies.	Tenn. Code Ann. §§ 50-6-405, 50-6-412.
TX	Yes, for public employers. Because coverage is elective only for private employers, insurance is not required of them.	Yes.	—	Tex. Lab. Code Ann. §§ 406.002, 406.003.
UT	Yes.	Yes.	An employer that fails to obtain coverage is liable to suit by an employee without benefit of certain defenses, and the employee obtains certain presumptions in his or her favor. Such an employer may be subject to an injunction preventing the conduct of business until the employer comes into compliance. An employer may also be subject to a penalty of $1,000 or 3 times the premium the employer would have paid during the period of noncompliance, whichever is greater.	Utah Code Ann. §§ 34A-2-201, 34A-2-207, 34A-2-210, 34A-2-211.
VT	Yes.	Yes.	Employers that fail to secure compensation are liable for administrative penalties of up to $50 per day of noncompliance but no more than $5,000. An employer that fails to secure insurance for another 5 days after being notified that it is not in compliance will be assessed an additional $150 per day of noncompliance. Employers also may face criminal sanctions of up to $2,500 in fines, up to 1 year of imprisonment, or both. The business of an employer that fails to obtain coverage within 2 years of the issuance of an order to do so will be suspended until it comes into compliance. The officers and majority stockholders of a corporate employer that fails to secure compensation at a time when an employee is injured are personally liable for any benefits owed to the worker.	Vt. Stat. Ann. tit. 21, §§ 687, 687a, 692.
VA	Yes.	Yes.	An employer that fails to file evidence of compliance with the law will be assessed a civil penalty ranging from $500 to $5,000 and loses the right to maintain certain otherwise-available defenses. In addition, an employer that knowingly and intentionally fails to comply with the law is guilty of a class 2 misdemeanor.	Va. Code Ann. §§ 65.2-800, 65.2-801, 65.2-804, 65.2-805.

State	Required	Penalties	Citation
WA	Yes, with state fund.	It is unlawful for an employer or one of its officers to engage in business without obtaining a certificate of coverage, and a person so doing is guilty of a gross misdemeanor. An employer that continues to engage in business after a certificate of coverage has been revoked is guilty of a class C felony. Where an employee is injured before the employer secures coverage, the employer is liable for a penalty of 50% to 100% of the cost of the injury. An employer that has failed to secure compensation may also be liable for a maximum penalty of $500 or double the amount of premiums incurred prior to compliance.	Wash. Rev. Code Ann. §§ 51.04.120, 51.14.010 *et seq.*, 51.48.010, 51.48.020, 51.48.103.
WV	Yes, with fund administered by the state.	Employers that willfully fail to insure are guilty of a felony and subject to a maximum fine of $10,000. For a second offense, the party is subject to imprisonment for 1 to 3 years and a fine of between $5,000 and $25,000. The state may levy on the property of an employer that has defaulted on premium payments. Employers that fail to pay premiums are liable for damages to injured employees and may not assert certain defenses. Late payments accrue interest at 18%.	W. Va. Code §§ 23-1-16, 23-2-1, 23-2-5a, 23-2-8, 23-2-13.
WI	Yes.	An employer that fails to insure coverage for 7 days or less will be liable for a maximum fine of $1,000. If an employer fails to comply for more than 7 days, the employer will be liable for up to $100 per day of violation. An employer who does not insure may be subject to an order to cease business until it obtains insurance. An employer that violates such an order may be fined a maximum of $10,000 or imprisoned for 2 years, or both. Repeat offenders may be subject to an additional $2,000 fine or 90 days in jail, or both. If an employer is uninsured and an employee dies as a result of an injury for which employer is liable, employer must pay the department $1,000.	Wis. Stat. Ann. §§ 102.28, 102.82, 102.85, 102.88.
WY	Yes, for enumerated industries, with state fund.	Employers that fail to pay their premiums are subject to interest of 2% or $50 per month, whichever is greater, to additional fines, and to suit by the state to recover any amounts due, and may be subject to an injunction preventing them from doing business.	Wyo. Stat. Ann. §§ 27-14-201–27-14-203.

§ 10.3 Coverage of Minors

States cover both legally and illegally employed minors under workers' compensation statutes. The age of majority differs from state to state, and different rules regarding workers' compensation coverage often apply to minors of different ages. In a number of states, the minor's future earning capacity must be considered in arriving at the amount of compensation to be provided to a minor who is injured on the job. Some states also have special rules regarding the validity of settlements of the workers' compensation claims of minors.

Table 10.3-1 provides information on whether minors are covered by state workers' compensation statutes and the age at which a worker is no longer considered a minor (the age of majority). The table also indicates whether future earning capacity must be considered in determining the amount of compensation to which a minor is entitled, and whether, and under what conditions, a minor's workers' compensation claim can be settled. Finally, the table lists other provisions of state workers' compensation laws that apply only to minors, such as exceptions from reductions of benefits, and extended statutes of limitations.

Table 10.3-1

COVERAGE OF MINORS

(See also text at § 10.3.)

	Are Minors Covered?	Age of Majority?	Is Future Earning Capacity Considered in Determining Amount of Award to Minor?	Are Settlements of a Minor's Claims Valid?	Exceptions or Other Provisions	Citations to Authority
AL	Yes.	19.	No specific statutory provision.	Yes.	If, at the time of the injury, the minor was employed in violation of, or contrary to, the law regulating the employment of minors, the compensation shall be 2 times what it would be if the employment had been legal.	Ala. Code §§ 25-5-34, 25-5-55, 26-1-1.
AK	Yes.	18. Note: An individual as young as age 14 may be considered an adult if he or she possesses a valid marriage license.	No specific statutory provision.	No specific statutory provision.	Statute of limitations does not run against minor without guardian.	Alaska Stat. §§ 23.30.105, 25.20.010, 25.20.020; *Whitney Fidalgo Seafoods, Inc. v. Home Ins. Co.,* 447 F. Supp. 393 (D. Alaska 1978).
AZ	Yes.	18.	Yes.	No specific statutory provision.	—	Ariz. Rev. Stat. Ann. §§ 8-101, 23-1042.
AR	Yes.	18.	No specific statutory provision.	No specific statutory provision.	—	Ark. Code Ann. §§ 9-25-101, 11-9-504.
CA	Yes.	18.	Yes.	No specific statutory provision.	If employee is under age 16 when injured, compensation will not be reduced by half in cases of serious and willful misconduct by a minor employee.	Cal. Lab. Code §§ 3351, 3352, 4455, 4551; Cal. Fam. Code § 6500.
CO	Yes.	18.	No specific statutory provision.	No specific statutory provision.	—	Colo. Rev. Stat. Ann. §§ 8-12-117, 13-22-101.
CT	Yes.	18.	No specific statutory provision.	No specific statutory provision.	—	Conn. Gen. Stat. Ann. §§ 1-1d, 31-318.
DE	Yes.	18.	No specific statutory provision.	No specific statutory provision.	—	Del. Code Ann. tit. 1, § 701; tit. 19, § 2315.

(Table continues.)

Table 10.3-1   PART 10—STATE WORKERS' COMPENSATION LAWS   10-62

Table 10.3-1 (cont'd)

COVERAGE OF MINORS

(See also text at § 10.3.)

	Are Minors Covered?	Age of Majority?	Is Future Earning Capacity Considered in Determining Amount of Award to Minor?	Are Settlements of a Minor's Claims Valid?	Exceptions or Other Provisions	Citations to Authority
DC	Yes.	18.	Yes.	No specific statutory provision.	—	D.C. Code Ann. §§ 30-401, 36-301(18), 36-311.
FL	Yes.	18.	Yes, where employee is under age 22 at time of injury or death and, under normal conditions, his or her wages would be expected to increase during the period of disability.	No specific statutory provision.	Statute of limitations does not run against minor without guardian.	Fla. Stat. Ann. §§ 440.02, 440.14, 440.19, 743.07.
GA	Yes.	18.	No specific statutory provision.	No specific statutory provision.	Statute of limitations does not run against minor without guardian.	Ga. Code Ann. §§ 34-9-85, 34-9-86.
HI	Yes.	18.	Yes.	No specific statutory provision.	Statute of limitations does not run against minor without guardian.	Haw. Rev. Stat. Ann. §§ 386-51, 386-84, 577-1.
ID	Yes.	18.	No specific statutory provision.	No specific statutory provision.	Statute of limitations does not run against minor without guardian.	Idaho Code §§ 32-101, 72-705.
IL	Yes.	18.	No specific statutory provision.	Yes, with approval of commission.	Minor may reject workers' compensation rights within 6 months in exchange for full common-law or statutory remedies.	755 Ill. Comp. Stat. Ann. 5/11-1; 820 Ill. Comp. Stat. Ann. 305/5, 305/23.
IN	Yes.	17.	No specific statutory provision.	No specific statutory provision.	Statute of limitations does not run against minor without guardian.	Ind. Code Ann. §§ 22-3-3-30, 22-3-6-1.
IA	Yes.	18.	No specific statutory provision.	No specific statutory provision.	—	Iowa Code Ann. §§ 85.61, 599.1.
KS	Yes.	18.	No specific statutory provision.	No specific statutory provision.	Statute of limitations does not run against minor without guardian.	Kan. Stat. Ann. §§ 38-101, 44-509.

KY	Yes.	18.	No specific statutory provision.	No specific statutory provision.	Statute of limitations does not run against minor without guardian. No benefits for unremunerated student trainees.	Ky. Rev. Stat. Ann. §§ 342.210, 342.640; Salvation Army v. Mathews, 847 S.W.2d 751 (Ky. Ct. App. 1993).
LA	Yes.	18.	No specific statutory provision.	No specific statutory provision.	—	La. Rev. Stat. Ann. § 23:1035; La. Civ. Code Ann. art. 29.
ME	Yes.	18.	No specific statutory provision.	No specific statutory provision.	Minor retains right of action at common law if illegally employed, in addition to workers' compensation.	Me. Rev. Stat. Ann. tit. 22, § 3472; tit. 39-A, § 408.
MD	Yes.	18.	No specific statutory provision.	No specific statutory provision.	—	Md. Code Ann., Lab. & Empl. § 9-103; Md. Const. art. 1, § 24.
MA	Yes.	18.	Yes.	No specific statutory provision.	—	Mass. Gen. Laws Ann. ch. 152, § 51; ch. 231, § 85P.
MI	Yes.	18.	No specific statutory provision.	No specific statutory provision.	—	Mich. Comp. Laws Ann. §§ 418.111, 722.52; Mich. Stat. Ann. §§ 17.237(111), 25.244(52).
MN	Yes.	18.	No specific statutory provision.	No specific statutory provision.	Minors with permanent total or compensable permanent partial disability receive maximum recovery.	Minn. Stat. Ann. §§ 176.011, 176.101, 645.451.
MS	Yes.	18.	No specific statutory provision.	No specific statutory provision.	—	Miss. Code Ann. § 71-3-107.
MO	Yes.	18.	Yes, for employees under age 21.	No specific statutory provision.	—	Mo. Rev. Stat. §§ 287.250, 431.055.
MT	Yes.	18.	No specific statutory provision.	No specific statutory provision.	Newspaper carrier not covered if parent, guardian, or minor acknowledges in writing lack of coverage.	Mont. Code Ann. §§ 39-71-118, 39-71-401, 41-1-101.
NE	Yes.	19. Married persons under the age of 19 are also considered to be adults.	No specific statutory provision.	No specific statutory provision.	—	Neb. Rev. Stat. Ann. §§ 43-2101, 48-132.
NV	Yes.	18.	No specific statutory provision.	No specific statutory provision.	—	Nev. Rev. Stat. Ann. §§ 129.010, 616D.290.
NH	Yes.	18.	No specific statutory provision.	No specific statutory provision.	—	N.H. Rev. Stat. Ann. § 21:44.
NJ	Yes.	18.	No specific statutory provision.	No specific statutory provision.	Minors retain common-law cause of action for employer's negligence.	N.J. Stat. Ann. §§ 9:17B-3, 34:15-10.

(Table continues.)

Table 10.3-1 (cont'd)

COVERAGE OF MINORS

(See also text at § 10.3.)

	Are Minors Covered?	Age of Majority?	Is Future Earning Capacity Considered in Determining Amount of Award to Minor?	Are Settlements of a Minor's Claims Valid?	Exceptions or Other Provisions	Citations to Authority
NM	Yes.	18.	No specific statutory provision.	No specific statutory provision.	—	N.M. Stat. Ann. §§ 28-6-1, 52-5-11.
NY	Yes.	18.	No specific statutory provision.	No specific statutory provision.	Statute of limitations does not run against minor without committee or guardian.	N.Y. Work. Comp. Law §§ 2, 115.
NC	Yes.	18.	No specific statutory provision.	No specific statutory provision.	Statute of limitations does not run against minor without guardian.	N.C. Gen. Stat. §§ 48A-2, 97-10.3, 97-50.
ND	Yes.	18.	No specific statutory provision.	No specific statutory provision.	—	N.D. Cent. Code §§ 14-10-01, 65-01-02.
OH	Yes.	18.	No specific statutory provision.	No specific statutory provision.	—	Ohio Rev. Code Ann. §§ 3109.01, 4123.89.
OK	Yes.	18.	No specific statutory provision.	No specific statutory provision.	Statute of limitations does not run against minor without guardian.	Okla. Stat. Ann. tit. 15, § 13; tit. 85, §§ 21, 106.
OR	Yes.	18.	No specific statutory provision.	No specific statutory provision.	—	Or. Rev. Stat. §§ 3.250, 656.132.
PA	Yes.	18.	No specific statutory provision.	No specific statutory provision.	The right of a minor to receive compensation for a compensable accident or injury is not affected if he or she obtained employment by misrepresenting his or her age.	Pa. Stat. Ann. tit. 23, § 5101; tit. 77, § 421.
RI	Yes.	18.	No specific statutory provision.	No specific statutory provision.	—	R.I. Gen. Laws §§ 15-21-1, 28-33-22.
SC	Yes.	18.	No specific statutory provision.	No specific statutory provision.	Statute of limitations does not run against minor without guardian.	S.C. Code Ann. §§ 20-7-30, 42-1-130, 42-15-50.
SD	Yes.	18.	No specific statutory provision.	No specific statutory provision.	—	S.D. Codified Laws §§ 26-1-1, 62-1-3.

TN	Yes.	18.	No specific statutory provision.	No specific statutory provision.	—	Tenn. Code Ann. §§ 1-3-105, 50-6-102.
TX	Yes.	18.	Yes, for minors whose earnings are limited due to apprenticeship, training, or education aimed at enhancing future wages.	No specific statutory provision.	—	Tex. Lab. Code Ann. § 408.044; Tex. Civ. Prac. & Rem. Code Ann. § 129.001.
UT	Yes.	18.	No specific statutory provision.	No specific statutory provision.	—	Utah Code Ann. §§ 15-2-1, 34A-2-104.
VT	Yes.	18.	No specific statutory provision.	No specific statutory provision.	Statute of limitations does not run against minor without guardian.	Vt. Stat. Ann. tit. 1, § 173; tit. 21, § 661.
VA	Yes.	18.	No specific statutory provision.	No specific statutory provision.	—	Va. Code Ann. §§ 1-13.42, 65.2-101.
WA	Yes.	18.	No specific statutory provision.	No specific statutory provision.	—	Wash. Rev. Code Ann. §§ 26.28.010, 51.04.070.
WV	Yes.	18.	No specific statutory provision.	No specific statutory provision.	—	W. Va. Code §§ 2-3-1, 23-2-1a.
WI	Yes.	18.	No specific statutory provision.	No specific statutory provision.	—	Wis. Stat. Ann. §§ 48.02, 102.07; *Harry Crow & Son, Inc. v. Industrial Comm'n*, 118 N.W.2d 841 (Wis. 1963).
WY	Yes.	18.	No specific statutory provision.	No specific statutory provision.	Statute of limitations does not run against minor without guardian.	Wyo. Stat. Ann. §§ 8-1-102, 27-14-102, 27-14-505.

§ 10.4 Compensation Required for Unlawfully Employed Minors

A number of states require additional compensation, often double and sometimes triple compensation, for unlawfully employed minors who are injured on the job. Significantly, many such penalties must be paid directly by the employer rather than by the employer's insurer. A number of states recognize certain exceptions to the requirement of additional compensation for unlawfully employed minors. In some states, additional compensation will not be required if the minor misrepresented his or her age to the employer. In other states, additional compensation will not be required if the minor employee had attained a certain age or was employed with the express consent of a parent.

A few jurisdictions allow minor employees to retain their common-law rights of action against an employer in whose employ they become injured. In states that allow a minor to retain common-law rights, employers face potential exposure to damage awards far beyond the restricted compensation typically authorized by workers' compensation statutes.

Table 10.4-1 shows whether the state requires additional compensation for unlawfully employed minors injured on the job, the amount of such required compensation, and the party responsible for payment of the additional compensation. The table also sets out exceptions to the additional compensation requirement and available employer defenses.

Table 10.4-1

COMPENSATION REQUIRED FOR UNLAWFULLY EMPLOYED MINORS

(See also text at § 10.4.)

	Does State Require Additional Compensation for Unlawfully Employed Minors?	What Amount of Additional Compensation Is Required?	Are There Exceptions to Additional Compensation Requirements?	Who Must Pay Additional Compensation?	Citations to Authority
AL	Yes.	Double.	Yes, violation of purely procedural statutes does not establish right to additional compensation.	No specific statutory provision.	Ala. Code §§ 25-5-34, 25-5-55, 26-1-1; *Willis v. Storey*, 105 So. 2d 128 (Ala. 1958).
AK	No, but illegally employed minor can avoid exclusive remedy provision.	—	—	—	*Whitney Fidalgo Seafoods, Inc. v. Home Ins. Co*, 447 F. Supp. 393 (D. Alaska 1978).
AZ	Yes.	50%.	—	Insurer entitled to recover any additional compensation paid from the employer.	Ariz. Rev. Stat. Ann. § 23-905.
AR	Yes.	Double.	Yes, additional compensation not required if minor misrepresented age to the employer in writing.	No specific statutory provision.	Ark. Code Ann. § 11-9-504.
CA	Yes, for employees under age 16.	50%.	Employer not liable for additional compensation if employee was hired pursuant to falsely obtained birth certificate, driver's license, or other reasonable evidence that employee is age 16 or older.	Employer.	Cal. Lab. Code § 4557; Cal. Ins. Code § 11661.5.
CO	No.	—	—	—	—
CT	No.	—	—	—	—
DE	No.	—	—	—	—
DC	No.	—	—	—	—
FL	Yes.	Judge's discretion, up to double.	—	Employer.	Fla. Stat. Ann. § 440.54.
GA	No.	—	—	—	—
HI	No.	—	—	—	—

(Table continues.)

Table 10.4-1   PART 10—STATE WORKERS' COMPENSATION LAWS   10-68

Table 10.4-1 (cont'd)
COMPENSATION REQUIRED
FOR UNLAWFULLY EMPLOYED MINORS

(See also text at § 10.4.)

	Does State Require Additional Compensation for Unlawfully Employed Minors?	What Amount of Additional Compensation Is Required?	Are There Exceptions to Additional Compensation Requirements?	Who Must Pay Additional Compensation?	Citations to Authority
ID	No.	—	—	—	—
IL	Yes, for minors under age 16.	50%.	If employer has on file employment certificate issued pursuant to the Child Labor Law or work permit issued pursuant to Fair Labor Standards Act, or a birth certificate properly and duly issued, such documentation is conclusive evidence of age for purposes of awarding additional compensation.	No specific statutory provision.	820 Ill. Comp. Stat. Ann. 305/7, 305/8.
IN	Yes, for minors under age 16.	Double.	Yes, exception for vocational education students; no double compensation for 16-year-olds.	Employer and insurer each pay half.	Ind. Code Ann. § 22-3-6-1.
IA	No.	—	—	—	—
KS	No.	—	—	—	—
KY	No.	—	—	—	—
LA	No.	—	—	—	—
ME	No.	—	—	—	Fanion v. McNeal, 577 A.2d 2 (Me. 1990).
MD	Yes.	May be doubled at judge's discretion.	Certificate of commissioner of labor and industry is conclusive evidence of the legality of a minor's employment.	Employer.	Md. Code Ann., Lab. & Empl. § 9-606.
MA	Yes.	Double.	No.	Employer.	Mass. Gen. Laws Ann. ch. 152, § 28.
MI	Yes.	Double.	Yes, for minor's fraudulent use of permits or certificates of age.	No specific statutory provision.	Mich. Comp. Laws Ann. § 418.161; Mich. Stat. Ann. § 17.237(161).
MN	No.	—	—	—	—

State					
MS	Yes.	Double.	No double compensation for student age 14 and over employed between semesters with written consent of parent or in on-the-job training as part of secondary school program with written consent of parent.	Employer.	Miss. Code Ann. § 71-3-107.
MO	Yes.	50%.	No.	No specific statutory provision.	Mo. Rev. Stat. § 287.250.
MT	No.	—	—	—	—
NE	No.	—	—	—	—
NV	Yes.	$300–$2,000.	No.	No specific statutory provision.	Nev. Rev. Stat. Ann. § 616D.290.
NH	Yes.	Double.	No.	Employer and insurer each pay half.	N.H. Rev. Stat. Ann. § 281-A:33.
NJ	Yes, for minor under age 14 unlawfully employed, those between ages 14 and 18 without an employment certificate or special permit if required by law, and a minor whose occupation is prohibited at the minor's age by law.	Double.	Duly issued employment certificate is conclusive evidence that minor had reached the age indicated therein, even if falsely provided, if employer can show that it accepted certificate in good faith and could not have, with reasonable diligence, discovered the fraud. Employees of certain summer camps are also excluded, as well as members of a junior firemen's auxiliary, employees of religious or charitable organizations, vocational education students, volunteers in Palisades Interstate Park, and volunteers with the Division of Parks and Forestry, the Division of Fish, Game and Wildlife, the New Jersey Natural Lands Trust, or the New Jersey Historic Trust, as authorized by the commissioner of environmental protection.	Employer.	N.J. Stat. Ann. § 34:15-10.
NM	No.	—	—	—	—
NY	Yes.	Double.	No.	Employer.	N.Y. Work. Comp. Law § 14-a.
NC	No.	—	—	—	N.C. Gen. Stat. § 97-10.3.
ND	No.	—	—	—	—
OH	Yes.	Double.	No, but a previously enacted version of this statute has been ruled unconstitutional.	No specific statutory provision.	Ohio Rev. Code Ann. § 4123.89; *Kantor Corp. v. Stringer*, 424 N.E.2d 282 (Ohio 1981).
OK	No.	—	—	—	—

(Table continues.)

Table 10.4-1   PART 10—STATE WORKERS' COMPENSATION LAWS   10-70

Table 10.4-1 (cont'd)
COMPENSATION REQUIRED
FOR UNLAWFULLY EMPLOYED MINORS

(See also text at § 10.4.)

	Does State Require Additional Compensation for Unlawfully Employed Minors?	What Amount of Additional Compensation Is Required?	Are There Exceptions to Additional Compensation Requirements?	Who Must Pay Additional Compensation?	Citations to Authority
OR	Yes.	25% penalty ($100–$500) paid to Insurance and Finance Fund if employer has no state certificate authorizing employment of minor.	No.	No specific statutory provision.	Or. Rev. Stat. § 656.132.
PA	Yes.	50%.	No.	Employer.	Pa. Stat. Ann. tit. 77, § 672.
RI	Yes.	Triple.	No.	No specific statutory provision.	R.I. Gen. Laws § 28-33-22.
SC	No.	—	—	—	—
SD	No.	—	—	—	—
TN	No.	—	—	—	—
TX	No.	—	—	—	—
UT	No.	—	—	—	—
VT	No.	—	—	—	—
VA	No.	—	—	—	—
WA	No.	—	—	—	—
WV	No.	—	—	—	—
WI	Yes.	Double if of permit age and without permit. Triple if under permit age, of permit age but engaged in prohibited employment, or of permit age but employed in job for which department of industry, labor and job development has resolved in writing not to issue permits.	No, but if employer is misled by fraudulent written evidence of age presented by minor, the extra compensation is paid to the state fund, rather than to the employee.	No specific statutory provision.	Wis. Stat. Ann. § 102.60.
WY	No.	—	—	—	—

§ 10.5 Required Medical Benefits and Providers

All states that require employers to insure against liability for worker injury mandate that the employer pay for a worker's medical treatment necessitated by the injury, in addition to any wage benefits to which the employee may be entitled. The extent of such required medical coverage differs from state to state. For example, virtually every state requires an employer to pay for the physical rehabilitation of an injured employee, but some states also require that the employer pay for retraining of the worker if an employment-related injury creates a permanent disability preventing the employee from returning to his or her previous job.

The party designated to select a health care provider also varies from state to state. Although the majority of states permit an injured employee to select a treating physician or provider, nine of those states (Georgia, Missouri, Nevada, New York, Pennsylvania, South Carolina, Tennessee, Texas, and Washington) limit an employee's choice to health care providers included on a state- or employer-compiled list. Other states, such as Alabama, Idaho, North Carolina, and Vermont, allow the employer to designate a health care provider, but establish a means by which an employee may petition for a change in physician if the employee is dissatisfied.

Table 10.5-1 lists some medical benefits employers must provide to their employees, indicating whether employers must supply injured workers with artificial devices or prostheses and the extent of the employer's responsibility for rehabilitation. The table also indicates whether the employer or the employee may choose a health care provider and whether chiropractic care is specifically covered under a state's act.

Table 10.5-1   PART 10—STATE WORKERS' COMPENSATION LAWS   10-72

Table 10.5-1

REQUIRED MEDICAL BENEFITS AND PROVIDERS

(See also text at § 10.5.)

	Who Chooses Physician?	Is Chiropractic Treatment Covered?	Are Rehabilitative Services Covered?	Are Medical Devices and Equipment Covered?	Other Provisions	Citations to Authority
AL	Employer, but objecting employee may select a second physician from panel of 4 selected by employer.	No specific statutory provision.	Employer must pay cost of physical rehabilitation.	Employer must pay cost of repair, refitting, or replacement of artificial members damaged in course of employment; employer must pay for crutches and artificial members.	Employee's right of compensation may be suspended for refusal to comply with reasonable request for examination or with medical treatment.	Ala. Code § 25-5-77.
AK	Employee.	Yes.	Yes.	Yes, for up to 2 years from date of injury or from employee's discovery of injury and its relationship to employment. Employer must pay the cost of all medical, surgical, and other required treatments, including medicine, crutches, and other apparatus.	Employee may not make more than one change in choice of physician without written consent of employer. If employee is unable to designate a physician in an emergency or fails to do so under any circumstances, employer must designate physician. An employer's designation does not prevent an employee from subsequently selecting another physician.	Alaska Stat. §§ 23.30.041, 23.30.095.
AZ	No specific statutory provision.	No specific statutory provision.	Yes, by state fund.	Employer must pay cost of surgical supplies, crutches, and artificial members reasonably required at the time of the injury and during the period of disability.	Employer is not liable for injury suffered by employee upon refusal to submit to treatment. Treatment by prayer or spiritual means is covered if approved by the workers' compensation commission.	Ariz. Rev. Stat. Ann. §§ 23-1027, 23-1061.01, 23-1062.

AR	If employer has a managed care organization (MCO), such organization specifies treating physician. Employee may petition for a change of physician within managed care network, unless unusual circumstances exist or employee has a history of treatment with an outside provider for same condition. If employer is not affiliated with an MCO, provider selected by whoever chooses first, employer or employee.	Yes.	Yes, employee who is entitled to receive benefits for permanent disability and who has not been offered either an opportunity to return to work or reemployment assistance must be paid reasonable expenses and costs of a program of vocational rehabilitation if program is found reasonable in relation to disability. Employer's maximum liability is 72 weeks.	Employer must promptly pay such medical, surgical, hospital, chiropractic, optometric, or podiatric costs as are reasonably necessary in connection with the injury received. Similarly, employer must pay for any and all reasonably necessary crutches, ambulatory devices, and artificial limbs.	Employer must supply eyeglasses, contact lenses, and hearing aids if reasonably necessary in connection with an injury received by an employee.	Ark. Code Ann. §§ 11-9-505, 11-9-508; Workers' Compensation Rule 33.
CA	Employer for first 30 days following worker's injury, employee thereafter; however, if employee notifies employer in writing prior to date of injury that he or she has a personal physician, employee may be treated by that physician from date of injury.	Yes.	Yes.		Employer must pay for X rays, laboratory fees, other diagnostic tests, medical reports, and medical records.	Cal. Lab. Code §§ 139.5, 4600.
CO	Employer chooses in first instance, but if services of a physician are not utilized at time of injury, employee may choose. Failure of employer to object to selection of employee's personal physician within 20 days waives any objections.	Yes, but only for 90 days after initial treatment or up to 12 treatments, whichever occurs first, unless chiropractor has received accreditation under workers' compensation law.	Yes, where employee is permanently and totally disabled, and is capable of being rehabilitated.		Employee may petition for a replacement of any device on grounds that employee has undergone anatomical change necessitating such replacement, where anatomical change is directly related to and caused by injury.	Colo. Rev. Stat. Ann. §§ 8-42-101, 8-42-111, 12-36-106.
CT	Employee chooses a physician from a list of approved doctors promulgated by the chairman of the workers' compensation commission.	Yes.	Yes.	Yes, employer liable for replacement or repair for accidental damage to artificial legs, feet, arms, or hands in course of employment; employer must also repair or replace eyeglasses, contact lenses, hearing aids, and artificial teeth where damage is accompanied by bodily injury to face or head.	Employee who refuses to accept and fails to obtain reasonable medical care loses all right to compensation under act during such refusal and failure. Direct payment for prescription medication is required.	Conn. Gen. Stat. Ann. §§ 31-275, 31-279, 31-283a, 31-294d, 31-294e, 31-311.

(Table continues.)

Table 10.5-1   PART 10—STATE WORKERS' COMPENSATION LAWS   10-74

Table 10.5-1 (cont'd)
REQUIRED MEDICAL BENEFITS AND PROVIDERS

(See also text at § 10.5.)

	Who Chooses Physician?	Is Chiropractic Treatment Covered?	Are Rehabilitative Services Covered?	Are Medical Devices and Equipment Covered?	Other Provisions	Citations to Authority
DE	Employee.	Yes.	Voluntary by employer.	Yes. Employer must repair or replace dentures, false eyes, and eyeglasses, and must provide hearing aids as needed.	Employer or its insurance obligated to replace or renew a defective or worn out prosthesis for life of injured person.	Del. Code Ann. tit. 19, §§ 2322, 2323.
DC	No specific statutory provision.	No specific statutory provision.	No specific statutory provision.	No specific statutory provision.	No specific statutory provision.	—
FL	Employer.	Yes, up to 18 treatments or up to 8 weeks beyond date of initial chiropractic treatment, whichever comes first, unless carrier authorizes further treatment and employee is catastrophically injured.	Yes.	Yes, including medical supplies, durable medical equipment, orthoses, prostheses, and other medically necessary apparatus.	Claims for specialist consultations, surgical operations, physiotherapeutic or occupational therapy procedures, X-ray examinations, or special diagnostic laboratory tests that cost more than $1,000 are not valid and reimbursable unless services have been expressly authorized by carrier or carrier has failed to respond to a request for authorization within 10 days.	Fla. Stat. Ann. § 440.13.
GA	Employee, from employer list.	An employer may request that the board order a change of physician or treatment and designate another physician or other treatment.	Yes, in event of catastrophic injury employer shall furnish employee with reasonable and necessary rehabilitation services.	Yes, including medical and surgical supplies, artificial members, and prosthetic devices and aids.	Refusal of employee without reasonable cause to accept rehabilitation entitles state to suspend or reduce compensation.	Ga. Code Ann. §§ 34-9-200, 34-9-200.1.
HI	Employee.	Yes.	Yes.	Yes, artificial members, eyeglasses, and any other aid, appliance, and apparatus certified as necessary to cure or relieve effects of an injury.	Employee may change physicians under rules promulgated by director of labor and industrial relations.	Haw. Rev. Stat. Ann. §§ 386-1, 386-21, 386-22, 386-25.

ID	Employer, but employee may petition for change of physician.	Yes.	Yes.	Yes. Employer must also furnish necessary replacements or repairs of appliances and prostheses, unless the need therefor is due to a lack of proper care by employee.	Christian Science treatment by practitioner covered under act. Employer responsible for travel to and from rehabilitation facility, or, if treatment is outpatient, for board, lodging, and transportation.	Idaho Code §§ 72-102, 72-432, 72-433.
IL	Employee selects a physician from a list provided by employer; however, employee retains the right to select an alternate physician if not satisfied with initial treatment.	No specific statutory provision.	Yes.	Yes.	Employer is liable for maintenance of an employee incidental to physical, mental, or vocational rehabilitation. Spiritual treatment permitted if agreed to by employer and employee.	820 Ill. Comp. Stat. Ann. 305/8.
IN	Employer.	No specific statutory provision.	Yes.	Yes.	Spiritual treatment may be permitted by employer in lieu of other medical treatment. Failure of employee to accept services and supplies provided by employer will bar employee from receiving any other benefits to which he or she is entitled until such time as the period of refusal ceases.	Ind. Code Ann. §§ 22-3-3-4, 22-3-12-1.
IA	Employer; however, employee may choose provider in emergency when employer cannot be reached. If dissatisfied by the care afforded by employer's designated physician, employee may petition the commissioner for an alternate physician.	Yes.	Yes.	Employer must furnish all reasonable and necessary crutches, artificial members, and appliances, and one set of permanent prosthetic devices.	—	Iowa Code Ann. § 85.27.
KS	Employer.	No specific statutory provision.	Yes, under direction of a state-appointed vocational rehabilitation administrator and by agreement of employer or carrier, employee may be referred to approved provider.	Yes.	Employee may rely solely or partially on treatment by prayer or spiritual means in accordance with tenets of church or denomination without loss of benefits.	Kan. Stat. Ann. §§ 44-510, 44-510g.

(Table continues.)

Table 10.5-1 PART 10—STATE WORKERS' COMPENSATION LAWS 10-76

Table 10.5-1 *(cont'd)*

REQUIRED MEDICAL BENEFITS
AND PROVIDERS

(See also text at § 10.5.)

	Who Chooses Physician?	Is Chiropractic Treatment Covered?	Are Rehabilitative Services Covered?	Are Medical Devices and Equipment Covered?	Other Provisions	Citations to Authority
KY	Employee, unless employer has designated a managed health care system.	Yes.	Yes, if because of injury employee is unable to perform work for which employee has had previous training or experience. Services will not extend beyond 52 weeks, except in unusual cases by order of an administrative law judge.	Yes.	Refusal to accept rehabilitation pursuant to an order will result in a 50% reduction in compensation for each week of refusal.	Ky. Rev. Stat. Ann. §§ 342.0011, 342.020.
LA	Employee.	No specific statutory provision.	Yes.	Yes.	After choosing physician, employee must obtain prior consent from employer or carrier for change of treating physician within same field. Employer liable for replacement of prostheses damaged in course of employment. Employer liable for travel expenses necessary for employee to obtain medical services.	La. Rev. Stat. Ann. §§ 23:1121, 23:1203, 23:1226.
ME	Employer; however, employee has right to choose after 10 days.	Yes.	Yes, when as a result of injury employee is unable to perform work for which employee has had previous training or experience, employee entitled to such rehabilitation as reasonably necessary to restore employee to suitable employment.	Yes.	Employer must replace or renew physical aids when necessary from wear and tear or physical change of employee. Treatment by prayer or spiritual means subject to agreement by employer.	Me. Rev. Stat. Ann. tit. 39-A, §§ 206, 217.

MD	Employee.	No specific statutory provision.	Yes. Vocational rehabilitation training limited to 24 months.	Yes.	Employer must repair or replace any prosthetic device or eyeglasses damaged or destroyed as a result of accident during course of employment.	Md. Code Ann., Lab. & Empl. §§ 9-660, 9-661, 9-670 et seq.
MA	Employee.	Yes.	Voluntary by employer.	Yes.	If employee refuses independent examination, right to compensation is suspended and may be forfeited.	Mass. Gen. Laws Ann. ch. 112, § 97; ch. 152, §§ 30, 30E et seq., 45.
MI	Employer; employee may select a physician 10 days after inception of medical care, but selection is subject to employer objection.	Yes.	Yes.	Yes.	On request, employee who filed the injury report must periodically submit to examination by employer-furnished physician. Employer is not obligated to provide certain optometric services.	Mich. Comp. Laws Ann. §§ 418:315, 418:319, 418:385; Mich. Stat. Ann. §§ 17.237(315), 17.237(319), 17.237(385).
MN	Employee, although employer may seek change of physician.	Yes.	Yes, employer must provide necessary physical and vocational rehabilitation; employer must provide qualified rehabilitation consultant to employee on request. If rehabilitation plan is prescribed and approved, employer is liable for cost of all services and supplies necessary for implementation of plan, but for no more than 156 weeks.	Yes.	Christian Science treatment is available at option of employee if notice is given at time of employment, unless employer files election with state not to be subject to requirement.	Minn. Stat. Ann. §§ 176.102, 176.135; Minn. R. 5221.0430 (1999).
MS	Employee.	No specific statutory provision.	Employees eligible for state rehabilitation program may receive an additional $10 a week for maintenance for a maximum of 52 weeks.	Yes.	Employee's chosen physician may refer to only one specialist in a given subject area; further referrals must be approved by employer or carrier.	Miss. Code Ann. §§ 71-3-15, 71-3-19.
MO	Employer; employee retains the right to select a physician but must pay those costs.	Yes.	Yes, administered by state, and benefits are payable for duration or program, which cannot exceed 52 weeks.	Yes.	Employer must provide all necessary and reasonable expenses to any employee required to undergo examination or treatment outside local area. Treatment by prayer and spiritual means is permitted if employer approves.	Mo. Rev. Stat. §§ 287.140, 287.141, 287.148.

(Table continues.)

Table 10.5-1 PART 10—STATE WORKERS' COMPENSATION LAWS 10-78

Table 10.5-1 (cont'd)

REQUIRED MEDICAL BENEFITS AND PROVIDERS

(See also text at § 10.5.)

	Who Chooses Physician?	Is Chiropractic Treatment Covered?	Are Rehabilitative Services Covered?	Are Medical Devices and Equipment Covered?	Other Provisions	Citations to Authority
MT	Employee.	Yes.	Yes, for workers who have a permanent impairment that precludes worker from returning to job held prior to injury, or for workers who as a result of a work-related injury have an impairment rating of 15% or greater. Worker must be subject to a rehabilitation plan agreed upon by insurer. Worker must begin plan within 78 weeks of reaching maximum medical healing, and must complete plan within 26 weeks of completion date specified in plan.	Yes.	Employer liable for repair or replacement of prosthesis furnished as a result of an industrial accident.	Mont. Code Ann. §§ 39-71-116, 39-71-704, 39-71-1006, 39-71-1101.
NE	Employee.	Yes.	Yes, for workers who as a result of injury are unable to perform suitable work for which they have had previous training or experience. Vocational rehabilitation is provided under auspices of Nebraska Workers' Compensation Court and must be administered by a certified vocational rehabilitation counselor pursuant to a rehabilitation plan. Such services are provided as reasonably necessary to restore worker to suitable employment.	Yes.	Employer must replace artificial devices and dental appliances, hearing aids, and eyeglasses if damaged during course of employee's sustaining a compensable injury. Employee who unreasonably refuses medical treatment may forfeit right to benefits.	Neb. Rev. Stat. Ann. §§ 48-120, 48-162.01; Neb. Admin. R. & Regs. 36–50.

State						Citation
NV	Employee, from state-approved list.	Yes.	Yes.	Yes.	Employee may elect treatment through prayer in lieu of medical treatment.	Nev. Rev. Stat. Ann. §§ 616C.040, 616C.090, 616C.120, 616C.245, 616C.275, 616C.530 et seq.
NH	Employee.	Yes.	Yes, for an employee who as a result of injury is unable to perform work for which employee has had previous training or experience. Services are provided as reasonably necessary to restore employee to suitable employment, and may not exceed 1 year except in unusual circumstances.	Yes.	Employee who refuses to cooperate with vocational rehabilitation may lose compensation. Employer is liable for repair or replacement of medical devices as a result of wear and tear or physical change in employee.	N.H. Rev. Stat. Ann. §§ 281-A:2, 281-A:23, 281-A:25.
NJ	Employer.	No specific statutory provision.	Yes, by state agency.	Yes.	Where damage occurs to an employee's prosthesis as a result of an accident compensable under act, employer is obligated to repair or replace device or pay cost or value of device.	N.J. Stat. Ann. §§ 34:15-12.7, 34:15-15, 34:16-20 et seq.
NM	Employer may initially select the health care provider or permit employee to make the selection. After 60 days, the party not making the selection may select the health care provider of his or her choice.	No specific statutory provision.	No.	Yes.	Employee who refuses to submit to an independent medical examination forfeits all benefits under act.	N.M. Stat. Ann. §§ 52-1-49, 52-1-51.
NY	Employee, from state-authorized list.	No specific statutory provision.	Yes, under auspices of state education department, although employer may be liable for an additional $30 a week for maintenance. Employers must contribute to state fund to finance vocational rehabilitation.	Yes.	Employer is liable for re-placement or repair of prostheses as a result of ordinary wear and tear when such devices were provided originally as a result of work-related injury.	N.Y. Work. Comp. Law §§ 13, 13-a, 15.
NC	Employer, but employee has option of selecting physician, subject to approval by state. If employer has contracted with a managed care organization, physician	Yes.	Yes.	Yes.	Refusal of employee to accept medical or other treatment when ordered by state bars employee from further compensation until employee agrees to treatment.	N.C. Gen. Stat. §§ 97-2, 97-25, 97-25.2, 97-25.5.

(cont'd)

(Table continues.)

Table 10.5-1 PART 10—STATE WORKERS' COMPENSATION LAWS 10-80

Table 10.5-1 (cont'd)
REQUIRED MEDICAL BENEFITS AND PROVIDERS

(See also text at § 10.5.)

	Who Chooses Physician?	Is Chiropractic Treatment Covered?	Are Rehabilitative Services Covered?	Are Medical Devices and Equipment Covered?	Other Provisions	Citations to Authority
NC (cont'd)	must be selected under rules of organization.					
ND	Employee.	Yes.	Yes, operated by state.	Yes.	Employers that maintain approved risk management programs under act may select a preferred provider in place of employee's choosing physician.	N.D. Cent. Code §§ 65-01-02, 65-05-07, 65-05-28, 65-05-28.1, 65-07.1-01 et seq.
OH	Employer is required to select a managed care organization (MCO) that is affiliated with certain providers. If employer fails to designate an MCO, state will select one for employer.	No specific statutory provision.	Yes, by employer or state.	Yes.	Where work-related accident causes damage to eyeglasses, artificial teeth, or hearing aid, state will replace or repair same.	Ohio Rev. Code Ann. §§ 4121.61 et seq., 4123.66; Ohio Admin. Code §§ 4123-6-01–4123-6-73.
OK	Employee.	Yes.	Yes, for a maximum 52 weeks, although period may be extended for an additional 52 weeks by court order.	Yes.	If employee refuses vocational rehabilitation or does not complete program in good faith, court, in its discretion, may deduct cost from employee benefits. Podiatric, dental, optometric, and osteopathic treatments are covered.	Okla. Stat. Ann. tit. 85, §§ 14–16.
OR	Employee.	No specific statutory provision.	Yes, for workers who are not able to return to their previous employment or to any other suitable employment with employer, and who have a substantial handicap. An employee actively	Yes.	Treatment by prayer or spiritual means is covered under act.	Or. Rev. Stat. §§ 656.010, 656.245, 656.340.

State						
PA	Employee, who must select from list of at least 6 health care providers selected by employer. At least 3 on list must be physicians, and no more than 4 may be coordinated care providers.	Yes.	Yes, by state program and fund.	engaged in training may receive temporary disability for a maximum of 16 months, although this may be extended to 21 months for good cause.	Yes.	If invasive surgery is prescribed by a physician designated by employer, employee is entitled to a second opinion by a physician of employee's choice. If second opinion differs from first, employee may choose course of action.	Pa. Stat. Ann. tit. 43, § 682.1 et seq.; tit. 77, § 531; Martin v. W.C.A.B. (Emmaus Bakery), 652 A.2d 1301 (Pa. 1995).
RI	Employee.	Yes.	Yes, by employer.	Yes. Hearing aids and other amplification devices are specifically excluded.	Employee's refusal to accept treatment bars employee from compensation during period of refusal. Dental, optical, and nursing services are covered.	R.I. Gen. Laws §§ 28-33-5, 28-33-6, 28-33-8, 28-33-41.
SC	Employer.	No specific statutory provision.	Yes, by state agency and fund.	Yes.	The right to compensation of any employee who refuses to submit to treatment or to independent physical examinations requested by employer is suspended until such time as employee complies with request. Employer must pay cost of repair of any prosthetic devices or eyeglasses damaged on the job.	S.C. Code Ann. §§ 42-15-60, 42-15-65, 42-15-80, 43-31-10 et seq.
SD	Employee.	Yes.	Yes, employee receives temporary total disability compensation while participating in rehabilitation program reasonably necessary to restore employee to suitable employment.	Yes.	Employer must repair or replace hearing aids, dentures, prescription eyeglasses, eyeglass frames, or contact lenses damaged or destroyed in a work-related accident also causing a compensable physical injury. Dental, optometric, and podiatric treatments are covered. If an injured employee unreasonably refuses or neglects to	S.D. Codified Laws §§ 62-1-1.1, 62-4-1, 62-4-5.1, 62-4-43.

(cont'd)

(Table continues.)

Table 10.5-1 (cont'd)
REQUIRED MEDICAL BENEFITS AND PROVIDERS

(See also text at § 10.5.)

	Who Chooses Physician?	Is Chiropractic Treatment Covered?	Are Rehabilitative Services Covered?	Are Medical Devices and Equipment Covered?	Other Provisions	Citations to Authority
SD (cont'd)					avail himself or herself of medical or surgical treatment, employer is not liable for an aggravation of such injury due to such refusal and neglect, and the department of labor may suspend, reduce, or limit the compensation otherwise payable.	
TN	Employee, who must choose from list of 3 physicians compiled by employer.	Yes.	Yes, under plan administered, and primarily funded, by state.	Yes.	Right to compensation of employee who refuses to comply with any reasonable request for examination or to accept medical services is suspended until employee complies.	Tenn. Code Ann. §§ 50-6-124, 50-6-204.
TX	Employee, from state-approved list.	No specific statutory provision.	Yes, employee is referred to state rehabilitation commission if it is determined that employee is entitled to supplemental benefits and employee could be materially assisted in returning to employment by vocational rehabilitation.	Yes.	If employee seeks a change from his or her initial choice of physician, he or she must request permission from state commission, which prescribes criteria to be used in selecting an alternate doctor.	Tex. Lab. Code Ann. §§ 408.022, 408.150.
UT	Most employers have a preferred provider, and employee must use this provider; however, if employer does not have a preferred provider, employee may select physician.	Yes.	If voluntarily undertaken by employer.	Yes.	Employer must replace or repair prosthesis or artificial device if injured in compensable injury.	Utah Code Ann. §§ 34A-2-413, 34A-2-418; *Fesler v. Industrial Comm'n,* 700 P.2d 1116 (Utah 1985).

VT	Employer, although employee may thereafter select another physician if dissatisfied.	No specific statutory provision.	Yes.	Yes.	Claimant who refuses to undergo independent physical examination is assessed cost of exam, and his or her benefits may be suspended.	Vt. Stat. Ann. tit. 21, §§ 640, 641, 667.
VA	Employee, from list of at least 3 physicians compiled by employer.	Yes.	Yes.	Yes, up to a maximum of $25,000 for equipment necessitated by any one accident.	Employer must repair or replace any prosthetic device damaged as a result of an accident otherwise compensable. Unjustified refusal of employee to accept medical treatment or vocational services will bar employee from receiving further compensation until refusal ceases.	Va. Code Ann. § 65.2-603.
WA	Employee.	Yes.	Yes, for 52 weeks unless extended up to 52 additional weeks at supervisor's discretion.	Yes.	Employer must repair or replace artificial devices damaged or destroyed in an accident.	Wash. Rev. Code §§ 51.32.095, 51.36.010, 51.36.015, 51.36.020.
WV	Employee.	No specific statutory provision.	Yes.	Yes.	The employer or state will provide for replacement of artificial limbs, crutches, hearing aids, eyeglasses, and other mechanical appliances provided under workers' compensation law that later wear out or need to be refitted, or that are broken in course of employment.	W. Va. Code Ann. §§ 23-4-3, 23-4-9.
WI	Employee.	Yes.	Yes.	Yes.	Christian Science treatment may be provided in lieu of medical treatment, but any employer may elect not to offer such treatment by filing written notice. Psychological, podiatric, and dental treatments are covered.	Wis. Stat. Ann. § 102.42.
WY	Employee. Employer may seek and receive a second opinion as to any course of treatment suggested by patient's physician.	Yes.	Yes.	Yes.	Employee's refusal to submit to medical treatment reasonably essential to promote recovery forfeits any right to compensation.	Wyo. Stat. Ann. §§ 27-14-102, 27-14-401, 27-14-402, 27-14-407, 27-14-408.

§ 10.6   Covered Occupational Diseases or Illnesses

General Provisions. Work-related diseases or illnesses are often covered under state workers' compensation statutes. The standard for determining whether a disease is work-related, however, differs from state to state. Some states merely require that the disease naturally arise out of the employment. Other states also require that it be due to hazards in excess of those ordinarily incident to employment in general. Under this standard, a disease will be considered work-related for purposes of workers' compensation statutes only if it is due to hazards peculiar to the particular occupation.

In some states, special rules apply to compensation for occupational diseases, and certain conditions may be imposed on compensation for occupational diseases that are otherwise not applicable. Finally, a number of states have special rules governing when claims for occupational diseases must be filed.

Table 10.6-1 Part A sets out the standard applied by each state for determining whether a disease or illness is work-related. The table also provides information on the amount of compensation, and any conditions placed on compensation for occupational diseases.

Specifically Covered Diseases or Illnesses. Some state workers' compensation statutes specify certain occupational diseases that are, or are not, covered under the statute. In some cases, certain occupational diseases are covered only for certain occupations. For example, in California, cancer is specifically covered under the state workers' compensation statute, but only for certain firefighters. Some states also have special rules for determining whether a particular occupational disease or illness is covered under the state's workers' compensation statute. For example, in Colorado, a heart attack is not a covered illness unless competent evidence shows that it was proximately caused by an unusual exertion arising out of and in the course of employment.

Table 10.6-1 Part B indicates whether certain occupational diseases or illnesses are covered under state workers' compensation laws. These include HIV/AIDS, heart disease, cancer, lung disease, and mental or emotional disease. Although a disease may not be specifically covered under a state's workers' compensation law, in some cases it may be covered under the general standard for determining whether an occupational disease is work-related.

Table 10.6-1 Part A

DISEASES OR ILLNESSES COVERED BY GENERAL PROVISIONS

(See also text at § 10.6.)

	Standard for Defining Whether Disease Is Work-Related	Compensation for Occupational Diseases	When Must Claim Be Filed?	Citations to Authority
AL	Arising out of and in the course of employment and as a result of the nature of the employment, and due to hazards in excess of those ordinarily incident to employment in general and peculiar to the occupation.	Same as for injury by accident.	Within 2 years after the date of injury. For death, within 2 years of death if death results proximately from the disease and occurs within 3 years of the date of injury. Date of injury means date of last exposure to the hazards of the disease in employment. For pneumoconiosis and radiation-related illness, date of injury is date of last exposure in employment of employer in whose employment the employee was last exposed to the hazards of the disease in each of at least 12 months within a period of 5 years prior to the date of injury.	Ala. Code §§ 25-5-110, 25-5-117, 25-5-119.
AK	Arising naturally out of the employment or naturally or unavoidably resulting from an accidental injury.	Same as for injury by accident.	Same as for injury by accident.	Alaska Stat. § 23.30.395.
AZ	Due to causes and conditions characteristic of and peculiar to a particular trade, occupation, process, or employment and is not an ordinary disease to which the general public is exposed. An occupational disease is deemed to have arisen out of employment only if (1) there is a direct and causal connection between the conditions under which the work is performed and the occupational disease; (2) the disease can be seen to have followed as a natural incident of the work as a result of the exposure occasioned by the employment; (3) the disease can be fairly traced to the employment as the proximate cause; (4) the disease does not come from a hazard to which workers would have been equally exposed outside of employment; (5) the disease is incidental to the character of the business and not independent of the relationship of employer and employee; and (6) the disease, after its contraction, appears to have had its origin in a risk *(cont'd)*	Same as for injury by accident.	Same as for injury by accident.	Ariz. Rev. Stat. Ann. §§ 23-901, 23-901.01, 23-901.05.

(Table continues.)

Table 10.6-1 Part A (cont'd)
DISEASES OR ILLNESSES COVERED BY GENERAL PROVISIONS

(See also text at § 10.6.)

	Standard for Defining Whether Disease Is Work-Related	Compensation for Occupational Diseases	When Must Claim Be Filed?	Citations to Authority
AZ (cont'd)	associated with the employment, and to have flowed from that source as a natural consequence, although it need not have been foreseen or expected. When an occupational disease is aggravated by any other disease or infirmity not itself compensable, the compensation payable shall be reduced and limited to such proportion of the compensation as would be payable if the occupational disease were the sole cause of the disability or death.			
AR	Arising out of and in the course of employment, or naturally following or unavoidably resulting from an injury. The causal connection between the job and the disease must be established by clear and convincing evidence. The disease must be due to the nature of an employment in which the hazards of the disease exist and are characteristic thereof and peculiar to the trade, occupation, process, or employment, and must be actually incurred in employment.	Same as for injury by accident and based on average weekly wage of employee when last injuriously exposed. In cases of silicosis or asbestosis, disability or death must result within 3 years. Disability or death must result within 1 year for other occupational diseases, except those caused by exposure to radiation. In cases of death, death must follow continuous disability from the disease, for which compensation has been paid or timely claim made, and death must result within 7 years of last exposure.	Same as for injury by accident.	Ark. Code Ann. § 11-9-601.
CA	Same as for injury by accident.	Same as for injury by accident.	Same as for injury by accident.	Cal. Lab. Code §§ 4407 et seq.
CO	Results directly from the employment or the conditions under which work was performed, can be seen to have followed as a natural incident of the work and resulted from the exposure occasioned by the nature of the employment, can be fairly traced to the employment as a proximate cause, and does not come from a hazard to which one would have been equally exposed outside the employment.	Same as for injury by accident.	Same as for injury by accident.	Colo. Rev. Stat. Ann. §§ 8-40-201, 8-43-102.
CT	Arising out of and in the course of employment, peculiar to the occupation in which the employee was engaged, and due to causes in excess of the ordinary hazards of employment.	Average weekly wage calculated as of the date of total or partial incapacity to work. Otherwise, same as for injury by accident.	Same as for injury by accident.	Conn. Gen. Stat. Ann. §§ 31-275, 31-306, 31-310c.

Jurisdiction	Definition	Time limitation	Citation
DE	Same as for injury by accident.	Within 1 year after employee first knew that the disability could have been caused by employment. In cases of death, 1 year after claimant knew or should have known of the possible relationship between the death and employment.	Del. Code Ann. tit. 19, §§ 2328, 2342, 2361.
DC	Statutory provision discusses pneumoconiosis (such as silicosis and asbestosis), radiation diseases, and "any other generally recognized occupational disease."	Same as for injury by accident.	D.C. Code Ann. § 36-310.
FL	Resulting from nature of the employment and actually contracted therein; the incidence of the disease is substantially higher in the occupation than in the usual run of occupations; disease is due to causes and conditions characteristic of and peculiar to a particular trade, occupation, process, or employment, excluding all ordinary diseases of life to which the general public is exposed, unless the incidence of such disease is substantially higher in the particular trade, occupation, process, or employment than in the general public.	Same as for injury by accident, except that in cases of death, unless death follows continuous disability, death must occur within 350 weeks of last exposure in order to be compensable.	Fla. Stat. Ann. § 440.151.
GA	Same as for injury by accident, except no compensation for partial loss of or partial loss of use of a member or for partial loss of vision in an eye. Partial loss of hearing due to industrial noise is not considered a compensable occupational disease. Psychiatric and psychological problems and heart and vascular diseases are not compensable occupational diseases unless they arise from a separate, distinct occupational disease.	Within 1 year of date employee knew or should have known of the disablement and its relationship to the employment, but in no event later than 7 years from last injurious exposure. In cases of asbestosis or mesothelioma, 1 year from date of first disablement after diagnosis of such disease. In case of death, within 1 year thereof.	Ga. Code Ann. §§ 34-9-280, 34-9-281, 34-9-283.
HI	Proximately caused by or resulting from the nature of the employment.	Same as for injury by accident.	Haw. Rev. Stat. Ann. § 386-3.
ID	Actually incurred in employer's employment; employee must have been exposed to the hazard of the disease for 60 days by same employer, and disease must be due to the nature of employment in which hazards of the disease actually exist and are characteristic of, and peculiar to, the trade, occupation, process, or employment. Does not include psychological injuries, disorders, or conditions unless accompanying a physical injury or occupational disease.	Within 1 year of death or first manifestation of disease.	Idaho Code §§ 72-102, 72-438, 72-439, 72-451.

(Table continues.)

Table 10.6-1 Part A (cont'd)

DISEASES OR ILLNESSES COVERED BY GENERAL PROVISIONS

(See also text at § 10.6.)

	Standard for Defining Whether Disease Is Work-Related	Compensation for Occupational Diseases	When Must Claim Be Filed?	Citations to Authority
IL	Arising out of and in the course of employment, which must have a direct causal connection to the disease, which must appear to have had its origin in a risk connected with the employment and to have flowed therefrom as a rational consequence. An employee is conclusively deemed to have been exposed to the hazards of an occupational disease when, for any length of time, he or she is employed in an occupation in which the hazard of the disease exists.	Same as for injury by accident, except no compensation unless disablement occurs within 2 years after the last day of exposure to the hazards of the disease; 3 years in cases of berylliosis, silicosis, or asbestos-related disease; 25 years in cases of exposure to radiation.	Same as for injury by accident.	820 Ill. Comp. Stat. Ann. 310/1, 310/7, 310/8.
IN	Arising out of and in the course of employment, not including ordinary diseases of life to which the general public is exposed; must be direct causal connection between the conditions of work and the disease, which can be seen to have followed as a natural incident of the work and to have had its origin in a risk connected therewith and to have flowed therefrom as a rational consequence.	None, unless disablement occurs within 2 years after last exposure to hazards of the disease, or within 3 years for silica dust– or coal dust–related disease. For radiation exposure, disablement must occur within 2 years from the date employee knew or should have known his or her disease was caused thereby. For asbestos-related disease, disablement must occur within 3, 20, or 35 years of last exposure depending on the date of last exposure. In cases of death, generally no compensation unless death results within 2 years after date of disablement. Otherwise, same as for injury by accident.	Within 2 years of disablement or death, as the case may be.	Ind. Code Ann. §§ 22-3-7-9, 22-3-7-10, 22-3-7-16, 22-3-7-32.
IA	Arising out of and in the course of employment, having direct causal connection with the employment, following as a natural incident thereto, and appearing to have had its origin in a risk connected with the employment. A disease that follows from a hazard to which employee has been, or would have been, equally exposed outside of his or her occupation is not compensable as an occupational disease.	Employee who contracts compensable occupational disease but is able to continue work must receive reasonable medical services therefor. To receive compensation, disablement or death must result within 3 years of last exposure for pneumoconiosis, or within 1 year for any other occupational disease. For latent or delayed pathological conditions due to radiation exposure, employer shall not be liable unless claim is filed within 90 days after disablement or death, or within 90 days after employee knew or should have known the disablement was caused by exposure to radiation and its relation to employment. Otherwise, same as for injury by accident.	Same as for injury by accident.	Iowa Code Ann. §§ 85A.5, 85A.8, 85A.12, 85A.18.

KS	Arising out of and in the course of employment, actually contracted while so engaged, and resulting from the nature of the employment.	No compensation for emphysema unless proven by clear and convincing evidence that it was caused solely by the employment; except, if employment aggravated existing emphysema, compensation is payable to extent such condition was aggravated by employment. No compensation unless after last injurious exposure disablement results within 1 year or death within 3 years in case of silicosis, or 1 year for any other occupational disease; or unless death follows continuous disability from an occupational disease commencing within the above period, for which compensation has been awarded or timely claim made, and death results within 7 years after last exposure. This time limit does not apply to death or disablement due to occupational exposure to radiation. Otherwise, same compensation as for injury by accident.	Same as for injury by accident.	Kan. Stat. Ann. § 44-5a01.
KY	Arising out of and in the course of employment, not including ordinary diseases of life to which the general public is exposed. There must be a direct causal connection between the conditions of work and the disease, which can be seen to have followed as a natural incident of the work, to have had its origin in a risk connected therewith, and to have flowed therefrom as a rational consequence.	Same as for injury by accident.	Within 3 years of last injurious exposure or after employee first experiences distinct manifestation of an occupational disease reasonably sufficient to apprise him or her that he or she has the disease, or within 3 years of death, but in no case later than 5 years since last injurious exposure. For radiation or asbestos exposure, within 20 years.	Ky. Rev. Stat. Ann. §§ 342.020, 342.316.
LA	Disease or illness that is due to causes and conditions characteristic of and peculiar to the particular trade, occupation, process, or employment in which the employee is exposed to such disease. If contracted within first year of employment, presumed not to have been contracted in the course of and arising out of employment, unless proven otherwise by a preponderance of evidence.	Same as for injury by accident.	For disability, within 1 year of disease manifesting itself, disablement, or when employee knows or has reasonable grounds to believe that the disease is occupationally related. For death, within 1 year of death or when claimant has reasonable grounds to believe death was due to occupational disease.	La. Rev. Stat. Ann. § 23:1031.1.
ME	Due to causes and conditions characteristic of a particular trade, occupation, process, or employment and arising out of and in the course of employment.	For incapacity, it must have resulted within 3 years after last injurious exposure to the occupational disease in employment. Otherwise, same as for injury by accident. Longer limitation periods are in place for asbestos-related diseases. These periods are determined with reference to when exposure occurred.	Same as for injury by accident.	Me. Rev. Stat. Ann. tit. 39-A, §§ 603, 609, 614.
MD	Disability is due to the nature of an employment in which hazards of the occupational disease exist and the covered employee was employed before the date of disablement, or has manifestations consistent with those known to result from exposure to an agent that is attributable to the type of employment and it may reasonably be concluded that the disease was incurred as a result of the employment.	Same as for injury by accident.	Within 2 years of death or disablement or when worker or claimant first had knowledge of the employment-related cause. The time period is 3 years for dust diseases.	Md. Code Ann., Lab. & Empl. §§ 9-502, 9-711.

(Table continues.)

Table 10.6-1 Part A   PART 10—STATE WORKERS' COMPENSATION LAWS   10-90

Table 10.6-1 Part A *(cont'd)*
DISEASES OR ILLNESSES COVERED BY GENERAL PROVISIONS

(See also text at § 10.6.)

	Standard for Defining Whether Disease Is Work-Related	Compensation for Occupational Diseases	When Must Claim Be Filed?	Citations to Authority
MA	Caused by the nature or circumstances of the employment.	Same as for injury by accident.	Same as for injury by accident.	Mass. Gen. Laws Ann. ch. 149, § 1.
MI	Due to the nature of the employment in which employee was engaged and contracted therein.	Same as for injury by accident.	Same as for injury by accident, except that limitations period commences from date claimant knew or should have known that disability or death was work-related and claims must be filed within 2 years of such time.	Mich. Comp. Laws Ann. §§ 418.415, 418.441; Mich. Stat. Ann. §§ 17.237(415), 17.237(441).
MN	Arising out of and in the course of employment, peculiar to the occupation, and due to causes in excess of the ordinary hazards of employment, including undulant fever; must be a direct causal connection between work conditions and the disease, which must follow as a natural incident to the employment.	66⅔% of employee's weekly wage on date of injury, subject to a maximum compensation equal to the maximum in effect on the date of last exposure.	Within 3 years after employee has knowledge of the cause of such injury and injury has resulted in disability, but not to exceed 6 years from the date of the accident.	Minn. Stat. Ann. §§ 176.011, 176.151, 176.66.
MS	Arising out of and in the course of employment where there is a direct causal connection between the work performed and the occupational disease.	Same as for injury by accident.	Same as for injury by accident.	Miss. Code Ann. § 71-3-7.
MO	Arising with or without human fault out of and in the course of employment; its contraction must appear to have had its origin in a risk connected with the employment and to have flowed from that source as a rational consequence. An employee is conclusively deemed to have been exposed to the hazards of an occupational disease when for any length of time, however short, he or she is employed in an occupation or process in which the hazard of disease exists.	Same as for injury by accident.	Same for injury by accident, but period begins running when it becomes reasonably discoverable that a compensable injury has been sustained.	Mo. Rev. Stat. §§ 287.063, 287.067.
MT	Arising out of and in the course of employment and caused by events occurring on more than a single day or work shift; must be direct causal connection between work conditions and disease, which follows as a natural incident to employment and was proximately caused thereby.	Same as for injury by accident, except in cases of pneumoconiosis.	Within 1 year from when claimant knew or should have known that the employee's condition or death resulted from an occupational disease. May be waived up to an additional 2 years by the department on reasonable showing that claimant could not have known that condition or death was related to an occupational disease.	Mont. Code Ann. §§ 39-72-103, 39-72-403, 39-72-408, 39-72-701.

NE	Due to causes and conditions that are characteristic of, and peculiar to, a particular trade, occupation, process, or employment. All ordinary diseases of life to which the general public is exposed are excluded.	Same as for injury by accident.	Same as for injury by accident.	Neb. Rev. Stat. Ann. §§ 48-101, 48-151.
NV	Preponderance of evidence must show: (1) that employee's occupational disease arose out of and in the course of employment; (2) a direct causal connection between work conditions and the disease that followed as a natural incident of the work; and (3) that the disease had its origin in a risk connected with the employment and flowed therefrom as a natural consequence.	Same as for injury by accident, except that for silicosis and asbestos-related diseases no compensation unless exposure to silicon or asbestos dust in employment lasted at least 1 year in Nevada.	For death, within 1 year of death. For disability, within 90 days after employee has knowledge of the disability and its relationship to employment. For silicosis or asbestos-related disease, within 1 year after claimant knew or should have known of the relationship between the disease and employment.	Nev. Rev. Stat. Ann. §§ 617.344, 617.358, 617.430, 617.440, 617.460.
NH	Arising out of and in the course of employment and due to causes and conditions characteristic of and peculiar to the particular trade, occupation, or employment. Includes disability resulting from radioactive properties or substances, or from exposure to ionizing radiation.	Same as for injury by accident.	Same as for injury by accident.	N.H. Rev. Stat. Ann. § 281-A:2.
NJ	Arising out of and in the course of employment, and due in material degree to causes and conditions characteristic of and peculiar to a particular trade, occupation, process, or place of employment.	Same as for injury by accident.	Once claimant knows of the nature of the disability and its relation to employment, all claims for compensation for occupational disease are barred unless filed within 2 years of such time.	N.J. Stat. Ann. §§ 34:15-30–34:15-34.
NM	Must be a direct causal connection between the disease and the conditions under which the work is performed; the exposure must be occasioned by the nature of the employment and traced to the employment as the proximate cause. The disease must be incidental to the character of the business.	Same as for injury by accident.	For death, within 1 year thereof. For disability, within 1 year thereof, except in cases of radiation injury the 1-year limitations period begins to run when injury sustained and employee knows or should know of its possible relation to employment.	N.M. Stat. Ann. §§ 52-3-14, 52-3-32, 52-3-42.
NY	Disease results from the nature of employment and was contracted therein.	Same as for injury by accident.	Within 2 years after disablement and claimant knew or should have known that the disease was due to the nature of the employment.	N.Y. Work. Comp. Law §§ 2(15), 28.
NC	Due to causes and conditions that are characteristic of and peculiar to a particular trade, occupation, or employment, but excluding all ordinary diseases of life to which the general public is equally exposed outside of the employment.	Same as for injury by accident.	Within 2 years of death or disablement, but in cases of radiation injury, within 2 years after employee first suffered incapacity from such exposure and knew or should have known that the occupational disease was caused by the employment.	N.C. Gen. Stat. §§ 97-52, 97-53, 97-58(c).
ND	Caused by hazard to which an employee is subjected in the course of employment, incidental to the character of the business, and not independent of the relation of employer and employee.	Same as for injury by accident.	Same as for injury by accident.	N.D. Cent. Code §§ 65-01-02, 65-05-01.

(Table continues.)

Table 10.6-1 Part A *(cont'd)*
DISEASES OR ILLNESSES COVERED BY GENERAL PROVISIONS

(See also text at § 10.6.)

	Standard for Defining Whether Disease Is Work-Related	Compensation for Occupational Diseases	When Must Claim Be Filed?	Citations to Authority
OH	Contracted in the course of employment, which created risk of contracting the disease in a greater degree and in a different manner from risk to public in general.	No compensation for partial disability due to silicosis, asbestosis, or pneumoconiosis. Otherwise, same as for accidents.	Within 2 years after disability commences, or within such longer period as does not exceed 6 months after diagnosis of the occupational disease by a licensed physician, or within 2 years after death occurs.	Ohio Rev. Code Ann. §§ 4123.01, 4123.68, 4123.85.
OK	Due to exposure to causes and conditions characteristic of or peculiar to the particular trade, occupation, process, or employment in which the employee is employed. An occupational disease arises out of the employment only if there is a direct causal connection between work conditions and the disease.	Same as for injury by accident.	Within 2 years of last exposure. For asbestosis, silicosis, and radiation-related disease: within 2 years from date condition first becomes manifest by a symptom or condition from which one learned in medicine could, with reasonable accuracy, diagnose such specific condition, whichever last occurs.	Okla. Stat. Ann. tit. 85, §§ 3, 43.
OR	Arising out of and in the course of employment, caused by substances or activities to which an employee is not ordinarily exposed, and requiring medical services or resulting in disability or death. Employment conditions must have been the major contributing cause of the disease.	Same as for injury by accident.	Within 1 year of date employee first discovered the occupational disease or should have, or within 1 year of date claimant first becomes disabled or is informed by a physician that the claimant is suffering from an occupational disease. In cases of death, within 1 year of date when claimant knew or should have known the cause of death was an occupational disease.	Or. Rev. Stat. §§ 656.802, 656.807.
PA	Claimant is exposed by reason of his employment, the disease is causally related to the industry or occupation, and the incidence of the disease is substantially greater in that industry or occupation than in the general population.	Same as for injury by accident.	Same as for injury by accident.	Pa. Stat. Ann. tit. 77, § 27.1.
RI	Disease is due to the nature of employment and contracted therein, and due to causes and conditions characteristic of and peculiar to a particular trade, occupation, process, or employment.	Same as for injury by accident.	Two years from date of disablement.	R.I. Gen. Laws §§ 28-34-1, 28-34-3, 28-34-4.
SC	Arising out of and in the course of employment, due to hazards in excess of those ordinarily incident to employment and peculiar to the occupation, and caused by hazard recognized as peculiar to a particular trade.	Same as for injury by accident.	Within 2 years of definitive diagnosis of an occupational disease and the employee having been notified thereof.	S.C. Code Ann. §§ 42-11-10, 42-11-40, 42-15-40.

SD	process, occupation, or employment and contracted as a direct result of continuous exposure to the normal working conditions thereof.	For silicosis, injurious exposure must have occurred for at least 2 years in the state, and there will be no compensation for partial disability therefrom. Otherwise, same as for injury by accident.	Claim must be filed within 2 years after disability or, in cases of death, within 2 years of death.	S.D. Codified Laws §§ 62-8-1, 62-8-11, 62-8-20.
TN	Disease is peculiar to the occupation and due to causes in excess of the ordinary hazards of employment. Includes any disease due or attributable to exposure to or contact with any radioactive material by an employee in the course of his or her employment.	Same as for injury by accident.	Within 1 year of beginning of incapacity for work or, in cases of death, within 1 year of death. For coal worker's pneumoconiosis, within 3 years of discovery of total disability or death.	Tenn. Code Ann. §§ 50-6-301, 50-6-303, 50-6-306.
TX	Arising out of and in the course of employment, disease is a natural incident of employment, proximate cause is shown, equal exposure does not exist outside the employment, the disease is incidental to the character of the employment, it originated from a risk connected therewith and flowed therefrom as a natural consequence, and a direct causal connection is established.	Same as for injury by accident.	Same as for injury by accident.	Tex. Lab. Code Ann. § 401.011.
UT	Arising out of and in the course of employment, and causing damage to physical structure of the body, including a repetitive trauma injury. Includes diseases or infections that naturally result from the work-related disease. Does not include ordinary diseases of life to which general public is exposed, unless incident to a compensable injury or occupational disease.	Same as for injury by accident.	For disability, within 6 years of the date the cause of action arises. For death, within 1 year of date deceased's dependents knew or should have known that employee's death was caused by an occupational disease, but in no case after 6 years since cause of action arose.	Utah Code Ann. §§ 34A-3-103, 34A-3-107, 34A-3-109.
VT	Arises out of and in the course of employment and is medically caused or aggravated by the employment.	Due to causes and conditions that are characteristic of and peculiar to a particular trade, occupation, process, or employment and to which an employee is not ordinarily subjected or exposed outside such employment, and arising out of and in the course of employment.	None, unless disablement results within 5 years after last injurious exposure in employment. None for death unless death occurs during employment or follows continuous disability from such disease and results within 12 years after last exposure. Otherwise, same as for injury by accident.	Within 1 year of injury or death.	Vt. Stat. Ann. tit. 21, §§ 1002, 1006, 1013.
VA	Arising out of and in the course of employment, and not an ordinary disease of life to which the general public is exposed; direct causal connection is established, disease is natural incident of employment, proximate cause is shown, disease is incidental to character of the business, and disease has its origin in a risk connected with employment and flowed therefrom as a natural consequence.	Same as for accidents, except that the period during which employer is required to furnish medical attention shall begin 15 days after the date of first communication of the diagnosis of the occupational disease to the employee.	For coal miner's pneumoconiosis, within 3 years of diagnosis or 5 years of last exposure, whichever is first. For byssinosis, 2 years after diagnosis or 7 years since last exposure, whichever comes first. For asbestosis, within 2 years of diagnosis. For HIV, within 2 years of positive test. For all other occupational diseases, within 2 years of diagnosis or 5 years of last injurious exposure in employment, whichever is first. In cases of death, within 3 years thereof.	Va. Code Ann. §§ 65.2-400, 65.2-403, 65.2-406.

(Table continues.)

Table 10.6-1 Part A *(cont'd)*

DISEASES OR ILLNESSES COVERED
BY GENERAL PROVISIONS

(See also text at § 10.6.)

	Standard for Defining Whether Disease Is Work-Related	Compensation for Occupational Diseases	When Must Claim Be Filed?	Citations to Authority
WA	Arising naturally and proximately out of employment.	Same as for injury by accident.	Within 2 years of notice in writing from physician of the existence of an occupational disease and stating that a claim for disability benefits may be filed within 2 years. In cases of death, within 2 years thereof.	Wash. Rev. Code Ann. §§ 51.08.140, 51.16.040, 51.28.055.
WV	Incurred in the course of and resulting from employment, and not including ordinary diseases of life to which the general public is exposed; a direct causal connection to employment is established, proximate cause is shown, the disease is incidental to the character of the business, and it originated in a risk connected with employment and flowed therefrom as a natural consequence. No disease is compensable if it was caused solely by nonphysical factors and did not result in any physical injury to the claimant.	Same as for injury by accident.	Within 6 months from the injury or death. For pneumoconiosis, within 3 years of last continuous period of 60 days of exposure, or 3 years from time employee knew or should have known he or she had the disease.	W. Va. Code §§ 23-4-1, 23-4-1f, 23-4-15.
WI	No specific statutory provision.	Same as for injury by accident.	No statute of limitations, except that benefits or treatment expenses due after 12 years from date of injury or death shall be paid from Work Injury Supplemental Fund.	Wis. Stat. Ann. §§ 102.01, 102.17.
WY	Arising out of and in the course of employment; risk of contracting disease must be increased by the nature of the employment, to which it has a direct and proximate causal connection; not including diseases to which one is equally exposed outside the employment; disease must be incidental to the character of employment.	Same as for injury by accident.	Within 1 year after diagnosis or within 3 years from date of last injurious exposure, except for radiation, for which there is no 3-year limit.	Wyo. Stat. Ann. §§ 27-14-102, 27-14-503, 27-14-603.

Table 10.6-1 Part B
SPECIFICALLY
COVERED DISEASES OR ILLNESSES

(See also text at § 10.6.)

NOTE: Although a disease may not be specifically covered under a state's workers' compensation law, in some cases the disease may be covered under the general standard for determining whether an occupational disease is work-related.

	Is HIV/AIDS Specifically Covered?	Is Heart Disease Specifically Covered?	Is Cancer Specifically Covered?	Lung Diseases Specifically Covered?	Is Mental or Emotional Disease Specifically Covered?	Citations to Authority
AL	No.	No.	No.	Pneumoconiosis, silicosis, siderosis, anthracosis, anthrasilicosis, anthracosilicosis, anthracotuberculosis, tuberculosilicosis, silico-tuberculosis, aluminosis, and other diseases caused by work-related dust inhalation.	No.	Ala. Code § 25-5-110.
AK	No.	No.	No.	No.	Mental injury caused by mental stress not covered unless it is established that work stress was extraordinary and unusual in comparison to the pressures and tensions of a comparable work environment. Mental injury is not considered to arise out of and in the course of employment if it results from a good-faith personnel action.	Alaska Stat. § 23.30.395.
AZ	Yes, if employee's regular course of employment involves handling or exposure to blood or body fluids other than tears, saliva, or perspiration. Employee must report to employer in writing possible exposure within 10 days, test *(cont'd)*	Heart-related or perivascular injury, illness, or death shall not be covered unless some injury, stress, or exertion related to the employment was a substantial contributing cause thereof.	No.	No.	Not covered unless some unexpected, unusual, or extraordinary stress related to the employment or some physical injury related to the employment was a substantial contributing cause of the mental injury, illness, or condition.	Ariz. Rev. Stat. Ann. §§ 23-901, 23-1043.01, 23-1043.02.

(Table continues.)

Table 10.6-1 Part B PART 10—STATE WORKERS' COMPENSATION LAWS 10-96

Table 10.6-1 Part B *(cont'd)*
SPECIFICALLY
COVERED DISEASES OR ILLNESSES

(See also text at § 10.6.)

NOTE: Although a disease may not be specifically covered under a state's workers' compensation law, in some cases the disease may be covered under the general standard for determining whether an occupational disease is work-related.

	Is HIV/AIDS Specifically Covered?	Is Heart Disease Specifically Covered?	Is Cancer Specifically Covered?	Lung Diseases Specifically Covered?	Is Mental or Emotional Disease Specifically Covered?	Citations to Authority
AZ *(cont'd)*	negative for HIV, and then test positive within 18 months to collect. Does not include exposure by sexual activity or illegal drug use.					
AR	No.	Yes, but only if an accident is the major cause of the physical harm. Stress will not be considered.	No.	Silicosis, asbestosis, including cases complicated by tuberculosis or some other disease.	Yes, but only if caused by physical injury, unless employee is a victim of a crime of violence. To be compensable, a mental injury or illness must also be diagnosed by a licensed psychiatrist or psychologist and the diagnosis of the condition must meet the criteria established in the most current edition of the *Diagnostic and Statistical Manual of Mental Disorders*.	Ark. Code Ann. §§ 11-9-113, 11-9-114, 11-9-601, 11-9-602.
CA	No.	Yes, for certain state custodial, supervisory, and security officers and municipal firefighters and law enforcement personnel.	Yes, for certain firefighters.	Asbestosis.	Psychiatric injuries covered if actual events of employment predominantly caused the injury. Employee must have been employed for 6 months. Not covered if caused by good-faith employment action.	Cal. Lab. Code §§ 3208.3, 3212, 3213, 4401–4406.

CO	No.	Heart attack not covered unless it is shown by competent evidence that it was proximately caused by an unusual exertion arising out of and in the course of employment.	No.	Silicosis, asbestosis, anthracosis.	Yes, if supported by testimony of a licensed physician or psychologist. Covered mental illness will not be considered to arise from good-faith employment action. Must arise primarily from the employee's job and place of employment and impairment must be sufficient alone to render employee temporarily or permanently disabled from pursuing the occupation or to require medical or psychiatric treatment.	Colo. Rev. Stat. Ann. §§ 8-41-301, 8-41-302, 8-41-304.
CT	No.	No.	No.	Yes, if a special panel of chest physicians determines it is a compensable condition.	No.	Conn. Gen. Stat. Ann. § 31-298a.
DE	No.	No.	No.	No.	No.	—
DC	No.	No.	No.	Pneumoconiosis, such as silicosis and asbestosis.	No.	D.C. Code Ann. § 36-310.
FL	No.	No.	No.	Dust diseases.	Mental or nervous injury due to stress, fright, or excitement only is not covered.	Fla. Stat. Ann. §§ 440.02, 440.151.
GA	No.	No.	Mesothelioma.	Asbestosis, mesothelioma.	No.	Ga. Code Ann. § 34-9-281.
HI	No.	No.	No.	No.	No.	—
ID	Yes, for occupations involving exposure to human blood or body fluids.	Yes, for paid firefighters.	No.	Silicosis in any occupation involving contact with silicon dioxide, and for firefighters, lung diseases in general.	Not covered unless caused by accident and physical injury or occupational disease or sudden and extraordinary event, not including personnel actions. Causative factors must really and objectively exist and causation must be proven by clear and convincing evidence. There must be accompanying physical injury.	Idaho Code §§ 72-438, 72-441–72-446, 72-451.
IL	No.	No.	No.	Berylliosis, silicosis, or any asbestos-related disease.	No.	820 Ill. Comp. Stat. Ann. 310/1.

(Table continues.)

Table 10.6-1 Part B | PART 10—STATE WORKERS' COMPENSATION LAWS | 10-98

Table 10.6-1 Part B *(cont'd)*
SPECIFICALLY COVERED DISEASES OR ILLNESSES

(See also text at § 10.6.)

NOTE: Although a disease may not be specifically covered under a state's workers' compensation law, in some cases the disease may be covered under the general standard for determining whether an occupational disease is work-related.

	Is HIV/AIDS Specifically Covered?	Is Heart Disease Specifically Covered?	Is Cancer Specifically Covered?	Lung Diseases Specifically Covered?	Is Mental or Emotional Disease Specifically Covered?	Citations to Authority
IN	No.	No.	No.	Yes.	No.	Ind. Code Ann. § 22-3-7-9.
IA	No.	No.	No.	Pneumoconiosis.	No.	Iowa Code Ann. §§ 85A.12, 85A.13.
KS	No.	No.	No.	Emphysema, silicosis.	No.	Kan. Stat. Ann. §§ 44-5a01, 44-5a09, 44-5a10, 44-5a13.
KY	Yes, provided the virus was contracted as a result of work-related exposure and employer was notified about the exposure.	No.	No.	Asbestosis, coal workers' pneumoconiosis.	No.	Ky. Rev. Stat. Ann. §§ 342.185, 342.316, 342.318.
LA	No.	Specifically excluded.	No.	No.	Specifically excluded.	La. Rev. Stat. Ann. § 23:1031.1.
ME	No.	No.	Yes, for firefighters whose last injurious exposure to carcinogens occurred after January 1, 1985.	Silicosis and asbestos-related diseases.	No.	Me. Rev. Stat. Ann. tit. 39-A, §§ 609, 613, 614.
MD	No.	No.	No.	Dust disease.	No.	Md. Code Ann., Lab. & Empl. § 9-711.
MA	No.	No.	No.	No.	No.	—
MI	No.	Yes, for firefighters and law enforcement officers.	No.	Silicosis, dust disease, and for firefighters and law enforcement officers, lung diseases in general.	No.	Mich. Comp. Laws Ann. §§ 418.405, 418.501; Mich. Stat. Ann. §§ 17.237(405), 17.237(501).
MN	No.	Yes, myocarditis and coronary sclerosis for certain enumerated state employees.	Yes, for firefighters.	Yes, pneumonia and its sequelae for certain enumerated state employees.	No.	Minn. Stat. Ann. § 176.011.

MS	No.	No.	No.	No.	No.	—
MO	No.	Yes, for firefighters.	Yes, for firefighters.	Yes, for firefighters.	No.	Mo. Rev. Stat. § 287.067.
MT	No.	No.	No.	Pneumoconiosis and silicosis.	Specifically excluded.	Mont. Code Ann. §§ 39-73-101 et seq., 39-73-509, 39-73-707.
NE	No.	No.	No.	No.	No.	—
NV	No.	Yes, for firefighters and law enforcement personnel.	Yes, for firefighters.	Silicosis, asbestos-related diseases, and any other respiratory occupational disease resulting from injurious exposure to dusts.	No.	Nev. Rev. Stat. Ann. §§ 617.453, 617.457, 617.460, 617.470.
NH	Yes, as are certain other blood-borne diseases.	Yes, for firefighters. Heart and cardiovascular conditions suffered by other employees are compensable only if they are contributed to, or aggravated by, another compensable injury or accident.	Yes, for firefighters.	Yes, for firefighters.	No. Diseases or death resulting from stress without an accompanying physical manifestation is specifically excluded. Also excluded are mental injuries resulting from any disciplinary action, work evaluation, job transfer, layoff, demotion, termination, or similar action, if taken in good faith by an employer.	N.H. Rev. Stat. Ann. §§ 281-A:2, 281-A:17.
NJ	No.	No.	No.	Asbestosis, silicosis, and similar diseases.	No.	N.J. Stat. Ann. § 34:15-34.
NM	No.	No.	No.	Silicosis.	No.	N.M. Stat. Ann. § 52-3-34.
NY	No.	No.	Yes, if malignancy is due to occupational exposure to, or contact with, arsenic, benzol, beryllium, zirconium, cadmium, chrome, lead, fluorine, X rays, radium, or ionizing radiation or other radioactive substances.	Silicosis and other dust diseases.	No.	N.Y. Work. Comp. Law § 28.
NC	No.	No.	Yes, for epitheliomatous cancer.	Asbestosis, silicosis, psittacosis.	No.	N.C. Gen. Stat. § 97-53.
ND	No.	Yes, when caused by employment with reasonable medical certainty and when unusual stress is at least 50% of the cause. Also (cont'd)	No.	Pneumoconiosis, and for firefighters and law enforcement personnel, lung diseases in general.	Yes, but only when caused by physical injury that is at least 50% of the cause.	N.D. Cent. Code §§ 65-01-01.1, 65-01-02, 65-01-15.1.

(Table continues.)

Table 10.6-1 Part B   PART 10—STATE WORKERS' COMPENSATION LAWS   10-100

Table 10.6-1 Part B *(cont'd)*
SPECIFICALLY COVERED DISEASES OR ILLNESSES

(See also text at § 10.6.)

NOTE: Although a disease may not be specifically covered under a state's workers' compensation law, in some cases the disease may be covered under the general standard for determining whether an occupational disease is work-related.

	Is HIV/AIDS Specifically Covered?	Is Heart Disease Specifically Covered?	Is Cancer Specifically Covered?	Lung Diseases Specifically Covered?	Is Mental or Emotional Disease Specifically Covered?	Citations to Authority
ND *(cont'd)*		covered for firefighters and law enforcement personnel.				
OH	No.	Yes, for firefighters and law enforcement personnel exposed to heat, smoke, toxic gases, chemical fumes, and other toxic substances.	Yes, for epithelion cancer.	Berylliosis, silicosis, coal miners' pneumoconiosis, and for firefighters and law enforcement personnel, lung diseases in general.	No.	Ohio Rev. Code Ann. § 4123.68.
OK	No.	No.	No.	Asbestosis, silicosis.	No.	Okla. Stat. Ann. tit. 85, § 43.
OR	No.	No.	No.	Yes, for firefighters.	Yes, if employment conditions producing it exist in a real and objective sense and are not generally inherent in every working situation. Normal personnel actions do not qualify. Disorder must be generally recognized in psychological or medical community. Claimant must prove by clear and convincing evidence that the condition arose out of and in the course of employment.	Or. Rev. Stat. § 656.802.
PA	No.	Yes, for certain firefighters.	Yes, epitheliomatous cancer and cancer due to asbestos exposure.	Pneumoconiosis, anthraco-silicosis, silicosis, asbestosis, and for firefighters, lung disease in general.	No.	Pa. Stat. Ann. tit. 77, § 27.1.

RI	No.	No.	Yes, epitheliomatous cancer.	Silicosis, asbestosis, pneumoconiosis, and respiratory disorders due to contact with petroleum.	Yes, if caused or accompanied by physical trauma, or by emotional stress resulting from a situation of greater dimensions than day-to-day emotional strain and tension that all employees encounter daily without serious mental injury.	R.I. Gen. Laws § 28-34-2.
SC	No.	Yes, for certain firefighters.	No.	Yes, for firefighters.	No.	S.C. Code Ann. § 42-11-30.
SD	No.	No.	No.	Silicosis.	No.	S.D. Codified Laws §§ 62-8-1, 62-8-14.
TN	No.	Specifically excluded.	No.	Coal miners' pneumoconiosis, if total disability or death results from exposure and eligible under federal Coal Mine Health & Safety Act and Black Lung Benefits Act.	No.	Tenn. Code Ann. §§ 50-6-301, 50-6-302.
TX	No.	Yes, heart attack, if caused by specific event occurring in the course and scope of employment, where medical evidence indicates the employee's work was substantial contributing factor and heart attack was not triggered solely by emotional or mental stress, unless precipitated by a sudden stimulus.	No.	No.	Yes. Mental or emotional injuries arising principally from a legitimate personnel action are not, however, compensable.	Tex. Lab. Code Ann. §§ 408.006, 408.008.
UT	No.	No.	No.	No.	Yes, but only when sufficient legal and medical causal connection between employee's disease and employment.	Utah Code Ann. § 34A-3-106.
VT	No.	No.	No.	No.	No.	—
VA	Yes.	Yes, for certain firefighters and law enforcement personnel.	Yes, for epitheliomatous cancer; for certain public employees, leukemia, pancreatic, prostate, rectal, and throat cancers.	Pneumoconiosis, byssinosis, asbestosis; for certain firefighters and emergency services personnel, lung diseases in general.	No.	Va. Code Ann. §§ 65.2-402, 65.2-406.
WA	No.	No.	No.	Asbestos-related diseases in maritime workers.	No.	Wash. Rev. Code Ann. § 51.12.102.

(Table continues.)

Table 10.6-1 Part B   PART 10—STATE WORKERS' COMPENSATION LAWS   10-102

Table 10.6-1 Part B *(cont'd)*

**SPECIFICALLY
COVERED DISEASES OR ILLNESSES**

(See also text at § 10.6.)

NOTE: Although a disease may not be specifically covered under a state's workers' compensation law, in some cases the disease may be covered under the general standard for determining whether an occupational disease is work-related.

	Is HIV/AIDS Specifically Covered?	Is Heart Disease Specifically Covered?	Is Cancer Specifically Covered?	Lung Diseases Specifically Covered?	Is Mental or Emotional Disease Specifically Covered?	Citations to Authority
WV	No.	No.	No.	Pneumoconiosis, silicosis, asbestosis, and similar respiratory diseases.	Not covered if solely caused by nonphysical factors and did not result in physical injury or disease.	W. Va. Code §§ 23-4-1, 23-4-1f.
WI	No.	No.	No.	No.	No.	—
WY	No.	Yes, heart attack, if caused by injury, or if direct causal connection and causative exertion clearly unusual to employees in that particular employment, and acute symptoms occur within 4 hours of alleged causative exertion.	No.	No.	Not unless proven by clear and convincing evidence and occurs with physical injury.	Wyo. Stat. Ann. §§ 27-14-102, 27-14-603.

§ 10.7 Compensation for Occupational Hearing and Vision Loss

Most jurisdictions provide payments through workers' compensation programs for loss of hearing or vision that occurs as a result of an accident or conditions at the workplace. In some cases, states have developed special statutes in addition to the generally applicable workers' compensation schedules to deal with such losses; in other cases, the information on recovery is part of the general workers' compensation statutes. Table 10.7-1 covers state laws dealing with hearing and vision loss.

Most state laws provide that a loss may be compensable whether it is partial or total. Many states allow payment of a percentage of the amount allowed for a total loss that equals the percentage of actual loss. Several states require that the loss be above a certain amount, usually expressed in terms of decibels, before any recovery may take place. A few states also set the exact decibel level that will be considered total hearing loss.

In some states, the workers' compensation board or industrial commission may use only the corrected hearing or vision of the worker to determine the extent of the loss, although under some statutes the loss determination is specifically required to be based on the uncorrected hearing or vision of the worker. In many states, the determination of whether corrected or uncorrected hearing or vision is used has been determined through case law. There may also be slight variations in these methods. For example, Georgia case law states that the commission should not consider the corrected vision of the worker if the worker had perfect vision before the loss was incurred. Indiana law provides that uncorrected vision should be used in calculating the loss, but if the loss is total without glasses and the worker has some vision with glasses, a reduced schedule of benefits should be used. A few states require a waiting period before some claims may be filed. For example, claimants in Georgia may file for loss of hearing only after six months has passed from the last time the worker was exposed to the harmful noise.

Most payments are expressed as compensation for a specified number of weeks, although that number may vary greatly from state to state. Once the number of weeks of compensation is determined, the general formula used by the state for compensation (often a number around 66 percent of the worker's prior average wage or the state average weekly wage) is used to determine the actual weekly payment amount. A few states allow for compensation as a lump sum rather than a weekly payment. One state, Wyoming, considers age, education level, and training, in addition to wage, in making the determination of compensation.

Loss of vision in both eyes usually creates a presumption that the worker is rendered totally disabled. In such a situation, the individual will usually continue to receive payments while disabled, often until the death of the person or the receipt of Social Security benefits. Some states may require a showing that the individual is in fact totally disabled, such as a showing that there are no jobs the person could perform.

A few states provide that if the worker is partially at fault for the loss, because of a failure to use a protective device, benefits may be reduced or eliminated.

Table 10.7-1 sets out how these various issues have been addressed by statute or case law in each state.

Table 10.7-1
COMPENSATION FOR OCCUPATIONAL HEARING AND VISION LOSS

(See also text at § 10.7.)

	What Losses Are Compensable?	Standard for Total Loss	When Can Claims Be Filed?	Compensation for Loss of Hearing in One Ear	Compensation for Loss of Vision in One Eye	Compensation for Loss of Hearing in Both Ears	Compensation for Loss of Vision in Both Eyes	Effect of Employee Failure to Use Protective Device	Citations to Authority
AL	No specific statutory provision.	No specific statutory provision.	No specific statutory provision.	53 weeks.	124 weeks.	163 weeks.	Total disability; employee is entitled to compensation for duration of disability.	No specific statutory provision.	Ala. Code § 25-5-57.
AK	Total and partial losses.	No specific statutory provision.	No specific statutory provision.	$135,000 multiplied by the percentage of permanent impairment with respect to the whole person.	$135,000 multiplied by the percentage of permanent impairment with respect to the whole person.	$135,000 multiplied by the percentage of permanent impairment with respect to the whole person.	Total disability; employee is entitled to compensation for duration of disability.	No specific statutory provision.	Alaska Stat. §§ 23.30.180, 23.30.190.
AZ	Total and partial losses.	No specific statutory provision.	No specific statutory provision.	20 months.	25 months (30 months in case of loss of eye by enucleation).	60 months.	Total disability; employee is entitled to compensation for duration of disability.	No specific statutory provision.	Ariz. Rev. Stat. Ann. §§ 23-1044, 23-1045, 23-1061.
AR	Total and partial losses.	No specific statutory provision. Corrected vision may be used in determining extent of vision loss.	No specific statutory provision.	42 weeks.	105 weeks (if enucleation).	158 weeks.	Total disability; employee is entitled to compensation for duration of disability. In any eye injury, a vision loss of 80% or more is considered a total loss.	No specific statutory provision.	Ark. Stat. Ann. §§ 11-9-519, 11-9-521; *Barnard v. B&M Constr.*, 915 S.W.2d 296 (Ark. Ct. App. 1996).

State									Citation
CA	Total and partial losses.	No specific statutory provision.	No specific statutory provision.	Sliding scale based on degree of impairment.	Sliding scale based on degree of impairment.	Sliding scale based on degree of impairment.	Total disability; employee is entitled to compensation for duration of disability.	If employee engages in serious and willful misconduct by disobeying a safety order, benefits may be reduced by up to 50%.	Cal. Lab. Code §§ 4551, 4553.1, 4658, 4662.
CO	Total and partial losses.	No specific statutory provision. Uncorrected vision should be used in making the determination of vision loss.	No specific statutory provision.	35 weeks.	104 weeks (139 weeks if enucleation).	139 weeks.	Total disability; employee is entitled to compensation for duration of disability.	No specific statutory provision.	Colo. Rev. Stat. Ann. §§ 8-42-105, 8-42-107; *Great Am. Indemnity Co. v. Industrial Comm'n*, 162 P.2d 413 (Colo. 1945).
CT	Total and partial losses.	No specific statutory provision for hearng. For vision, reduction of sight to one-tenth or less of normal vision.	No specific statutory provision.	35 weeks.	157 weeks.	104 weeks.	Total incapacity; employee is entitled to compensation for duration of disability.	No specific statutory provision.	Conn. Gen. Stat. Ann. §§ 31-307, 31-308; *Reilly v. Carroll*, 134 A. 68 (Conn. 1926).
DE	Total and partial losses. Loss of equilibrium due to injury of the inner ear is covered.	No specific statutory provision. Uncorrected vision should be used to determine extent of vision loss.	No specific statutory provision.	75 weeks.	200 weeks.	175 weeks.	Total disability; employee is entitled to compensation for duration of disability.	No specific statutory provision.	Del. Code Ann. tit. 19, § 2326; *Keith v. Dover City Cab Co.*, 427 A.2d 896 (Del. Super. Ct. 1981); *Delle Donne v. Marcozi Radio & TV*, 263 A.2d 306 (Del. Super. Ct. 1970); *Alessandro Petrillo Co. v. Marioni*, 131 A.2d 164 (Del. Super. Ct. 1925).

(Table continues.)

Table 10.7-1 (cont'd)
COMPENSATION FOR OCCUPATIONAL HEARING AND VISION LOSS

(See also text at § 10.7.)

	What Losses Are Compensable?	Standard for Total Loss	When Can Claims Be Filed?	Compensation for Loss of Hearing in One Ear	Compensation for Loss of Vision in One Eye	Compensation for Loss of Hearing in Both Ears	Compensation for Loss of Vision in Both Eyes	Effect of Employee Failure to Use Protective Device	Citations to Authority
DC	No specific statutory provision.	For hearing, no specific statutory provision. For vision, 80% loss or more.	For hearing, 6 months after removal from injurious work environment. For vision, no specific statutory provision.	52 weeks.	160 weeks.	200 weeks.	Total disability; employee is entitled to compensation for duration of disability.	No specific statutory provision.	D.C. Code Ann. § 36-308.
FL	No specific statutory provision.	No specific statutory provision.	No specific statutory provision.	Compensation as provided by state panel.	Compensation as provided by state panel.	Compensation as provided by state panel.	Total disability; employee is entitled to compensation for duration of disability.	Compensation award reduced by 50%.	Fla. Stat. Ann. §§ 440.09, 440.15.
GA	For hearing, greater than 15 decibels (26 decibels ANSI or ISO). For vision, no specific statutory provision.	For hearing, 82 decibels (93 decibels ANSI or ISO). For vision, no specific statutory provision. For vision, uncorrected vision should be used to determine extent of loss.	For hearing, 6 months after last exposure to harmful noise. For vision, no specific statutory provision.	75 weeks.	150 weeks.	150 weeks.	Total disability; employee is entitled to compensation for duration of disability.	Compensation not payable.	Ga. Code Ann. §§ 34-9-261, 34-9-263, 34-9-264; Georgia Cas. & Sur. Co. v. Speller, 177 S.E.2d 491 (Ga. Ct. App. 1970).

HI	No specific statutory provision.	For hearing, no specific statutory provision. For vision, loss of binocular vision or loss of 80% of vision.	No specific statutory provision.	52 weeks.	140 weeks (160 weeks if loss of eye by enucleation).	200 weeks.	Total disability; employee is entitled to compensation for duration of disability.	No specific statutory provision.	Haw. Rev. Stat. Ann. §§ 386-31, 386-32.
ID	No specific statutory provision.	No specific statutory provision. Uncorrected vision should be considered in determining loss.	No specific statutory provision.	No specific statutory provision.	150 weeks (175 weeks if loss of eye by enucleation).	175 weeks for total loss of binaural hearing.	Total disability; employee is entitled to compensation for duration of disability.	No specific statutory provision.	Idaho Code §§ 72-407, 72-428; *Kelley v. Prouty*, 30 P.2d 769 (Idaho 1934).
IL	For hearing, greater than 30 decibels. For vision, no specific statutory provision.	For hearing, greater than 85 decibels. For vision, no specific statutory provision. Industrial commission has the discretion to determine whether corrected or uncorrected vision should be used to determine extent of vision loss.	No specific statutory provision.	50 weeks.	150 weeks (160 weeks if loss of eye by enucleation).	200 weeks.	Total disability; employee is entitled to compensation for duration of disability.	No specific statutory provision.	820 Ill. Comp. Stat. Ann. 305/8; *Brooks v. Industrial Comm'n*, 637 N.E.2d 114 (Ill. App. Ct. 1993).
IN	Total and partial losses.	For hearing, no specific statutory provision. For vision, reduction to one-tenth *(cont'd)*	No specific statutory provision.	Flat rate based on degree of impairment plus weekly compensation for up to 125 weeks.	150 weeks.	200 weeks.	500 weeks.	No specific statutory provision.	Ind. Code Ann. § 22-3-7-16.

(Table continues.)

Table 10.7-1 (cont'd)

COMPENSATION FOR OCCUPATIONAL HEARING AND VISION LOSS

(See also text at § 10.7.)

	What Losses Are Compensable?	Standard for Total Loss	When Can Claims Be Filed?	Compensation for Loss of Hearing in One Ear	Compensation for Loss of Vision in One Eye	Compensation for Loss of Hearing in Both Ears	Compensation for Loss of Vision in Both Eyes	Effect of Employee Failure to Use Protective Device	Citations to Authority
IN (cont'd)		normal vision. Uncorrected vision should be used to determine extent of vision loss, but if loss is 100% without correction and greater than 100% with correction, compensation should not be paid as for total loss.							
IA	For hearing, greater than 25 decibels (ANSI/ISO). Uncorrected hearing should be used to determine extent of hearing loss. Loss of hearing attributable to age or any other	For hearing, 92 decibels (ANSI/ISO). For vision, no specific statutory provision.	For hearing, 6 months after separation from employment. For vision, no specific statutory provision.	50 weeks.	140 weeks. If, at the time of vision loss, employee is already suffering from a loss of vision in the other eye, 200 weeks.	175 weeks.	Total disability; employee is entitled to compensation for duration of disability.	No specific statutory provision.	Iowa Code Ann. §§ 85.34, 85B.1 et seq.

	condition, or to exposure not arising out of and in the course of employment, is not compensable. For vision, partial and total losses.								
KS	Total and partial losses.	No specific statutory provision.	No specific statutory provision.	30 weeks.	120 weeks.	110 weeks.	Total disability; employee is entitled to compensation for duration of disability.	No specific statutory provision.	Kan. Stat. Ann. §§ 44-510c, 44-510d.
KY	Binaural hearing loss converted to impairment of the whole person must result in at least an 8% total impairment.	No specific statutory provision.	No specific statutory provision.	Compensation based on impairment factor.	Compensation based on impairment factor.	Compensation based on impairment factor.	Compensation based on impairment factor.	No specific statutory provision.	Ky. Rev. Stat. Ann. §§ 342.730, 342.7305.
LA	No specific statutory provision.	No specific statutory provision.	No specific statutory provision.	100 weeks.	100 weeks.	No specific statutory provision.	Total disability; employee is entitled to compensation for duration of disability.	No specific statutory provision.	La. Rev. Stat. § 23:1221; *Ryan v. Aetna Cas. & Sur. Co.*, 161 So. 2d 286 (La. Ct. App. 1964).
ME	For hearing, greater than 25 decibels ANSI (15 decibels ASA). For vision, no specific statutory provision.	For hearing, 92 decibels ANSI (82 decibels ASA). Uncorrected hearing should be used to determine extent of hearing loss. In determining an employee's hearing loss, in *(cont'd)*	For hearing, 30 days after separation from the occupational noise. For vision, no specific statutory provision.	50 weeks.	162 weeks.	200 weeks.	Total disability; employee is entitled to compensation for duration of disability and no less than 800 weeks.	No specific statutory provision.	Me. Rev. Stat. Ann. tit. 39-A, §§ 212, 612.

(Table continues.)

Table 10.7-1 PART 10—STATE WORKERS' COMPENSATION LAWS 10-110

Table 10.7-1 (cont'd)
COMPENSATION FOR OCCUPATIONAL HEARING AND VISION LOSS

(See also text at § 10.7.)

	What Losses Are Compensable?	Standard for Total Loss	When Can Claims Be Filed?	Compensation for Loss of Hearing in One Ear	Compensation for Loss of Vision in One Eye	Compensation for Loss of Hearing in Both Ears	Compensation for Loss of Vision in Both Eyes	Effect of Employee Failure to Use Protective Device	Citations to Authority
ME (cont'd)		order to account for "normal, age-related hearing loss," ½ decibel is deducted from the total average decibel loss for each year of employee's age over 40 at the time of the last exposure to industrial noise. For vision, 80% loss or more.							
MD	For hearing, greater than 15 decibels. For vision, total or partial loss.	For hearing, 82 decibels. For vision, no specific statutory provision. Uncorrected vision should be used to determine extent of vision loss.	No specific statutory provision.	125 weeks.	250 weeks.	250 weeks.	Total disability; employee is entitled to compensation for duration of disability.	No specific statutory provision.	Md. Code Ann., Lab. & Empl. §§ 9-627, 9-636, 9-637, 9-649 et seq.

MA	Total or partial losses.	For hearing, no specific statutory provision, but case law indicates that loss does not have to be 100%. For vision, 20/70 of normal vision. Corrected vision should be considered to determine extent of vision loss.	No specific statutory provision.	29 times state average weekly wage.	39 times state average weekly wage.	77 times state average weekly wage.	Total disability; employee is entitled to compensation for duration of disability.	No specific statutory provision.	Mass. Gen. Laws Ann. ch. 152, § 36; *Vouniseas' Case,* 324 N.E.2d 916 (Mass. App. Ct. 1975).
MI	No specific statutory provision.	For hearing, no specific statutory provision. For vision, 80% loss or more in one eye.	No specific statutory provision.	No specific statutory provision.	162 weeks.	No specific statutory provision.	Total disability; employee is entitled to compensation for duration of disability; total disability presumed for at least 800 weeks.	No specific statutory provision.	Mich. Comp. Laws Ann. §§ 418.351, 418.361; Mich. Stat. Ann. §§ 17.237(351), 17.237(361).
MN	Total and partial losses.	No specific statutory provision. Corrected vision should be used to determine extent of vision loss.	No specific statutory provision.	Flat rate based on an impairment rating (1–100%) times amount ranging from $25,000 to $400,000.	Flat rate based on an impairment rating (1–100%) times amount ranging from $25,000 to $400,000.	Flat rate based on an impairment rating (1–100%) times amount ranging from $25,000 to $400,000.	Total disability; employee is entitled to compensation for duration of disability.	No specific statutory provision.	Minn. Stat. Ann. § 176.191; *Flint v. American Can Co.,* 426 N.W.2d 190 (Minn. 1980); *Yureko v. Prospect Foundry Co.,* 115 N.W.2d 477 (Minn. 1962).
MS	Total and partial losses.	For hearing, no specific statutory provision. For vision, 80% loss of vision or loss of binocular vision.	No specific statutory provision.	40 weeks.	100 weeks.	150 weeks.	Total disability; employee is entitled to compensation for duration of disability, at least 450 weeks.	No specific statutory provision.	Miss. Code Ann. § 71-3-17.

(Table continues.)

Table 10.7-1   PART 10—STATE WORKERS' COMPENSATION LAWS   10-112

Table 10.7-1 *(cont'd)*
COMPENSATION FOR OCCUPATIONAL HEARING AND VISION LOSS

(See also text at § 10.7.)

	What Losses Are Compensable?	*Standard for Total Loss*	*When Can Claims Be Filed?*	*Compensation for Loss of Hearing in One Ear*	*Compensation for Loss of Vision in One Eye*	*Compensation for Loss of Hearing in Both Ears*	*Compensation for Loss of Vision in Both Eyes*	*Effect of Employee Failure to Use Protective Device*	*Citations to Authority*
MO	For hearing, greater than 15 decibels. For vision, no specific statutory provision.	For hearing, 82 decibels. For vision, no specific statutory provision. Uncorrected vision should be used to determine extent of vision loss.	For hearing, 6 months after last exposure to noisy work. For vision, no specific statutory provision.	For partial occupational hearing loss, 40 weeks. For total hearing loss, 44 weeks.	140 weeks.	For partial occupational hearing loss, 180 weeks. For total hearing loss, 180 weeks.	No specific statutory provision.	No specific statutory provision.	Mo. Rev. Stat. §§ 287.190, 287.197; *Graf v. National Steel Prods. Co.*, 38 S.W.2d 518 (Mo. Ct. App. 1931).
MT	Total and partial losses. For hearing, greater than 25 decibels (ISO).	For hearing, 92 decibels (ISO). Uncorrected hearing should be used to determine extent of hearing loss. For vision, no specific statutory provision.	For hearing, 6 months after removal from noisy employment. For vision, no specific statutory provision.	40 weeks.	350 weeks.	200 weeks.	Total disability; employee is entitled to compensation for duration of disability.	No specific statutory provision.	Mont. Code Ann. §§ 39-71-702, 39-71-703, 39-71-801 *et seq.*

	Total and partial losses	Hearing/Vision provision	Waiting period			Hearing	Vision		Citation
NE	Total and partial losses.	No specific statutory provision.	No specific statutory provision.	50 weeks. An employee who loses an ear in an accident receives compensation equal to 25 weeks' pay.	125 weeks.	If total loss of hearing, total disability; employee is entitled to compensation for duration of disability.	If total loss of vision, total disability; employee is entitled to compensation for duration of disability.	No specific statutory provision.	Neb. Rev. Stat. Ann. § 48-121.
NV	Total and partial losses.	No specific statutory provision.	No specific statutory provision.	Formula based on percentage impairment times percentage of employee's wages.	Formula based on percentage impairment times percentage of employee's wages.	Formula based on percentage impairment times percentage of employee's wages.	Total disability; employee is entitled to compensation for duration of disability.	No specific statutory provision.	Nev. Rev. Stat. Ann. §§ 616C.435, 616C.440, 616C.490.
NH	Total and partial losses.	For hearing, no specific statutory provision. For vision, 80% loss or more. Uncorrected vision should be used to determine extent of vision loss.	No specific statutory provision.	30 weeks.	84 weeks.	123 weeks.	300 weeks.	No specific statutory provision.	N.H. Rev. Stat. Ann. § 281-A:32.
NJ	Total and partial losses. For hearing, loss must be greater than 30 decibels ANSI (20 decibels ASA).	No specific statutory provision.	For hearing, 4 weeks after removal from exposure to hazardous noise in employment. For vision, no specific statutory provision.	60 weeks.	200 weeks (225 if enucleation).	200 weeks.	Total disability; employee is entitled to compensation for duration of disability, at least 450 weeks.	Compensation not payable.	N.J. Stat. Ann. §§ 34:15-7, 34:15-12, 34:15-35.10 et seq.
NM	Total and partial losses.	No specific statutory provision. Uncorrected vision should be used to determine extent of vision loss.	No specific statutory provision.	40 weeks.	120 weeks (130 if enucleation).	150 weeks.	Total disability; employee is entitled to compensation for life.	No specific statutory provision.	N.M. Stat. Ann. §§ 52-1-41, 52-1-43.

(Table continues.)

Table 10.7-1 PART 10—STATE WORKERS' COMPENSATION LAWS 10-114

Table 10.7-1 (cont'd)
COMPENSATION FOR OCCUPATIONAL HEARING AND VISION LOSS

(See also text at § 10.7.)

	What Losses Are Compensable?	Standard for Total Loss	When Can Claims Be Filed?	Compensation for Loss of Hearing in One Ear	Compensation for Loss of Vision in One Eye	Compensation for Loss of Hearing in Both Ears	Compensation for Loss of Vision in Both Eyes	Effect of Employee Failure to Use Protective Device	Citations to Authority
NY	Total and partial losses.	For hearing, no specific statutory provision. For vision, 80% loss or more or loss of binocular vision.	For hearing, 3 months after removal from exposure to harmful noise in employment. For vision, no specific statutory provision.	60 weeks.	160 weeks.	150 weeks.	Total disability; employee is entitled to compensation for duration of disability.	No specific statutory provision.	N.Y. Work. Comp. Law §§ 15, 49-aa-49-hh.
NC	Total and partial losses.	For hearing, no specific statutory provision. For vision, 85% loss or more.	No specific statutory provision.	70 weeks.	120 weeks.	150 weeks.	Total disability; employee is entitled to compensation for life.	No specific statutory provision.	N.C. Gen. Stat. §§ 97-29, 97-31.
ND	Total and partial losses.	No specific statutory provision.	No specific statutory provision.	50 weeks.	150 weeks.	200 weeks.	Total disability; employee is entitled to compensation for duration of disability.	No specific statutory provision.	N.D. Cent. Code §§ 65-05-09, 65-05-12– 65-05-14.

OH	Total and partial losses. Case law, now codified in the statute, indicates that vision loss must be at least 25%. *(cont'd)*	No specific statutory provision. Uncorrected vision should be used to determine extent of vision loss. *(cont'd)*	No specific statutory provision.	25 weeks.	125 weeks.	125 weeks.	Total disability; employee is entitled to compensation for life.	No specific statutory provision.	Ohio Rev. Code Ann. §§ 4123.57, 4123.58; *State ex rel. Swander v. Indus. Comm'n*, 468 N.E.2d 913 (Ohio Ct. App. 1983); *Industrial Comm'n v. Whitlatch*, 21 Ohio Law Abs. 34 (Ohio Ct. App. 1935).
OK	Total and partial losses.	No specific statutory provision. Industrial commission need not consider corrected vision to determine extent of vision loss.	No specific statutory provision.	105 weeks; 110 weeks after 1/1/03..	263 weeks.	315 weeks; 330 weeks after 1/1/03.	Total disability; employee is entitled to compensation for duration of disability.	No specific statutory provision.	Okla. Stat. Ann. tit. 85, § 22; *Parrott Motor Co. v. Jolls*, 31 P.2d 925 (Okla. 1934).
OR	Total and partial losses.	No specific statutory provision. Maximum corrected vision should be used to determine extent of vision loss.	No specific statutory provision.	Flat rate based on degree of impairment.	Flat rate based on degree of impairment.	Flat rate based on degree of impairment.	Total disability; employee is entitled to compensation for duration of disability.	No specific statutory provision.	Or. Rev. Stat. §§ 656.206, 656.214.
PA	For hearing, greater than 10% binaural loss. For vision, no specific statutory provision.	No specific statutory provision.	For industrial loss of hearing, compensation based on percentage of binaural loss. For total hearing loss, 60 weeks.		275 weeks.	260 weeks.	Total disability; employee is entitled to compensation for duration of disability.	No specific statutory provision.	Pa. Stat. Ann. tit. 77, §§ 511, 513.
RI	For hearing, greater than 15 decibels. For vision, no specific statutory provision.	For hearing, 82 decibels. For vision, one-tenth or less of *(cont'd)*	For hearing, 6 months after separation from the noisy *(cont'd)*	75 weeks for total occupational deafness.	160 weeks.	44 weeks for total deafness.	Total disability; employee is entitled to compensation for duration of disability, plus *(cont'd)*	No specific statutory provision.	R.I. Gen. Laws §§ 28-33-17, 28-33-19.

(Table continues.)

Table 10.7-1   PART 10—STATE WORKERS' COMPENSATION LAWS   10-116

Table 10.7-1 *(cont'd)*

COMPENSATION FOR OCCUPATIONAL HEARING AND VISION LOSS

(See also text at § 10.7.)

	What Losses Are Compensable?	Standard for Total Loss	When Can Claims Be Filed?	Compensation for Loss of Hearing in One Ear	Compensation for Loss of Vision in One Eye	Compensation for Loss of Hearing in Both Ears	Compensation for Loss of Vision in Both Eyes	Effect of Employee Failure to Use Protective Device	Citations to Authority
RI *(cont'd)*		normal vision. Corrected vision should be used to determine extent of vision loss.	employment. For vision, no specific statutory provision.				additional compensation for up to 312 weeks.		
SC	Total and partial losses.	No specific statutory provision; case law for vision indicates total loss of vision may be less than 100% loss.	No specific statutory provision.	80 weeks.	140 weeks.	165 weeks.	Total disability; employee is entitled to compensation for duration of disability.	No specific statutory provision.	S.C. Code Ann. §§ 42-9-10, 42-9-30; *Dykes v. Daniel Constr. Co.*, 202 S.E.2d 646 (S.C. 1974).
SD	Total and partial losses. Hearing loss must be greater than 25 decibels (ANSI).	For hearing, 92 decibels (ANSI). For vision, no specific statutory provision.	For hearing, 6 months after last exposure to excessive occupational noise. For vision, no specific statutory provision.	50 weeks.	150 weeks.	150 weeks.	Total disability; employee is entitled to compensation for duration of disability.	For hearing, compensation not payable. For vision, no specific statutory provision.	S.D. Codified Laws §§ 62-4-6, 62-4-7, 62-9-3, 62-9-6, 62-9-8.

State									
TN	Total and partial losses.	No specific statutory provision.	No specific statutory provision.	No specific statutory provision.	100 weeks.	150 weeks.	400 weeks. If totally disabled, employee is entitled to compensation for life.	No specific statutory provision.	Tenn. Code Ann. § 50-6-207.
TX	Total and partial losses.	No specific statutory provision. Uncorrected vision should be used to determine extent of vision loss.	No specific statutory provision.	Compensation based on impairment rating.	Compensation based on impairment rating.	Compensation based on impairment rating.	If total disability, employee is entitled to compensation for life.	No specific statutory provision.	Tex. Lab. Code Ann. §§ 408.124, 408.161; National Union Fire Ins. Co. of Pittsburgh v. Lucio, 674 S.W.2d 487 (Tex. App. 1984).
UT	For hearing, greater than 25 decibels. For vision, no specific statutory provision.	No specific statutory provision.	For hearing, 6 weeks after termination of exposure to harmful industrial noise.	Proportional.	100 weeks (120 weeks if enucleation).	109 weeks.	Total disability; employee is entitled to compensation for duration of disability.	No specific statutory provision.	Utah Code Ann. §§ 34A-2-412, 34A-2-501, 34A-2-505, 34A-2-507.
VT	Total and partial losses.	No specific statutory provision.	No specific statutory provision.	Rate determined by multiplying the percentage impairment of the whole person times 330 weeks.	Rate determined by multiplying the percentage impairment of the whole person times 330 weeks.	Rate determined by multiplying the percentage impairment of the whole person times 330 weeks.	Total disability; employee is entitled to compensation for duration of disability.	No specific statutory provision.	Vt. Stat. Ann. tit. 21, §§ 644, 648.
VA	Total and partial losses. Hearing loss must be at least 27 decibels (ASA). Vision loss must be at least 5% or more (20/25 Snellen).	For hearing, 90 decibels. Uncorrected hearing should be used to determine extent of hearing loss. For vision, 20/200 (Snellen).	No specific statutory provision.	50 weeks.	100 weeks.	No specific statutory provision.	Total disability; employee is entitled to compensation for duration of disability.	No specific statutory provision.	Va. Code Ann. §§ 65.2-500, 65.2-503; 16 Va. Admin. Code §§ 30-50-130, 30-50-140.

(Table continues.)

Table 10.7-1 PART 10—STATE WORKERS' COMPENSATION LAWS 10-118

Table 10.7-1 *(cont'd)*

COMPENSATION FOR OCCUPATIONAL HEARING AND VISION LOSS

(See also text at § 10.7.)

	What Losses Are Compensable?	Standard for Total Loss	When Can Claims Be Filed?	Compensation for Loss of Hearing in One Ear	Compensation for Loss of Vision in One Eye	Compensation for Loss of Hearing in Both Ears	Compensation for Loss of Vision in Both Eyes	Effect of Employee Failure to Use Protective Device	Citations to Authority
WA	Total and partial losses.	For hearing, complete loss. For vision, loss of central visual acuity.	No specific statutory provision.	$7,200.*	$18,000* ($21,600* if enucleation).	$43,200.*	If total disability, employee is entitled to compensation for duration of disability.	No specific statutory provision.	Wash. Rev. Code Ann. §§ 51.08.160, 51.32.060, 51.32.080.
	*These amounts are increased annually by an amount equal to the rise in CPI.								
WV	Total and partial losses. Hearing loss must be greater than 27.5 decibels.	For hearing, 90 decibels. For vision, no specific statutory provision.	No specific statutory provision.	90 weeks.	132 weeks.	220 weeks.	Total disability; employee is entitled to compensation until Social Security age is reached.	No specific statutory provision.	W. Va. Code §§ 23-4-6, 23-4-6b.
WI	Total and partial losses. Hearing loss must be greater than 20% binaural hearing loss.	No specific statutory provision.	For hearing, 7 days after removal from noisy employment. For vision, no specific statutory provision.	For occupational deafness, 36 weeks; for total deafness, 55 weeks.	250 weeks (275 if enucleation).	For occupational deafness, 216 weeks; for total deafness, 330 weeks.	Total disability; employee is entitled to compensation for duration of disability.	No specific statutory provision.	Wis. Stat. Ann. §§ 102.43, 102.52, 102.555.
WY	Total and partial losses.	No specific statutory provision.	No specific statutory provision.	Number of months calculated by formula using factors including employee's age, education level, occupation, training, etc.	Number of months calculated by formula using factors including employee's age, education level, occupation, training, etc.	Number of months calculated by formula using factors including employee's age, education level, occupation, training, etc.	No specific statutory provision.	Injuries due solely to the culpable negligence of the employee are not compensable.	Wyo. Stat. Ann. §§ 27-14-102, 27-14-405.

§ 10.8 Total Disability Benefits

Total disabilities under state workers' compensation laws are divided into temporary total disability and permanent total disability. *Permanent total disability* generally indicates that the individual is totally and permanently unable to return to employment. *Temporary total disability* benefits are available to covered employees who are totally disabled for a period but are expected to recover and return to employment.

Benefit amounts for temporary or permanent total disability under state workers' compensation laws are generally computed based on a percentage of the employee's average weekly wage (AWW). The majority of states set minimum and maximum weekly benefit amounts. In most states the maximum amount is expressed as a percentage of the state average weekly wage (SAWW). Some states, including Alaska, Georgia, and New York, set the maximum amount by statute. Additionally, most states limit the number of weeks and the aggregate dollar amount of total disability benefits. Most states provide permanent total disability benefits for the lifetime of the employee. Many states also reduce workers' compensation benefits for total disability by benefits from other sources, including Social Security disability benefits.

Table 10.8-1 sets out the amount of benefits payable upon a covered worker's total disability, including formulas for calculating the benefit amount and maximum and minimum weekly benefit amounts payable to disabled workers.

Table 10.8-2 sets out the limitations on the amount of time benefits will be paid, the maximum total amount of total disability benefits to be paid to a covered worker, and any offsets against the available benefit under the state's workers' compensation laws as a result of benefits received from other sources.

Table 10.8-1   PART 10—STATE WORKERS' COMPENSATION LAWS   10-120

Table 10.8-1
CALCULATION OF BENEFITS FOR TOTAL DISABILITY

(See also text at § 10.8.)

	Percentage of Wages Paid as Benefit	Maximum Weekly Benefit Amount	Maximum Weekly Benefit Rate	Minimum Weekly Benefit Amount	Minimum Weekly Benefit Rate	Citations to Authority
AL	66⅔% of employee's average weekly earnings received at the time of injury.	$531.	100% of state's average weekly wage.	$146 unless at the time of the accident employee was receiving earnings of less than the minimum rate; then employee shall receive his or her actual wage.	27½% of state's average weekly wage.	Ala. Code §§ 25-5-57, 25-5-58, 25-5-68.
AK	80% of employee's spendable weekly wages.	$700.	State has no specific statutory authority.	$110 ($154 in cases of employees who have furnished proof of wages). If employee's spendable weekly wages are less than $154, then employer may adjust the weekly rate of compensation to a rate equal to employee's spendable weekly wages.	State has no specific statutory authority.	Alaska Stat. §§ 23.30.175, 23.30.180, 23.30.185.
AZ	66⅔%.	$327.95.	State has no specific statutory authority.	State has no specific statutory authority.	State has no specific statutory authority.	Ariz. Rev. Stat. Ann. § 23-901 *et seq.*
AR	66⅔% of weekly wages.	$410.	85% of state's average weekly wage.	$20.	State has no specific statutory authority.	Ark. Code Ann. §§ 11-9-518, 11-9-519.
CA	66⅔% of average weekly earnings.	$490; $602 after 1/1/03; $728 after 1/1/04; $840 after 1/1/05.	State has no specific statutory authority.	*Temporary total disability:* $126 or employee's average weekly earnings from all employers, whichever is less. *Permanent total disability:* $112.	State has no specific statutory authority.	Cal. Lab. Code §§ 4453, 4653, 4658.
CO	66⅔%.	$593.81.	91% of state's average weekly wage.	State has no specific statutory authority.	State has no specific statutory authority.	Colo. Rev. Stat. Ann. §§ 8-42-102, 8-42-105, 8-42-111.
CT	75% of weekly wages after tax.	$838.	100% of state's average weekly wage.	Lesser of $167.60 or 75% of employee's average weekly wage.	Lesser of 20% of the maximum or 75% of employee's average weekly wage.	Conn. Gen. Stat. Ann. §§ 31-307, 31-309.

DE	66⅔% of weekly wages.	$449.60.	66⅔% of state's average weekly wage.	$149.87.	22⅔% of state's average weekly wage or 100% of employee's average weekly wage, whichever is less.	Del. Code Ann. tit. 19, § 2324.
DC	66⅔% of weekly wages.	$948.76.	100% of average weekly wage of insured employees in the District of Columbia.	$237.19.	25% of average weekly wage of insured employees in the District of Columbia.	D.C. Code Ann. §§ 36-305, 36-308, 36-311.
FL	66⅔% of employee's weekly wages.	$571.	100% of state's average weekly wage.	$20 or employee's weekly wages, whichever is less.	State has no specific statutory authority.	Fla. Stat. Ann. §§ 440.12(2), 440.15.
GA	66⅔% of employee's weekly wages.	$375.	State has no specific statutory authority.	$37.50.	State has no specific statutory authority.	Ga. Code Ann. § 34-9-261.
HI	66⅔% of average weekly wage.	$547.	100% of state's average weekly wage.	$137.	*Temporary total disability:* 25% of state's average weekly wage or $38, whichever is higher, or if the employee's average weekly wages are less than the prescribed minimum weekly benefit, at the rate of 100% of the employee's average weekly wages. *Permanent total disability:* 25% of state's average weekly wage or $38, whichever is higher.	Haw. Rev. Stat. Ann. § 386-31.
ID	67% of employee's average weekly wage.	$445.50.	90% of state's average weekly wage.	$222.75.	45% of state's average weekly wage or 90% of employee's average weekly wage, whichever is less.	Idaho Code §§ 72-408, 72-409.
IL	66⅔% of average weekly wage.	$972.12.	133⅓% of state's average weekly wage.	*Temporary total disability:* $100.90 for unmarried employee and up to $124.30 if employee has at least 4 children. Minimum amount shall not exceed 100% of employee's average weekly wage. *Permanent total disability:* $358.62.	*Permanent total disability:* 50% of state's average weekly wage.	820 Ill. Comp. Stat. Ann. 305/8.
IN	66⅔% of weekly wages.	$508.	State has no specific statutory authority.	$50; however, the weekly compensation payable shall not exceed employee's aver- *(cont'd)*	State has no specific statutory authority.	Ind. Code Ann. §§ 22-3-3-7, 22-3-3-8, 22-3-3-10, 22-3-3-22.

(Table continues.)

Table 10.8-1 PART 10—STATE WORKERS' COMPENSATION LAWS 10-122

Table 10.8-1 (*cont'd*)
CALCULATION OF BENEFITS FOR TOTAL DISABILITY

(See also text at § 10.8.)

	Percentage of Wages Paid as Benefit	Maximum Weekly Benefit Amount	Maximum Weekly Benefit Rate	Minimum Weekly Benefit Amount	Minimum Weekly Benefit Rate	Citations to Authority
IN (cont'd)				age weekly wage at the time of the injury.		
IA	80% of weekly earnings after payroll deductions.	$1,031.	200% of state's average weekly wage.	*Temporary total disability:* $174 or employee's average weekly spendable wage, whichever is less. *Permanent total disability:* $121.38.	35% of state's average weekly wage.	Iowa Code Ann. §§ 85.32, 85.34, 85.36, 85.37.
KS	66⅔% of employee's average weekly wage.	$401.	75% of state's average weekly wage.	$25.	State has no specific statutory authority.	Kan. Stat. Ann. § 44-510c.
KY	66⅔% of employee's average weekly wage.	$530.07.	75% of state's average weekly wage.	$106.01.	20% of state's average weekly wage.	Ky. Rev. Stat. Ann. § 342.730.
LA	66⅔% of employee's average weekly wage.	$388.	75% of state's average weekly wage.	$104 or employee's average weekly wage, whichever is less.	20% of state's average weekly wage.	La. Rev. Stat. Ann. §§ 23:1202, 23:1221.
ME	80% of average after-tax weekly earnings.	$471.76.	90% of state's average weekly wage.	State has no specific statutory authority.	State has no specific statutory authority.	Me. Rev. Stat. Ann. tit. 39-A, §§ 211, 212.
MD	66⅔% of employee's average weekly wage.	$668.	100% of state's average weekly wage.	*Temporary total disability:* $50 or employee's average weekly wage, whichever is less. *Permanent total disability:* $25 or employee's average weekly wage, whichever is less.	State has no specific statutory authority.	Md. Code Ann., Lab. & Empl. §§ 9-621, 9-637.
MA	*Temporary total disability:* 60% of employee's average weekly wage. *Permanent total disability:* 66⅔% of employee's average weekly wage.	$830.89.	100% of state's average weekly wage.	*Temporary total disability:* $166.18 or employee's average weekly wage, whichever is less. *Permanent total disability:* $166.18.	20% of state's average weekly wage.	Mass. Gen. Laws Ann. ch. 152, §§ 34, 34A.

State						Citation
MI	80% of employee's after-tax average weekly wage.	$644.	90% of state's average weekly wage.	State has no specific statutory authority.	25% of state's average weekly wage.	Mich. Comp. Laws Ann. §§ 418.351, 418.355; Mich. Stat. Ann. §§ 17.237(351), 17.237(355).
MN	66⅔% of employee's weekly wage.	$750.	State has no specific statutory rate.	*Temporary total disability:* $104 or employee's actual weekly wage, whichever is less.	*Permanent total disability:* 65% of state's average weekly wage.	Minn. Stat. Ann. § 176.101.
MS	66⅔% of employee's average weekly wages.	$316.46.	66⅔% of state's average weekly wage.	$25.	State has no specific statutory authority.	Miss. Code Ann. §§ 71-3-13, 71-3-17.
MO	66⅔% of employee's average weekly wage.	$599.96.	105% of state's average weekly wage.	$40.	State has no specific statutory authority.	Mo. Rev. Stat. §§ 287.170, 287.200.
MT	66⅔% of employee's weekly wages.	$396.	100% of state's average weekly wage.	$192.	State has no specific statutory authority.	Mont. Code Ann. §§ 39-71-701, 39-71-702.
NE	66⅔% of employee's weekly wages.	$487.	100% of state's average weekly wage.	$49 or employee's weekly wage, whichever is less.	State has no specific statutory authority.	Neb. Rev. Stat. Ann. §§ 48-121, 48-121.01.
NV	66⅔% of employees average monthly wage.	$580.72.	150% of state's average weekly wage.	State has no specific statutory authority.	State has no specific statutory authority.	Nev. Rev. Stat. Ann. §§ 616C.440, 616C.475.
NH	60% of employee's weekly wages.	$926.	150% of state's average weekly wage.	$184.60 or 90% of employee's after-tax earnings, whichever is less.	30% of state's average weekly wage or 90% of employee's after-tax earnings, whichever is less.	N.H. Rev. Stat. Ann. §§ 281-A:28, 281-A:28-a.
NJ	70% of employee's weekly wages.	$591.	75% of state's average weekly wage.	$158.	20% of state's average weekly wage.	N.J. Stat. Ann. § 34:15-12.
NM	66⅔% of weekly wages.	$492.98.	85% of state's average weekly wage.	$36 or employee's weekly wage, whichever is less.	State has no specific statutory authority.	N.M. Stat. Ann. § 52-1-41.
NY	66⅔% of weekly wages.	$400.	State has no specific statutory authority.	$40 or employee's weekly wage, whichever is less.	State has no specific statutory authority.	N.Y. Work. Comp. Law § 15.
NC	66⅔% of employee's weekly wages.	$654.	110% of state's average weekly wage.	$30.	State has no specific statutory authority.	N.C. Gen. Stat. §§ 96-8(22), 97-29.
ND	66⅔% of weekly wages.	$497.	100% of state's average weekly wage.	$271.	60% of state's average weekly wage or employee's weekly wage after deductions for Social Security and federal income tax, whichever is less.	N.D. Cent. Code § 65-05-09.

(Table continues.)

Table 10.8-1 *(cont'd)*
CALCULATION OF BENEFITS FOR TOTAL DISABILITY

(See also text at § 10.8.)

	Percentage of Wages Paid as Benefit	Maximum Weekly Benefit Amount	Maximum Weekly Benefit Rate	Minimum Weekly Benefit Amount	Minimum Weekly Benefit Rate	Citations to Authority
OH	*Temporary total disability:* 72% of weekly wages for first 12 weeks of disability, 66⅔% for additional weeks. *Permanent total disability:* 66⅔% of weekly wages.	$618.	*Temporary total disability:* 100% of state's average weekly wage. During the first 12 weeks, the maximum benefit is the lesser of 100% of state's average weekly wage or 100% of employee's net wages. *Permanent total disability:* 66⅔% unless compensation benefits combined with disability benefits received pursuant to the Social Security Act are less than state's average weekly wage; then the maximum compensation shall be 100% of state's average weekly wage.	$309.	*Temporary total disability:* 33⅓% of state's average weekly wage or 100% of weekly wages, whichever is less. *Permanent total disability:* 50% of state's average weekly wage.	Ohio Rev. Code Ann. §§ 4123.56, 4123.58.
OK	70% of employee's weekly wages.	$473.	100% of state's average weekly wage.	$30 or employee's average weekly wage, whichever is less.	State has no specific statutory authority.	Okla. Stat. Ann. tit. 85, § 22.
OR	*Temporary total disability:* 66⅔% of employee's wages. *Permanent total disability:* 66⅔% of employee's wages plus $5 per week for each additional beneficiary, not to exceed 5.	*Temporary total disability:* $576.64. *Permanent total disability:* $628.64 plus $5 per week for each additional child.	*Temporary total disability:* 133% of state's average weekly wage. *Permanent total disability:* 100% of state's average weekly wage plus $5 per week for each additional child.	$50 or 90% of state's average weekly wage, whichever is less.	90% of state's average weekly wage or $50, whichever is less.	Or. Rev. Stat. §§ 656.206, 656.210.
PA	66⅔% of weekly wages.	$644.	66⅔% of state's average weekly wage.	$357.78.	50% of state's average weekly wage or 90% of worker's average weekly wage, whichever is less.	Pa. Stat. Ann. tit. 77, §§ 25.1, 25.2, 511.

State	Percentage of Wages	Maximum Weekly Payment	Maximum (% of state average weekly wage)	Minimum Weekly Payment	Minimum	Statutory Reference
RI	75% of spendable weekly wages.	$572.24 plus $15 per dependent (total benefits may not exceed 80% of employee's average weekly wage).	100% of state's average weekly wage.		State has no specific statutory authority.	R.I. Gen. Laws §§ 28-33-17, 28-44-6.
SC	66⅔% of employee's weekly wages.	$532.77.	100% of state's average weekly wage.	Lesser of $75 or employee's average weekly salary.	State has no specific statutory authority.	S.C. Code Ann. § 42-9-10.
SD	66⅔% of weekly wages.	$448.	100% of state's average weekly wage.	$224.	Lesser of 50% of state's average weekly wage or employee's actual wages.	S.D. Codified Laws §§ 62-4-3, 62-4-7.
TN	66⅔% of weekly wages.	$562.	100% of state's average weekly wage (for injuries occurring on or after July 1, 1997).	$84.30.	15% of state's average weekly wage (for injuries occurring on or after July 1, 1997).	Tenn. Code Ann. §§ 50-6-102, 50-6-207.
TX	70% of weekly wages (75% of wages for employees receiving temporary benefits who earn less than $8.50 an hour).	$533.	100% of state's average weekly wage (determined by Texas Employment Commission).	$80.	15% of state's average weekly wage.	Tex. Lab. Code Ann. §§ 408.061, 408.062, 408.103.
UT	66⅔% of weekly wages.	Temporary total disability: $509. Permanent total disability: $450.	Temporary total disability: 100% of state's average weekly wage. Permanent total disability: 85% of state's average weekly wage.	$45 plus $5 for a dependent spouse and $5 for each dependent child under the age of 18, up to a maximum of 4 children, but not to exceed employee's average weekly wage at the time of the injury.	After the initial 312 weeks, the minimum compensation rate for permanent total disability shall be 36% of the current state's average weekly wage.	Utah Code Ann. §§ 34A-2-410, 34A-2-413.
VT	66⅔% of weekly wages.	$790.	150% of state's average weekly wage.	$263.	The lesser of 50% of state's average weekly wage or employee's actual weekly wage.	Vt. Stat. Ann. tit. 21, §§ 601, 645, 650.
VA	66⅔% of employee's average weekly wage.	$606.	100% of commonwealth's average weekly wage.	$151.50.	25% of commonwealth's average weekly wage or employee's actual wage if less.	Va. Code Ann. § 65.2-500.
WA	60% to 75% of employee's wages depending on marital status and number of dependents. 60% of wages plus additional 5% of wages for spouse and an additional 2% of wages for each child up to a maximum of 5 children.	$821.77.	120% of state's average weekly wage.	$42.69. Minimum amount varies depending on marital status and number of dependents.	State has no specific statutory authority.	Wash. Rev. Code Ann. § 51.32.060.

(Table continues.)

Table 10.8-1 *(cont'd)*

CALCULATION OF BENEFITS
FOR TOTAL DISABILITY

(See also text at § 10.8.)

	Percentage of Wages Paid as Benefit	Maximum Weekly Benefit Amount	Maximum Weekly Benefit Rate	Minimum Weekly Benefit Amount	Minimum Weekly Benefit Rate	Citations to Authority
WV	*Temporary total disability:* 70% of average weekly wage earnings. *Permanent total disability:* 66⅔% of employee's weekly wages.	$490.55.	100% of state's average weekly wage.	$163.52.	33⅓% of state's average weekly wage.	W. Va. Code § 23-4-6.
WI	66⅔% of weekly wages.	$582.	100% of state's average weekly wage.	$30.	State has no specific statutory authority.	Wis. Stat. Ann. §§ 102.11, 102.43.
WY	*Temporary total disability:* 66⅔% of injured employee's actual wages, but not to exceed state's average monthly wage. *Permanent total disability:* For employees whose actual earnings are less than 73% of state's average wage, the award shall be 92% of employee's actual monthly earnings. For employees whose wages are equal to or greater than 73% of state's average monthly wage but less than state's average monthly wage, the award shall be 66⅔% of statewide average monthly wage. For employees whose actual wages equal or exceed statewide average monthly wage, the award shall be 66⅔% of employee's actual wages.	$504.88.	100% of state's average weekly wage.	State has no specific statutory authority.	State has no specific statutory authority.	Wyo. Stat. Ann. § 27-14-403.

Table 10.8-2

TOTAL DISABILITY
BENEFIT CAPS AND REDUCTIONS

(See also text at § 10.8.)

	Maximum Allowable Time for Receipt of Benefits	Maximum Amount of Total Benefits	Are Workers' Compensation Benefits Reduced by Benefits from Other Sources?	Other Provisions	Citations to Authority
AL	Period of total disability.	State has no specific statutory authority.	State has no specific statutory authority.	Minimum and maximum benefits that are in effect on the date of the accident shall be applicable for the full period during which compensation is payable. If an employee receives an injury for which compensation is payable while he or she is still receiving or entitled to receive compensation for a previous injury in the same employment, employee shall not be entitled to compensation for both injuries, unless the latter is a permanent injury.	Ala. Code §§ 25-5-57, 25-5-58.
AK	Period of disability.	State has no specific statutory authority.	Workers' compensation is not available for a week in which the employee receives unemployment benefits. Compensation is reduced by one-half of Social Security benefits for a week and reduced by amounts paid or payable to worker under a qualified pension or profit-sharing plan.	State has no specific statutory authority.	Alaska Stat. §§ 23.30.180, 23.30.185, 23.30.187, 23.30.225.
AZ	*Temporary total disability:* Period of disability. *Permanent total disability:* Lifetime of employee.	State has no specific statutory authority.	State has no specific statutory authority.	Coverage is not extended for self-inflicted injuries.	Ariz. Rev. Stat. Ann. §§ 23-901 *et seq.*
AR	Period of total disability.	State has no specific statutory authority.	*Permanent total disability:* Disability benefits payable shall be reduced dollar for dollar by the amount of benefits the injured worker is eligible to *(cont'd)*	Lump-sum settlements are allowed if workers' compensation commission determines that they are in the best interest of the parties involved.	Ark. Code Ann. §§ 11-9-519, 11-9-804.

(Table continues.)

Table 10.8-2   PART 10—STATE WORKERS' COMPENSATION LAWS   10-128

Table 10.8-2 (cont'd)
TOTAL DISABILITY
BENEFIT CAPS AND REDUCTIONS

(See also text at § 10.8.)

	Maximum Allowable Time for Receipt of Benefits	Maximum Amount of Total Benefits	Are Workers' Compensation Benefits Reduced by Benefits from Other Sources?	Other Provisions	Citations to Authority
AR (cont'd)			receive from a publicly or privately funded retirement or pension plan, not including employee contributions to a privately funded retirement or pension plan.		
CA	*Temporary total disability:* Period of disability. *Permanent total disability:* Life of injured employee.	State has no specific statutory authority.	State has no specific statutory authority.	Benefit limits in effect on the date of injury shall remain in effect for the duration of any disability resulting from the injury. Loss of sight in both eyes, loss of both hands, practical total paralysis, and injury resulting in imbecility or insanity are presumed to be total in character. In all other cases, permanent total disability shall be determined in accordance with fact.	Cal. Lab. Code §§ 4453, 4659, 4662.
CO	*Temporary total disability:* Benefits shall continue until the employee reaches the maximum medical improvement, returns to work, or receives written release from attending physician to return to work, or until employee receives written release for modified employment, such employment is offered by employer, and employee fails to begin modified employment. *Permanent total disability:* Life of employee.	State has no specific statutory authority.	State has no specific statutory authority.	Coverage is not extended to self-inflicted injuries. Coverage shall be reduced 50% where injury results from the intoxication of the employee.	Colo. Rev. Stat. §§ 8-42-103, 8-42-111, 8-42-112.

CT	Period of total disability.	State has no specific statutory authority.	Total disability compensation shall be reduced while the employee is entitled to receive old-age insurance benefits pursuant to the Social Security Act.	Self-inflicted injuries and injuries that result from substance abuse on the job are not covered.	Conn. Gen. Stat. Ann. § 31-307.
DE	Period of disability.	State has no specific statutory authority.		Self-inflicted injuries and injuries that result from substance abuse on the job are not covered.	Del. Code Ann. tit. 19, §§ 2324, 2353.
DC	Period of disability.	District has no specific statutory authority.	Limitation on disability benefits based on amounts received by employee from federal old-age and survivors benefit insurance, employee benefit plans subject to ERISA, and income maintenance plans funded solely by employer.	Self-inflicted injuries and injuries that result from substance abuse on the job are not covered.	D.C. Code Ann. § 36-308.
FL	*Temporary total disability:* 104 weeks. Employee may be entitled to permanent impairment or wage loss benefits subsequent to 104-week period. *Permanent total disability:* Period of disability.	State has no specific statutory authority.	Disability benefits are reduced for employees eligible for benefits under the federal Old-Age, Survivors, and Disability Insurance Act. No total disability compensation benefits shall be payable for weeks in which the injured employee has received or is receiving unemployment compensation benefits.	Self-inflicted injuries and injuries that result from substance abuse on the job are not covered.	Fla. Stat. Ann. § 440.15.
GA	*Noncatastrophic:* 400 weeks. *Catastrophic:* Period of disability, defined as that period of time until employee undergoes a change in condition for the better.	State has no specific statutory authority.		Catastrophic injuries include: spinal cord injuries involving paralysis of an appendage; amputation of an appendage; and severe brain or head injury. Injuries that result from substance abuse on the job are not covered.	Ga. Code Ann. §§ 34-9-200.1, 34-9-261.
HI	Period of disability.	State has no specific statutory authority.		Payment of temporary total disability benefits payments shall be terminated only upon order of the director of labor and industrial relations or if the employee is able to resume work.	Haw. Rev. Stat. Ann. § 386-31.
ID	Period of disability.	State has no specific statutory authority.		Benefits are subject to cost-of-living adjustment prior to 52 weeks of disability payments.	Idaho Code § 72-408.

(Table continues.)

Table 10.8-2   PART 10—STATE WORKERS' COMPENSATION LAWS   10-130

Table 10.8-2 *(cont'd)*
TOTAL DISABILITY
BENEFIT CAPS AND REDUCTIONS

(See also text at § 10.8.)

	Maximum Allowable Time for Receipt of Benefits	Maximum Amount of Total Benefits	Are Workers' Compensation Benefits Reduced by Benefits from Other Sources?	Other Provisions	Citations to Authority
IL	*Temporary total disability:* Period of disability. *Permanent total disability:* Life of employee.	State has no specific statutory authority.	State has no specific statutory authority.	—	820 Ill. Comp. Stat. Ann. 305/8.
IN	500 weeks.	With respect to injury occurring between July 1, 1998, and June 30, 1999, the maximum compensation amount, exclusive of medical benefits, is $234,000. For injuries occurring between July 1, 1999, and June 30, 2000, the maximum amount is $254,000.	State has no specific statutory authority.	Minimum total benefit for permanent total disability shall not be less than $75,000.	Ind. Code Ann. §§ 22-3-3-22, 22-3-3-32.
IA	Period of disability.	State has no specific statutory authority.	State has no specific statutory authority.	—	Iowa Code Ann. §§ 85.33, 85.34.
KS	Period of disability.	State has no specific statutory authority.	Retirement benefits under federal Social Security Act and retirement benefits provided by employer against which the claim is being made.	—	Kan. Stat. Ann. §§ 44-501, 44-510c.
KY	Period of disability.	State has no specific statutory authority.	Income benefits are offset by unemployment insurance benefits and exclusively employer-funded disability or sickness plan benefits unless plan contains an internal offset provision.	All income benefits terminate at the date on which the employee qualifies for normal old-age Social Security retirement benefits.	Ky. Rev. Stat. Ann. § 342.730.
LA	Period of disability.	State has no specific statutory authority.	No compensation benefits for temporary or permanent total disability for any week in	Employee receiving permanent total disability benefits will not be eligible for benefits if	La. Rev. Stat. Ann. §§ 23:1221, 23:1225.

ME	Duration of incapacity.	State has no specific statutory authority.	…which employee received or is receiving unemployment compensation benefits. If employee receives benefits from Social Security, disability benefits under plan funded by employer, or other federal and state workers' compensation, then compensation benefits will be reduced so that the aggregate remuneration from these sources does not exceed 66⅔% of employee's average weekly wage.		employee has or receives earnings but may be eligible for supplemental earnings benefits.	Me. Rev. Stat. Ann. tit. 39-A, §§ 201, 212, 220, 221.
MD	Period of disability.	$45,000 for permanent total disability. Notwithstanding the limitation, the employer or insurer shall pay the benefit for the period that the covered employee is permanently totally disabled.	Compensation is reduced to the extent of avoiding diminution of Social Security benefits.	—	Compensation prohibited when injury was willful or resulted from employee's intoxication.	Md. Code Ann., Lab. & Empl. §§ 9-621, 9-637, 9-638.
MA	*Temporary total disability:* 156 weeks. *Permanent total disability:* Period of disability.	State has no specific statutory authority.	No compensation benefits for any week in which employee has received or is receiving unemployment compensation benefits.		No savings or benefits derived from source other than insurer shall be considered in determining compensation payable.	Mass. Gen. Laws Ann. ch. 152, §§ 34, 34A, 36B, 38.
MI	*Temporary total disability:* Period of disability. *Permanent total disability:* Conclusive presumption of total and permanent disability does not extend beyond 800 weeks from the date of injury, and thereafter the question of total and permanent disability shall be determined in accordance with the current facts.	State has no specific statutory authority.	Unemployment compensation; old-age insurance benefits; payments under a self-insurance plan, wage continuation plan, or disability insurance plan provided by employer; or pension or retirement payments pursuant to a plan established or maintained by employer reduce the amount of workers' compensation benefits.		Weekly benefits are reduced by 5% each year following employee's 65th birthday until employee's 75th birthday. Once employee reaches age 75, there are no further reductions in his or her benefits.	Mich. Comp. Laws Ann. §§ 418.351, 418.354, 418.357, 418.358; Mich. Stat. Ann. §§ 17.237(351), 17.237(354), 17.237(357), 17.237(358).

(Table continues.)

Table 10.8-2   PART 10—STATE WORKERS' COMPENSATION LAWS   10-132

Table 10.8-2 (cont'd)
TOTAL DISABILITY
BENEFIT CAPS AND REDUCTIONS

(See also text at § 10.8.)

	Maximum Allowable Time for Receipt of Benefits	Maximum Amount of Total Benefits	Are Workers' Compensation Benefits Reduced by Benefits from Other Sources?	Other Provisions	Citations to Authority
MN	Period of disability. Temporary total disability benefits shall cease at retirement.	State has no specific statutory requirements.	After $25,000 of weekly compensation has been paid, permanent disability benefits shall be reduced by the amount of any government disability benefit program if the disability benefits are occasioned by the same injury.	—	Minn. Stat. Ann. § 176.101.
MS	450 weeks.	450 times 66⅔% of state's average weekly wage.	State has no specific statutory authority.	Lump-sum payments shall not be made except when determined by workers' compensation commission to be in best interest of employee.	Miss. Code Ann. §§ 71-3-13, 71-3-17, 71-3-37.
MO	*Temporary total disability:* 400 weeks. *Permanent total disability:* Lifetime of injured employee.	State has no specific statutory authority.	State has no specific statutory authority.	Lump-sum payments are allowed when commission determines it is in the best interest of employee.	Mo. Rev. Stat. §§ 287.170, 287.200, 287.530.
MT	Duration of disability. Permanent total disability payments cease when employee is eligible to receive full Social Security retirement benefits.	State has no specific statutory authority.	Social Security benefits payable as a result of the injury reduce compensation benefits by an amount equal to one-half of the federal benefits.	Employees may not receive more than 10 annual cost-of-living adjustments.	Mont. Code Ann. §§ 39-71-701, 39-71-702, 39-71-710.
NE	Duration of disability.	State has no specific statutory authority.	State has no specific statutory authority.	—	Neb. Rev. Stat. Ann. § 48-121.
NV	Period of disability.	State has no specific statutory authority.	Compensation reduced by amount of Social Security disability benefits.	Compensation may be reduced or suspended if employee is participating in an unsanitary or injurious practice that threatens or retards recovery.	Nev. Rev. Stat. Ann. §§ 616C.320, 616C.430, 616C.440, 616C.475.
NH	Period of disability.	State has no specific statutory authority.	State has no specific statutory authority.	Employees entitled to Social Security are not entitled to adjustments in their weekly compensation.	N.H. Rev. Stat. Ann. §§ 281-A:28, 281-A:28-a, 281-A:29.

NJ	*Temporary total disability:* 400 weeks. *Permanent total disability:* 450 weeks.	State has no specific statutory requirements.	Compensation reduced by Social Security benefits.	—	N.J. Stat. Ann. § 34:15-12.
NM	*Temporary total disability:* Worker is not entitled to temporary total disability benefits if worker returns to work at pre-injury wage. If worker returns to work prior to maximum medical improvement at less than pre-injury wage, then worker is disabled and shall receive benefits of 66⅔% of the difference between current wage and pre-injury wage. *Permanent total disability:* Worker shall receive total disability benefits for life, except in the case of mental impairment, which is limited to 100 weeks, or for the maximum period allowable for the disability produced by the physical impairment, whichever is greater.	State has no specific statutory authority.	Total disability benefits shall be offset by any unemployment compensation benefits. Sum of total benefits shall not exceed the amount of total disability benefits that would otherwise be payable.	State has no specific statutory authority.	N.M. Stat. Ann. §§ 52-1-25.1, 52-1-41, 52-1-70.
NY	Period of disability.	State has no specific statutory authority.	Generally, no benefits, savings, or insurance of injured employee shall be considered in determining workers' compensation benefits. *Permanent total disability:* Social Security disability benefits are offset against the workers' compensation benefit to the extent that the aggregate benefit exceeds employee's weekly benefit amount. There shall be no offset if the claim for disability benefits is based on a disability other than the permanent disability for which the permanent disability benefit was granted.	State has no specific statutory authority.	N.Y. Work. Comp. Law §§ 15, 30, 206.
NC	*Temporary total disability:* Period of disability. *Permanent total disability:* Life of employee.	State has no specific statutory authority.	State has no specific statutory authority.	State has no specific statutory authority.	N.C. Gen. Stat. § 97-29.

(Table continues.)

Table 10.8-2 (cont'd)
TOTAL DISABILITY
BENEFIT CAPS AND REDUCTIONS

(See also text at § 10.8.)

	Maximum Allowable Time for Receipt of Benefits	Maximum Amount of Total Benefits	Are Workers' Compensation Benefits Reduced by Benefits from Other Sources?	Other Provisions	Citations to Authority
ND	Period of disability or retirement. Individual is considered retired if he or she is receiving retirement benefits or is 65 and is eligible to receive Social Security retirement benefits.	State has no specific statutory authority.	Aggregate benefits are reduced by any Social Security disability and retirement benefits.	If employee is permanently and totally disabled, the workers' compensation bureau may pay employee a lump sum equal to the present value of all future payments of compensation. If employee is disabled due to an injury, employee's benefits will be determined based on the benefit rates in effect on the date of the first disability.	N.D. Cent. Code §§ 65-05-09, 65-05-09.1–65-05-09.3, 65-05-23.
OH	*Temporary total disability:* Period of disability. *Permanent total disability:* Life of employee.	State has no specific statutory authority.	Workers' compensation benefits from other states shall be credited against the amount of any award of compensation or benefits. Compensation awards are further reduced in proportion to the benefits received under an act of Congress or federal program providing benefits for civil defense workers.	State has no specific statutory authority.	Ohio Rev. Code Ann. §§ 4123.54, 4123.541, 4123.571.
OK	*Temporary total disability:* Period of disability, but not in excess of 150 weeks. After compensation has been paid for 140 weeks, employee may request a review of the case for continued temporary total disability benefits. On a finding that benefits should be extended beyond the initial 150 weeks, compensation may be continued for an additional 150 weeks. *Permanent total disability:* Period of disability.	State has no specific statutory authority.	No benefits, savings, or insurance of the injured employee, independent of the provisions of the statute, shall be considered in determining the compensation or benefit to be paid under the statute. No employee may receive temporary total disability benefits covering the same period of time as unemployment compensation received by the employee.	Total permanent disability awards shall not be commuted to a lump-sum payment.	Okla. Stat. Ann. tit. 85, §§ 22, 41, 45.

State					Statutory Reference
OR	Period of disability.	State has no specific statutory authority.	Amount of any permanent total disability benefits payable to an injured worker shall be reduced by the amount of any disability benefits the worker receives from Social Security.	Benefits may be suspended or reduced if worker commits unsanitary or injurious practices that tend either to imperil or to retard recovery.	Or. Rev. Stat. §§ 656.206, 656.209, 656.210, 656.325.
PA	Period of disability.	State has no specific statutory authority.	State has no specific statutory authority.	Payment of benefits during periods of incarceration after a conviction or during periods where employee is receiving wages equal to or greater than prior earnings is not required.	Pa. Stat. Ann. tit. 77, §§ 511, 511.2.
RI	Period of disability.	State has no specific statutory authority.	State has no specific statutory authority.	Payments to totally incapacitated employees shall be increased on an annual basis by an amount equal to the increase in the annual consumer price index.	R.I. Gen. Laws § 28-33-17.
SC	500 weeks. Paraplegics, quadriplegics, and persons suffering physical brain damage are not subject to 500-week limitation and receive benefits for life.	State has no specific statutory authority.	State has no specific statutory authority.	No lump-sum payment may be ordered where the injured employee is entitled to lifetime benefits.	S.C. Code Ann. § 42-9-10.
SD	*Temporary total disability:* Period of disability. *Permanent total disability:* Life, with up to a 3% cost-of-living increase each year.	State has no specific statutory authority.	If employee is entitled to Social Security benefits, the compensation payable for permanent total disability shall be 150% of the compensation payable by statute less the old-age insurance benefit.	State has no specific statutory authority.	S.D. Codified Laws § 62-4-7.
TN	*Temporary total disability:* Period of disability. *Permanent total disability:* Benefits payable until employee reaches age 65, provided that with respect to injuries occurring after the age of 60, regardless of the age of the employee, benefits are payable for 260 weeks.	*Temporary total disability:* 400 times maximum weekly benefit.	State has no specific statutory authority.	State has no specific statutory authority.	Tenn. Code Ann. §§ 50-6-102, 50-6-207.
TX	Employee's eligibility for temporary income benefits, impairment income benefits, and supplemental income benefits terminates on the expiration of 401 weeks after the date of the injury. Benefits continue for life, at amount equal to 75% of employee's average wage, in *(cont'd)*	State has no specific statutory authority.	State has no specific statutory authority.	The minimum and maximum weekly income benefits in effect on the date of the injury are applicable for the entire time that income benefits are payable.	Tex. Lab. Code Ann. §§ 408.062, 408.083.

(Table continues.)

Table 10.8-2 *(cont'd)*

TOTAL DISABILITY
BENEFIT CAPS AND REDUCTIONS

(See also text at § 10.8.)

	Maximum Allowable Time for Receipt of Benefits	Maximum Amount of Total Benefits	Are Workers' Compensation Benefits Reduced by Benefits from Other Sources?	Other Provisions	Citations to Authority
TX *(cont'd)*	cases of loss of 2 limbs, permanent and total loss of sight in both eyes, or injury to skull resulting in insanity.				
UT	*Temporary total disability:* 312 weeks at the rate of 100% of state's average weekly wage at time of injury over a period of 8 years from time of injury. *Permanent total disability:* Period of disability.	State has no specific statutory authority.	Yes, for Social Security benefits.	State has no specific statutory authority.	Utah Code Ann. § 34A-2-410.
VT	Period of disability, but in no event shall employee receive benefits for less than 330 weeks. Benefits will continue beyond 330 weeks if the injury results in the loss of actual earnings or earning capacity.	State has no specific statutory authority.	State has no specific statutory authority.	Injured employee shall receive $10 a week for each dependent child who is unmarried and under the age of 21, provided the weekly benefits under the statute shall not exceed employee's weekly net income.	Vt. Stat. Ann. tit. 21, §§ 642, 645.
VA	*Temporary total disability:* Period of disability. *Permanent total disability:* Lifetime of employee.	No limit as to total amount.	State has no specific statutory authority.	State has no specific statutory authority.	Va. Code Ann. § 65.2-500.
WA	Period of disability.	State has no specific statutory authority.	For employees under age 65, workers' compensation benefits will be reduced by amount equal to Social Security benefits payable.	Workers with a permanent total disability may elect actuarially determined death benefit option and may also be entitled to compensation for a personal attendant.	Wash. Rev. Code Ann. §§ 51.32.060, 51.32.067, 51.32.160.

WV	Period of disability.	State has no specific statutory authority.	No permanent total disability benefits shall be awarded to any claimant who terminates active employment and is receiving full old-age retirement benefits under the Social Security Act.	No person shall be entitled to temporary total disability benefits for periods of incarceration in excess of 3 days.	W. Va. Code §§ 23-4-1 *et seq.*
WI	Period of disability.	State has no specific statutory authority.	In cases where Social Security benefits are paid to the employee because of disability, workers' compensation benefits shall be reduced accordingly.	No lump-sum payment shall be allowed in cases of permanent total disability except with the consent of all parties.	Wis. Stat. Ann. §§ 102.32, 102.43, 102.44.
WY	*Temporary total disability:* 24 months or time of disability (the workers' compensation division in its discretion may award additional benefits). *Permanent total disability:* 80 months.	State has no specific statutory authority.	State has no specific statutory authority.	If an injured employee participates in an unsanitary or injurious practice that retards employee's recovery, employee forfeits all rights to compensation under workers' compensation act.	Wyo. Stat. Ann. §§ 27-14-406, 27-14-407.

§ 10.9 Death Benefits and Burial Expenses

In most states, the relationship of an individual to the deceased worker determines both whether the individual is entitled to benefits and the amount of benefits to which he or she is entitled. Such benefits are usually provided only to individuals who were, at the time of death, dependent on the deceased worker. Other states look to the time of the injury to determine whether the individual was dependent on the deceased worker.

The majority of states employ a presumption that the spouse of a deceased worker is wholly dependent, and therefore entitled to benefits. Many states place a limitation on the presumption requiring a spouse to be living with the decedent at the time of injury or living apart for justifiable reasons. There is, however, no presumption of dependency for the spouse in several states, including California and North Carolina; in these states, dependency is determined in accordance with the facts at the time of injury. The surviving spouse is usually entitled to benefits for life or until remarriage, and many states provide that the spouse is entitled to a lump-sum payment on remarriage. Two states (Rhode Island and Tennessee) expressly discontinue a surviving spouse's eligibility on his or her remarriage.

In the majority of states, unmarried children are also presumed to be dependent on the deceased if the child is under the age of 18. This presumption is expanded in a number of states to include children who are physically or mentally incapacitated from earning or those enrolled in college or vocational school. Siblings, parents, and grandchildren are often entitled to benefits if there is no surviving spouse or children or by a showing of actual dependency.

Several states, including Kentucky, Minnesota, New York, and Utah, reduce death benefits based on amounts received from the federal government under the Social Security Act.

Table 10.9-1 sets out the statutory provisions regarding individuals who are presumed to be wholly dependent on the deceased worker, and which individuals are entitled to benefits.

Table 10.9-2 sets out the amount of benefits payable on a covered worker's death, including maximum and minimum weekly benefits and burial expenses.

Table 10.9-1

DEATH BENEFITS AND BURIAL EXPENSES: DEPENDENTS ENTITLED TO BENEFITS

(See also text at § 10.9.)

	Is Spouse Presumed Wholly Dependent?	Are Children Presumed Wholly Dependent?	Are Siblings Entitled to Benefits?	Are Parents Entitled to Benefits?	Are Grandchildren Entitled to Benefits?	Citations to Authority
AL	Yes, unless spouse was voluntarily living apart from employee at time of injury or death or unless employee did not contribute to spouse's support for the 12 months preceding the injury or death. Spouse is no longer entitled to benefits after death or remarriage.	Yes, if under age 18, or over 18 and physically or mentally incapacitated from earning.	Yes. Siblings wholly or partially supported by deceased employee at time of death and for a reasonable period of time immediately prior to death shall be considered employee's dependents.	Yes. Parents wholly or partially supported by deceased employee at time of death and for a reasonable period of time immediately prior to death shall be considered employee's dependents.	Yes. Grandchildren wholly or partially supported by deceased employee at time of death and for a reasonable period of time immediately prior to death shall be considered employee's dependents.	Ala. Code §§ 25-5-61, 25-5-62, 25-5-64–25-5-66.
AK	Yes. On remarriage, spouse is entitled to lump-sum payment equal to 2 years of compensation as full and final settlement for all sums due spouse.	Yes, if under age 19, currently enrolled in high school, or attending the first 4 years of vocational school, trade school, or college.	Yes, if there is no surviving spouse or child and sibling was dependent on deceased at time of injury.	Yes, if there is no surviving spouse or child and parent was dependent on deceased at time of injury.	Yes, if there is no surviving spouse or child and grandchild was dependent on deceased at time of injury.	Alaska Stat. §§ 23.30.215, 23.30.395.
AZ	Yes. On remarriage, spouse is entitled to 2 years' compensation in 1 sum.	Yes, if children are under age 18, or until age 22 if child is enrolled as a full-time student in any accredited educational institution.	Yes, if there is no surviving spouse, child, or dependent parent and sibling is wholly or partially dependent on deceased at time of death.	Yes, if there is no surviving spouse or child and parent is wholly or partially dependent on deceased at time of death.	State has no specific statutory authority.	Ariz. Rev. Stat. Ann. § 23-1046.
AR	Yes. Dependent spouse is entitled to benefits until death or remarriage. If dependent spouse remarries, he or she shall receive a lump-sum payment equal to compensation for 104 weeks.	Yes, if child is under age 18, or enrolled as a full-time student and has reached age 25, or physically or mentally incapacitated to earn a livelihood.	Yes, if dependent sibling is physically or mentally incapacitated.	Yes, if dependent parent is physically or mentally incapacitated.	Yes, if dependent grandchild is physically or mentally incapacitated.	Ark. Stat. Ann. § 11-9-527.

(Table continues.)

Table 10.9-1   PART 10—STATE WORKERS' COMPENSATION LAWS   10-140

Table 10.9-1 *(cont'd)*

DEATH BENEFITS AND BURIAL EXPENSES: DEPENDENTS ENTITLED TO BENEFITS

(See also text at § 10.9.)

	Is Spouse Presumed Wholly Dependent?	Are Children Presumed Wholly Dependent?	Are Siblings Entitled to Benefits?	Are Parents Entitled to Benefits?	Are Grandchildren Entitled to Benefits?	Citations to Authority
CA	Yes, if spouse earned $30,000 or less in the 12 months immediately preceding the death.	Yes. Children under age 18 or over age 18 if physically or mentally incapacitated from earning shall be presumed to be wholly dependent if living with decedent at time of injury or for whose maintenance the decedent was legally liable at time of injury.	Question of dependency shall be determined in accordance with facts at the time of injury.	If no person qualifies as a total or partial dependent of a deceased employee, the surviving parent or parents of the employee shall be conclusively presumed to be wholly dependent for support upon the deceased employee.	Question of dependency shall be determined in accordance with facts at the time of injury.	Cal. Lab. Code §§ 3501, 3502, 4700 *et seq.*; *Department of Highway Patrol v. W.C.A.B*, 40 Cal. Rptr. 2d 188 (Cal. Ct. App. 1995); *Wings W. Airlines v. W.C.A.B.*, 232 Cal. Rptr. 343 (Cal. Ct. App. 1986); *Industrial Indem. Co. v. Industrial Accident Comm'n*, 220 P.2d 765 (Cal. Ct. App. 1950); *Granell v. Industrial Accident Comm'n*, 153 P.2d 358 (Cal. 1944).
CO	Yes, unless spouse was voluntarily separated and living apart from spouse at time of injury or death. On remarriage, spouse shall receive a 2-year lump-sum benefit.	Yes, if under age 18, or under age 21 and actually dependent on deceased for support, or under age 21 and engaged as a full-time student at an accredited school.	Yes, if wholly or partially supported by deceased and incapable or actually disabled from earning their own living.	Yes, if wholly or partially supported by deceased and incapable or actually disabled from earning their own living.	Yes, if wholly or partially supported by deceased and incapable or actually disabled from earning their own living.	Colo. Rev. Stat. Ann. §§ 8-41-502, 8-42-120.
CT	Yes. Surviving spouse is eligible for benefits until death or remarriage.	Yes, if under age 18, or over age 18 and physically or mentally incapacitated from wage earning. Payments to incapacitated children shall continue for the full period of their incapacity. Full-time, unmarried students are eligible for benefits until attainment of age 22.	Siblings are not presumptive dependents but may be wholly or partially dependent in fact.	Parents are not presumptive dependents but may be wholly or partially dependent in fact.	Grandchildren are not presumptive dependents but may be wholly or partially dependent in fact.	Conn. Gen. Stat. Ann. § 31-306.

DE	Yes, if living with deceased at time of death, receiving support at time of death, or deserted prior to and at time of death. On remarriage, surviving spouse shall receive a 2-year lump-sum benefit.	Yes, if under age 18, or under age 25 and enrolled full-time in an accredited educational institution, or physically or mentally handicapped and actually dependent on deceased for at least 50% of their support at time of death.	Yes, if sibling is under age 18 and was actually dependent on the deceased for at least 50% of his or her support.	Yes, if actually dependent on the deceased for at least 50% of their support at the time of death.	State has no specific statutory authority.	Del. Code Ann. tit. 19, § 2330.
DC	Yes, if living with or dependent for support on the decedent at time of death, or living apart for justifiable cause.	Yes, if under age 18, or under age 23 and full-time student in approved educational program, or physically or mentally incapable of self-support.	Yes, if there is no surviving spouse or child or if amounts payable are less than 66⅔% of deceased's wages and sibling was wholly dependent on deceased.	Yes, if there is no surviving spouse or child or if amounts payable are less than 66⅔% of deceased's wages and parent was wholly dependent on deceased.	Yes, if there is no surviving spouse or child or if amounts payable are less than 66⅔% of deceased's wages and grandchild was wholly dependent on deceased.	D.C. Code Ann. §§ 301, 309.
FL	Yes. On remarriage, spouse is entitled to a lump-sum payment equal to 26 weeks of compensation at 50% of the state's average weekly wage.	Yes, if under age 18, or under age 22 and enrolled as a full-time student in an accredited educational institution, or physically or mentally incapacitated from earning a livelihood.	Yes, if dependent on deceased.	Yes, if dependent on deceased.	Yes, if dependent on deceased.	Fla. Stat. Ann. § 440.16.
GA	Yes, if spouse had not voluntarily abandoned employee at time of accident. Dependency terminates with remarriage or cohabitation in a meretricious relationship; at age 65; or after payment of benefits for 400 weeks, whichever provides greater benefits.	Yes, if the child is under age 18 or enrolled full-time in high school, or over age 18 and physically or mentally incapable of earning a livelihood, or under age 22 and a full-time student in good standing at post-secondary institution of higher learning.	State has no specific statutory authority.	State has no specific statutory authority.	State has no specific statutory authority.	Ga. Code Ann. § 34-9-13.
HI	Yes until death or remarriage with 2 years' compensation in 1 lump sum on remarriage.	Yes, if unmarried and under age 18, or under age 20 and attending vocational, business, or high school full-time, or under age 22 and a full-time undergraduate student at a college, or over age 18 and incapable of self-support as a result of disability.	Yes, if sibling was dependent on deceased and there is no dependent widow, widower, child, parent, or grandparent.	Yes, if parent was dependent on deceased and there is no dependent widow, widower, child, parent, or grandparent.	Yes, if grandchild was dependent on deceased and there is no dependent widow, widower, child, parent, or grandparent.	Haw. Rev. Stat. Ann. §§ 386-41, 386-43.

(Table continues.)

Table 10.9-1 (cont'd)
DEATH BENEFITS AND BURIAL EXPENSES: DEPENDENTS ENTITLED TO BENEFITS

(See also text at § 10.9.)

	Is Spouse Presumed Wholly Dependent?	Are Children Presumed Wholly Dependent?	Are Siblings Entitled to Benefits?	Are Parents Entitled to Benefits?	Are Grandchildren Entitled to Benefits?	Citations to Authority
ID	Yes, if living with deceased or living apart from deceased for justifiable cause, or actually dependent on deceased. Benefits cease on remarriage and after payment of benefits for 500 weeks. On remarriage, spouse will receive a lump-sum payment equal to the lesser of 100 payments or total benefits for the remainder of the 500 weeks.	Yes, if under age 18 or incapable of self-support and unmarried.	Yes, if under age 18, or incapable of self-support, and wholly dependent upon deceased.	Yes, if actually dependent on deceased.	Yes, if under age 18, or incapable of self-support, and wholly dependent on deceased.	Idaho Code §§ 72-410, 72-412, 72-413, 72-413A.
IL	Yes. In the event of remarriage where decedent did not leave surviving children who at time of remarriage are entitled to compensation benefits under workers' compensation act, surviving spouse shall be paid a lump-sum payment equal to 2 years' compensation benefits.	Yes, if under age 18, or physically or mentally incapable of engaging in gainful employment, or under age 25 and a full-time student in an accredited educational institution.	Yes, if sibling was dependent on employee's earnings to the extent of 50% or more of total dependency.	Yes, if at time of accident parent was totally dependent on the earnings of decedent.	Yes, if grandchild was dependent on employee's earnings to the extent of 50% or more of total dependency.	820 Ill. Comp. Stat. Ann. 305/7 et seq.
IN	Yes. Spouses are conclusively presumed to be wholly dependent if living with decedent at time of death or if state imposes obligation of spousal support on decedent. A surviving spouse who is the only surviving dependent is entitled to receive on	Yes, unmarried children under age 21; physically or mentally incapacitated from earning; or over age 21 if child has never been married, is living with parents, and is not gainfully employed. Benefits of child over age 21 who is not gainfully employed will	Yes. Any blood relative who is actually totally or partially dependent on deceased employee is entitled to compensation as a dependent in fact.	Yes. Any blood relative who is actually totally or partially dependent on deceased employee is entitled to compensation as a dependent in fact.	Yes. Any blood relative who is actually totally or partially dependent on deceased employee is entitled to compensation as a dependent in fact.	Ind. Code Ann. §§ 22-3-3-17 et seq.

State	Surviving Spouse	Children	Other Dependents	Other Dependents	Statute
IA	[remarriage a lump-sum payment equal to the smaller of 104 weeks of compensation or the remainder of the maximum statutory compensation period.] Yes, if wholly dependent on the earnings of employee for support at the time of injury. On remarriage, 2 years' benefits shall be paid to surviving spouse in a lump sum if there are no children entitled to benefits.	[terminate as such child becomes gainfully employed or marries.] Yes, if under age 18 or under age 25 and actually dependent on employee. The fact that child is under age 25 and is enrolled as a full-time student in an accredited educational institution shall be a prima facie showing of actual dependence. Children who are physically or mentally incapacitated from earning at the time of employee's injury shall be entitled to benefits for the duration of their incapacity.	Yes, if actually dependent on the earnings of employee for support at the time of injury or mentally or physically incapacitated from earning. Such status shall be determined in accordance with the facts at the time of injury.	Yes, if actually dependent on the earnings of employee for support at the time of injury or mentally or physically incapacitated from earning. Such status shall be determined in accordance with the facts at the time of injury.	Iowa Code Ann. §§ 85.31, 85.44.
KS	Yes. Surviving legal spouse is entitled to benefits for life or until remarriage. On remarriage, surviving legal spouse shall be entitled to 100 weeks of benefits paid in 1 lump sum.	Yes, if wholly dependent and under age 18, or physically or mentally incapacitated from obtaining gainful employment, or under age 23 and enrolled full-time in an institution of higher learning or vocational school.	Yes, if employee leaves no legal spouse or dependent children, such dependents who are wholly dependent on employee's earnings shall receive weekly compensation benefits, up to a maximum of $18,500.	Yes, if employee leaves no legal spouse or dependent children, such dependents who are wholly dependent on employee's earnings shall receive weekly compensation benefits, up to maximum of $18,500.	Kan. Stat. Ann. § 44-510b.
KY	Yes. On remarriage, spouse is entitled to 2 years of benefits paid in 1 lump sum.	Yes, if child is unmarried and under age 18, physically or mentally incapable of self-support, or under age 22 and enrolled full-time in an accredited educational institution.	Yes, if actually dependent.	Yes, if actually dependent.	Ky. Rev. Stat. Ann. § 342.750.
LA	Yes. Spouse is entitled to weekly benefits until death or remarriage. If spouse remarries, 2 years' compensation payments shall be payable in 1 lump sum.	Yes, if physically or mentally incapacitated from earning; or unmarried and under age 18; or unmarried, under age 23, and attending an accredited educational institution full-time.	Dependency shall be determined in accordance with the facts at the time of employee's death.	Dependency shall be determined in accordance with the facts at the time of employee's death. If the employee leaves no legal dependents entitled to benefits under any state or federal compensation	La. Rev. Stat. Ann. §§ 23:1231, 23:1232 et seq.

(cont'd)

(Table continues.)

Table 10.9-1 (cont'd)
DEATH BENEFITS AND BURIAL EXPENSES: DEPENDENTS ENTITLED TO BENEFITS

(See also text at § 10.9.)

	Is Spouse Presumed Wholly Dependent?	Are Children Presumed Wholly Dependent?	Are Siblings Entitled to Benefits?	Are Parents Entitled to Benefits?	Are Grandchildren Entitled to Benefits?	Citations to Authority
LA (cont'd)				system, a lump sum of $75,000 shall be paid to each surviving parent of the deceased employee.		
ME	Yes, if living with employee, separated for justifiable cause, or actually dependent on employee at time of injury. On remarriage, spouse is entitled to remainder of benefits due, not to exceed $500.	Yes, if under age 18, or under age 23 if a full-time student, or over age 18 but physically or mentally incapacitated from earning and dependent on employee.	Yes, if wholly or partially dependent on earnings of employee for support at the time of the injury.	Yes, if wholly or partially dependent on earnings of employee for support at the time of the injury.	Yes, if wholly or partially dependent on earnings of employee for support at the time of the injury.	Me. Rev. Stat. Ann. tit. 39-A, §§ 102, 216.
MD	Yes. Wholly dependent surviving spouse is entitled to benefits during the period of total dependency or until spouse remarries. Wholly dependent surviving spouses are entitled to benefits for 2 years after the date of remarriage.	Yes, if the child is under age 18, or over age 18 and incapable of self-support because of a mental or physical disability, or under age 23 and attending school full-time.	State has no specific statutory authority.	State has no specific statutory authority.	State has no specific statutory authority.	Md. Code Ann., Lab. & Empl. § 9-681.
MA	Yes, if living with employee at time of death. Wife is entitled to benefits if living apart from employee at time of death for justifiable reasons.	Yes, if dependent on employee at time of death and if under age 18, or over age 18 and physically or mentally incapacitated from earning.	Dependency shall be determined in accordance with facts at the time of death.	Dependency shall be determined in accordance with facts at the time of death.	Dependency shall be determined in accordance with facts at the time of death.	Mass. Gen. Laws Ann. ch. 152, § 32.
MI	Yes, if wholly or partially dependent on employee. Spouse living with employee at time of death or separated for justifiable reasons is	Yes, if wholly or partially dependent on employee. Children under age 16, or over age 16 and physically or mentally incapacitated from	State has no specific statutory authority.	State has no specific statutory authority.	State has no specific statutory authority.	Mich. Comp. Laws Ann. §§ 418.331, 418.335, 418.341; Mich. Stat. Ann. §§ 17.237(331), 17.237(335), 17.237(341).

MN	... earning, are conclusively presumed to be wholly dependent. ... conclusively presumed to be wholly dependent. On remarriage, spouse is entitled to balance of compensation not to exceed $500.	Yes, unless it can be proven that spouse and decedent were voluntarily living apart at the time of death.	Yes, if under age 18, or over age 18 when physically incapacitated from earning, or under age 25 and enrolled full-time in a high school, college, or vocational school.	Yes, if wholly or partially supported.	Yes, if wholly or partially supported.	Yes, if wholly or partially supported.	Minn. Stat. Ann. § 176.111.
MS		Yes. In addition to other benefits, spouse is entitled to a lump-sum payment of $250 at time of death.	Yes, if under age 18, or over age 18 and wholly dependent and incapable of self-support by reason of physical or mental disability, or under age 23 and wholly dependent and pursuing a full-time education.	Question of dependency shall be considered as the facts may warrant.	Question of dependency shall be considered as the facts may warrant.	Question of dependency shall be considered as the facts may warrant.	Miss. Code Ann. §§ 71-3-3, 71-3-25.
MO		Yes. Spouse is entitled to benefits for life or until spouse remarries. In the event of remarriage, a lump-sum payment equal to the benefits due for a period of 2 years shall be paid to the widow or widower.	Yes, if under age 18, or over age 18 and physically or mentally incapacitated from wage earning. Payment of benefits will cease when child attains age 18, dies, or becomes physically and mentally capable of wage earning over that age, or until age 22 if child is attending any accredited educational institution full-time or if at age 18 child is a member of the armed forces on active duty. Children on active duty who commence full-time attendance at an accredited institution immediately on cessation of active duty and prior to attaining age 23 are entitled to benefits during four years of full-time attendance.	Dependent shall be construed to mean a relative by blood or marriage who is actually dependent for support, in whole or in part, at the time of employee's injury.	Dependent shall be construed to mean a relative by blood or marriage who is actually dependent for support, in whole or in part, at the time of employee's injury.	Dependent shall be construed to mean a relative by blood or marriage who is actually dependent for support, in whole or in part, at the time of employee's injury.	Mo. Rev. Stat. §§ 287.230, 287.240.

(Table continues.)

Table 10.9-1   PART 10—STATE WORKERS' COMPENSATION LAWS   10-146

Table 10.9-1 (cont'd)
DEATH BENEFITS AND BURIAL EXPENSES: DEPENDENTS ENTITLED TO BENEFITS

(See also text at § 10.9.)

	Is Spouse Presumed Wholly Dependent?	Are Children Presumed Wholly Dependent?	Are Siblings Entitled to Benefits?	Are Parents Entitled to Benefits?	Are Grandchildren Entitled to Benefits?	Citations to Authority
MT	Yes, if living with or legally entitled to be supported by decedent at the time of injury. Benefits are paid to spouse for 500 weeks or until spouse remarries.	Yes, if unmarried and under age 18, or if unmarried, under age 22, and enrolled as a full-time student in an accredited program.	Yes, if under age 18 and dependent on deceased.	Yes, if dependent on deceased at time of injury.	State has no specific statutory authority.	Mont. Code Ann. §§ 39-71-116, 39-71-720.
NE	Yes, if living with deceased employee at time of death or if actually dependent on deceased at time of injury or death. Spouse will receive 2 years' indemnity benefits in 1 lump sum on remarriage.	Yes, if under age 18, or over such age and mentally or physically incapable of self-support, or age 18 or over and actually dependent, or under age 25 and enrolled as full-time student in an accredited educational institution.	Yes, if actually dependent.	Yes, if actually dependent.	Yes, if actually dependent.	Neb. Rev. Stat. Ann. § 48-122 *et seq.*
NV	Yes. On remarriage, spouse will receive 2 years' compensation payable in 1 lump sum.	Yes, if under age 18.	Yes, if under age 18 and dependent on employee and there is no surviving spouse or children.	Yes, if dependent on employee and there is no surviving spouse or children.	State has no specific statutory authority.	Nev. Rev. Stat. Ann. § 616C.505.
NH	Yes. In the case of remarriage of a widow or widower without dependent children, compensation payments shall cease.	Yes, if under age 18, over age 18 and physically or mentally incapacitated, or under age 25 and enrolled as a full-time student in an accredited educational institution.	State has no specific statutory authority.	State has no specific statutory authority.	State has no specific statutory authority.	N.H. Rev. Stat. Ann. § 281-A:26.
NJ	Yes, if dependent on deceased at the time of the accident. Dependency shall be conclusively presumed for spouse. On remarriage, spouse is entitled to remainder of the compensation that	Yes, if dependent on deceased at the time of the accident, or under age 18, or under age 23 and enrolled as full-time student, or part of decedent's household at time of decedent's death.	Yes, if dependent on the deceased at the time of the accident.	Yes, if dependent on the deceased at the time of the accident.	Yes, if dependent on the deceased at the time of the accident.	N.J. Stat. Ann. § 34:15-13.

Jurisdiction	Spouse	Children	Brothers and Sisters	Parents	Grandchildren / Other	Statutory Reference
NM	Yes, if living with employee at time of injury or legally entitled to support, including a divorced spouse entitled to alimony. Spouse is entitled to 2 years' compensation benefits in 1 lump sum on remarriage. [...] would have been due spouse had spouse not remarried or 100 times the amount of weekly compensation, whichever is less.	Yes, if under age 18 or incapable of self-support and unmarried, or under age 23 and enrolled as a full-time student in any accredited educational institution.	Yes, if there is no spouse, child, or grandparent, compensation may be paid to siblings who were dependent to any extent on deceased for support.	Yes, if there is no spouse or children, compensation may be paid to parents who were dependent to any extent on deceased for support.	Yes, if there is no spouse, child, or grandparent, compensation may be paid to grandchildren who were dependent to any extent on the deceased for support.	N.M. Stat. Ann. §§ 52-1-17, 52-1-46.
NY	Yes, if spouse had not abandoned deceased. On remarriage, spouse shall receive 2 years' compensation in 1 lump sum.	Yes, if under age 18, under age 23 and enrolled full-time in an accredited institution, or dependent blind or physically disabled.	Yes, if sibling was dependent on deceased and there is no surviving spouse or dependent child.	Yes, if there is no surviving spouse, eligible child, or disabled blind or physically disabled sibling or grandchild, surviving parents are entitled to a lump-sum payment of $50,000.	Yes, if grandchild was dependent on deceased and there is no surviving spouse or dependent child.	N.Y. Work. Comp. Law § 16.
NC	No. Persons wholly dependent for support on the earnings of deceased at the time of the accident shall be entitled to receive the entire compensation payable share and share alike.	No. Persons wholly dependent for support on the earnings of deceased at the time of the accident shall be entitled to receive the entire compensation payable share and share alike.	Persons wholly dependent for support on the earnings of deceased at the time of the accident shall be entitled to receive the entire compensation share and share alike.	Persons wholly dependent for support on the earnings of deceased at the time of the accident shall be entitled to receive the entire compensation share and share alike.	Persons wholly dependent for support on the earnings of deceased at the time of the accident shall be entitled to receive the entire compensation share and share alike.	N.C. Gen. Stat. § 97-38.
ND	Yes, if living with decedent or dependent on decedent for support at time of injury. On remarriage, spouse is entitled to a lump-sum payment equal to 104 weeks of compensation.	Yes, if under age 18 and residing in employee's household, or over age 18 and physically or mentally incapable of self-support and actually dependent on employee, or under age 22 and enrolled as a full-time student in any accredited educational institution.	State has no specific statutory requirements.	State has no specific statutory requirements.	State has no specific statutory requirements.	N.D. Cent. Code §§ 65-01-02, 65-05-17.
OH	Yes, if living with employee at time of accident or living apart as a result of aggression by employee. If dependent spouse remarries, an amount equal to 2 years _(cont'd)_	Yes, if under age 18, or under age 25 and pursuing a full-time educational program, or over said age if physically or mentally incapacitated from earning.	May be considered a prospective dependent if actually dependent on deceased. Total award may not exceed $3,000.	May be considered a prospective dependent if actually dependent on deceased.	May be considered a prospective dependent if actually dependent on deceased. Total award may not exceed $3,000.	Ohio Rev. Code Ann. §§ 4123.59, 4123.60.

(Table continues.)

Table 10.9-1   PART 10—STATE WORKERS' COMPENSATION LAWS   10-148

Table 10.9-1 (cont'd)
DEATH BENEFITS AND BURIAL EXPENSES: DEPENDENTS ENTITLED TO BENEFITS

(See also text at § 10.9.)

	Is Spouse Presumed Wholly Dependent?	Are Children Presumed Wholly Dependent?	Are Siblings Entitled to Benefits?	Are Parents Entitled to Benefits?	Are Grandchildren Entitled to Benefits?	Citations to Authority
OH (cont'd)	of compensation benefits shall be paid in 1 lump sum and no further compensation shall be paid to such spouse.					
OK	Yes, if spouse received more than half of his or her support from employee. Surviving spouse is entitled to an immediate lump-sum payment of $20,000 on death of employee. Spouse is entitled to 2 years' indemnity benefit payable in 1 lump sum on remarriage.	Yes, if under age 18, or over age 18 and physically or mentally incapable of self-support, or under age 23 and enrolled full-time in an accredited educational institution. Surviving child is entitled to an immediate lump-sum payment of $5,000 on death of employee, not to exceed 2 children.	Yes, if actually dependent.	Yes, if actually dependent.	Yes, if actually dependent.	Okla. Stat. Ann. tit. 85, § 22.
OR	Yes. On remarriage, surviving spouse shall be paid 24 times the monthly benefit in a lump sum as final payment of the claim.	Yes, if under age 18, or under age 23 and enrolled full-time at an institution of higher learning.	State has no specific statutory authority.	State has no specific statutory authority.	State has no specific statutory authority.	Or. Rev. Stat. § 656.204.
PA	Yes, if widow was living with spouse at time of death or actually dependent on husband and receiving substantial support. Widower is not entitled to compensation unless incapable of self-support at time of wife's death and dependent on wife for support	Yes, if disabled, or under age 18, or under age 23 and enrolled as full-time student in an accredited educational institution.	If there is no surviving spouse, child, or dependent parent entitled to compensation, then siblings dependent on employee are entitled to compensation.	If there is neither surviving spouse nor child, then parent dependent to any extent on employee is entitled to compensation.	State has no specific statutory authority.	Pa. Stat. Ann. tit. 77, §§ 561, 562.

State					
	at such time. On remarriage, widow is entitled to 104 weeks of compensation in 1 lump sum. Widower's benefits cease on remarriage or should he become capable of self-support.				
RI	Yes. A wife living with the employee, or living apart for justifiable cause, or dependent on husband at time of death, is presumed to be wholly dependent. A husband living with wife or dependent on wife at time of death is presumed to be wholly dependent. Benefit payments cease on remarriage of surviving spouse.	Yes, if under age 18, or over that age but physically or mentally incapacitated from earning and dependent on employee at time of death of employee, or under age 23 and enrolled as a full-time student in an accredited institution of learning.	Question of dependency shall be determined in accordance with the facts as the facts may have been at the time of the injury.	Question of dependency shall be determined in accordance with the facts as the facts may have been at the time of the injury.	R.I. Gen. Laws §§ 28-33-12–28-33-14.
SC	Yes.	Yes, if under age 18, or under age 23 and enrolled full-time in an accredited educational institution, or physically or mentally incapable of self-support. Death benefits vest at death of employee and payments continue to be paid for 500 weeks regardless of child's age.	State has no specific statutory authority.	State has no specific statutory authority.	S.C. Code Ann. § 42-9-290.
SD	Yes. On remarriage, spouse shall be paid 2 years' benefits in 1 lump sum.	Yes, if under age 18, or under age 22 and enrolled as full-time student in an accredited educational institution, or over age 18 and physically or mentally incapable of self-support.	Yes, if there is no surviving spouse or qualifying child.	Yes, if there is no surviving spouse or qualifying child.	S.D. Codified Laws §§ 62-4-3, 62-4-8, 62-4-12, 62-4-14.
TN	Yes, unless surviving spouse was voluntarily living apart from his or her spouse at the time of injury. Benefits cease on remarriage of surviving spouse.	Yes, if under age 18, or over age 18 and physically or mentally incapable of self-support, or under age 22 and attending a recognized educational institution.	Yes, if wholly supported by deceased at time of injury.	Yes, if wholly supported by deceased at time of injury.	Tenn. Code Ann. § 50-6-210.

(Table continues.)

Table 10.9-1 *(cont'd)*

DEATH BENEFITS AND BURIAL EXPENSES: DEPENDENTS ENTITLED TO BENEFITS

(See also text at § 10.9.)

	Is Spouse Presumed Wholly Dependent?	Are Children Presumed Wholly Dependent?	Are Siblings Entitled to Benefits?	Are Parents Entitled to Benefits?	Are Grandchildren Entitled to Benefits?	Citations to Authority
TX	Yes, unless spouse abandoned deceased employee without good cause for longer than a year immediately preceding employee's death. Spouse is entitled to death benefits for life or until remarriage. On remarriage, spouse is entitled to receive 104 weeks of death benefits.	Yes, if child is a minor, enrolled as a full-time student in an accredited educational institution, and less than age 25, or is dependent on deceased employee at the time of employee's death.	If there is no eligible spouse, no eligible child, and no eligible grandchild, death benefits shall be paid in equal shares to surviving dependents who are parents, stepparents, siblings, or grandparents of deceased.	If there is no eligible spouse, no eligible child, and no eligible grandchild, death benefits shall be paid in equal shares to surviving dependents who are parents, stepparents, siblings, or grandparents of deceased.	If an eligible child has predeceased employee, death benefits that would have been paid to the child shall be paid in equal shares to the children of the deceased child. If there is a dependent grandchild whose parent is not an eligible child and there is no eligible spouse, benefits shall be paid to the eligible grandchild.	Tex. Lab. Code Ann. §§ 408.182, 408.183.
UT	Yes, if surviving spouse lived with deceased employee at time of employee's death. On remarriage, surviving spouse will receive the lesser of 52 weeks of compensation or the balance of weekly compensation payments unpaid from time of remarriage to the end of 312 weeks or 6 years from the date of the injury in which death resulted.	Yes, if under age 18, or over age 18 and physically and mentally incapacitated and dependent on parent.	Sibling may be considered as a dependent.	Parent may be considered as a dependent.	Grandchild may be considered as a dependent.	Utah Code Ann. §§ 34A-2-403, 34A-2-413, 34A-2-414.
VT	Yes. Spouse is entitled to benefits until he or she attains age 62 or remarries. Balance of 330 weeks times the maximum compensation is payable in 1 lump sum upon attaining the age of 62 or remarrying.	Yes, if under age 18, or incapable of support and unmarried, or regularly enrolled in an approved vocational or educational program.	Yes, if there is no spouse, child, parent, or grandparent and grandchild is a dependent of deceased.	Yes, if there is neither spouse nor child and parent is a dependent of deceased.	Yes, if there is no spouse, child, parent, or grandparent and grandchild is a dependent of deceased.	Vt. Stat. Ann. tit. 21, §§ 632, 634, 635.

State						Statutory Authority
VA	Yes, if surviving spouse has not voluntarily deserted employee or is actually dependent on employee.	Yes, if under age 18, or over such age and physically incapacitated from earning, or under age 23 and enrolled as full-time student in any accredited educational institution.	State has no specific statutory authority.	Yes, if parent is in destitute circumstances and there is no dependent child or spouse.	State has no specific statutory authority.	Va. Code Ann. § 65.2-515.
WA	Yes. On remarriage, spouse is entitled to lump-sum payment equal to 24 months of benefits.	Yes, if under age 18, or over such age and a dependent invalid child, or under age 23 and enrolled full-time in an accredited institution.	State has no specific statutory authority.	State has no specific statutory authority.	State has no specific statutory authority.	Wash. Rev. Code Ann. §§ 51.32.010, 51.32.040.
WV	Yes.	Yes, if under age 18, or over such age and an invalid, or under age 25 and enrolled full-time in an accredited institution.	State has no specific statutory authority.	Yes, if wholly dependent and there is no dependent spouse or child.	State has no specific statutory authority.	W. Va. Code § 23-4-10.
WI	Yes, if living with employee at time of death.	Yes, if under age 18, or over age 18 and physically or mentally incapacitated.	Yes, if dependent on employee at time of death.	Yes, if dependent on employee at time of death.	Yes, if dependent on employee at time of death.	Wis. Stat. Ann. § 102.51.
WY	Yes. Benefits cease if spouse remarries.	Yes, if under age 21 and physically or mentally incapacitated.	State has no specific statutory authority.	Yes, if there is no surviving spouse or dependent child and parent received substantially all of his or her financial support from employee at the time of injury.	State has no specific statutory authority.	Wyo. Stat. Ann. § 27-14-403.

Table 10.9-2   PART 10—STATE WORKERS' COMPENSATION LAWS   10-152

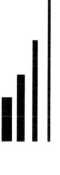

Table 10.9-2
DEATH BENEFITS AND BURIAL EXPENSES: BENEFIT AMOUNTS

(See also text at § 10.9.)

	Income Benefits	Maximum Weekly Benefits	Minimum Weekly Benefits	Maximum Burial Expenses	Death Benefits Offset by Benefits from Other Sources	Citations to Authority
AL	*No dependents:* Lump-sum payment of $7,500 to employee's estate. *1 dependent:* 50% of employee's average weekly wage for period of dependency not to exceed 500 weeks. *2 or more dependents:* 66⅔% of employee's average weekly wage for period of dependency not to exceed 500 weeks.	100% of state's average weekly wage.	27½% of state's average weekly wage, or actual wages if less.	$3,000.	State has no specific statutory authority.	Ala. Code §§ 25-5-60, 25-5-63, 25-5-67, 25-5-68.
AK	80% of employee's spendable weekly wages.	$700.	$110 (or $154 if documentary proof of employee's spendable weekly wages is provided) or employee's spendable weekly wages, whichever is greater. Total weekly compensation may not be less than $75 for a widow or widower nor less than $25 weekly to a child or $50 for children.	$2,500.	State has no specific statutory authority.	Alaska Stat. §§ 23.30.175, 23.30.215.
AZ	35% of average wage of deceased to the spouse if there are no children. 25% of average wage for a single surviving child. The weekly benefit is increased by 15% for each additional surviving child, but not exceeding a total of 66⅔% of average wage.	In computing average monthly wage, amounts in excess of $2,100 shall be excluded from the calculation of income benefits payable.	Compensation shall be paid on the basis of a minimum monthly wage of $200 for employees age 18 or over.	$5,000.	State has no specific statutory authority.	Ariz. Rev. Stat. Ann. §§ 23-1041, 23-1046.

State	Benefit	Maximum Weekly	Minimum Weekly	Burial Expenses	Other	Statutory Authority
AR	35% to the spouse if there is no child; an additional 15% on account of each child. 50% to a surviving child and an additional 15% for each additional child. 15% to dependent parents, siblings, grandchildren, and grandparents. Partial dependents shall receive compensation for a period not to exceed 450 weeks.	85% of state's average weekly wage.	$20.	$6,000.	State has no specific statutory authority.	Ark. Stat. Ann. §§ 11-9-501, 11-9-527.
CA	Maximum total benefit is $160,000 for 3 or more total dependents, $145,000 for 2 or more total dependents, and $125,000 for 1 total dependent. In the case of 1 or more totally dependent minor children and notwithstanding the maximum limitations, death benefits of 66⅔% of employee's average weekly wage shall continue until youngest child reaches age 18. Benefits are lifelong for children who are physically or mentally incapacitated from earning.	Same as for temporary total disability: $490; $602 after 1/1/03; $728 after 1/1/04; $840 after 1/1/05.	$224.	$5,000.	State has no specific statutory authority.	Cal. Lab. Code §§ 4455, 4700 et seq.
CO	66⅔% of deceased's average weekly wage.	91% of state's average weekly wage.	25% of state's average weekly wage.	$7,500.	Aggregate benefits payable for death shall be reduced by Social Security benefits and workers' compensation benefits from another state or federal government.	Colo. Rev. Stat. Ann. §§ 8-42-114, 8-42-123.
CT	75% of employee's after-tax average weekly wage.	100% of state's average weekly wage.	State has no specific statutory authority.	$4,000.	State has no specific statutory authority.	Conn. Gen. Stat. Ann. §§ 31-306, 31-309.
DE	66⅔% of wages of deceased for 400 weeks. If there are surviving children, a maximum of 80% of deceased's wages. Compensation for children shall continue after period of 400 weeks until child reaches age 18, or age 25 if enrolled full-time in accredited educational institution.	100% of state's average weekly wage.	22²/₉% of state's average weekly wage.	$3,500. Additional funeral expenses may be approved by the industrial accident board.		Del. Code Ann. tit. 19, §§ 2330, 2331.

(Table continues.)

Table 10.9-2   PART 10—STATE WORKERS' COMPENSATION LAWS   10-154

Table 10.9-2 *(cont'd)*
DEATH BENEFITS AND BURIAL EXPENSES: BENEFIT AMOUNTS

(See also text at § 10.9.)

	Income Benefits	Maximum Weekly Benefits	Minimum Weekly Benefits	Maximum Burial Expenses	Death Benefits Offset by Benefits from Other Sources	Citations to Authority
DC	*If survived by spouse and at least 1 child:* 66⅔% of employee's average weekly wage. *If survived only by spouse or child:* 50% of employee's average weekly wage.	100% of average weekly wage of insured employees in District of Columbia.	No specific statutory authority.	$5,000.	No specific statutory authority.	D.C. Code Ann. §§ 308, 309.
FL	*Spouse and child:* 66⅔% of employee's average weekly wage. *Spouse only:* 50% of employee's average weekly wage. *Children only:* 33⅓% of employee's average weekly wage to each child. Total benefits shall not exceed $100,000. Surviving spouse entitled to student fees at community college or vocational school.	100% of state's average weekly wage.	$20 or weekly wages, whichever is less.	$5,000.	State has no specific statutory authority.	Fla. Stat. Ann. §§ 440.12, 440.16.
GA	66⅔% of employee's average weekly wage.	$350. Total benefits shall not exceed $100,000 for a surviving spouse when there is no other dependent for more than 1 year.	$35 or weekly wages, whichever is less.	$7,500.	State has no specific statutory authority.	Ga. Code Ann. §§ 34-9-261, 34-9-265.
HI	66⅔% of employee's weekly wage to dependent widow or widower if there are 1 or more dependent children of deceased. 50% of employee's weekly wage to dependent widow or widower if there are no dependent children.	100% of state's average weekly wage.	25% of state's average weekly wage.	Funeral expenses shall not exceed 10 times state's average weekly wage and burial expenses are not to exceed 5 times state's average weekly wage.	State has no specific statutory authority.	Haw. Rev. Stat. Ann. §§ 386-31, 386-41.

State	Death Benefit	Maximum	Minimum	Burial Expense	Other	Statutory Authority
ID	40% of employee's weekly wage if 1 dependent child and 66⅔% if more than 1 dependent child. 45% of state's average weekly wage to dependent spouse; an additional 5% of state's average weekly wage for each dependent child up to a total of 3 children. 30% for dependent child when there is no dependent spouse; an additional 10% for each additional child up to a total of 3 children. *(cont'd)*	Benefits are fixed as percentage of state's average weekly wage. Maximum payable to all beneficiaries shall not exceed 60% of state's average weekly wage.	Benefits are fixed as percentage of state's average weekly wage.	$6,000, plus actual expenses of transportation of body to place of residence.	State has no specific statutory authority.	Idaho Code §§ 72-102, 72-413, 72-416, 72-417, 72-436.
IL	66⅔% of employee's average weekly wage.	133⅓% of state's average weekly wage. Total compensation payable shall not exceed the greater of $250,000 or 20 years.	50% of state's average weekly wage.	$4,200.	State has no specific statutory authority.	820 Ill. Comp. Stat. Ann. 305/7 et seq.
IN	66⅔% of deceased's average weekly wage for a maximum of 500 weeks.	$762.	$75.	$6,000.	State has no specific statutory authority.	Ind. Code Ann. § 22-3-3-22.
IA	80% of employee's average weekly spendable wages.	200% of state's average weekly wage.	Equal to the weekly benefit amount of a person whose gross weekly earnings are 35% of state's average weekly wage.	$5,000.	State has no specific statutory authority.	Iowa Code Ann. §§ 85.28, 85.31.
KS	66⅔% of employee's average gross weekly wage.	75% of state's average weekly wage. Maximum amount of total compensation to any or all dependents shall not exceed $200,000.	$25.	$5,000.	State has no specific statutory authority.	Kan. Stat. Ann. §§ 44-510b, 44-510c.
KY	*Widow or widower and no children:* 50% of employee's average weekly wage. *Children living with spouse:* 45% of employee's average weekly wage plus 15% of employee's average weekly wage for each child. *(cont'd)*	75% of state's average weekly wage.	State has no specific statutory authority.	$4,000.	All benefits shall terminate when such spouse and dependents qualify for benefits under the U.S. Social Security Act by reason of the fact that the worker on whose earnings entitlement is based would *(cont'd)*	Ky. Rev. Stat. Ann. §§ 342.730, 342.750.

(Table continues.)

Table 10.9-2 PART 10—STATE WORKERS' COMPENSATION LAWS 10-156

Table 10.9-2 *(cont'd)*
DEATH BENEFITS AND BURIAL EXPENSES: BENEFIT AMOUNTS

(See also text at § 10.9.)

	Income Benefits	Maximum Weekly Benefits	Minimum Weekly Benefits	Maximum Burial Expenses	Death Benefits Offset by Benefits from Other Sources	Citations to Authority
KY *(cont'd)*	*Children not living with spouse:* 40% of employee's average weekly wage to spouse; 15% of employee's average weekly wage for each child. *Children with no surviving parent:* 50% of average weekly wage for 1 child; 15% of average weekly wage for each additional child, share and share alike.				have qualified for normal old-age Social Security retirement benefits.	
LA	*Spouse or child alone:* 32½% of wages. *Spouse and 1 child or 2 children:* 46¼% of wages. *Spouse and 2 or more children:* 65% of wages.	75% of state's average weekly wage.	20% of state's average weekly wage or actual wages, whichever is less.	$7,500.	State has no specific statutory authority.	La. Rev. Stat. Ann. § 23:1210 et seq.
ME	80% of average weekly wage.	$441 or 90% of state's average weekly wage, whichever is higher. Benefits shall not be paid for more than 500 weeks unless at the expiration of the 500 weeks any dependent is less than age 18; then benefits will be paid until dependent reaches age 18.	State has no specific statutory authority.	$4,000. In addition to burial expenses, employer shall pay $3,000 as incidental compensation to employee's estate.	State has no specific statutory authority.	Me. Rev. Stat. Ann. tit. 39-A, §§ 211, 216.
MD	66⅔% of average weekly wage of deceased employee.	100% of state's average weekly wage.	$25 or state's average weekly wage, whichever is less.	$5,000 unless additional amounts (up to $45,000) are approved by the workers' com-	State has no specific statutory authority.	Md. Code Ann., Lab. & Empl. §§ 9-681, 9-689.

Jurisdiction	Percentage of Wages	Maximum	Minimum	Burial Expenses	Other	Statutory References
MA	66⅔% of average weekly wage of employee.	100% of state's average weekly wage. Total benefits shall not exceed 100% of state's average weekly wage multiplied by 250 weeks plus any cost-of-living increases, except that payments for dependent children shall be continued during their dependency.	$110.	pension commission. Burial expenses are paid if employee dies as a result of and within 7 years of accidental personal injury. $4,000.	State has no specific statutory authority.	Mass. Gen. Laws Ann. ch. 152, §§ 31, 33.
MI	80% of employee's after-tax average weekly wage.	80% of state's average weekly wage paid for a maximum of 500 weeks. If dependent is less than age 21, workers' compensation magistrate may order additional payments.	State has no specific statutory authority.	$6,000.	State has no specific statutory authority.	Mich. Comp. Laws Ann. §§ 418.321, 418.345; Mich. Stat. Ann. §§ 17.237(321), 17.237(345).
MN	*Spouse with no dependent children:* 50% of weekly wages. *Spouse with 1 dependent child:* 60% of weekly wages. *Spouse with 2 or more dependent children:* 66⅔% of weekly wages.	$615.	State has no specific statutory authority.	$7,500.	Combined total of weekly government survivor benefits and workers' compensation death benefits shall not exceed 100% of the weekly wage being earned by deceased at time of injury.	Minn. Stat. Ann. §§ 176.101, 176.111.
MS	35% of deceased's average weekly wage for surviving spouse and no child with an additional 10% of average weekly wage for each child, provided the total amount payable shall not exceed 66⅔% of deceased's average weekly wage. If there are surviving children but no surviving spouse, each child shall receive 25% of deceased's average weekly wage provided the total amount payable shall not exceed 66⅔% of average weekly wage.	66⅔% of the state's average weekly wage. Benefits shall not be paid for a period longer than 450 weeks.	State has no specific statutory authority.	$2,000.	State has no specific statutory authority.	Miss. Code Ann. § 71-3-25.

(Table continues.)

Table 10.9-2   PART 10—STATE WORKERS' COMPENSATION LAWS   10-158

Table 10.9-2 *(cont'd)*

DEATH BENEFITS AND BURIAL EXPENSES: BENEFIT AMOUNTS

(See also text at § 10.9.)

	Income Benefits	Maximum Weekly Benefits	Minimum Weekly Benefits	Maximum Burial Expenses	Death Benefits Offset by Benefits from Other Sources	Citations to Authority
MO	66⅔% of employee's average weekly earnings.	105% of state's average weekly wage.	$40.	$5,000.	State has no specific statutory authority.	Mo. Rev. Stat. §§ 287.230, 287.240.
MT	66⅔% of decedent's weekly wages.	100% of state's average weekly wage.	50% of state's average weekly wage or actual wage of decedent, whichever is less.	$4,000.	State has no specific statutory authority.	Mont. Code Ann. § 39-71-720.
NE	*Spouse with no dependent children:* 66⅔% of decedent's weekly wages. *Spouse with dependent children:* 60% of decedent's weekly wages plus 15% for each dependent child. Total benefits shall not exceed 75% of decedent's weekly wages.	100% of state's average weekly wage.	$49 or weekly wages of deceased, whichever is less.	$6,000.	State has no specific statutory authority.	Neb. Rev. Stat. Ann. § 48-121.01 *et seq.*
NV	66⅔% of employee's average monthly wage.	State has no specific statutory authority.	State has no specific statutory authority.	$5,000.	State has no specific statutory authority.	Nev. Rev. Stat. Ann. § 616C.505.
NH	60% of employee's weekly wage.	150% of state's average weekly wage.	30% of state's average weekly wage or employee's average weekly wage, whichever is less.	$5,000.	State has no specific statutory authority.	N.H. Rev. Stat. Ann. §§ 281-A:26, 281-A:28.
NJ	*1 dependent:* 50% of wages. *2 dependents:* 55% of wages. *3 dependents:* 60% of wages. *4 dependents:* 65% of wages. *5 or more dependents:* 70% of wages.	75% of state's average weekly wage. Benefits shall cease after 450 weeks unless there is a dependent under age 18, in which case compensation shall continue until dependent reaches age 18.	20% of state's average weekly wage.	$3,500.	State has no specific statutory authority.	N.J. Stat. Ann. §§ 34:15-12, 34:15-13.

NM	66⅔% of employee's average weekly wage.	85% of state's average weekly wage. Total compensation shall not exceed 700 times the maximum weekly benefit payable at the time of the accident.	$36 or deceased employee's average weekly wage, whichever is lower.	$7,500.	State has no specific statutory authority.	N.M. Stat. Ann. §§ 52-1-42, 52-1-46, 52-1-47.
NY	66⅔% of average weekly wage.	$400.	$30.	$2,000.	Benefits will be reduced by survivor's benefits under the Social Security Act. In computing offsets, any increase in Social Security benefits after the date of death shall not be considered.	N.Y. Work. Comp. Law § 16.
NC	66⅔% of average weekly wage of decedent.	110% of state's average weekly wage. Benefits will continue for 400 weeks except in cases where spouse is unable to support himself or herself because of a disability that existed at time of employee's death; in such case, compensation payments shall continue until death or remarriage and compensation payments due a dependent child shall be continued until such child reaches age 18.	$30.	$3,500.	State has no specific statutory authority.	N.C. Gen. Stat. §§ 97-29, 97-38.
ND	66⅔% of weekly wage of decedent.	100% of state's average weekly wage. Total benefits may not exceed $197,000.	60% of state's average weekly wage.	$6,500.	State has no specific statutory authority.	N.D. Cent. Code §§ 65-05-17, 65-05-26.
OH	66⅔% of employee's average weekly wage.	100% of state's average weekly wage.	50% of state's average weekly wage.	$3,200.	State has no specific statutory authority.	Ohio Rev. Code Ann. §§ 4123.59, 4123.60, 4123.66.
OK	Surviving spouse with no dependent children: 70% of employee's average weekly wage. Surviving spouse with children: Additional 15% of employee's average weekly wage for each dependent child. (cont'd)	Average weekly wage of employee shall be taken as not more than state's average weekly wage. If the average weekly wage of the employee equal or exceed the average weekly wage of the state, aggregate bene- (cont'd)	State has no specific statutory authority.	$5,000.	State has no specific statutory authority.	Okla. Stat. Ann. tit. 85, § 22.

(Table continues.)

Table 10.9-2 (cont'd)
DEATH BENEFITS AND BURIAL EXPENSES: BENEFIT AMOUNTS

(See also text at § 10.9.)

	Income Benefits	Maximum Weekly Benefits	Minimum Weekly Benefits	Maximum Burial Expenses	Death Benefits Offset by Benefits from Other Sources	Citations to Authority
OK (cont'd)	*Children with no surviving spouse:* 50% of employee's average weekly wage for 1 child and 20% of average weekly wage for each additional child, not to exceed 100% of average weekly wage.	fits may not exceed the average weekly wage of the state. If the average weekly wages of the employee are less than the average weekly wage of the state, aggregate benefits may not exceed 100% of the average weekly wages of the employee.				
OR	66⅔% of state's average weekly wage for surviving spouse plus an additional 10% of state's average weekly wage for dependent children. If there is no surviving spouse, each dependent child is entitled to 25% of state's average weekly wage.	133⅓% of state's average weekly wage.	State has no specific statutory authority.	10 times state's average weekly wage.	State has no specific statutory authority.	Or. Rev. Stat. § 656.204.
PA	*Spouse only:* 51% of employee's average weekly wage. *Spouse and 1 child:* 60% of average weekly wage. *Spouse and 2 or more children:* 66⅔% of employee's average weekly wage. *No surviving spouse and 1 child:* 32% of employee's average weekly wage.	100% of state's average weekly wage.	Wages of deceased shall not be taken to be less than 50% of state's average weekly wage.	$3,000.	State has no specific statutory authority.	Pa. Stat. Ann. tit. 77, § 561.

State						
(cont'd)	*No surviving spouse and 2 children:* 42% of employee's average weekly wage. *No surviving spouse and 3 children:* 52% of employee's average weekly wage. *No surviving spouse and 4 children:* 62% of employee's average weekly wage. *No surviving spouse and 5 children:* 64% of employee's average weekly wage. *No surviving spouse and 6 or more children:* 66⅔% of employee's average weekly wage.					
RI	75% of employee's average spendable base wage exclusive of overtime pay. Surviving spouse is entitled to receive an additional $20 per week for each dependent child, and if there is no surviving spouse, $20 shall be paid for each additional dependent child.	100% of state's average weekly wage plus $20 for each dependent child.	State has no specific statutory authority.	$5,000.	State has no specific statutory authority.	R.I. Gen. Laws §§ 28-33-12, 28-33-16, 28-33-17.
SC	66⅔% of employee's average weekly wage.	100% of state's average weekly wage. Payments shall be made for a period of no more than 500 weeks.	$75 or employee's average weekly wage, whichever is less.	$2,500.	State has no specific statutory authority.	S.C. Code Ann. § 42-9-290.
SD	66⅔% of employee's earnings plus an additional $50 for each child under age 18.	100% of state's average weekly wage plus additional $50 for each child under age 18.	50% of state's average weekly wage or actual after-tax wages, whichever is less.	$5,000 plus additional allowance for transportation of body if death occurs outside the community in which the body is to be buried.	State has no specific statutory authority.	S.D. Codified Laws §§ 62-4-3, 62-4-12, 62-4-13, 62-4-16.
TN	*Surviving spouse and child:* 66⅔% of average weekly wage. *Surviving spouse only:* 50% of average weekly wage. *1 dependent orphan:* 50% of average weekly wage.	100% of state's average weekly wage. Maximum total benefit is 400 times the maximum weekly benefit.	15% of state's average weekly wage.	$7,500.	State has no specific statutory authority.	Tenn. Code Ann. §§ 50-6-102, 50-6-204, 50-6-210.

(Table continues.)

Table 10.9-2   PART 10—STATE WORKERS' COMPENSATION LAWS   10-162

Table 10.9-2 *(cont'd)*

DEATH BENEFITS AND BURIAL EXPENSES:
BENEFIT AMOUNTS

(See also text at § 10.9.)

Income Benefits	Maximum Weekly Benefits	Minimum Weekly Benefits	Maximum Burial Expenses	Death Benefits Offset by Benefits from Other Sources	Citations to Authority
TN *(cont'd)*					
2 or more dependent orphans: 66⅔% of average weekly wage.					
No surviving spouse or children and 1 dependent parent: 25% of average weekly wage.					
No surviving spouse or children and 2 dependent parents: 35% of average weekly wage.					
No surviving spouse, children, or parents and 1 surviving grandparent, sibling, or in-law: 20% of average weekly wage.					
No surviving spouse, children, or parents and more than 1 surviving grandparent, sibling, or in-law: 25% of average weekly wage, share and share alike.					
TX 75% of employee's average weekly wage.	100% of state's average weekly wage.	15% of state's average weekly wage.	$2,500 plus reasonable transportation cost if employee died away from usual place of employment.	State has no specific statutory authority.	Tex. Lab. Code Ann. §§ 408.061, 408.181, 408.186.
UT 66⅔% of employee's average weekly wage plus $5 for each dependent child under age 18, up to a maximum of 4 children.	85% of state's average weekly wage at time of injury.	36% of state's average weekly wage.	$4,000.	After 312 weeks, compensation shall be reduced by the dollar amount of 50% of Social Security benefits.	Utah Code Ann. §§ 34A-2-403, 34A-2-413, 34A-2-414.

VT	Spouse with no dependent children: 66⅔% of wages. Spouse and 1 dependent child: 71⅔% of wages. Spouse with more than 1 dependent child: 76⅔% of wages. No spouse but dependent child or children: Children are entitled to receive amounts payable to a spouse with the same number of dependent children.	150% of state's average weekly wage.	50% of state's average weekly wage.	$5,500 plus expenses, not to exceed $1,000 for out-of-state transportation of decedent to burial.	State has no specific statutory authority.	Vt. Stat. Ann. tit. 21, §§ 601, 632.
VA	66⅔% of employee's average weekly wage for a period of 500 weeks from date of injury.	100% of state's average weekly wage.	25% of state's average weekly wage.	$10,000. An additional amount up to $1,000 for reasonable transportation expenses.	State has no specific statutory authority.	Va. Code Ann. § 65.2-512.
WA	Surviving spouse and no dependent children: 60% of wages. Surviving spouse and 1 child: 62% of wages. Surviving spouse and 2 children: 64% of wages. Surviving spouse and 3 children: 66% of wages. Surviving spouse and 4 children: 68% of wages. Surviving spouse and 5 or more children: 70% of wages. Child and no surviving spouse: 35% of wages for 1 child and an additional 15% for each additional child.	120% of state's average weekly wage.	$185 for spouse with no dependent children.	200% of SAWW.	State has no specific statutory authority.	Wash. Rev. Code Ann. § 51.32.040.
WV	66⅔% of wages.	100% of state's average weekly wage.	33⅓% of state's average weekly wage.	$5,000.	State has no specific statutory authority.	W. Va. Code §§ 23-4-4, 23-4-6, 23-4-10.
WI	66⅔% of average weekly wage of employee. Surviving parent shall also receive a death benefit of $6,500.	100% of state's average weekly wage or $538, whichever is lower.	33⅓% of state's average weekly wage.	$6,000.	State has no specific statutory authority.	Wis. Stat. Ann. §§ 102.46 et seq.

(Table continues.)

Table 10.9-2 PART 10—STATE WORKERS' COMPENSATION LAWS 10-164

Table 10.9-2 *(cont'd)*

DEATH BENEFITS AND BURIAL EXPENSES: BENEFIT AMOUNTS

(See also text at § 10.9.)

	Income Benefits	Maximum Weekly Benefits	Minimum Weekly Benefits	Maximum Burial Expenses	Death Benefits Offset by Benefits from Other Sources	Citations to Authority
WY	66⅔% of employee's average weekly wage. Each child shall be paid $100 per month until child dies or reaches majority, or if the child is physically or mentally incapacitated, until child reaches age 21. Surviving spouse shall receive benefits for 54 months.	100% of state's average weekly wage.	80% of state's average weekly wage.	$2,500 for burial expenses plus an additional $2,500 to cover other related expenses.	State has no specific statutory authority.	Wyo. Stat. Ann. § 27-14-403.

§ 10.10 Notice Requirements Imposed on Employees

Most states require employees to provide notification to the employer of any workplace accident or injury. In many states, such notice must be in writing. The time within which such notice must be given varies widely from state to state. In some states, notice must be provided immediately or shortly after the accident or injury; in other states, an employee may have 30 to 90 days to provide notice. In some states, there is no separate requirement for providing notice to the employer apart from the time limits in which the employee must file a claim for compensation. Where notice to the employer is required, however, an employee's failure to comply may be costly. In a number of states, an employee can lose the right to compensation by failing to provide the required notice, although most states recognize liberal exceptions to the rule.

Table 10.10-1 sets out the provisions of state laws requiring notice to employers, including whether written notice is required, when notice must be given, what exceptions to the notice requirement are recognized, and the consequences of failure to comply.

Table 10.10-1   PART 10—STATE WORKERS' COMPENSATION LAWS   10-166

Table 10.10-1

NOTICE REQUIREMENTS
IMPOSED ON EMPLOYEES

(See also text at § 10.10.)

	Must Employee Give Notice of Injury or Illness to Employer?	Must Notice Be in Writing?	When Must Notice Be Given?	Exceptions to Notice Requirements	Effect of Failure to Notify Employer	Other Provisions	Citations to Authority
AL	Yes.	Yes.	Within 5 days of the accident or injury.	Excused if shown that employee or other party responsible for giving notice was prevented from doing so by reason of physical or mental incapacity for first 90 days after injury or death.	No claim allowed if written notice not provided within 90 days of injury or death.	For the notice provided to be deemed adequate, it must advise employer that a certain employee, by name, received a specified injury in the course of his or her employment on or about a specified time, at or near a specified place.	Ala. Code §§ 25-5-78, 25-5-79.
AK	Yes.	Yes.	Within 30 days after the date of injury or death.	If employer has knowledge of the injury or death and is not prejudiced by lack of notice, or if the workers' compensation board excuses the failure to report on the ground that there is a satisfactory reason for employee's failure to report.	Claim may be barred.	—	Alaska Stat. § 23.30.100.
AZ	Yes.	—	Forthwith.	If employee is legally incapacitated, the statute is tolled for the duration of the incapacity.	Claim may be barred if employer has not begun payment of compensation.	—	Ariz. Rev. Stat. Ann. §§ 23-908, 23-1061.
AR	Yes.	—	Immediately, or as soon as practicable.	Employer's knowledge of accident or death, or inability of employee to report.	Claim may be barred.	—	Ark. Code Ann. § 11-9-701.

State						Statute
CA	Yes.	No.	As soon as possible, but within 1 year.	None.	Employee will, if able, fill out a section of the form required to be submitted by the treating physician.	Cal. Lab. Code §§ 3550, 6409.
CO	Yes.	Yes.	Within 4 days of the injury.	If employee is unable to give written notice, requirement is waived.	For each day that employee fails to give notice, employee may lose 1 day of compensation. —	Colo. Rev. Stat. Ann. § 8-43-102.
CT	Yes.	No.	Immediately.	Failure to report may be excused by the workers' compensation commission.	May result in reduction of compensation. —	Conn. Gen. Stat. Ann. § 31-294b.
DE	Yes.	No.	Within 90 days of injury or death.	If employer has knowledge of the injury or death.	No compensation will be paid until notice is provided. —	Del. Code Ann. tit. 19, § 2341.
DC	Yes.	Yes.	Within 30 days of injury or death, or 30 days of when employee or beneficiary becomes aware of the relationship between the employment and the injury or death.	If employer had knowledge of the injury or death, or the relationship between the employment and the injury or death. The mayor may excuse the failure to give notice if employee was unable to give notice.	May bar compensation. —	D.C. Code Ann. § 36-313.
FL	Yes.	No.	Within 30 days of the date or initial manifestation of the injury.	Employer or employer's agent had actual knowledge of the injury, or employer failed to post notice of the requirements of the statute, or other exceptional circumstances.	Petition for compensation shall be barred. —	Fla. Stat. Ann. § 440.185.
GA	Yes.	Yes, if notice is not given by employee or his or her agent within 30 days of the accident.	Immediately.	If employer had knowledge of the accident, or employee was unable to give notice.	No compensation shall be paid until notice is given. —	Ga. Code Ann. § 34-9-80.

(Table continues.)

Table 10.10-1 PART 10—STATE WORKERS' COMPENSATION LAWS 10-168

Table 10.10-1 *(cont'd)*

NOTICE REQUIREMENTS
IMPOSED ON EMPLOYEES

(See also text at § 10.10.)

	Must Employee Give Notice of Injury or Illness to Employer?	Must Notice Be in Writing?	When Must Notice Be Given?	Exceptions to Notice Requirements	Effect of Failure to Notify Employer	Other Provisions	Citations to Authority
HI	Yes.	No.	As soon as practicable.	If employer has knowledge; if medical, surgical, or hospital services have been provided by employer; or if employee has a satisfactory reason for failure to give notice and employer has not been unduly prejudiced by such failure.	Claim may be barred.	If employer fails to object to lack of notice at the first hearing of the claim, the requirement for notice shall be deemed to be waived.	Haw. Rev. Stat. Ann. § 386-81.
ID	Yes.	Yes.	As soon as practicable, but not later than 60 days after the injury.	If payments for compensation have been made voluntarily, or if an application requesting a hearing has been filed with the workers' compensation commission.	Claim proceeding shall be barred.	—	Idaho Code §§ 72-701, 72-702.
IL	Yes.	No.	As soon as practicable, but not more than 45 days after the accident.	If employee is under a legal disability, the time for giving notice to employer is tolled until the disability has been removed; if the injury is exposure to radiological materials, employee has 90 days to give notice.	Claim may be barred.	—	820 Ill. Comp. Stat. Ann. 305/6.

State							Citation
IN	Yes.	Yes.	As soon as practicable.	Unless employer is unduly prejudiced by lack of notice, lack of notice shall not bar payment of compensation.	If no notice is given within 30 days of the accident or injury, no compensation shall be paid until and from the date notice is given.	—	Ind. Code Ann. § 22-3-3-1.
IA	Yes.	No.	Within 90 days of the injury.	If employer receives actual notice within 90 days of the injury.	Compensation will be barred.	—	Iowa Code Ann. § 85.23.
KS	Yes.	No.	Within 10 days of the accident; in no event shall proceedings for compensation occur unless notice of the injury is given to employer within 75 days of the accident, unless (1) employer had actual knowledge of the injury; (2) employer was unavailable to receive notice; or (3) employee was physically unable to give notice.	If employer has actual knowledge of the accident.	Claim for compensation barred.	—	Kan. Stat. Ann. § 44-520.
KY	Yes.	No.	As soon as practicable.	—	Claim may be barred.	—	Ky. Rev. Stat. Ann. § 342.185.
LA	Yes.	No.	Within 30 days after the accident.	If employer fails to post notice of employees' reporting requirements, the period for reporting to employer may be extended to 12 months; case law indicates that failure to give notice may be excused for good reason, so long as employer is not unduly prejudiced by the lack of notice.	Compensation barred.	—	La. Rev. Stat. Ann. §§ 23:1301, 23:1302; *Jackson v. Savant Ins. Co.*, 694 So. 2d 1178 (La. Ct. App. 1997).
ME	Yes.	No.	Within 90 days of the injury; within 3 months in the event of death.	If employer has knowledge of the injury, if employee is unable to give notice by reason of mental or physical incapacity, or if *(cont'd)*	Claim for compensation is barred.	—	Me. Rev. Stat. Ann. tit. 39-A, §§ 301, 302.

(Table continues.)

Table 10.10-1   PART 10—STATE WORKERS' COMPENSATION LAWS   10-170

Table 10.10-1 (cont'd)

NOTICE REQUIREMENTS IMPOSED ON EMPLOYEES

(See also text at § 10.10.)

	Must Employee Give Notice of Injury or Illness to Employer?	Must Notice Be in Writing?	When Must Notice Be Given?	Exceptions to Notice Requirements	Effect of Failure to Notify Employer	Other Provisions	Citations to Authority
ME (cont'd)				employee fails to give notice because of a mistake of fact.			
MD	Yes.	No.	For injury, within 10 days of the accident; for death, within 30 days.	If the commission of labor and industry finds sufficient reason for the failure to give notice, or if employer or its insurer has not been prejudiced by the failure to comply.	Claim for compensation may be barred.	—	Md. Code Ann., Lab. & Empl. §§ 9-704, 9-706.
MA	Yes.	Yes.	As soon as practicable.	—	—	—	Mass. Gen. Laws Ann. ch. 152, §§ 41, 42.
MI	Yes.	No.	Within 90 days of the accident, or within 90 days of when employee knew, or should have known, of the injury.	Excusable unless employer can show that he or she was prejudiced by the failure to give notice.	—	—	Mich. Comp. Laws Ann. § 418.381; Mich. Stat. Ann. § 17.237(381).
MN	Yes.	Yes.	Within 14 days of the injury; if notice is given or knowledge is gained within 30 days of the injury, compensation shall not be barred on account of want of such notice unless employer shows prejudice and then only to the extent of the prejudice. If notice is given or knowledge ob-	If employer has knowledge of injury.	Compensation may be barred.	—	Minn. Stat. Ann. § 176.141.

State							Citation
MS	Yes.	tained within 180 days, and if the failure to provide notice was due to mistake, inadvertence, ignorance of fact or law, or inability, or to the fraud, misrepresentation, or deceit of employer or agent, then compensation may be allowed. Unless notice or knowledge is obtained within 180 days of the injury, no compensation shall be allowed, except that an employee who is unable because of incapacity must give notice within 180 days of the time the incapacity ceases. Within 30 days after the occurrence of the injury.	No.	If employer had knowledge of the injury and was not prejudiced by employee's failure to provide notice; if employee is legally incompetent or is a minor.	May bar claim for compensation.	—	Miss. Code Ann. § 71-3-35.
MO	Yes.	As soon as practicable, but not more than 30 days after the accident.	Yes.	If the workers' compensation commission finds there was good cause for the failure to give notice, or the employer was not prejudiced by the lack of notice.	Claim for compensation shall be barred.	—	Mo. Rev. Stat. § 287.420.
MT	Yes.	Within 30 days after the injury.	No.	If employer has actual knowledge.	Claim is not compensable.	—	Mont. Code Ann. § 39-71-603.
NE	Yes.	As soon as practicable.	Yes.	If employer has notice or knowledge of injury.	Compensation proceedings may not be maintained without notice.	Notice must be served on employer or an agent thereof and must state, in ordinary language, the time, place, and cause of the injury.	Neb. Rev. Stat. Ann. § 48-133.

(Table continues.)

Table 10.10-1 *(cont'd)*
NOTICE REQUIREMENTS IMPOSED ON EMPLOYEES

(See also text at § 10.10.)

	Must Employee Give Notice of Injury or Illness to Employer?	Must Notice Be in Writing?	When Must Notice Be Given?	Exceptions to Notice Requirements	Effect of Failure to Notify Employer	Other Provisions	Citations to Authority
NV	Yes.	Yes.	As soon as practicable, but at least within 7 days of the accident.	Notice is not required if the notice was not given because of the following: the injury or another cause beyond the control of employee prevented the filing of notice; mistake or ignorance of fact or law; physical or mental inability to give notice; fraud, misrepresentation, or deceit.	The claim for compensation will be barred.	—	Nev. Rev. Stat. Ann. §§ 616C.015, 616C.020, 616C.025.
NH	Yes.	Yes.	Within 2 years of the date of the injury. If, however, the injury and its possible relationship to the employment are not known to employee, the time for filing notice does not begin to run until (1) the date employee knows, or by reasonable diligence should know, of the nature of the injury and its possible relationship to the employment; or (2) in the event of death, the date any dependent knows, or by reasonable diligence should know,	—	Claim for compensation shall be barred.	Employee must execute the notice in writing and sign both copies. After receipt of notice, employer must sign both copies and employee retains the duplicate.	N.H. Rev. Stat. Ann. §§ 281-A:19, 281-A:20.

State			Time for Notice	Excuse / Waiver	Consequence	Additional Provisions	Statute
NJ	Yes.	No.	of the nature of the injury and its possible relationship to employee's employment. Within 14 days of the injury.	If employee can show that the failure to give notice was the result of mistake, inadvertence, ignorance of fact or law, or inability, or was due to the fraud, misrepresentation, or deceit of another person, or any other reasonable cause or excuse, and that employer was not prejudiced by the lack of notice.	Compensation may be barred.	Regardless of other provisions, if employer has not received notice within 90 days, compensation will be barred.	N.J. Stat. Ann. §§ 34:15-17, 34:15-18.
NM	Yes.	Yes.	Within 15 days after worker knew, or should have known, of the injury's occurrence.	If employer has knowledge of the injury, or if employer has failed to post notice of statute.	Compensation may be barred.	Even when 15-day notice requirement is waived, notice must still be provided within no more than 60 days of the accident.	N.M. Stat. Ann. § 52-1-29.
NY	Yes.	Yes.	Within 30 days of the accident or death.	If employee is unable to give notice, or is otherwise excused by the workers' compensation board, or if employer had knowledge of the injury, or was not prejudiced by the lack of notice.	Unless excused, lack of notice shall bar compensation.	—	N.Y. Work. Comp. Law § 18.
NC	Yes.	Yes.	Immediately after the accident, or as soon as possible thereafter.	Industrial commission may waive requirement if reasonable excuse for failure to provide notice is offered. The notice requirement is waived if employee is incapacitated.	If notice not given within 30 days, claim for compensation may be barred.	—	N.C. Gen. Stat. § 97-22.

(Table continues.)

Table 10.10-1 *(cont'd)*

NOTICE REQUIREMENTS
IMPOSED ON EMPLOYEES

(See also text at § 10.10.)

	Must Employee Give Notice of Injury or Illness to Employer?	Must Notice Be in Writing?	When Must Notice Be Given?	Exceptions to Notice Requirements	Effect of Failure to Notify Employer	Other Provisions	Citations to Authority
ND	Yes.	No.	Notice must be given within 7 days absent good cause.	—	Failure to provide notice will be considered by the workers' compensation bureau in determining whether the injury is compensable.	—	N.D. Cent. Code §§ 65-05-01.2, 65-05-01.3.
OH	Yes.	Employee must submit First Report of Injury form.	Claims must be filed within 2 years. Bureau of workers' compensation recommends that report be submitted within 7–10 working days.	None.	Failure to file claim within 2 years will bar compensation.	—	Ohio Rev. Code Ann. § 4123.84; Ohio Admin. Code § 4123-03-08.
OK	Yes.	No.	Within 30 days of the injury. Notice of cumulative trauma or occupational disease must be given within 90 days of separation from employment.	If employer has knowledge of the injury.	Presumption that injury was not employment related. This presumption must be overcome by a preponderance of the evidence.	—	Okla. Stat. Ann. tit. 85, § 24.2.
OR	Yes.	Yes.	Immediately, but not more than 30 days after the accident.	Failure to give notice may be excused if employer had knowledge; if employer has begun paying compensation; or if notice is given within 1 year, and employee had good cause for not giving notice.	Claim may be barred if failure to give notice is not excused.	If employer fails to object to lack of notice at the first hearing, the notice requirement is waived.	Or. Rev. Stat. § 656.265.

State							Citation
PA	Yes.	No.	Within 21 days of the injury.	No notice required if employer has knowledge of injury. If injury is the result of ionizing radiation, notice is not required until such time as employee knows, or, by the exercise of reasonable diligence, should know, of the injury.	No compensation shall be due until notice is given. If no notice is given within 120 days, no compensation is allowed.	—	Pa. Stat. Ann. tit. 77, § 631.
RI	Yes.	No.	Within 30 days of the injury's occurrence or the illness's manifestation.	—	Claim for compensation may be barred.	—	R.I. Gen. Laws § 28-33-30.
SC	Yes.	No.	Immediately, or as soon as practicable, but not later than 90 days after the injury.	If employer has knowledge; if employee is mentally or physically incapacitated; or in cases of fraud or deceit of some third person.	If no notice is given within 90 days, claim for compensation shall be barred, unless employee can present reasonable excuse to the workers' compensation commission for failure to provide notice and employer has not been prejudiced.	—	S.C. Code Ann. § 42-15-20.
SD	Yes.	Yes.	No later than 3 business days after the occurrence of the injury.	Employer or employer's agent has actual knowledge, or employee can show good cause for failing to give notice within the 3-day period.	Claim for compensation prohibited.	—	S.D. Codified Laws § 62-7-10.
TN	Yes.	Yes.	Immediately, or as soon as practicable and reasonable after the accident or injury has occurred. No later than within 30 days of the accident or injury.	If employer has actual notice of the accident or injury, or employee can satisfactorily demonstrate that he or she had a reasonable excuse for failing to notify employer.	If notice is not given to employer within 30 days, the right to compensation ceases.	Claim must be made within 1 year of injury.	Tenn. Code Ann. § 50-6-201.

(Table continues.)

Table 10.10-1 (*cont'd*)

NOTICE REQUIREMENTS IMPOSED ON EMPLOYEES

(See also text at § 10.10.)

	Must Employee Give Notice of Injury or Illness to Employer?	Must Notice Be in Writing?	When Must Notice Be Given?	Exceptions to Notice Requirements	Effect of Failure to Notify Employer	Other Provisions	Citations to Authority
TX	Yes.	No.	Not later than the 30th day after the injury occurs.	Employer has actual knowledge; workers' compensation commission determines good cause exists for the failure to provide notice; employer or employer's insurance carrier does not contest the claim.	Claim for compensation is barred.	—	Tex. Lab. Code Ann. §§ 409.001, 409.002.
UT	Yes.	No.	Promptly.	—	If no notice is given within 180 days, claim for compensation is barred.	—	Utah Code Ann. § 34A-2-407.
VT	Yes.	Yes.	As soon as practicable after an injury; within 6 months of death.	If employer has voluntarily begun payment of compensation.	Claim for compensation is barred.	No claim for compensation may be maintained more than 6 months after the injury occurs. Filing of a false claim may result in a fine of $1,000 and no compensation.	Vt. Stat. Ann. tit. 21, §§ 656, 658, 708.
VA	Yes.	Yes.	Immediately, or as soon as practicable.	—	—	—	Va. Code Ann. § 65.2-600.
WA	Yes.	No.	Forthwith.	—	—	—	Wash. Rev. Code Ann. § 51.28.010.
WV	Yes.	Yes.	Notice must be given immediately after employee sustains the injury, or as soon thereafter as possible.	None.	—	—	W. Va. Code § 23-4-1a.

WI	Yes.	—	Within 30 days of the occurrence of the injury, or within 30 days of when employee knew or should have known of the disability and its relation to the employment. If no claim is filed with the department of industry, labor and job development within 2 years of injury or death, the claim is barred, unless employer had reason to know or should have known that employee had sustained the injury on which the claim is based.	Absence of notice does not bar recovery if it is shown that employer was not misled.	None, unless employer was misled by the absence of notice.	—	Wis. Stat. Ann. § 102.12.
WY	Yes.	Either in writing or by other means approved by the department of employment.	As soon as practical, but not more than 72 hours after the general nature of the injury becomes apparent.	—	Rebuttable presumption that the claim will be denied.	Employer must acknowledge the receipt of written notice of the injury in writing, on the report or on a copy of the report.	Wyo. Stat. Ann. § 27-14-502.

§ 10.11 Employer Recordkeeping and Reporting Requirements

As part of their workers' compensation statutory schemes, most states require employers to keep certain records and make certain reports regarding workplace accidents and injuries. Most states also require employers to make a report of any workplace accident or injury to the state workers' compensation commission or other responsible agency. In some states, these recordkeeping and reporting requirements also cover workplace illnesses or diseases. Such reports must be made within certain time limits, which vary from state to state. Although in some states such a report must be made within 30 days of the accident, most states require reports to be made within 10 to 15 days. In some states, however, the employer is required to make the report immediately or within as few as 2 to 5 days. Penalties for failure to keep required records or to make required reports include fines of as much as $500 per offense, or the payment of additional compensation to employees.

Table 10.11-1 identifies states with recordkeeping and reporting requirements and sets out penalties for failure to comply.

Table 10.11-1
EMPLOYER RECORDKEEPING AND REPORTING REQUIREMENTS

(See also text at § 10.11.)

	Must Employers Maintain Records of Accidents or Injuries?	Must Employers Report Injuries?	When Must Report Be Made?	Penalties for Failure to Report	Citations to Authority
AL	Yes.	Yes.	Within 15 days of report of injury or death.	—	Ala. Code § 25-5-4.
AK	Yes.	Yes.	Within 10 days of the date employer has knowledge of the injury or death, or 10 days from the date employer has knowledge of disease or infection alleged by employee to have arisen out of or in the course of employment.	Employee or other person entitled to benefits shall receive an additional award equal to 20% of the amounts that were unpaid when due.	Alaska Stat. § 23.30.070.
AZ	Yes.	Yes.	Within 10 days after receiving notice of the accident.	Petty offense.	Ariz. Rev. Stat. Ann. §§ 23-908, 23-1061.
AR	Yes.	Yes, any injury.	Within 10 days of notice of injury or death.	Up to $500 for each refusal to submit required reports.	Ark. Code Ann. §§ 11-9-528, 11-9-529.
CA	Yes.	Yes, all injuries resulting in lost time beyond the date of the injury or illness, or requiring medical treatment beyond first aid.	Within 1 day after employer gains knowledge of injury, or immediately after death.	May be punished by appeals board as contempt.	Cal. Lab. Code §§ 3760, 6409.1.
CO	Yes, all injuries resulting in fatality or permanent physical impairment, or lost time from work for employee in excess of 3 shifts or calendar days.	Yes.	Within 10 days of notice or knowledge that an employee has contracted an occupational disease disability, or suffered a permanent physical impairment or lost-time injury, or immediately after a fatality. Other injuries need only be reported to insurer, which reports monthly.	—	Colo. Rev. Stat. Ann. § 8-43-101.
CT	Yes.	Yes, all injuries resulting in incapacity for 1 day or more.	Reports submitted weekly, or as directed by the workers' compensation commission.	Awards to injured workers may be increased by the workers' compensation commission.	Conn. Gen. Stat. Ann. § 31-316.
DE	Yes.	Yes, all injuries, fatal or otherwise.	Within 10 days of when employer has knowledge of the injury's occurrence.	Not less than $100 and not more than $250 for each offense.	Del. Code Ann. tit. 19, § 2313.

(Table continues.)

Table 10.11-1　　　PART 10—STATE WORKERS' COMPENSATION LAWS　　　10-180

Table 10.11-1 (cont'd)
EMPLOYER RECORDKEEPING AND REPORTING REQUIREMENTS

(See also text at § 10.11.)

	Must Employers Maintain Records of Accidents or Injuries?	Must Employers Report Injuries?	When Must Report Be Made?	Penalties for Failure to Report	Citations to Authority
DC	Yes.	Yes.	Within 10 days of the injury or death.	$1,000 civil penalty for each failure to report.	D.C. Code Ann. §§ 36-331, 36-332.
FL	Yes.	Yes.	Within 7 days of injury, or within 24 hours, by telephone or telegraph, of death. The 24-hour requirement is waived where death occurs subsequent to the submission of a previous injury report.	$500 for each failure or refusal to report.	Fla. Stat. Ann. § 440.185.
GA	Yes.	Yes, injuries requiring medical or surgical treatment, or causing absence from work for more than 7 days.	Within 10 days after receiving notice of the accident.	Not more than $100 for each refusal or instance of willful neglect.	Ga. Code Ann. § 34-9-12.
HI	Yes, all injuries, fatal or otherwise.	Yes, all injuries requiring an absence from work of 1 day or more, or requiring medical treatment beyond ordinary first aid. When an injury results in immediate death, employer shall report the accident within 48 hours by telephone.	Within 7 working days, or within 48 hours, by telephone, of death.	Willful refusal or neglect to report shall be fined not more than $5,000.	Haw. Rev. Stat. Ann. § 386-95.
ID	Yes, all accidents or injuries, fatal or otherwise, of which employer has notice.	Yes, any injury requiring treatment by a physician, or resulting in an absence from work for more than 1 day.	As soon as practicable, but not more than 10 days after the occurrence of the injury.	Willful failure or refusal to report is a misdemeanor. In such cases, the limitation period shall not run against the claim of any person seeking compensation until the report has been filed.	Idaho Code §§ 72-601, 72-602, 72-604.
IL	Yes.	Yes, all injuries involving medical treatment, transfer to another position, loss of consciousness, restriction of movement, or the loss of more than 3 scheduled workdays. An employer need not report	2 working days after an accidental death, or between the 15th and 25th of each month, unless required sooner by rule of the industrial commission.	Petty offense.	820 Ill. Comp. Stat. Ann. 305/6.

State	Records Required	Reports Required	Time for Report	Penalty	Statute
IN	Yes. [minor injuries requiring no more medical attention than on-site first-aid treatment.]	Yes, all injuries resulting in death or absence from work for more than 1 day.	Within 7 days of learning of the injury.	Class C infraction. Violators are also subject to a civil penalty of $50 per violation.	Ind. Code Ann. § 22-3-4-13.
IA	Yes, all injuries causing incapacity for more than 1 day.	Yes, all injuries resulting in incapacity for more than 3 days.	Within 4 days of the injury, not counting Sundays and legal holidays.	Civil penalty of up to $100 for each occurrence.	Iowa Code Ann. §§ 86.11, 86.12.
KS	Not required by statute.	Yes, all injuries that incapacitate employee for more than the remainder of the shift or day must be reported within 28 days of receiving knowledge of the injury. If employee subsequently dies, additional supplemental report must be submitted within 28 days of employer's knowledge of death.	Within 28 days.	Civil penalty not to exceed $250.	Kan. Stat. Ann. § 44-557.
KY	Yes.	Yes, all injuries causing an employee's absence from work for 1 day or more.	Within 1 week after occurrence and employer's knowledge of the accident.	—	Ky. Rev. Stat. Ann. § 342.038.
LA	Yes.	Yes, any accident or injury resulting in death or lost time in excess of 1 week. Employers with 10 or more employees who are subject to recordkeeping requirements under 29 U.S.C. § 655 must report any accident involving death, loss of consciousness, restriction of work or motion, transfer to another position, or any medical treatment beyond first aid.	Within 10 days of actual knowledge of the injury or death. Employers with 10 or more employees who are subject to recordkeeping requirements under 29 U.S.C. § 655 must file a report within 90 days of the accident.	—	La. Rev. Stat. Ann. §§ 23:1292, 23:1306.
ME	Yes.	Yes, any injury resulting in employee's loss of a day's work.	Within 7 days of when employer receives notice of the injury.	—	Me. Rev. Stat. Ann. tit. 39-A, § 303.
MD	Not required by statute.	Yes, all injuries resulting in death or 3 or more days of disability.	Within 10 days of receiving notice.	Misdemeanor—fine not to exceed $50; period for employee to file claim is tolled.	Md. Code Ann., Lab. & Empl. §§ 9-707, 9-708, 9-1102.
MA	Yes.	Yes, any injury resulting in the incapacity of employee from earning full wages for 5 or more calendar days.	Within 7 calendar days, not including Sundays or legal holidays, of receipt of notice of occurrence of injury.	More than 3 violations per year results in a fine of $100 for each violation; failure to pay the fine within 30 days constitutes a separate violation.	Mass. Gen. Laws Ann. ch. 152, § 6.

(Table continues.)

Table 10.11-1   PART 10—STATE WORKERS' COMPENSATION LAWS   10-182

Table 10.11-1 (cont'd)
EMPLOYER RECORDKEEPING AND REPORTING REQUIREMENTS

(See also text at § 10.11.)

	Must Employers Maintain Records of Accidents or Injuries?	Must Employers Report Injuries?	When Must Report Be Made?	Penalties for Failure to Report	Citations to Authority
MI	Yes, all injuries causing death or disability.	Yes, all injuries causing death or disability.	At such times and in such manner as the director may reasonably require.	Failure to report to carrier results in fine of $50 per day, but may not exceed $1,500.	Mich. Comp. Laws Ann. §§ 418.801(2), 418.801(5), 418.805; Mich. Stat. Ann. §§ 17.237(801)(2), 17.237(801)(5), 17.237(805); *Shaw v. General Motors Corp.*, 31 N.W.2d 75 (Mich. 1948).
MN	Yes.	Yes, all accidents resulting in injury or death.	In the case of serious injury or death, report by telephone must be made within 48 hours and a written report must be filed within 7 days. For incapacitating injuries resulting in inability to work for 3 calendar days or more, report shall be made within 10 days. Self-insured employer must report the injury no later than 14 days after its occurrence. If an injury is reported and death subsequently occurs, employer shall report within 48 hours of receiving notice, followed by a written report within 7 days.	Up to $500 for each failure to report.	Minn. Stat. Ann. § 176.231.
MS	Yes, all injuries.	Yes, all resulting in death or disability for 5 days or more.	Within 10 days of injury and death. Injuries resulting in permanent disfigurement of the head or face, even if they do not result in 5 days of lost time, must be reported. Injuries resulting in medical compensation, but not 5 or more days of lost time, need not be reported, though records shall be maintained.	Up to $100 civil penalty, and judge may award additional $100 award to injured employee.	Miss. Code Ann. §§ 71-3-65, 71-3-67.

MO	Not required by statute.	Within 10 days of the injury.	Fine of not less than $50 nor more than $500, or by imprisonment in the county jail for not less than 1 week nor more than 1 year, or by both fine and imprisonment.	Mo. Rev. Stat. § 287.380.
MT	Yes.	Within 6 days of receiving notification of injury.	Penalty of not less than $200 and not more than $500 for each offense.	Mont. Code Ann. § 39-71-307; Mont. Admin. R. 24.29.801.
NE	Yes, all fatalities, no matter the length of time between injury and death; lost-workday cases; cases resulting in job transfers, restriction of work or motion, loss of consciousness, or termination of employment.	Within 48 hours of death, or within 7 days of other reportable injury.	Class II misdemeanor.	Neb. Rev. Stat. Ann. §§ 48-144.01, 48-144.04.
NV	Yes.	Within 6 days of receiving notice of employee's claim.	$1,000 for each violation.	Nev. Rev. Stat. Ann. § 616C.045.
NH	Yes.	As soon as possible, but no later than 5 days after employer learns of the occurrence of the injury. If the injury results in a disability of 3 days or more, employer shall file a supplemental report as soon as possible, but no more than 7 days after the injury.	Civil penalty of not more than $100.	N.H. Rev. Stat. Ann. § 281-A:53.
NJ	Yes, all injuries resulting in 7 or more days lost from work.	Immediately on employer's knowledge of the accident. Second report to be made 3 weeks after the accident.	Not less than $10, nor more than $50 per violation.	N.J. Stat. Ann. §§ 34:15-14, 34:15-96, 34:15-97, 34:15-101.
NM	Yes, all injuries resulting in 7 days or more lost time from work.	Within 10 days after employer has knowledge of the injury.	Not less than $25 nor more than $1,000.	N.M. Stat. Ann. §§ 52-1-58, 52-1-61.
NY	Yes, all injuries resulting in the loss of more than 1 day from work, or medical treatment beyond first aid, or more than 2 treatments by a physician.	Within 10 days of the injury.	Misdemeanor; a fine of not more than $1,000 may be imposed for refusal or neglect to keep records or file required reports. A fine of up to $2,500 may be imposed by the workers' compensation board for refusal or neglect to make the required reports.	N.Y. Work. Comp. Law § 110.

(Table continues.)

Table 10.11-1 PART 10—STATE WORKERS' COMPENSATION LAWS 10-184

Table 10.11-1 *(cont'd)*

EMPLOYER RECORDKEEPING AND REPORTING REQUIREMENTS

(See also text at § 10.11.)

	Must Employers Maintain Records of Accidents or Injuries?	Must Employers Report Injuries?	When Must Report Be Made?	Penalties for Failure to Report	Citations to Authority
NC	Yes, all injuries, fatal and otherwise.	Yes, all injuries resulting in an absence from work of 1 day or more, or medical claims in excess of $2,000. Supplementary reports are required at the termination of the disability, or if the disability extends beyond 60 days.	Within 5 days after the occurrence and knowledge thereof.	Not less than $5, and not more than $25, for each offense.	N.C. Gen. Stat. § 97-92.
ND	Yes.	Yes, all injuries.	Within 7 days from the date employer receives notice of the injury.	Failure to file is deemed an admission that the injury is compensable.	N.D. Cent. Code § 65-05-01.4.
OH	Yes, all injuries resulting in 7 days or more of total disability or in death.	Yes, all injuries resulting in 7 days or more of total disability or in death.	Within 1 week of learning of the injury or death.	4th-degree misdemeanor.	Ohio Rev. Code Ann. §§ 4123.28, 4123.99.
OK	Yes.	Yes, all injuries that result in loss of time for more than 1 shift or medical treatment away from the job site.	Within 10 days.	An employer that refuses or neglects to file a report is liable for an administrative violation and is subject to a fine of not more than $1,000.	Okla. Stat. Ann. tit. 85, § 24.1.
OR	Yes. Self-insured employers must maintain records.	Yes. Self-insured employers must report all claims; other employers shall report to their insurers.	Self-insured employers shall report within 21 days of receiving knowledge or notice of the injury. Other employers shall report to their insurers within 5 days.	$250 each day.	Or. Rev. Stat. §§ 656.262, 656.455, 656.750.
PA	Yes.	Yes.	Within 48 hours of receiving report of injury resulting in death; within 7 days for all other injuries resulting in disability lasting more than 1 day.	10% of the amount payable; if delays are unreasonable or excessive, penalty may be increased to 50%.	Pa. Stat. Ann. tit. 77, §§ 991, 994, 995.

State	Recordkeeping	Reporting	Penalty	Citation
RI	Not required by statute.	Within 10 days of the employer's having knowledge of the injury, or within 48 hours of an injury resulting in death, even if the death does not occur immediately after the injury.	Fine of $250 for each offense.	R.I. Gen. Laws §§ 28-32-1, 28-32-2.
SC	Yes.	Within 10 days of having knowledge or receiving notice thereof.	Not less than $10 nor more than $100 for each refusal or neglect.	S.C. Code Ann. §§ 42-19-10, 42-19-30; S.C. Code Ann. Regs. 67-412.
SD	Yes, all injuries, fatal or otherwise, must be recorded and maintained for at least 4 years after the injury.	Within 7 days (not counting Sundays and holidays) of the employer's having knowledge of the injury.	Class 2 misdemeanor and an administative fine of $100.	S.D. Codified Laws §§ 62-6-1, 62-6-2.
TN	No.	Report must be made as soon as possible, but not later than 14 days after the accident, where there is a permanent disability or the employee does not return to work within 7 days. Where there is no permanent impairment and the employee returns in less than 7 days, report must be made by the 15th day of the following month.	$25 for each 15 days past the required date for filing.	Tenn. Code Ann. § 50-6-102; Tenn. Admin. R. ch. 0800-2-1-.06.
TX	Yes.	Not later than the 8th day after the employee's absence from work for 1 day or more as a result of an injury.	Class D administrative violation.	Tex. Lab. Code Ann. §§ 409.005, 409.006.
UT	Yes.	Within 7 days after the injury or when employer has knowledge.	Class C misdemeanor and civil assessment.	Utah Code Ann. § 34A-2-407.
VT	Yes.	Within 72 hours, Sundays and holidays excluded, after the injury.	$100 per violation. Failure to file annual statistical report upon request of commissioner of labor and industry may result in $1,000 fine. Willful false statements or representations in order to receive lower workers' compensation premium may result in penalty of not more than $5,000.	Vt. Stat. Ann. tit. 21, §§ 701, 702, 708.

(Table continues.)

Table 10.11-1 *(cont'd)*

EMPLOYER RECORDKEEPING AND REPORTING REQUIREMENTS

(See also text at § 10.11.)

	Must Employers Maintain Records of Accidents or Injuries?	Must Employers Report Injuries?	When Must Report Be Made?	Penalties for Failure to Report	Citations to Authority
VA	Yes.	Yes, all injuries or deaths.	Within 10 days.	Civil penalty of not more than $500; if the workers' compensation commission determines the failure to report was willful, the penalty shall be not less than $500, and not more than $5,000.	Va. Code Ann. §§ 65.2-900, 65.2-902.
WA	No.	Yes, all injuries resulting in treatment by a physician, disability from work, hospitalization, or death.	Immediately.	Penalty not to exceed $250.	Wash. Rev. Code Ann. § 51.28.025.
WV	No.	Yes.	Within 5 days of receiving employee's notice of injury.	Employer deemed to have waived right to object to any interim payment of temporary total disability benefits paid by the commissioner.	W. Va. Code § 23-4-1b.
WI	Every employer of 3 or more persons and every employer subject to statute must keep a record of all accidents causing death or disability of any employee while performing services incidental to or growing out of the employment.	Fatalities must be reported within 24 hours; all other injuries are reported to insurance carrier.	—	—	Wis Stat. Ann. § 102.37; Wis. Admin. Code § 80.70.
WY	Yes.	Yes.	Within 10 days of receiving notification.	Fine of $750, or imprisonment for 6 months, or both.	Wyo. Stat. Ann. § 27-14-506.

§ 10.12 Subsequent Injury Funds

Employers are sometimes reticent to hire employees with previous workplace injuries because of fear of future expenses or related injuries. A failure to hire an employee because of such concerns may violate the Americans with Disabilities Act. Nevertheless, to ameliorate the negative consequences of this reluctance to hire employees who have suffered previous workplace injuries, many states have passed legislation designed to allocate more fairly the costs associated with employees who suffer second or subsequent injuries after they have changed jobs. To accomplish this goal, states establish funds that pay a certain portion of the cost of subsequent injuries and establish rules for determining what portion of the costs is paid by the employer.

Table 10.12-1 identifies which states have subsequent injury funds, provides information on which injuries are covered, and details how costs are allocated between the fund, if any, and the employer. The table also identifies the sources of revenue for the fund.

Table 10.12-1

SUBSEQUENT INJURY FUNDS

(See also text at § 10.12.)

	Which Injuries Are Covered by Subsequent Injury Funds?	What Portion of Compensation Is Allocated to Employers?	What Portion of Compensation Is Allocated to Fund?	What Are the Revenue Sources for the Fund?	Citations to Authority
AL	Reimbursement for subsequent injuries abolished.	—	—	—	—
AK	Subsequent injury that, combined with a preexisting permanent physical impairment, causes a substantially greater disability than that caused by the second injury alone.	That portion of the disability caused by the subsequent injury, for the first 104 weeks following the injury.	That portion of the disability caused by the subsequent injury, after 104 weeks.	$10,000 paid into fund per no-dependent death case. Certain fines and civil penalties are collected. Assessment against carriers and self-insured employers of up to 6% of total premiums received, depending on fund's balance.	Alaska Stat. §§ 23.30.040, 23.30.205.
AZ	Subsequent injury that, combined with a preexisting work-related impairment or one of the 25 specified nonindustrial preexisting physical impairments, causes a greater disability than that caused by the subsequent injury alone. Employer must have had knowledge of any nonindustrial physical impairment, but is presumed to have had such knowledge in regard to any of the 25 enumerated impairments.	That portion of the disability caused by the subsequent injury.	Employer and "Special Fund" are equally liable for difference remaining between that compensation payable for the subsequent injury and that compensation payable for the combined disability.	Up to 1.5% assessment on all insurance carrier premiums and costs of self-insurance.	Ariz. Rev. Stat. Ann. § 23-1065.
AR	Subsequent injury that, combined with a previous permanent partial disability or impairment, results in an additional impairment or disability that is greater than that caused by the subsequent injury alone.	That portion of the impairment or disability caused by the subsequent injury. Employer is liable for costs associated with both injuries if suffered in the same employment.	The difference between the compensation payable for the subsequent injury and the compensation payable for the permanent disability.	A portion of an insurance premium tax is allocated to the fund, as is a portion of those fines and penalties assessed against violators of various workers' compensation laws.	Ark. Code Ann. §§ 11-9-301, 11-9-525.

State					
CA	Subsequent permanent partial injury that, combined with a preexisting permanent partial disability, results in a permanent disability of 70% or greater. The subsequent injury must account for at least 35% of the total disability unless the prior disability involved a major member and the subsequent injury involved the opposite and corresponding member and accounts for at least 5% of the total disability.	That portion of the disability caused by the subsequent injury.	The difference between the compensation payable for the subsequent injury and the compensation payable for the permanent disability.	$50,000 or the unpaid balance is paid into fund in each no-dependent death case.	Cal. Lab. Code §§ 4750, 4751, 4755.
CO	Subsequent injury that, combined with a preexisting permanent partial disability, results in a permanent total disability. The statute includes in its coverage various industrial diseases resulting from long-term exposure to toxic substances.	That portion of the disability caused by the subsequent injury.	The difference between the compensation payable as a result of the subsequent injury and the compensation payable as a result of the permanent total disability. If injured employee gains employment while collecting compensation from the subsequent injury fund, the fund may reduce its payments by 50%.	$15,000 payments made by employer or insurance carrier in all no-dependent death cases; or that portion of $15,000 left over after settlement in partial dependent claims. A portion of tax, not to exceed 3.25%, levied on all premiums received by insurance carriers. Applicable surcharges assessed on insurance carriers and self-insurers. Portions of those monies paid as fines and penalties for violation of the workers' compensation statutes.	Colo. Rev. Stat. Ann. §§ 8-43-306, 8-46-101, 8-46-102.
CT	Subsequent injury or occupational disease that, combined with a preexisting injury or disease, causes a permanent disability that is materially and substantially greater than that disability caused by the subsequent injury alone.	Compensatory benefits during the first 104 weeks following the injury.	Compensatory benefits beyond the first 104 weeks following the injury. The amount is reduced by that portion of the cost caused by the prior injury.	Fund liabilities are allocated between self-insured employers and insurance carriers. The method of assessment for self-insured employers is based on paid losses while insurance carriers are assessed a surcharge based on premiums received. The fund also collects fines on its behalf.	Conn. Gen. Stat. Ann. §§ 31-348g, 31-349, 31-355a.
DE	Subsequent injury or disease that, combined with a preexisting permanent injury, results in a permanent total disability.	That portion of the disability caused by the subsequent injury.	The difference between the compensation payable as a result of the subsequent injury and the compensation payable as a result of the permanent disability.	$500–$2,500 fines assessed insurance carriers and self-insured employers who neglect or refuse to make compensation payments within 15 days of a compensable worker's injury. Tax assessed, not to exceed 1%, against premiums received by insurance carriers. A similar charge is assessed against self-insured employers.	Del. Code Ann. tit. 19, §§ 2327, 2362, 2395.

(Table continues.)

Table 10.12-1 *(cont'd)*

SUBSEQUENT INJURY FUNDS

(See also text at § 10.12.)

	Which Injuries Are Covered by Subsequent Injury Funds?	*What Portion of Compensation Is Allocated to Employers?*	*What Portion of Compensation Is Allocated to Fund?*	*What Are the Revenue Sources for the Fund?*	*Citations to Authority*
DC	Subsequent injury or occupational disease that, combined with a preexisting physical impairment, results in a permanent disability substantially greater than that caused by the second injury alone.	Lost wages and medical costs caused by the subsequent injury for the first 104 weeks following the injury.	Lost wages beyond the first 104 weeks and the difference between compensation payable for the subsequent injury and the permanent disability. For injuries occurring on or after March 16, 1991, the fund reimburses only for lost wages, and employer remains liable for cost of medical care.	$5,000 payments in all no-dependent death cases and unpaid awards. Insurance carriers and self-insured employers are assessed an amount based on losses paid. Various fines and penalties are also collected for workers' compensation violations.	D.C. Code Ann. §§ 36-308, 36-340, 36-341.
FL	Subsequent injury or occupational disease that, combined with a preexisting permanent physical impairment, results in a substantially greater disability than that caused by the second injury alone. No reimbursement is allowed unless employer reached an informed conclusion prior to the occurrence of the subsequent injury or occupational disease that the preexisting physical impairment was, or likely would be, a significant hindrance to employment. Reimbursement is not allowed unless employer knew of the preexisting permanent physical impairment and such impairment is one of 26 enumerated injuries or conditions.	Compensation payable for second injury up to $10,000, and 50% of the payable compensation thereafter.	The fund reimburses employers for 50% of all benefits paid over and above $10,000. A "Preferred Worker Program" reimburses employer for the cost of insuring a previously injured and impaired worker for up to 3 years of continuous employment.	Insurance carriers and self-insured employers are assessed an average of the sum disbursed for the prior 3 calendar years plus twice the disbursements from the most recent calendar year.	Fla. Stat. Ann. §§ 440.15(5), 440.49.

GA	Subsequent injury that, combined with a prior permanent physical impairment of which employer was aware, results in a disability greater than the one caused by subsequent injury alone.	That portion of the disability caused by the subsequent injury, for the first 104 weeks following the injury.	Employers are reimbursed for 50% of medical and rehabilitative expenses greater than $5,000 but less than $10,000. After $10,000, the fund reimburses 100% of those costs. The fund pays all lost wages after the first 104 weeks.	Fund's administrator and custodian execute an official surety bond of not less than $50,000 payable to the "Subsequent Injury Trust Fund." Insurance carriers and self-insured employers make payments in an amount equal to 175% of the total disbursement made by the fund in the preceding calendar year, less the amount of the net assets in the fund as of 12/31 of the preceding year, which the total workers' compensation claims paid by the insurers bears to the total workers' compensation claims paid by all insurance carriers and self-insured employers during the previous calendar year. The fund is also composed of penalties and assessments for delinquent reporting. The lesser of one-half of the benefits paid or $10,000 in all no-dependent cases is transferred to the fund.	Ga. Code Ann. §§ 34-9-58-34-9-61, 34-9-241, 34-9-352, 34-9-353, 34-9-358.
HI	Subsequent injury that, combined with a preexisting disability, results in a greater permanent partial disability, permanent total disability, or death.	Disability benefits during first 104 weeks after the injury.	Disability benefits after the first 104 weeks.	25% of 312 times the then-effective maximum weekly benefit rate is paid to the fund in all no-dependent death cases, as is the unpaid balance of compensation due in all permanent total and permanent partial disability cases with no dependents. Insurance carriers and self-insured employers are assessed a percentage fee.	Haw. Rev. Stat. §§ 386-33, 386-34(5), 386-41(d), 386-151-386-154.5.
ID	Subsequent injury that, combined with a preexisting permanent physical impairment, results in a permanent total disability.	That portion of the disability caused by the subsequent injury.	The difference between the compensation payable for the subsequent injury and that payable for the permanent total disability.	A pro rata apportionment of twice the fund's previous annual expense is assessed against all "responsible" persons or entities.	Idaho Code §§ 72-323, 72-327, 72-332.
IL	Subsequent injury involving loss of, or loss of use of, a major member or eye that, combined with a preexisting loss of, or loss of use of, a member, causes a permanent total disability.	That portion of the disability caused by the subsequent injury. Employer retains full liability if the subsequent injury is, by itself, permanent and total without regard to the prior injury.	The difference between the compensation payable as a result of the subsequent injury and that payable as a result of the permanent total disability.	Semiannual payments by employers of up to 0.125% of all compensation payments paid. Actual amount depends on fund's balance.	820 Ill. Comp. Stat. Ann. 305/7, 305/8.

(Table continues.)

Table 10.12-1 *(cont'd)*

SUBSEQUENT INJURY FUNDS

(See also text at § 10.12.)

	Which Injuries Are Covered by Subsequent Injury Funds?	*What Portion of Compensation Is Allocated to Employers?*	*What Portion of Compensation Is Allocated to Fund?*	*What Are the Revenue Sources for the Fund?*	*Citations to Authority*
IN	Subsequent injury involving loss of, or loss of use of, a hand, arm, foot, leg, or eye that, combined with a preexisting loss of, or loss of use of, a hand, arm, foot, leg, or eye, causes a permanent total disability.	That portion of the disability caused by the subsequent injury.	The difference between the compensation payable as a result of the subsequent injury and that payable as a result of the permanent total disability.	1.5% of all compensation payments made by insurance carriers and self-employed employers in the previous calendar year.	Ind. Code Ann. § 22-3-3-13.
IA	Subsequent injury involving the loss of, or loss of use of, a hand, arm, foot, leg, or eye that, combined with a previous loss of, or loss of use of, a hand, arm, foot, leg, or eye, results in a permanent total disability.	That portion of the disability caused by the subsequent injury.	The difference between the compensation payable for the subsequent injury and that payable for the permanent disability, less the value of the member or organ previously disabled or lost.	$12,000 payments in all dependent death cases; $45,000 payments in all no-dependent death cases. Any and all contributions made by the United States.	Iowa Code Ann. §§ 85.64, 85.65, 85.69.
KS	Subsequent injury causing increased disability above and beyond that already suffered as a result of the preexisting disability. Employer must show that it employed the disabled employee after receiving knowledge of that disability.	The difference between the fund's payment and the maximum disability payment.	That compensation attributable to the preexisting injury.	Pro rata assessment against insurance carriers and self-insured employees determined by the amount paid out. $18,500 payments in no-dependent death cases.	Kan. Stat. Ann. §§ 44-501, 44-567.
KY	—	—	—	—	—
LA	Subsequent injury that, combined with a known prior permanent disability, causes death or a disability that is materially and substantially greater than that caused by the subsequent injury alone.	All disability benefits for the first 104 weeks following the subsequent injury. In cases resulting in death of employee, all disability benefits for the first 175 weeks. All medical benefits up to $5,000; 50% of costs greater than $5,000 but less than $10,000; 100% of medical costs after $10,000.	Employer is reimbursed by the fund for all disability compensation after the first 104 weeks; if injury causes death, after 175 weeks. No employer or insurer is entitled to reimbursement unless it is clearly established that employer or insurer had actual knowledge of employee's preexisting permanent partial disability prior to the subsequent injury, and that employer or insurer con-	Insurance carriers and self-insured employers are assessed an amount based on benefits paid. The total assessment may not be more than 125% of the fund's disbursements in the prior fiscal year.	La. Rev. Stat. Ann. §§ 23:1371, 23:1377, 23:1378.

ME	—	—	—	sidered it to be a hindrance or obstacle to employment. The statute enumerates 30 conditions whereby employer or insurer is presumed to have so known and considered.	—
MD	Subsequent accidental personal injury, occupational disease, or compensable hernia resulting in a permanent total disability that is substantially greater because of the combined effects of the previous impairment and the subsequent compensable event than it would have been from the subsequent compensable event alone.	That portion of the disability caused by the subsequent injury.	If the permanent disability disables more than 50% of employee's body as a whole, employee is entitled to receive additional compensation from the fund. The prior and subsequent injuries must have been compensable for at least 125 weeks each.	Assessment of 5.0% paid to fund in all awards and settlement agreements.	Md. Code Ann., Lab. & Empl. §§ 9-802, 9-806, 10-204.
MA	Subsequent injury that, combined with a preexisting physical impairment, causes death or a substantially greater disability.	All benefits for first 104 weeks following the injury.	Fund reimburses employers 75% of benefits after 104 weeks. An employer is not eligible for reimbursement unless it had personal knowledge of the existence of the preexisting physical impairment within 30 days of employment or retention from either a physical examination, an employment application questionnaire, or an employee statement.	Pro rata assessment against insurance carriers and self-insured employers based on losses paid in the preceding year.	Mass. Gen. Laws Ann. ch. 152, §§ 37, 65 et seq.
MI	Subsequent injury involving the loss of a hand, arm, foot, leg, or eye that, combined with a preexisting loss of a hand, arm, foot, leg, or eye, results in a permanent total disability.	That portion of the disability caused by the subsequent injury.	The difference between compensation payable for the subsequent injury and that payable for the permanent total disability. The fund pays benefits for all workers certified as "vocationally handicapped" after 52 weeks.	Assessments against insurance carriers and self-insured employers bearing the same relationship as the total compensation benefits paid by each carrier and self-insurer in the state bears to the total compensation benefits paid by all carriers and self-insurers in the state.	Mich. Comp. Laws Ann. §§ 418.501, 418.521, 418.551, 418.901, 418.905, 418.921; Mich. Stat. Ann. §§ 17.237(501), 17.237(521), 17.237(551), 17.237(901), 17.237(905), 17.237(921).
MN	—	—	—	—	—
MS	Subsequent injury involving the loss of, or loss of use of, a hand, arm, foot, leg, or eye that, combined with a preexisting loss of, or loss of use of, a hand, arm, foot, leg, or eye, results in a permanent total disability.	That portion of the disability caused by the subsequent injury.	The difference between the compensation payable for the subsequent injury and that payable for the permanent disability.	$500 payments in all no-dependent death cases; $300 in all death cases with dependents. The workers' compensation commissioner is also authorized to make transfers of up to $200,000 from the "Administrative Expense Fund."	Miss. Code Ann. §§ 71-3-73, 71-3-95.

(Table continues.)

Table 10.12-1   PART 10—STATE WORKERS' COMPENSATION LAWS   10-194

Table 10.12-1 (cont'd)

SUBSEQUENT INJURY FUNDS

(See also text at § 10.12.)

	Which Injuries Are Covered by Subsequent Injury Funds?	What Portion of Compensation Is Allocated to Employers?	What Portion of Compensation Is Allocated to Fund?	What Are the Revenue Sources for the Fund?	Citations to Authority
MO	Subsequent injury causing at least a 15% disability of a major extremity where a prior permanent partial industrial disability of at least 15% to a major extremity already existed.	That portion of the disability caused by the subsequent injury.	The difference between the compensation payable as a result of the subsequent injury and the cost of the compounded disability.	A surcharge is assessed annually on the basis of a formula set by statute. The surcharge may at no time exceed 3% of all premiums paid in the state.	Mo. Rev. Stat. §§ 287.220, 287.715.
MT	Any compensable injury suffered by an employee certified as a "person with a disability."	Medical benefits and indemnity benefits for the first 104 weeks following the injury.	The fund reimburses employers after the first 104 weeks.	An assessment against insurance carriers and self-insured employers based on paid losses during the previous calendar year is collected.	Mont. Code Ann. §§ 39-71-119, 39-71-905, 39-71-907, 39-71-915.
NE	Subsequent injury that, combined with a preexisting permanent disability, causes a disability that is substantially greater in degree or percentage than that caused by the subsequent injury alone. The preexisting disability must authorize at least a 25% earnings loss or 90 weeks of benefits. Employer must have known of the preexisting permanent disability.	That portion of the disability caused by the subsequent injury.	The difference between the compensation payable for the subsequent injury and that payable for the resulting disability as a whole.	There is an assessment of 2% against all benefits paid by insurance carriers or self-insured employers, with a floor of at least $25.	Neb. Rev. Stat. Ann. § 48-128; *Norris v. Iowa Beef Processors*, 402 N.W.2d 658 (Neb. 1987).
NV	Subsequent injury that, combined with any previous permanent physical disability, causes a substantially greater disability. The preexisting disability must affect at least 6% of employee's entire body, and employer must have had prior knowledge of the impairment.	Compensation is allocated between insurance carriers, self-insured employers, and the fund as determined yearly.	Self-insured employers and insurance carriers contribute to and may receive reimbursement from the fund. Fines and penalties collected by the state also go to the fund.	Assessment against insurance carriers and self-insured employers reflecting the relative hazards of covered employers.	Nev. Rev. Stat. Ann. §§ 616B.540, 616B.587.

	Injury covered	Fund liability	Funding	Citation
NH	Subsequent injury that, combined with any preexisting disability, causes a substantially greater disability.	That portion of the disability caused by the subsequent injury.	The fund reimburses employers in full for benefits paid after the first 104 weeks following the injury and reimburses 50% of all benefits over $10,000 during the first 104 weeks. The fund will also reimburse an employer 50% of the cost of any modification made in order to retain an injured worker, up to $5,000 total.	Each insurance carrier and self-insurer makes payments to the fund in an amount equal to 175% of the total obligation of the fund during the preceding 12 months, less current net assets.	N.H. Rev. Stat. Ann. §§ 281-A-54, 281-A-55.
NJ	Subsequent injury that, combined with any preexisting partial disability, causes a permanent total disability.	That portion of the disability caused by the subsequent injury.	The difference between the compensation payable for the subsequent injury and that payable for the total disability.	Policyholders and self-insured employers are assessed a pro rata percentage of 150% of the estimated payments made by the fund in the previous year. The assessment is reduced if the fund's year-end balance exceeds $5 million. The assessment is paid quarterly.	N.J. Stat. Ann. §§ 34:15-94, 34:15-95.
NM	—	—	—	—	—
NY	Subsequent injury that, combined with a preexisting permanent physical impairment, causes a permanent disability that is materially and substantially greater than that which would have resulted from the second injury alone.	Death or disability benefits for the first 260 weeks following the injury.	Fund reimburses employer after the first 260 weeks following the injury.	Assessment against insurance carriers and self-insured employers equal to 150% of the total compensation payment made by all carriers and self-insured employers.	N.Y. Work. Comp. Law § 15.
NC	Subsequent injury involving a member that, combined with a preexisting permanent disability, causes a permanent total disability. The original and increased disabilities must have caused at least 20% disability each to the member. By statute, epilepsy is considered a preexisting permanent disability.	That portion of the disability caused by the subsequent injury.	The difference between the compensation payable for the subsequent injury and that payable for the permanent total disability.	Insurance carriers and self-insured employers are assessed, for each permanent partial disability, up to $250 for the loss of, or loss of use of, a "minor" member, and up to $750 for the loss of, or loss of use of, a "major" member (hearing, back, eye, arm, foot, leg, hand).	N.C. Gen. Stat. § 97-40.1.
ND	Subsequent injury or aggravation of a prior condition or injury that causes a greater disability than previously suffered.	That portion of the disability caused by the subsequent injury or aggravation.	That percentage of the total disability attributable to the prior injury or condition.	Compensation payments come from a "Benefit Fund" supported by taxation of insurance carriers and self-insurers.	N.D. Cent. Code § 65-04-19.
OH	Subsequent injury or occupational disease that aggravates a preexisting condition or disease and causes death, permanent total disability, or temporary total disability.	That portion of the disability attributable to the subsequent injury or occupational disease.	That portion of the disability or death attributable to the preexisting injury or occupational disease.	A reserve from which compensation is paid is set aside from a statutory surplus fund.	Ohio Rev. Code Ann. §§ 4123.34, 4123.341.

(Table continues.)

Table 10.12-1   PART 10—STATE WORKERS' COMPENSATION LAWS   10-196

Table 10.12-1 (cont'd)

SUBSEQUENT INJURY FUNDS

(See also text at § 10.12.)

	Which Injuries Are Covered by Subsequent Injury Funds?	What Portion of Compensation Is Allocated to Employers?	What Portion of Compensation Is Allocated to Fund?	What Are the Revenue Sources for the Fund?	Citations to Authority
OK	Subsequent injury to a person who, by accident, disease, birth, military action, or any other cause, has suffered the loss of, or loss of use of, an eye, hand, arm, foot, or leg that is readily observable by an ordinary lay person.	That portion of the disability caused by the subsequent injury.	The difference between the compensation payable as a result of the subsequent injury and that payable as a result of the combined injuries. Compensation is payable by the fund for 5 years or until the injured employee reaches age 65, whichever period is longer.	Payments of 5% of all permanent disability compensation paid by insurance carriers, self-insured employers, and the Multiple Injury Trust Fund.	Okla. Stat. Ann. tit. 85, § 172.
OR	Any subsequent injury suffered by an injured worker within 3 years of hire as a "preferred worker."	None.	Various fund programs pay for the subsequent injury, ergonomic research, wage subsidies of 50% for the first 6 months, work-site modifications up to $25,000, and insurance premiums during the first 3 years.	"Preferred worker" and employer pay $0.011 per hour each into the Workers' Benefit Fund.	Or. Rev. Stat. §§ 656.273, 656.506, 656.605, 656.622.
PA	Subsequent injury involving the loss of, or loss of use of, a hand, arm, foot, leg, or eye that, combined with a preexisting loss of, or loss of use of, a hand, arm, foot, leg, or eye, causes a permanent total disability.	Benefits set by statutory schedule relating to the subsequent injury.	The difference between the compensation payable as a result of the subsequent injury and the compensation payable as a result of the total disability.	An assessment against insurance carriers and self-insurers proportionate to the total amount paid in compensation per year.	Pa. Stat. Ann. tit. 71, § 578; tit. 77, § 517.
RI	Subsequent injury that, combined with a preexisting work-related disability, causes death or a greater disability.	For claims filed after September 1, 1990, benefits for the first 26 weeks following the injury.	For claims filed after September 1, 1990, benefits after the first 26 weeks following the injury. To obtain reimbursement, employer must prove knowledge of the preexisting injury unless employee purposefully failed to disclose it.	Insurance carriers and self-insurers are assessed an amount as determined by the fund director on or before March 15 of each year. Additionally, employers and/or insurers must pay into the fund $7,500 in the event of a compensable death case.	R.I. Gen. Laws § 28-37-13.

State	Definition of Subsequent Injury	Fund Pays	Reimbursement/Liability	Financing	Citation
SC	Subsequent injury that, combined with any preexisting permanent physical disability likely to cause a hindrance to employment, causes death or a substantially greater disability.	All benefits for the first 78 weeks following the injury, subject to limited reimbursement during that time.	Employer is reimbursed for all costs after the first 78 weeks following the injury and for 50% of the costs over $3,000 during the first 78 weeks.	All unpaid benefits in no-dependent death cases are paid to the fund. Insurance carriers and self-insured employers are assessed an amount equal to the amount the fund paid on their behalf in the preceding year.	S.C. Code Ann. §§ 42-7-200, 42-7-310, 42-9-400, 42-9-410.
SD	—	—	—	—	S.D. Codified Laws § 62-4-34.7. Reimbursement for subsequent injuries abolished. Any claim filed after June 30, 1999, is now barred.
TN	Subsequent injury involving loss of, or loss of use of, a hand, arm, foot, leg, or eye that, combined with a preexisting loss of, or loss of use of, such a member, causes a permanent total disability.	That portion of the disability caused by the subsequent injury.	The difference between compensation payable as a result of the subsequent injury and the compensation payable as a result of the total disability as a whole.	One-half of the revenue gathered from the 4% tax assessed on all insurance carriers and self-insured employers. The Second Injury Fund also comprises various penalties collected by the division for violations of its promulgated rules.	Tenn. Code Ann. §§ 50-6-118, 50-6-206, 50-6-208.
TX	Subsequent injury that, combined with a preexisting disability, entitles employee to lifetime income benefits.	Those benefits that would have been payable had the subsequent injury but not the preexisting disability existed.	All lifetime income benefits to which injured employee is entitled, less those benefits payable as a result of the subsequent injury alone.	Payments equal to 364 weeks of the death benefit otherwise payable in each no-dependent death case, supplemented, if necessary, by a maintenance tax on insurance carriers.	Tex. Lab. Code Ann. §§ 403.006, 403.007.
UT	Subsequent injury that, combined with a previous permanent incapacity caused by accident, disease, or congenital condition, causes a permanent total disability. The injury must have occurred on or before July 1, 1994.	The first 6 years of the permanent total disability payments, unless the preexisting condition caused at least a 10% disability prior to the subsequent injury. If the preexisting injury accounted for at least a 10% disability prior to the subsequent injury, employer pays the first $20,000 of all medical benefits and only the first 3 years of the disability benefits.	50% of the medical benefits in excess of $20,000 and the permanent total disability compensation payable after the initial 3- or 6-year period.	An assessment, not to exceed 7.25%, against insurance carriers and self-insured employers, tied to total compensation paid.	Utah Code Ann. §§ 34A-2-410 et seq.
VT	—	—	—	—	Vt. Stat. Ann. tit. 21a, §§ 683–685.
VA	Subsequent injury involving the 20% loss of, or loss of use of, a foot, leg, hand, arm, or eye that, combined with a preexisting disability of at least 20%, causes a partial or total temporary disability.	That portion of the disability caused by the subsequent injury.	Employers are reimbursed for disability benefits necessitated by the effect of the preexisting disability and up to $7,500 for medical and vocational rehabilitation benefits.	Insurance carriers and self-insured employers are assessed a 0.25% tax on premiums.	Va. Code Ann. §§ 65.2-1100–65.2-1106.

(Table continues.)

Table 10.12-1 (cont'd)

SUBSEQUENT INJURY FUNDS

(See also text at § 10.12.)

	Which Injuries Are Covered by Subsequent Injury Funds?	What Portion of Compensation Is Allocated to Employers?	What Portion of Compensation Is Allocated to Fund?	What Are the Revenue Sources for the Fund?	Citations to Authority
WA	Subsequent injury or occupational disease that, combined with a preexisting injury or disease, causes death or permanent total disability.	That portion of the disability caused by the subsequent injury.	The difference between the compensation payable as a result of the subsequent injury and the compensation payable as a result of the death or permanent disability.	Insurance carriers and self-insured employers are assessed an amount tied to claims paid.	Wash. Rev. Code Ann. §§ 51.16.120, 51.32.250, 51.44.040.
WV	Subsequent injury that, combined with a definitively ascertainable physical disability caused by a previous injury, causes a permanent total disability.	That portion of the disability caused by the subsequent injury. Self-insured employers are liable in full if they elect not to pay into the fund.	The difference between the compensation payable as a result of the subsequent injury and that payable as a result of the permanent disability.	Self-insured employers are assessed an amount that increases as the inherent danger of the industry in which they do business increases.	W. Va. Code § 23-3-1.
WI	Subsequent injury causing at least 200 weeks of permanent disability that occurs to an employee with a preexisting disability of at least equal degree.	That portion of the disability caused by the subsequent injury.	The disability caused by the lesser of the two injuries. If the combined effects of the two injuries result in a permanent total disability, the fund will pay the difference between the compensation payable for the subsequent injury and the compensation payable for the permanent total disability.	$5,000 payments in all death cases; 100% of all benefits payable in no-dependent death cases; $7,000 payments in all loss-of-member cases.	Wis. Stat. Ann. §§ 102.11, 102.59.
WY	—	—	—	—	—